Asia's Transformations
Edited by Mark Selden, *Cornell University, USA*

The books in this series explore the political, social, economic and cultural consequences of Asia's transformations in the twentieth and twenty-first centuries. The series emphasizes the tumultuous interplay of local, national, regional and global forces as Asia bids to become the hub of the world economy. While focusing on the contemporary, it also looks back to analyze the antecedents of Asia's contested rise.

This series comprises several strands:

Asia's Transformations

Titles include:

1. **Debating Human Rights***
   Critical essays from the United States and Asia
   Edited by Peter Van Ness
2. **Hong Kong's History***
   State and society under colonial rule
   Edited by Tak-Wing Ngo
3. **Japan's Comfort Women***
   Sexual slavery and prostitution during World War II and the US occupation
   Yuki Tanaka
4. **Opium, Empire and the Global Political Economy***
   Carl A. Trocki
5. **Chinese Society***
   Change, conflict and resistance
   Edited by Elizabeth J. Perry and Mark Selden
6. **Mao's Children in the New China***
   Voices from the Red Guard generation
   Yarong Jiang and David Ashley
7. **Remaking the Chinese State***
   Strategies, society and security
   Edited by Chien-min Chao and Bruce J. Dickson
8. **Korean Society***
   Civil society, democracy and the state
   Edited by Charles K. Armstrong
9. **The Making of Modern Korea***
   Adrian Buzo
10. **The Resurgence of East Asia***
    500, 150 and 50 year perspectives
    Edited by Giovanni Arrighi, Takeshi Hamashita and Mark Selden
11. **Chinese Society, second edition***
    Change, conflict and resistance
    Edited by Elizabeth J. Perry and Mark Selden
12. **Ethnicity in Asia***
    Edited by Colin Mackerras
13. **The Battle for Asia***
    From decolonization to globalization
    Mark T. Berger

The Political Economy of Affect and Emotion in East Asia

When thinking about the culture and economy of East Asia, many attri to the region a range of dispositions, including a preference for consensus social harmony, loyalty and respect towards superiors and government, fa values, collectivism and communitarianism. Affect is central to these cepts, and yet the role of affect and its animated or imagined potentiali the political economy of East Asia has not been systematically studied. book examines the affective dimensions of power and economy in East It illuminates the dynamics of contemporary governance and ways of coming common Western assumptions about East Asian societies. Here, is defined as felt quality that gives meaning and imagination to social, tical and economic processes and, as this book demonstrates, it can pr an analytical tool for a nuanced and enriched analysis of social, politica economic transformations in East Asia.

Through ethnographic and media analyses, this book provides a framewo analyzing emerging phenomena in East Asia, such as happiness promo therapeutic governance, the psychologization of social issues, the rise o help genres, transnational labor migration, new ideologies of gender ar family, and mass-mediated affective communities. Through the lens of theory, the contributors explore changing political configurations, eco engagements, modes of belonging and forms of subjectivity in East Asi use ethnographic research and discourse analysis to illustrate the af dimensions of state and economic power and the way affect inform inspires action.

This interdisciplinary book will be of great interest to students and sc of Asian studies, anthropology, sociology, media studies, history, c studies, and gender and women's studies.

Jie Yang is Assistant Professor of Anthropology at Simon Fraser Uni Canada.

14. **State and Society in 21st Century China***
Edited by Peter Hays Gries and Stanley Rosen

15. **Japan's Quiet Transformation***
Social change and civil society in the 21st century
Jeff Kingston

16. **Confronting the Bush Doctrine***
Critical views from the Asia-Pacific
Edited by Mel Gurtov and Peter Van Ness

17. **China in War and Revolution, 1895–1949***
Peter Zarrow

18. **The Future of US-Korean Relations***
The imbalance of power
Edited by John Feffer

19. **Working in China***
Ethnographies of labor and workplace transformations
Edited by Ching Kwan Lee

20. **Korean Society, second edition***
Civil society, democracy and the state
Edited by Charles K. Armstrong

21. **Singapore***
The state and the culture of excess
Souchou Yao

22. **Pan-Asianism in Modern Japanese History***
Colonialism, regionalism and borders
Edited by Sven Saaler and J. Victor Koschmann

23. **The Making of Modern Korea, 2nd Edition***
Adrian Buzo

24. **Re-writing Culture in Taiwan***
Edited by Fang-long Shih, Stuart Thompson and Paul-François Tremlett

25. **Reclaiming Chinese Society***
The new social activism
Edited by You-tien Hsing and Ching Kwan Lee

26. **Girl Reading Girl in Japan***
Edited by Tomoko Aoyama and Barbara Hartley

27. **Chinese Politics***
State, society and the market
Edited by Peter Hays Gries and Stanley Rosen

28. **Chinese Society, third edition***
Change, conflict and resistance
Edited by Elizabeth J. Perry and Mark Selden

29. **Mapping Modernity in Shanghai**
Space, gender, and visual culture in the sojourners' city, 1853–98
Samuel Y. Liang

30. **Minorities and Multiculturalism in Japanese Education**
An interactive perspective
Edited by Ryoko Tsuneyoshi, Kaori H. Okano and Sarane Boocock

31. **Japan's Wartime Medical Atrocities**
Comparative inquiries in science, history, and ethics
Edited by Jing-Bao Nie, Nanyan Guo, Mark Selden and Arthur Kleinman

32. **State and Society in Modern Rangoon**
    Donald M. Seekins

33. **Learning Chinese, Turning Chinese***
    Becoming sinophone in a globalised world
    Edward McDonald

34. **Aesthetic Constructions of Korean Nationalism**
    Spectacle, politics and history
    Hong Kal

35. **Popular Culture and the State in East and Southeast Asia**
    Edited by Nissim Otmazgin and Eyal Ben Ari

36. **Japan's Outcaste Abolition**
    The struggle for national inclusion and the making of the modern state
    Noah Y. McCormack

37. **The Market and Temple Fairs of Rural China**
    Red fire
    Gene Cooper

38. **The Role of American NGOs in China's Modernization**
    Invited influence
    Norton Wheeler

39. **State, Society and the Market in Contemporary Vietnam**
    Property, power and values
    Edited by Hue-Tam Ho Tai and Mark Sidel

40. **East Asia Beyond the History Wars**
    Confronting the ghosts of violence
    Tessa Morris-Suzuki, Morris Low, Leonid Petrov and Timothy Yun Hui Tsu

41. **China**
    How the empire fell
    Joseph W. Esherick and C.X. George Wei

42. **The Political Economy of Affect and Emotion in East Asia**
    Jie Yang

Asia's Great Cities

Each volume aims to capture the heartbeat of the contemporary city from multiple perspectives emblematic of the authors' own deep familiarity with the distinctive faces of the city, its history, society, culture, politics and economics, and its evolving position in national, regional and global frameworks. While most volumes emphasize urban developments since the Second World War, some pay close attention to the legacy of the longue durée in shaping the contemporary. Thematic and comparative volumes address such themes as urbanization, economic and financial linkages, architecture and space, wealth and power, gendered relationships, planning and anarchy, and ethnographies in national and regional perspective. Titles include:

1. **Bangkok***
   Place, practice and representation
   Marc Askew

2. **Representing Calcutta***
   Modernity, nationalism and the colonial uncanny
   Swati Chattopadhyay

3. **Singapore***
Wealth, power and the culture of control
Carl A. Trocki

4. **The City in South Asia**
James Heitzman

5. **Global Shanghai, 1850–2010***
A history in fragments
Jeffrey N. Wasserstrom

6. **Hong Kong***
Becoming a global city
Stephen Chiu and Tai-Lok Lui

Asia.com

Asia.com is a series that focuses on the ways in which new information and communication technologies are influencing politics, society and culture in Asia. Titles include:

1. **Japanese Cybercultures***
Edited by Mark McLelland and Nanette Gottlieb

2. **Asia.com***
Asia encounters the Internet
Edited by K.C. Ho, Randolph Kluver and Kenneth C.C. Yang

4. **The Internet in Indonesia's New Democracy***
David T. Hill and Krishna Sen

5. **Chinese Cyberspaces***
Technological changes and political effects
Edited by Jens Damm and Simona Thomas

6. **Mobile Media in the Asia-Pacific**
Gender and the art of being mobile
Larissa Hjorth

7. **Online@AsiaPacific**
Mobile, social and locative media in the Asia-Pacific
Larissa Hjorth and Michael Arnold

Literature and Society

Literature and Society is a series that seeks to demonstrate the ways in which Asian literature is influenced by the politics, society and culture in which it is produced. Titles include:

1. **The Body in Postwar Japanese Fiction**
Douglas N. Slaymaker

2. **Chinese Women Writers and the Feminist Imagination, 1905–48***
Haiping Yan

3. **Okinawan War Memory**
Transgenerational Trauma and the War Fiction of Medoruma Shun
Kyle Ikeda

Routledge Studies in Asia's Transformations

Routledge Studies in Asia's Transformations is a forum for innovative new research intended for a high-level specialist readership. Titles include:

1. **The American Occupation of Japan and Okinawa***
   Literature and memory
   Michael Molasky

2. **Koreans in Japan***
   Critical voices from the margin
   Edited by Sonia Ryang

3. **Internationalizing the Pacific**
   The United States, Japan and the Institute of Pacific Relations in war and peace, 1919–1945
   Tomoko Akami

4. **Imperialism in South East Asia***
   "A fleeting, passing phase"
   Nicholas Tarling

5. **Chinese Media, Global Contexts***
   Edited by Chin-Chuan Lee

6. **Remaking Citizenship in Hong Kong***
   Community, nation and the global city
   Edited by Agnes S. Ku and Ngai Pun

7. **Japanese Industrial Governance**
   Protectionism and the licensing state
   Yul Sohn

8. **Developmental Dilemmas***
   Land reform and institutional change in China
   Edited by Peter Ho

9. **Genders, Transgenders and Sexualities in Japan***
   Edited by Mark McLelland and Romit Dasgupta

10. **Fertility, Family Planning and Population Policy in China***
    Edited by Dudley L. Poston, Che-Fu Lee, Chiung-Fang Chang, Sherry L. McKibben and Carol S. Walther

11. **Japanese Diasporas***
    Unsung pasts, conflicting presents and uncertain futures
    Edited by Nobuko Adachi

12. **How China Works***
    Perspectives on the twentieth-century industrial workplace
    Edited by Jacob Eyferth

13. **Remolding and Resistance among Writers of the Chinese Prison Camp**
    Disciplined and published
    Edited by Philip F. Williams and Yenna Wu

14. **Popular Culture, Globalization and Japan***
    Edited by Matthew Allen and Rumi Sakamoto

15. **medi@sia***
    Global media/tion in and out of context
    Edited by Todd Joseph Miles Holden and Timothy J. Scrase

16. **Vientiane***
    Transformations of a Lao landscape
    Marc Askew, William S. Logan and Colin Long

17. **State Formation and Radical Democracy in India**
    Manali Desai

18. **Democracy in Occupied Japan***
The US occupation and Japanese politics and society
Edited by Mark E. Caprio and Yoneyuki Sugita

19. **Globalization, Culture and Society in Laos***
Boike Rehbein

20. **Transcultural Japan***
At the borderlands of race, gender, and identity
Edited by David Blake Willis and Stephen Murphy-Shigematsu

21. **Post-Conflict Heritage, Post-Colonial Tourism**
Culture, politics and development at Angkor
Tim Winter

22. **Education and Reform in China***
Emily Hannum and Albert Park

23. **Writing Okinawa**
Narrative acts of identity and resistance
Davinder L. Bhowmik

24. **Maid in China***
Media, morality, and the cultural politics of boundaries
Wanning Sun

25. **Northern Territories, Asia-Pacific Regional Conflicts and the Åland Experience**
Untying the Kurillian knot
Edited by Kimie Hara and Geoffrey Jukes

26. **Reconciling Indonesia**
Grassroots agency for peace
Birgit Bräuchler

27. **Singapore in the Malay World***
Building and breaching regional bridges
Lily Zubaidah Rahim

28. **Pirate Modernity***
Delhi's media urbanism
Ravi Sundaram

29. **The World Bank and the post-Washington Consensus in Vietnam and Indonesia**
Inheritance of loss
Susan Engel

30. **China on Video**
Smaller screen realities
Paola Voci

31. **Overseas Chinese, Ethnic Minorities and Nationalism**
De-centering China
Elena Barabantseva

32. **The Education of Migrant Children and China's Future**
The urban left behind
Holly H. Ming

Critical Asian Scholarship

Critical Asian Scholarship is a series intended to showcase the most important individual contributions to scholarship in Asian Studies. Each of the volumes presents a leading Asian scholar addressing themes that are central to his or her most significant and lasting contribution to Asian Studies. The series is committed to the rich variety of research and writing on Asia, and is not restricted to any particular discipline, theoretical approach or geographical expertise.

1. **Southeast Asia***
   A testament
   George McT. Kahin

2. **Women and the Family in Chinese History***
   Patricia Buckley Ebrey

3. **China Unbound***
   Evolving perspectives on the Chinese past
   Paul A. Cohen

4. **China's Past, China's Future***
   Energy, food, environment
   Vaclav Smil

5. **The Chinese State in Ming Society***
   Timothy Brook

6. **China, East Asia and the Global Economy***
   Regional and historical perspectives
   Takeshi Hamashita
   Edited by Mark Selden and Linda Grove

7. **The Global and Regional in China's Nation-Formation***
   Prasenjit Duara

8. **Decoding Subaltern Politics***
   Ideology, disguise, and resistance in agrarian politics
   James C. Scott

9. **Mapping China and Managing the World***
   Culture, cartography and cosmology in late Imperial times
   Richard J. Smith

10. **Technology, Gender and History in Imperial China***
    Great transformations reconsidered
    Francesca Bray

* Available in paperback

The Political Economy of Affect and Emotion in East Asia

Edited by Jie Yang

Routledge
Taylor & Francis Group
LONDON AND NEW YORK

First published 2014
by Routledge
2 Park Square, Milton Park, Abingdon, Oxon OX14 4RN

and by Routledge
711 Third Avenue, New York, NY 10017

Routledge is an imprint of the Taylor & Francis Group, an informa business

British Library Cataloguing in Publication Data
A catalogue record for this book is available from the British Library

Library of Congress Cataloging in Publication Data
The political economy of affect and emotion in East Asia / [edited by] Jie Yang.
pages cm. -- (Asia's transformations ; 42)
Includes bibliographical references and index.
1. East Asia--Civilization--21st century. 2. East Asia--History--21st century. 3. East Asia--Social conditions--21st century. 4. Emotions--Social aspects.
5. Economics--Political aspects.
DS509.3.P65 2014
950.4'3--dc23
2013042083

ISBN: 978-0-415-70970-5 (hbk)
ISBN: 978-1-315-88539-1 (ebk)

Typeset in Times New Roman
by Taylor & Francis Books

MIX
Paper from responsible sources
FSC www.fsc.org FSC® C013604

Printed and bound by CPI Group (UK) Ltd, Croydon, CR0 4YY

Contents

List of figures

List of contributors

Shuyu Kong is Associate Professor of Humanities and Director of the Asia-Canada program at Simon Fraser University, Canada. She received her BA in Chinese literature, MA in comparative Literature, both from Peking University, and a PhD in Asian Studies from University of British Columbia. She has lived, studied and worked in China, Canada and Australia, and keeps herself busy with cross-cultural teaching, bilingual writing and cross-continental travelling. Shuyu's research interests encompass both Chinese literary and cultural studies and Chinese diaspora studies. Besides numerous articles in referred journals such as *Positions: East Asia Cultures Critique*, *Asian Cinema*, *China Journal*, and *Modern Chinese Literature & Culture*, Shuyu is the author of two books: *Consuming Literature: Bestsellers and the Commercialization of Literary Production in Contemporary China* (Stanford University Press, 2005), and *Popular Media, Social Emotion and Public Discourse in Contemporary China* (Routledge, 2014). She is also co-translator of *Beijing Women* (with Colin S. Hawes, MerwinAsia Publishing, 2013). Shuyu's current research project focuses on Chinese-language television in Canada.

Teresa Kuan is Assistant Professor in the Department of Anthropology at the Chinese University of Hong Kong. She takes interest in the cultural life of psychological ideas and she is currently developing a new project on the localization of family therapy in China. She has published in *The China Journal* and *Positions*, and her book on popular advice for parents in China is forthcoming with the University of California Press.

Craig MacKie is a sociologist, a health services researcher, a communist and a writer of speculative fiction. He recently graduated from Concordia University where he wrote his thesis on the political economy of affect in North Korea and studied the theological turn in Marxism, emphasizing the writings of Terry Eagleton, Slavoj Žižek and Alain Badiou. His latest publications include an analysis of the discourses of medical risk regarding pregnancy and a statistical corpus analysis of the works of Dr. Seuss. He lives in Montreal, Canada where he reads and works.

Sung Kil Min graduated from Yonsei University, Seoul, Korea with an MD in 1968, in 1975 with a PhD from the same university, and trained in psychiatry at Yonsei University Severance Hospital. He had study visits to Copenhagen University, Tuebingen University and Illinois State University. From 1976, he was a professor of psychiatry, Yonsei University, served as chair of the department of psychiatry in 1994–2000, and retired as a professor emeritus in 2009. Throughout the years he held special positions such as the president of the Korean Neuropsychiatric Association, president of the Korean Society of Social Psychiatry, director of the Institute of Korea Unification Study, Yonsei University, medical consultant for President Kim Dae-jung and his family, member of the board of directors of the Pacific Rim College of Psychiatrists, lifetime member of the National Academy of Medicine of Korea, and superintendent of Seoul Metropolitan Eunpyeong Hospital. He has published numerous articles and books on psychiatry, including on *hwa-byung*, the culture-related anger syndrome observed among Koreans, and the psycho-social adaptation of communist North Korean defectors in capitalistic South Korea, and he has edited a Korean textbook of psychiatry.

Momoko Nakamura, PhD, is Professor of English at Kanto Gakuin University in Yokohama, Japan. Her recent publications include *Onna kotoba wa tsukurareru* (Constructing Women's Language) (winner, 27th Yamakawa Kikue Award), *Sei to Nihongo*: *Kotoba ga tsukuru onna to otoko* (Sex and Japanese Language: Woman and Man Constructed by Language), *Onna kotoba to Nihongo* (Women's Language and Japanese Language), and *Honyaku ga tsukuru Nihongo: Hiroin wa onna kotoba o hanashi tsuzukeru* (Translation and Japanese Language: Heroines Speak Women's Language). She contributed "Women's and Men's Languages as Heterosexual Resource: Power and Intimacy in Japanese Spam e-mail," in *Femininity, Feminism and Gendered Discourse*, edited by Janet Holmes and Meredith Marra; "Creating Indexicality: Schoolgirl Speech in Meiji Japan," in *The Language and Sexuality Reader*, edited by Deborah Cameron and Don Kulick; and "Let's Dress a Little Girlishly! or Conquer Short Pants!: Constructing Gendered Communities in Fashion Magazines for Young People," in *Japanese Language, Gender, and Ideology: Cultural Models and Real People*, edited by Shigeko Okamoto and Janet S. Shibamoto Smith. She also edited *Jendaa de manabu gengogaku* (Learning Linguistics by Gender), and translated into Japanese *Language and Sexuality*, written by Deborah Cameron and Don Kulick.

Shiho Satsuka is Assistant Professor of Anthropology at the University of Toronto. Her research concerns the significance of nature in producing imaginaries of global connection and the cultural politics of knowledge translation, especially that of the natural environment. Her book *Nature in Translation* is forthcoming from Duke University Press, and examines how the Japanese tour guides living in Banff—Canada's iconic national park—translate various notions of nature to tourists from Japan, and how the guides' translation practices have been shaped by the changing work relations in Japan reflecting the larger power dynamics in post-Cold War geopolitics. She is currently working on the emerging global networks of science, commerce and environmental movements regarding the *matsutake* wild mushroom highly treasured in Japan, as a member of the Matsutake Worlds Research Group.

Toshiko Tsujimoto is a sessional lecturer and researcher of labor history in the Center for Culture and International Studies at SungKongHoe University in South Korea. She completed her MA at Osaka University of Foreign Studies. In 2006, she obtained her PhD from the graduate school of sociology at SungKongHoe University. In her doctoral research, she studied the diaspora experiences of migrant Filipino women in Korea with the occupations and status of factory worker, domestic worker, entertainer, and spouse of a Korean citizen. Tsujimoto received the post-doctoral fellowship from the government of Canada between 2009 and 2010, and she was affiliated with the Centre for the Study of Korea, Munk School of Global Affairs at the University of Toronto. In her post-doctoral program, she conducted research on transnationalism of migrant Filipino workers and their experiences of re-emigration from the former host countries in East Asia to Canada.

Daniel White is Assistant Professor of Anthropology and Media Studies in the Department of Global and Interdisciplinary Studies at Hosei University, Tokyo. His research interests focus on affect, the public sphere, and the politics and ethics of cultural production in Japan. Most recently he has published in the journal *Pan-Japan* (2012) on the political appropriation of author Murakami Haruki, and is currently writing a book on the emotional dimensions of bureaucracy and public diplomacy within Japan's government agencies of national culture.

Jie Yang is Assistant Professor of Anthropology at Simon Fraser University. Her research interests include language, gender, privatization and neoliberal restructuring, happiness and well-being and mental health in China. She has published in journals such as *American Ethnologist*, *Anthropological Quarterly*, *Signs*, *Ethos*, *Ethnography*, *Social Analysis*, *Social Semiotics*, *Language and Communication*, and *Gender and Language*. Her monograph titled *Unknotting the Heart: Gender, Unemployment and Psychotherapy in China* is currently under review.

Ayaka Yoshimizu is a doctoral student of the School of Communication at Simon Fraser University. Her current research interests include transnational migration, urban memory, diaspora identity and culture, body and affect. Her dissertation research examines the displacement of transnational migrant sex workers from the port city of Yokohama, Japan, and reconstructs its cultural landscape by unearthing memories of the sex workers through her ethnographic work. She has also been engaged in a cross-Pacific, historical project on the formation and regulation of communities of sex-workers in former brothel districts of Yokohama, Japan and Vancouver, Canada. She has published widely in cultural studies, literary studies, anthropology and human geography.

Yanhua Zhang is Associate Professor of Chinese and Anthropology at Clemson University, United States, where she also directs the CU in China Summer Study Abroad Program. Trained as a cultural and medical anthropologist, her research interests center on medical and linguistic anthropology, and the interplay among Chinese philosophical thought, language use and contemporary practice of traditional Chinese medicine in China. Her publications include *Transforming Emotions with Chinese Medicine: An Ethnographic Account from Contemporary China* (SUNY Press, 2007).

Acknowledgements

I am grateful to Mark Selden for his encouragement, support and insightful comments on the project at different stages of writing. His expertise in Asia Studies has shaped the whole project. His virtuosic editing is truly a gift. At Routledge, I thank Stephanie Rogers, Hannah Mack, Ruth Bradley and Alison Neale for their patience, professionalism and kind support throughout the review and production process. I also appreciate extremely helpful comments from the two anonymous reviewers.

The book is derived from a conference panel and workshop I organized in 2009. I thank the Department of Sociology and Anthropology, Faculty of Arts and Sciences and the David Lam Center at Simon Fraser University for financial and logistic support. Not all the participants contributed their papers to this volume, but Alan Smart, Jesook Song, Alison Bailey, Mun Young Cho, Judy Juhui Han, Huang Xin, Francis Cody, Charles Crawford, Jan Walls and Mary Lynn Stewart were part of the conversation and their insights indirectly shaped the chapters here. Keynote speeches delivered by Bonnie McElhinny and Lisa Rofel offered theoretical insights and analytical frameworks for the book. Edith Lo and Paul Crowe at the David Lam Center and Jeanne Persoon in the Department of Sociology and Anthropology provided helpful logistical and administrative assistance. Xing Guoxin, Ryan Brown, Ayaka Yoshimizu and Peter Muirhead read and commented on chapters and provided wonderful research and editorial assistance. George Zhao, Teresa Kuan and Craig MacKie helped with the search for the cover image. A publication grant from Simon Fraser University generously assisted the editing, index and copyright clearance.

Sara Ahmed's insightful and penetrating comments on an early draft of the introduction have compelled me to shift direction. Her reference guidance on the feminist scholarship of emotion benefits both my general understanding of affect and the writing and editing of the book. I very much appreciate her serious scholarship and am grateful to her generosity with her time and expertise. I also want to thank my colleague Dara Culhane for her kind suggestions and reference guidance at the beginning of the project. Wendy Chan's advice, support and editorial suggestions have sustained me throughout the project. Janice Matsumura and Kirsten McAllister provided warm encouragement and helpful suggestions for the organization of the workshop.

Janet Dixon Keller and Marguerite Pigeon offered excellent comments and superb editorial improvements on the Introduction. I am indebted to the following colleagues and friends for their insightful comments and inspiring conversations: Alison Bailey, Mun Young Cho, Shuyu Kong, Teresa Kuan, Daromir Rudnyckyj, Alan Smart, Hans Steinmuller, Daniel White, and Yanhua Zhang. I would also like to thank all the contributors for their patience, hard work and continued dialogue on affect and emotion.

Jie Yang
November 2013

Foreword

Starting and Startling

Sara Ahmed

Are we witnessing the emergence of a new field called "affect studies"? If so, what would be its primary objects of study, what are its tools or methods of analysis? What intellectual genealogies would we offer if we were to map this field? Where is this field, and where is it going?

I begin with these questions as these questions are about how to begin. For me, at least, it is the last of these questions, the *where* questions, that have the most potential to startle. It encourages us to think about whether gathering a field called "affect studies" involves its own orientation devices, such that a field, in being given contours and edges, points in some directions more than others. In this important collection of essays, *The Political Economy of Affect and Emotion in East Asia*, the project is two-fold: firstly to explore the potential of affect as an analytic tool; and secondly to rethink the nature of contemporary governance in East Asia in such a way that moves beyond, as Jie Yang describes in her introduction, "common Western assumptions about Asian governmentality."

What is the relation between these two folds? Perhaps it is the gap between them that registers something significant and timely about this volume. For affect studies, it could be argued, the field has emerged in or even as a set of "common Western assumptions." Of course to describe the field in these terms might be to stabilise and reduce the field prematurely. Or we might be describing how a field emerges through such acts of stabilisation. Take for example Melissa Gregg and Gregory J. Seigworth's introduction to *The Affect Theory Reader*, "An Inventory of Shimmers." They identify two essays first published in 1995 as "watershed moments" for the "interest and intrigue regarding affect," one by Eve Sedgwick and Adam Frank, the other by Brian Massumi. Just to be clear: a watershed is a line separating waters that flow into different rivers. These essays are taken up as directing the flow of traffic along two distinct lines. Gregg and Seigworth suggest that they "have given substantial shape to the two dominant vectors of affect study in the humanities" relating either to the work of Silvan Tomkins, or to the work of Gilles Deleuze and through Deleuze, Spinoza (2010: 5).

I have no doubt about the influence and importance of these two intellectual genealogies within "affect studies" and beyond. But how often in describing a shape that is given we are giving a shape. We often register the contours of a shape when we are not folded into it. As a scholar writing about affect and emotion in the humanities, I could not and would not see myself as part of either of these "vectors of affect study." My own starting point would be the work of Black feminist Audre Lorde who wrote in 1984, over a decade before these watershed moments, of anger as loaded with information and energy.

Of course it is hard to give a history of the emergence of an interest without creating a shape that does not accommodate all of those who share this interest. Gregg and Seigworth attempt in their introduction to offer a complex and nuanced account of the emergence of "affect theory" by giving us seven different "affectual orientations." One of these "affectual orientations" is described as "politically engaged work – perhaps most often undertaken by feminists, queer theorists, disability activists, and subaltern peoples living under the thumb of a normatizing power" (7).[1] Interestingly, this is the only one of the seven affectual orientations listed in which no individual authors are named. Here "the others" appear rather like a faceless mass, perhaps repeating in the form of the argument some of the erasures that "politically engaged" work might describe.

When "affect studies" is given a white male European intellectual genealogy, with two lines of descent, one from Deleuze, the other from Tomkins, we might end up where we started from. Although some of the individual essays in this volume do start from these same points (my point is not that they are wrong as starting points just that there are other starting points), the overall effect of this volume is one of disruption, a way of dislocating an emergent field by relocating it. We get a sense from this collection how "affect studies" pulls from many different directions, including ones that take us beyond "the West" as an affectual orientation.

A dialogue between literatures that unfold from different starting points often requires acts of translation; and translation is never perfect. Many of the insights of this collective contribution are predicated on examples that are hard to translate, including examples of "emotion words" that do not find an exact match in other languages (such as *haan* in Korean). Researching affects and emotions can mean attending to mismatches. As we learn from Gayatri Spivak (1995) translation becomes a necessary and painstaking form of intellectual labour given the impossibility of meaning simply moving across languages and domains. Affect as a tool can do different things in different hands; the idea of affect (rather like affects) when passed around, does not always pass smoothly.[2]

The introduction to this book refers to a "long standing literature" that understands social relations in Japan, Korea and China as "more rooted in (and articulated in terms of) affect and emotion than in the West." What follows is thus a dialogue and encounter between different literatures that allow a critical reappraisal of the affective dimensions of power and governance, of how power operates as much through charm and charisma as it does through coercion. We learn about the creation of new hybrid forms: how through old and new media platforms Confucian teachings can be translated into market based neo-liberal ideologies and affective practices. We learn about new styles of pedagogy; about the rise of the discipline of psychology; about increasing concerns with personal happiness as a social aspiration. Throughout, the study of affects and emotions is related to different groups of subjects: from "the affective child" in China, to care workers in Japan, to Filipino domestic workers in Korea. Subjects are addressed as embodied as well as embedded in local, national and transnational axes of difference. The volume as a whole thus attends to the messy nature of social and affective landscapes: contributions address questions of gender (for example by considering how women who have been laid off are represented in television dramas in China or by reflecting on the specific affective pull of women's language in Japan); and race and ethnicity (for example in the consideration of the "affective foreigners" in Japan) as well as class relations and the impact of neoliberalism in the generalisation of precarity.

As with all productive dialogues across bodies of literature that have different starting points, there is room for disagreement. As a reader, I appreciated how questions of definition are not resolved: each contribution defines affect somewhat differently; for example, some authors assume a distinction between affect and emotion, whilst others do not. This means that the chapters not only pull from many different directions but that the volume as a whole includes feminist and queer work on emotions as part of affect studies.[3] Some contributions reflect on public emotions (for example in national uses of happiness), thus showing how emotions are narrated and performed collectively, whilst others explore the body as sensorium, taking up tears, for instance, as a way of thinking about bodies. And whilst some chapters address how affects and emotions become tools that can strengthen the hold of existing regimes of power, other chapters emphasise subversion, play and possibility. Rethinking governmentality through the lens of affect theories, in all their divergences and complexities, allows us to ask what affects can and do "do."

The Political Economy of Affect and Emotion in East Asia is a very welcome addition to the expanding of affect studies. More than this: it points us in some new directions. To begin a journey with different starting points can mean to be more open to being startled en route. The word "startle" derives from start: it implies being moved suddenly, perhaps by surprise or fear. In this context, I am thinking of the affective quality of being startled as more akin to surprise. As a whole, I would suggest, this volume can be taken up as a reorientation device; it offers a restart, a way of beginning our travels again.

Notes

1 I should note that explicit reference is made to individuals as feminist philosophers (Grosz, Lloyd, Gatens, Braidotti) as part of the general description of non-humanist philosophy, although they do not list any of the most significant feminist scholars

who have written on emotion (Lorde, Hochschild, Spelman, Jaggar). Their list, I would add, is also a very white list (of the almost fifty individual scholars who are named in full only two are not white, Frantz Fanon and Paul Gilroy). I would speculate that it is through an exploration of the psychic effects of slavery and colonialism that many of us who work in the West, but are marked as racially other, became interested in affect and emotion.

2 In *The Promise of Happiness* (2010) I suggested that models of affective contagion tend to imply that when affects are passed around, they pass smoothly (shame when contagious means we are all "caught up" by shame). I used as a thought exercise the example of a game called *Telephone* where you are seated in a circle, and one person whispers a message, which then gets passed around. The point of the game is the pleasure of deviation: of hearing how far the message is different at the end point from the starting point (2010: 240). As I pointed out in the text, when I was growing up in Australia, this game was called *Chinese Whispers.* As Rosalind Ballaster notes, "the sinophobic name points to the centuries old tradition in Europe of representing spoken Chinese as the incomprehensible and unpronounceable combination of sounds" (2005: 203–3). Writing this foreword, now, I am thinking how fitting it is to think with this: how the deviant travels of affects relates to the difficult histories of mistranslation.

3 In the afterword to the second edition of my book, *The Cultural Politics of Emotion* (2014) I note how Michael Hart's preface to Patricia Clough's *The Affective Turn*, describes feminist work on the body and queer work on emotions as "precursors" to the affective turn rather than part of that turn. For Hardt: "A focus on affect certainly does draw attention to the body and emotions, but it also introduces an important shift" (2007: ix). Hardt suggests that the turn to affect requires a different "synthesis" than the study of the body and emotions because affects "refer equally to the body and mind" and because they "involve both reason and the passions" (ix). When the affective turn becomes a turn to affect, feminist and queer work are no longer positioned as part of that turn. Even if they are acknowledged as precursors a shift *to* affect signals a shift *from* this work. Feminist theories of emotion opened up a critical space to rethink the relation between mind and body; and much work in feminist theory (some of which is also explicitly engaged with philosophical debates about minds and bodies) did precisely the kind of work that Hardt seems to assume that affect as a concept was required in order to do.

References

Ahmed, Sara. 2010. *The Promise of Happiness.* Durham, NC: Duke University Press.

——2014. "Emotions and Their Objects." *The Cultural Politics of Emotion.* Edinburgh: Edinburgh University Press.

Ballaster, Rosalind. 2005. *Fabulous Orients: Fictions of the East in England, 1622–1785.* Oxford: Oxford University Press.

Gregg, Melissa and Gregory Seigworth. 2010. "An Inventory of Shimmers." In *The Affect Theory* Reader. Durham, NC: Duke University Press, 1–25.

Hardt, Michael. 2007. "Foreword: What Affects are Good For." In Patricia Clough with Jean Halley (eds), *The Affective Turn*: *Theorizing the Social.* Durham, NC: Duke University Press.

Lorde, Audre.1984. *Sister Outsider: Essays and Speeches.* Trumansburg: The Crossing Press.

Spivak, Gayatri Chakravorty. 1995. "Translators Preface." *Imaginary Maps.* London: Routledge.

Part I

Introduction

The politics of affect and emotion

Imagination, potentiality and anticipation in East Asia

Jie Yang

The study of East Asian economic growth has ranged from research that emphasizes context-neutral economic policies (cf. Stiglitz and Yusuf 2001; Pomfret 2011) to cultural analysis (cf. Tai 1989; Yao 2002; Yasushi and McConnell 2008).[1] In their book *Culture and Economy: The Shaping of Capitalism in Eastern Asia*, Timothy Brook and Hy Van Luong (1997) unite these two approaches by examining how culture as both a meaning system and a historically situated ideology is shaped by, and shapes, the political economy of Eastern Asia. At the end of the book, they invite social scientists to "think anew about the unanticipated reconfigurations of economic and political power … in Eastern Asia and about the strategies that ordinary people will develop to survive in the presence of that power" (Brook and Luong 1997: 20). This volume takes a first step toward answering that call. However, instead of focusing on culture as an analytical framework, we address affect as both an analytical tool and a force for reconfiguring power and achieving political and economic objectives in East Asia (including China, Japan, South Korea and North Korea).

When thinking about the culture and economy of East Asia, many people attribute to the region a range of dispositions, including a preference for consensus and social harmony, loyalty and respect toward superiors and government, family values, collectivism and communitarianism. These emotionally grounded perceptions also underlie research and writings about East Asia and have shaped notions such as "Asian values," "soft power," "Confucian capitalism," or "*guanxi* capitalism." Many of these qualities are affective registers at which emotional bonds are animated, cultivated and valorized. Such affective dynamics closely shape the material and ideological processes of everyday life. Though key to the concepts mentioned above, the role of affect and its animated or imagined potentialities in the political economy of East Asia have not been systematically examined. The concepts of Asian values, soft power and Confucian capitalism emerge largely from the West to be used locally in Asia by those in power. Scholars have criticized the ways in which these concepts have been mobilized by politicians and governments in Asian countries to help legitimate (repressive) policies and practices (Bell 2008; Chin-Dahler 2010). By engaging the affective dimensions of power and economy in East

Asia through ethnographic and media analyses, we intend this book to help readers better understand the dynamics of contemporary governance in East Asia and to distinguish these processes from common Western assumptions about East Asian societies.

Affect, Asian values and soft power

Scholars have noted the role of emotion in shaping nationalities and economies in East Asia. Masahiko Fujiwara, for example, in his 2006 Japanese bestseller, *The Dignity of a State*, criticizes the emphasis on Western logic in Japanese society and calls for a return to ancient Japanese virtues. He argues that Japan overemphasizes logic, reason and rationality—Western constructs that have brought social ruin to Japan—and the Japanese meaning of nationhood has been lost amidst the forces of Americanization and internationalization. He sees globalism as a strategy of the United States for seeking world domination and the market economy as a system that destroys the country's egalitarianism and divides the society into a minority of winners and a majority of losers. He claims that Japan and the Japanese are unique; Japan is the only civilization of emotion in the world. Fujiwara states that Japanese do not have a religion such as Christianity or Islam, but need something else: deep emotion. Although this analysis not only simplifies the "West" but also essentializes emotions as something unique to Japan, his claim might be useful if interpreted as calling for a return to indigenous emotional registers and concepts to develop local models of democracy and ways of living.

In his study of a Japanese bank in Tokyo, Rohlen (1974) demonstrates that work at the bank means more than contractual relations. It requires loyalty, trust, friendship and responsibility. More than a workplace, the bank is viewed by both employers and employees as a household and family. Rohlen suggests that economic development and modernization in East Asia should not be seen solely as the product of Westernization or economic modernization, but as shaped (particularly in Japan and China) by a long history of successful (Confucian) bureaucracies and their continued existence and transformations in contemporary organizations (ibid.: 60). Likewise in a study of the public sphere in Japan, Daniel White (Chapter 5, this volume) observes that tears saturate Japanese TV production and consumption. He then uses tears as a methodological tool to trace the moral economy of emotion in Japanese TV. By challenging the emphasis on reason and rationality in early Western literature on the public sphere, White examines how those invested in the possibilities of a public sphere in Japan argue for its legitimacy by appropriating, contextualizing and problematizing emotions.

As for Asian values, underlying the so-called authoritarianism or strong state presence in economic operations in East Asia is a bond between the state and the people, and between superiors and subordinates. This bond does not endure solely through coercive force. Other means are required: strategies that encourage people to accept policies due to positive feelings (i.e. hope, happiness), or other affective registers (i.e. anger, fear). For example, happiness is a corollary to the Chinese political project of building "a harmonious society" envisioned in 2004 by Chinese President Hu Jintao and Premier Wen Jiabao. Because of ubiquitous propaganda, the notion of happiness or social harmony in this project has become affective in centralizing people's attention towards projects of sustaining symbolic, social and political stability.

Similarly, Rohlen (1974) illustrates in his ethnographic study of a Japanese bank that social concord is a highly valued quality expressed in the term *wa*. The bank's motto is *wa to chikara*, meaning "harmony and strength." However, Rohlen points out the difficulty in translating *wa* as it is neither a metaphor nor an abstract or logical part of a system of distinctions:

> Rather it is a quality of relationship … and it refers to the cooperation, trust, sharing, warmth, morale, and hard work of efficient, pleasant, and purposeful fellowship … Thus *wa* is far from a concept of static harmony. It is a directly tangible thing that easily accommodates human frailties and differences as long as participants share a devotion to the success of the common effort and a respect for one another as partners in the enterprise.
>
> (Rohlen 1974: 47)

Wa is a means to social improvement and, as a bond between individuals and their communities, it is an end in itself. *Wa* constitutes an affective vector that activates, enhances and expands the kind of family-like teamwork typical of a Japanese corporation.

Several chapters in this volume consider the family as an affective site and attend to shifts in the notion of family as new niche markets are created. For example, in Japan and South Korea where caring for the old was traditionally undertaken by family members, daughters and daughters-in-law, is now transforming as gender roles change and market competition allows women to go out to work, simultaneously opening new doors for domestic care of the elderly. In this context, both Japan and South Korea turn to international immigrant women for care labor. Toshiko Tsujimoto and Ayaka Yoshimizu both depict the emotional labor of immigrant care workers from the Philippines and Indonesia. In historically and culturally specific contexts where family members traditionally have been care givers, emotional labor is not always seen as a mode of exploitation (cf. Hochschild 1983), but rather as a gendered virtue that gives immigrant care workers market advantages, particularly in South Korea (see Chapter 8).

The notion of the family is also key to social imagination and nation building. In this volume, Craig MacKie (Chapter 11) examines the notion of the family—more precisely, the unified ethnic family (of Korea)—as a happy object of imagination and a source of pleasure and promises. In North Korea, the family is not only an affective site for constructing political subjects and generating political allegiance but also a mode of imagining the happy family state that might emerge by defeating South Korea (and its American ally) and uniting the two Koreas. Such family-rooted political imagination propels current governing from propaganda to military drills in North Korea. This notion of the family is also crucial in the governance shift in China. In her study of how a Chinese academic-turned-celebrity, Yu Dan, interprets and popularizes Confucius's *Analects*, Yanhua Zhang argues that Yu's maternal and emotive approach to Confucian narratives does not challenge the Chinese political imagination rooted in the Confucian family-centered tradition, but rather, Yu's interpretation mediates (or dampens) people's criticism by conflating the nation-state as polity with nation-culture as a symbolic and affective source of identity. Yu's reading of Confucianism helps shift attention from the paternalistic moral order to maternal affective affinity; the government is thus not to be judged morally on obligations for providing for the people, but to be embraced as the object of love and loyalty, and the source of spiritual growth and psychological comfort.

There is a longstanding literature that sees social relations in Japan, Korea, and China as more rooted in (and articulated in terms of) affect and emotion than in the West. For example, the notion of "Confucian capitalism" or "*guanxi* capitalism" relies upon affective connections in contrast to contractual relations that supposedly characterize business and politics in the West. Existing literature emphasizes culture and emotional and ethical bonds (cf. Rohlen 1974; Yang 1984; Smart 1993; Allison 1994; Yan 1996; Kipnis 1997). The literature highlights the affective and ethical dimensions of social connections or *guanxi* in China in terms of *renqing* (Yang 1984; Yan 1996) and *ganqing* (Kipnis 1997), both roughly translated as "human feelings." While Yang (1984) argues that *guanxi* is not only a historically specific cultural practice but also a ubiquitous discourse, Kipnis (1997) goes beyond the discursive dimension by demonstrating that *guanxi* can be articulated through non-representational ethics. By examining the affective-ethical dimension of *guanxi* practices, Kipnis suggests that subjects can be formed not merely in and through language but can be constructed more holistically, for example, through social relations and bodily feelings. In general, scholars on Asian social relations focus on the role of emotions in defining, limiting or expanding social, political and ethical boundaries. In this book contributors build on this attention to emotional bonds but diverge from the charting of relationships and boundaries to explore potential and imagination. We see affect as a felt quality that gives meanings and imaginative potential to political and economic transformations, and we focus on how affect triggers change, releases energy and imagination, and intensifies connectivity between objects, people and events.

Unlike affect explored in terms of *guanxi*, social ties and networks in China, where it operates as almost a separate system from bureaucratic power, supporting or subverting it, this volume pays particular attention to how state power works through affective modes of engagement or individual desires and feelings. As Hippler (2011) points out, according to Spinoza, power is twofold: on the one hand, there is physical power, the force of coercive strength that exists between one body and another, or between the state and the individual; on the other hand, power is imaginary and affective, relying on the manipulations of human passions. Hippler suggests that what we call "politics" is the collective agency of people's imaginative power, because political power is based on the force of an imagined association between social life and affects, between a world of individuals and their collective imagination (ibid.: 71).

Another widely cited concept that is frequently applied to East Asia is the notion of soft power (cf. Nye 2004, 2008a, 2008b; Bell 2008; Yasushi and McConnell 2008). Joseph Nye (2004) introduces the notion of soft power into the study of international politics. It is "an agent-focused definition of power" and "the ability to influence others to obtain the outcomes one wants" (Nye 2008a: x).[2] Nye (2004: 5–6) writes that soft power is "leading by example and attracting others to do what you want." This attractiveness, Nye argues, can be conveyed through various means, via a country's popular and elite culture, its public diplomacy, its businesses' actions abroad, international perceptions of its government's policies, and the gravitational pull of a nation's economic strength, among other factors. While Nye originally calls on the United States to apply soft power in its foreign affairs, the notion of soft power has now been widely used by analysts and politicians in international relationships. China's growing soft power, for example, has been described as "charm offensive," and as the most potent weapon in its foreign policy arsenal in recent years (Kurlantzick 2007: 5).[3] To the extent that soft power concerns the ability to create desire for others, it is an affective apparatus. However, Nye sees soft power as twisting *minds* rather than twisting arms. He writes: "Power defined in behavioral terms is a relationship, and soft power depends more on the subject's role in that relationship than does hard power. Attraction depends on what is happening *in the mind of the subject*" (Nye 2008a: xiii, emphasis added). With Nye's emphasis on "minds," soft power operates as a cognitive process; it can be exercised, for example, through "reasoned persuasion" (Nye 2008a: xiii). However, if soft power is about attraction, intersubjectivity, or interconnectivity, it can be captured more fully by including an analysis of its affective dimension that goes beyond reason: how that "softness" is manifested, felt or experienced and imagined, and how potentialities animated by that softness guide and shape what is currently unfolding.

MacKie in this volume touches on this topic through the notion of "charismatic affect." He suggests that charismatic affect is not an office but a role to be embodied. The charismatic affect of the North Korean leader is based on an appeal to the notion of the family. It enables people to personify the incomprehensible unity of a disintegrated group identity (North and South Korea) into the body of an existing person. He argues that while the Kim family dynasty stands as an example of a successful application of charismatic affect, its very existence as a dynasty without the assurance of the divine mandates of yore, has produced contradictions in its governing, which can be reflected in the phenomenon of people faking emotional authenticity in the mourning of Kim Jong-il.

Another example of such soft power and charm offensive is found in the recent rise of China's First Lady Peng Liyuan. Between March and June in 2013, Peng accompanied her husband, the new President Xi Jinping on two important foreign visits; she stole the limelight of the international political stage, at times even overshadowing her husband. Both foreign and Chinese media commented that Peng gives China a much needed soft power boost, signaling China's move from its traditionally isolationist foreign policy to being more engaged and proactive in international politics. However, during the two visits on which Peng accompanied her husband the president, she spoke little. Rather, her image—her body, her posture, her smile as well as her fashion sense—made for powerful "speech." Images are affective. She debuted her husband's and China's attention to soft power. While the presentation of Peng reflects the party's emphasis on "face," Xi uses his wife to start a quest for Chinese (and international) hearts and minds by presenting himself as a loving husband and a family man. Also, Peng's story, her humble family background, her success as a self-made popular folk vocal artist, and her army experiences—what she was, what she symbolizes and what she inspires—appear to be what the party desperately needs at the moment. She could emerge as a savior of a party whose image has been tarnished with corruption, alienating neoliberal policies and a widening income gap. Peng herself has become an affective vector, stimulating imagination and desire among ordinary people who join their government in "China's dream." Xi has announced "China's dream" as a new governing blueprint and technology to propel current socialist projects, mobilize people to identify with state interests and visions, and encourage the release of positive energy. This notion of China's dream focuses less on control and stability and more on people embracing government initiatives and potentialities. It is more affectively compelling than coercive.

This book is intended as a contribution to a new understanding of emerging modes of governmentality in East Asia through the lens of affect theory. It offers a framework for analyzing emerging (and relatively understudied) phenomena in East Asia—the psychologization of social issues, the rise of self-help genres, transnational labor migration, new ideologies of gender and the family, and mass-mediated affective communities. Authors apply affect theory to understand changing political configurations, economic engagements, modes of belonging and forms of subjectivity in East Asia. They use ethnographic research and discourse analysis to illustrate the affective dimensions of state and economic power and the way affect informs and inspires action. Given the importance of emotion and affect to prior models of sociality and power in East Asia, this volume sheds new light on well-established themes in the study of East Asia. In what follows, I first define affect as it is used throughout the book. I then discuss the main themes of the volume—affect and its relation to ideology, governmentality, subjectivity, the body and biopolitical economy as they manifest through the chapters.

Affect and emotion

In the literature there have been diverse and multiple genealogies and definitions of affect (see McElhinny 2010; Gregg and Selgworth 2010). Many think of *affect* as another way of saying *emotion*. Indeed, scholars often use emotion and affect interchangeably (see Gorton 2007 for a review of works on this use). Given the significance and long history of the study of emotions in feminist scholarship, I will start with reviewing their notions of emotion and affect. For example, in reclaiming the erotic as a form of affective power that has been degraded under a hetero-patriarchal regime of power, Audre Lorde writes:

> The erotic is a measure between the beginnings of our sense of self and the chaos of our strongest feelings. It is an internal sense of satisfaction to which, once we have experienced it, we know we can aspire. For having experienced the fullness of this depth of feeling and recognizing its power, in honor and self-respect we can require no less of ourselves.
>
> (Lorde 1978: 54)

In this account, "the fullness of this depth of feeling" points to affect as volume or intensity. This fullness and depth is something that we can work to achieve. In achieving this state, we can look back on the process of accomplishment as the creation of possibility. This felt space of possibility is a process of becoming subjects for ourselves. Here affect refers to both cognition and bodily sensation (see also Ahmed 2004; Gorton 2007). While acknowledging the bodily sensation of emotions, feminist scholars also emphasize the usefulness of a cognitive approach to emotions for developing critique on inequality. For example, in studying the politics of anger, Elizabeth V. Spelman (1989) adopts the cognitivist theory for capturing situations in the Western cultures where although reason has long been associated with members of dominant groups, emotion with members of subordinate groups, the anger of subordinate groups is not tolerated. She argues that dominant groups place limits on the kinds of emotional responses appropriate to those subordinate to them and the systematic denial of anger can be seen as a mechanism of subordination. She thus calls on people to express anger as an act of insubordination (ibid.: 270). Similarly, Alison Jaggar (1989), by disputing the gendered dichotomy between reason and emotion (emotions are often associated with women and subordinate groups while rationality with men and dominant groups), argues that rationality needs emotion, as emotions constitute cognitive processes and modes of knowledge production. Jaggar criticizes the downplaying by dominant groups of the role of emotion (and its alleged association with women and subordinate groups) in contributing to knowledge production and social inequality.

Unlike these feminist scholars who view emotion or affect as both cognitive and sensational, scholars like Brian Massumi (2002) suggest a sharp distinction between affect and emotion. He sees emotion as a cognitive process that can be linguistically represented, while affect is a bodily experience of intensity that cannot be captured by narration (Massumi 2002: 28; Grossberg 1992: 81). For Massumi, affect is the connecting thread of experience. It is the animating force behind all "natural" and "social" phenomena. This notion of affect offers new perspectives for anthropologists to examine the physiological, the concrete and the nonconscious processes of social life. In her study of the quality education reform in China, Teresa Kuan (Chapter 3, this volume) adopts this notion of affect. Through analyzing an experiential exercise at the Summer Palace through which a summer camp teacher asked her students to deposit sensory-emotion banknotes to their bodies for future use, Kuan examines this bodily and sensory experiment and its significance in contributing to the broader discussion on education reform, economic development and national strength in China. She suggests that the body of a child and its capacity to be affected can be mobilized into a power to affect in a given historical context. That is, a body's capacity to act and to affect constitutes a major focus of discursive concern and pedagogical intervention in China's education reform. While Kuan focuses on the indeterminate and the undefined that can be instrumental for value extraction, she combines this affective study with ethnographic and discourse analyses.

However, for Massumi (2002: 35–36), affect is autonomous and can only be felt and perceived as escape. Such non-representational features of affect may pose a methodological challenge for anthropologists to document the affective dimension of social life. Massumi (2002) then argues that even though affect is experienced as intensity and cannot be directly analyzed, the effect of affect can be analyzed. Indeed, people may experience the effects of affect, but the way they articulate such effects may differ because of their ways of existence—status, biography, or lifestyle. The way one comes to know oneself and others as subjects—that is, subjectivity itself—is contingent on such differences. Affect, as a primary element in social relations, thus needs to be contextualized and examined culturally, historically and politically. Instead of seeing affect as pure potentiality or intensity as described by Massumi (2002), I focus on affect as harnessed to the service of politics and economy, taking up approaches that are more suited for ethnographic analysis.

For example, Sara Ahmed (2004, 2010), instead of asking what emotions are, focuses on what emotions do. This shift of framing allows her approach to be well suited to anthropological inquiry as it enables anthropologists to see what happens on the ground. As she suggests, "emotions are not simply something 'we' have. Rather, it is through emotions, or how we respond to objects and others, that surfaces or boundaries are made: the 'I' and the 'we' are shaped by, and even take the shape of, contact with others" (Ahmed 2004: 10). Her mode of affective contagion focuses on "how emotions create the very surfaces and boundaries that allow all kinds of objects to be delineated" (Ahmed 2004: 10). Emotion, for Ahmed, seems to be an aura that envelops bodies and objects, which move, connect with and transform one another, accumulating values (ibid.: 11). She examines the "sociality" of emotion: "feelings do not reside in subjects or objects, but are produced as effects of circulation" (ibid.: 8). The circulation of emotions between subjects thus creates the effect of a collective. All contributors explicitly or implicitly take on this relational approach to emotions; instead of defining affect, we focus on what affects do in specific contexts.

Similarly, Bonnie McElhinny (2010), rather than offering a fixed definition, invites scholars to consider what the proliferation of definitions might reflect about differences in intellectual genealogies and their various epistemological and political claims and implications. Following Raymond Williams (1977), she treats *affect* as a keyword (McElhinny 2010: 310; see also Stewart 2007), a key site at which identities and social experiences (including feelings) are constructed, negotiated and contested (McElhinny 2007). In this volume, Sung Kil Min (Chapter 10) views the unique Korean cultural phenomenon of *haan* (roughly suppressed anger and feelings of unfairness) as a keyword. He suggests that any type of *haan* encompasses at least two processes: one is years of accumulated and layered feelings of being unfairly treated, oppressed or devalued; the other, the gradual dissolving or resolving of *haan* through various means correlating with specific causes of that type of *haan*. While it is normatively considered as a physical or psychological disorder, Min focuses on *haan* as a political affect, as a force mobilized by the government for political and economic purposes.

Contributors to this volume also take on Sianne Ngai's approach, which treats the differences between affect and emotion as a matter of degree:

> [A]ffects are less formed and structured than emotions, but not lacking form or structure altogether; less "sociolinguistically fixed," but by no means code-free or meaningless; less "organized in response to our interpretations of situations," but by no means entirely devoid of organization or diagnostic powers.
>
> (Ngai 2005: 27)

This affect-emotion relational approach allows analysis of a process—the transitions between affect and emotion, particularly the transition whereby affects acquire the semantic density and narrative complexity of emotions. For example, in studying the affective dimension of Japanese TV production and consumption, White argues that tears are nonconscious, physiological responses of the body which resist narration, but that tears are also cultural. Instead of taking the physiological for granted, he pays equal attention to the physical manifestations of tears as well as their cultural meaning (e.g. shame, loss, sadness or happiness) and the way they shape one another. In general, contributors to this volume see affect as a felt quality that gives meanings and imaginative potential to social, political and economic transformations. It is the force or energy that circulates and mediates within, between and around bodies and worlds, organizing or structuring social, economic and political activities.[4] It is bodily, but cannot be entirely contained or embodied. It has its own autonomy but can be partially captured by language. In particular, the works collected here treat affect and its animated potentionalities as objects of governance and sites for value extraction. Rather than seeing affect and emotion as a totalizing or essentializing force, contributors investigate the ways each emotion or affect does in historically specific social and cultural contexts.

More than using ideological or rational structuring to support ways of living that affirm their power, those who govern also use strategies that call upon affectivity, emotions, enjoyment, happiness and fun (see Prada 2010). For example, nationalism, communism, or even fascism as an ideological premise and practice also encompasses emotional appeals. However, there is incongruence between what affect is and what it can do. There is inevitably a misfit between individual identities and potentialities and the dispositions society desires for its members (see Ahmed 2010). Affect, in the employ of government agents, can be intended to address this gap and enable the reshaping of citizens. The authors contributing to this volume explore the twists and misfits between different affective registers in terms of both power and subject formation. They seek to untangle the complex and intricate ways that affect and emotion may be insinuated within and contribute to the reproduction of subjectivity, power and economy. Specifically, the chapters explore various ways that affect mediates and transforms relations of signification (representation and language), market economy (affective labor and consumption), and power and ideology in East Asia.

Taken together the works collected here emphasize the advantages of ethnographic analyses of the political economy of affect in East Asia for understanding the dynamics of affective registers; it is not only the effects of affective power that are at issue but also the historical and cultural shaping of specific contexts where these affective vectors are formed and operate and where affective subjectivities are constructed.

Happiness, optimism and therapeutic governance

Like her approach to emotions, rather than defining happiness, Sara Ahmed (2010) focuses on what happiness does. This powerful framing allows her to move away from the elusiveness and fluidity of happiness and focus on "how [the everyday habits of happiness] involve ways of thinking about the world that shape how the world coheres" (ibid.: 15). For Ahmed, happiness is a form of world making—happiness participates in the creation of social form—and a political technology that produces social norms. Her approach to happiness enables ethnographers to examine how people pursue and perform happiness as well as use happiness to justify ideological representations, distract and downplay inequalities in specific contexts.

Ahmed (2010) explores how the promise of happiness inspires and directs our actions and compels current practice. "The promise of happiness is what makes certain objects proximate, affecting how the world gathers around us"

(Ahmed 2010: 14). She considers how happiness is attributed to objects (ibid.: 17). Happiness involves affect, intentionality and evaluation or judgment. If happiness creates its objects, such objects are passed around, accumulating positive affective value as social good (ibid.: 21). The happy object is both intentional and anticipatory, being something we deliberately turn ourselves towards in hopes of future pleasure or benefit. Adopting this dimension of happiness, MacKie (this volume) argues that the concept of the family, or more specifically the reunified Korean ethnic family, is the anticipated happy object—affectively rooted promise—in North Korea's affective training. He suggests that this unified, happy Korean family as the *prime* happy object lends positive affect to objects around it such as Kim Il-sung, socialism, the military, etc. However, as both North and South Korea are pitted against each other in a conflict of national identity, this very conflict simultaneously frustrates the "promise" of the national community itself, the state of happiness, flourishing or belonging.

Ahmed (2010) also discusses positive psychology as a happiness turn within psychology. She suggests that instead of assuming happiness as found in "happy persons," we consider how claims to happiness make certain forms of personhood valuable. "Attributions of happiness might be how social norms and ideals become affective, as if relative proximity to those norms and ideals creates happiness" (Ahmed 2010: 11). In this book, both Yoshimizu and Jie Yang adopt this notion of happiness through analysis of the happiness of marginalized individuals promoted by the Japanese and Chinese governments. Both view happiness as a site of ideological investment for legitimating broader political and economic agendas.

Lauren Berlant (2008, 2011) examines another "positive" affect, optimism. She uses the notion of cruel optimism to discuss affect and unconscious fantasies in relation to ideologies of the good life that were made available for optimism in the post-war economic bubble in the United States. As she states, "cruel optimism is the condition of *maintaining* an attachment to a problematic object" (Berlant 2008: 33, emphasis original). These problematic objects—embodied in a cluster of promises—sustain *and* destroy people. For example, although capital may in fact threaten our well-being and happiness, but facilitate "the good life," we are willing to continue the relationship with this object rather than disassociate from it because of the belief that it is somehow integral to our existence and sense of continuity. The notion attends attachment to compromised conditions, where the attachment is necessary or desirable for maintaining a conception of one's place in the world, but the promise the attachment holds is patently unrealistic, either impossible, or too easy, to attain.

For Berlant (2008), cruel optimism lies in its synchronicity. Optimism persists, even if cruel, because loss of the object's promise carries the menace of destabilizing hope entirely (ibid.: 33). The cruel optimism in Ashbery's poem is that of the American Dream, in which the individual has lost her awareness of the world in exchange only for the promise of, in this case, the suburban good life (ibid.: 38). Through Ashbery's narrator, Berlant points to the way of escaping cruelty—that is, openness to disruptive encounter, to a promise of the suspension of habituated attachment to the cruelty of middle-class optimism (ibid.: 42). Such openness is not about forming less cruel optimistic attachments, but rather about recognizing the subversive potential of optimism's interruptions. While these disruptions interfere with optimism's synchronicity, they do not seem to posit any alternative scheme of attachment to the possible. In this context, Hirokazu Miyazaki's view of hope as a cultural force may suggest some resolution to this tension.[5] In his ethnography of hope among Suvavou people in Fiji, Miyazaki examines how Suvavou people have kept hope alive over the last one hundred years, and their capacity to create hopeful moments across different facets of their life ranging from petitions to the government to gift-giving rituals, church services and business activities. His notion of hope is derived from the impossibility he perceives in reconciling a progressive view of history, and Suvavou people's understanding of their experience of it (Miyazaki 2004: 22–23). For Miyazaki, hope can be a methodological stance, a way of generating knowledge (ibid.: 7–12); this approach offers a useful framework for ethnographic inquiry into hope and optimism.

In studying state-led re-employment counseling programs in China, which are imbued with psychologically infused ideologies and practices to promote happiness and optimism among unemployed workers, Yang suggests that this notion of happiness is a governing technology that delivers "therapy" in order to "heal" and integrate those who have been displaced and impoverished by privatization into the market economy. Such happiness also generates cruel optimism: impoverished workers hope to see the fulfillment of the promises the state claims to deliver through tokenistic welfare programs (as a political technique of bearing optimism), which, however, are creating new vulnerabilities for those workers. This notion of happiness as therapy is a form of psychologization—translating socioeconomic issues in psychological terms—which can be invoked to blame individuals for their unemployment and poverty. Such happiness promotions in China also gesture the emerging therapeutic governance. In the name of healing, the state and its arms increase profits and control over those whom they displaced and impoverished. Such strategies point to complicity between the state and market.

The above-mentioned works on happiness, hope and optimism offer important insights for us to reconsider the nature of the emerging modes of governing in East Asia, for example, through psychological self-help. Such self-help literature allows readers to enjoy psychological insights without being stigmatized as mentally ill. Based on the information they consume, individuals become "experts" on their own and learn to help themselves. This "free choice" is nevertheless an illusion because powerful groups and governments pull the strings behind the scenes and direct people towards their "choices" (Rose 1996). However, there are distinctive features in the development of psychological self-help, for example, in China: besides importing Western psychological self-help literature, Chinese cultural tradition such as Confucianism, Daoism and Buddhism is also mobilized as part of psychological self-help.[6]

Zhang's chapter, for example, engages a notion of happiness based on new interpretations of Confucius's *Analects*. Zhang focuses on how Yu Dan as a cultural nanny uses happiness and her femininity as media to translate the Confucian tradition into a meaning-making, affective practice which is further mobilized by the government to achieve various social, political and economic objectives. Zhang argues that happiness is not only an important goal and a practical concern in everyday life, but is employed as a neoliberal technology of governance. Yu Dan's Confucian lectures on happiness could be understood as a process of neoliberal localization, seeking to articulate neoliberal self-governance in terms of Confucian self-cultivation. In other words, Yu Dan offers a Confucian solution that supplements the neoliberal technology of self by focusing on how to deal with one's self.

Affect, body and subjectivity

Feelings affect the body. Affect offers a unique way of thinking about subjectivity by not just what we think of ourselves but also by how we feel and how our bodies respond to feelings. Perceived as felt quality, affect offers a particular way to feel or imagine the world and the subject, or to feel the feeling of the subject. Protevi (2009: 50) uses a notion of "bodies politic" to capture the relationship between politics and affect. To illustrate the emergent character of subjectivity and different relations of subjectification "intersecting populations of bodies with genetic diversity and with developmental plasticity" (ibid.: 42), Protevi suggests that bodies are necessarily embedded and embodied in an ecosocial matrix of other bodies, being affected by and affecting them. Subjects and bodies negotiate ecosocial situations by "feeling" through the world. Contrary to the belief that bodies simply represent the features of the world to themselves (cultural representationalism in anthropology), feeling through the world allows for three possible outcomes: first, the enhancement of power in one body and a decrease in another; second, a decrease in both bodies; and third, a mutual enhancement of power. Affect thus offers a particular way of rendering the world intelligible through bodily engagement and its power dynamics. The existing literature on Asian values, Confucian capitalism, or soft power captures such processes by emphasizing the discursive and ideological modes of subject formation (cf. Brook and Luong 1997). The study of affect opens a new space to study the forming and formative process of subjectivity in terms of its bodily mode or the dynamics in which subjectivity *becomes* visible or invisible, formed or transformed, circulated or (re)distributed.

Subject formation through affect also offers a critique of feminist Lacanians' positioning of subjects in and through language (cf. Henriques *et al.* 1984; Mahoney and Yngvesson 1992). Subjects exist not only in language or discourse but also in ongoing social and bodily interactions (cf. Lyon 1995; Ness 2011). Michael Jackson (1983), for example, suggests that the meaning of body praxis or bodily feelings is not always reducible to cognitive or semantic operations; bodily engagement can do more than words. Kipnis (1997) points out that as much as in language, feelings with their physical, bodily and social richness are forming and shaping subjectivity.

Recent feminist scholarship treats the body not as an enclosed entity but as fluid and continuous with its environment (cf. Haraway 1991; Wissinger 2007). Their conceptualization of the body opens to the flow of energy or as a site of the interface of affects. Through nuanced ethnographic and media analyses, contributors examine how affective regimes are articulated by non-Western bodies and subjects. Instead of theorizing power as *effects* and allowing its pervasiveness to deconstruct selves, contributors of this volume use affect to deconstruct power and track down its *origins*. As a whole, the volume also seeks to shed light on how affect can constitute the potential for subversion. We locate resistive affects, for example, anger or *haan* in South Korea (Min, Chapter 10) and tears of laid-off women represented in Chinese television melodrama (Shuyu Kong, Chapter 6), and explore how these affects offer a way of analyzing the formation of racialized, classed and gendered subjects, and how those who find themselves in these subject categories "feel" through the world and "muster" their feelings and desires to cope with and sometimes transform their positionality.

In this volume, both Kuan and Shiho Satsuka (Chapter 4) examine the body's interaction with the natural, cultural and economic environments. Through analysis of the notion of a "sensory-emotion bank," improvised by a summer camp teacher at Beijing's Summer Palace, Kuan discusses the quality education reform in China. The teacher instructed students to store valuable sensory "banknotes" in their sensory organs—that is, a more holistic approach to experiential learning, which goes beyond the traditional educational model that emphasizes, for example, test-taking. Kuan sees the body as world-connecting thread of experience, and a site where affective forces could be put into play in the changing of a country's future, for example, through sensory engagements with the material world. She treats affect as a milieu, an in-between space that must be facilitated, through the management of fragile social relationship. It is a process of becoming, a hope that inspires youth to actualize their full potential.

Similarly, through an ethnographic study of affective subject formation and embodiment of Japanese tour guides in the Canadian Rockies, Satsuka analyzes how local Japanese tour guides become both "commodities" *and* active agents of enacting the affective economy of enjoyment. The guides as residents in the idealized natural landscape of the Rockies embodied Japanese cosmopolitan desire, free from the social pressures and communal obligations in Japan. These guides' full-bodied approach to tour guidance and their dedication to clients became an integral part of their subjectivity formation. However, when those grateful tourists tried to reconnect them through gifts and memory cards, a practice encouraged by tour companies to attract repeat tourists, the guides were nevertheless detached from these tourists. Satsuka argues that such detachment constituted an unintentional critique of the circular logic in the gift or commodity economy of this hospitality industry. In this sense, she suggests that the excess generated by guides' bodies—for tourists to experience full-bodied affect in the nature and culture of the Canadian Rockies, without expecting any return—goes beyond the enclosed machine of economy.

As Hippler (2011) points out, the individual is not a fixed entity but a process within a "web of reference." For example, the individual is not a given and stable matter of politics; rather, individuation is a process coextensive with political engagement. Moreover, the individual is subject to fluxes of affects; a specific place and configuration within a web of imaginary and affective relations. Individuality is thus trans-individuality. Both individuals and the multitude rely on communication of affects and subjective communication through affects (Hippler 2011: 71). Indeed, affect can direct people to act in ways that support (or challenge) power, because affect structures encounters as a series of modifications that can dispose bodies for action in a given way. As Sedgwick writes:

> Affects can be, and are, attached to things, people, ideas, sensations, relations, activities, ambitions, institutions, and any other number of others things, including other affects. Thus one can be excited by anger, disgusted by shame, or surprised by joy.
>
> (Sedgwick 2003: 19)

Authors in this volume examine the unequal production and circulation of affects and their attachment to certain bodies as political processes, linking varied distributions of affects to class, gender and other social stratifications (see Ahmed 2004, 2010).

Contributions to this volume also examine the use of affect as a tool (one developed in the West) to analyze affective regimes in East Asia. For example, Min examines *haan*, which could develop into a serious disease or could be channeled as a cathartic force for political and economic purposes. Viewing *haan* as both sensational and cognitive, Min argues that *haan* is a political affect that intensifies people's attachment to the world and contributes to South Korea's nationalist discourse and nation-building efforts.

The contributors pay particular attention to gender as an affective vector and its attachment to emotions (happiness, sorrow, tears) (see also Lutz 1988; Ahmed 2004), and how emotions mediate, shape, and are shaped by, gender ideologies (see Chapters 1, 6, 7, 8, 9). Using gender as a lens, these authors are able to conceptualize insightfully aspects of the political economies of East Asia. For example, by paying attention to how positive representations of foreign care workers and their happiness render invisible migrant care workers' subjectivities, Yoshimizu sees Indonesian women and their happiness represented by Japanese media as a way for the Japanese government to manage the declining appeal of traditional feminine virtues—for example, embodied by daughters or "good wife, wise mother"—and as a new trend in Japanese biopolitics which draws resources from its colonial past. She argues that such biopolitical strategies rely on existing racial and sexual stereotypes of the ex-colonized, and by exploiting these subordinate bodies, reinforce racist and sexist structures.

Like Yoshimizu's chapter on the moral, economic and political implications of the recent deployment of Southeast Asian care workers in Japan, Tsujimoto analyzes Filipino care workers in South Korea. She demonstrates that Filipino care workers do not see emotional labor as a source of exploitation, but as a way of allocating resources to fulfill themselves and legitimating and expanding a niche market for domestic care in a country where care givers have traditionally been family members. In the same process these women must manage their transnational intimacy with families left behind, legitimating as best they can the tragic irony that they care for their own families by leaving them to care for other families.

Diverging from Yoshimizu's notion of happiness which downplays immigrant women's subjectivities, Zhang discusses the gendered dimension of psychologization in China through analyzing how Yu Dan mobilizes her femininity and happiness to accord Confucian stories an affective appeal. Such an affective turn mirrors and contributes to the governance shift in China from a paternalistic polity which is supposed to provide for its people to a maternal and emotive role which only constitutes the object of love and loyalty and a symbolic source of identity.

Unlike White's emphasis on tears and crying as a seemingly common practice for both men and women in Japanese television, Kong examines the gendered dimension of tears—those of women workers laid off from the state sector—in a way to critique both state policies and patriarchy in devastating the living conditions of those unemployed women. Kong focuses on the emotional performativity of tears in shaping social imagination and mediating the social experience of change. She suggests that tears construct an affective space and emotional realism. Kong contextualizes her analysis of tears in the Chinese melodramatic narrative tradition, which sees women's suffering and tears as significant device for social criticism, and within the Confucian notion of *ku*: women's crying presents their struggle between political ideals and emotional frustrations in a patriarchal society.

While Kong examines the performativity of tears and gender, Momoko Nakamura (Chapter 9) focuses on the performativity of language and gender through analysis of Japanese "women's language." She views gender not only as a site for affective and ideological investment but also as a political technology for the government to enact colonial rule and strengthen nation-state. Highlighting the performativity of language and its ability to affect people's sense of self and place in the world (see Riley 2005), Nakamura examines how emotion takes over the linguistic power and concomitant affect it has on Japan's colonial agenda. To legitimate linguistic colonization of East Asian countries during World War II, women's language was suddenly praised as an imperial tradition which facilitated Japan's colonial rule. After the war, under occupation by the US Army which denied both the emperor and patriarchal system, Japanese linguists redefined women's language as a natural reflection of "innate" femininity. De-politicized and naturalized, women's language became one of the few ideologies used to represent imperial tradition and patriarchy but survived the defeat in the war and the US occupation. The Japanese government and intellectuals thus viewed women's language as a felt space of possibility to recover Japanese social order and national identity.

Ideology, imagination and affective governmentality

Louis Althusser conceptualizes what he calls the ideological state apparatus (ISA) (i.e. schools, churches, parties, families, media), which embodies or transmits the ideology of the ruling class, interpellating subjects into being (e.g. as Christians, as citizens). He views ideology not as an accurate representation of human conditions of existence, but as their relation to those conditions of existence that are represented to them in ideology (Althusser 1971: 124). In other words, ideology is how subjects come to understand or recognize themselves in relation to the conditions and relations of production. In this sense, ideology involves elements of perception and imagination.

Imagination is more than mere fantasy, as Bottici and Challand (2011) point out. Imagination includes the capacity to represent what does not exist, but is not limited to this function. It also produces images of existing and non-existing objects (ibid.: 3). Without such production of images, there could be no utopia or ideology in the sense of false consciousness. Bottici and Challand (2011: 4) define politics as "a struggle for people's imagination." Indeed, as Hippler (2011) observes, those who hold power often see imagination and passion as causes of social disharmony. Hippler then identifies hope and fear as the passions that are most often used by power for social pacification: hope for a better life in the future and fear of punishment. However, since human nature will not submit to absolute repression, it is more useful for political powers to rely on hope than fear. Imagination provides the link between the social creation of hope and the stability of the state (ibid.: 61). Working from within imagination, power is not felt directly, but indirectly, through the intensity of an affective experience, like the power of hope. Because this is the case, Bugliani (2011: 83) suggests, instead of looking for power in terms of its location (who wields power), researchers should look for power in the limits placed on people's faculties of imagining and in how these constraints are imposed.

For example, state-sanctioned representations of happiness among particular individuals of the underprivileged in China encourage people to imagine and work toward a better future by adopting the represented emotions or thought processes attached to ideas of a good life, which nevertheless constitutes a type of cruel optimism in Berlant's term (Chapter 2, this volume).

Alternatively, the tears of laid-off women saturating TV dramas in China make it possible for people to imagine shared suffering and thus engender comfort, solidarity and stability (Chapter 6, this volume).

The authors of work collected here investigate how imagination reverberates in various elements of social and political life to affect people's capacity to form images that have affective potential. Control over image-making is a key political objective. Yoshimizu, for example, analyzes the happy image of the Southeast Asian care workers depicted by Japanese media as a way to downplay gendered exploitation in the care labor market and legitimate a new trend of Japan's biopolitics (by drawing on human resources from its former colonies).

While Althusser's notion of ideology emphasizes the structural relationship between individuals and the ideological state apparatus, with affect transcending institutional and programmatic boundaries, the study of affect may reveal new political registers and intensities that go beyond the (neat, logically based) conceptual framework of ideology (Thrift 2007: 173). Authors contributing to this volume identify and examine (new) affective regimes and affective registers that are not reducible to, though entangled with, discursive and ideological orders.

For example, Kong suggests that tears in Chinese TV drama on laid-off women workers complicate the ideological messages conveyed in the official promotion of neoliberal inspiration and upward mobility in a new market economy. Despite the positive message of aspiration and happy endings on the surface of the TV dramas on unemployed workers, Kong argues that there is a theme of suffering and salvation expressed in a melodramatic style and a deep-seated emotional antagonism grounded in popular discontent and resentment expressed through the characterization of laid-off female workers as crying subjects. In this sense, tears represent contentious voices from the victims' point of view, which opens up a subtle critique of heightened social inequality and the new dominance of capital over all other values. Similarly, Zhang suggests that the popularized Confucian wisdom for happiness promoted by Yu Dan at China Central Television (CCTV) programs is both ideological and emotive, and is crafted, prescribed and appropriated to mediate between how to "feel" as a cultural subject of Chinese person and to "live" in everyday life as a modern neoliberal individual in the globalized market era in China.

Sites where one can witness the work of these affective regimes, be it the body, language, care labor, television dramas, or government programs, can entail and reveal technologies of governance. Through them, an emotional tone can be embedded in social or state structures. Nakamura, for example, suggests that the emotional attachment to Japanese women's language—polite, indirect and soft women's language—can be mobilized into the possibility to believe that Japanese tradition, pride and social order are safely inherited and secured. That is, the feelings, belief, anticipation and possibility attached to women's language not only intensify people's attachments to it, but also enable people to confirm themselves that there is a space in which Japanese social order and identity can be reproduced, preserved and sustained.

This emotional tone can also resonate with increasingly emotional, psychological, or therapeutic forms of selfhood (see Kleinman 2010). The individual is encouraged to escape from within or to refer to the language of emotions as a problem-solving technique or as a means of self-understanding. This emotionally based understanding of self and society shapes the way individuals participate and communicate in social life (Nolan 1998: 6). This volume examines such emotive or therapeutic sensibilities and their relations to subject formation in East Asia from multiple vantage points such as emotion-provoking TV programs, propaganda and language in China, Japan and North Korea, the promotion of the happiness of the marginalized in China and Japan, and *haan* in South Korea.

Power can form or mobilize affective regimes to win over the hearts of the people by tapping into individual desires or emotions. Nigel Thrift's (2007: 188) notion of "velvet dictatorship," for example, refers to this kind of affective strategy (or therapeutic governance): its civil, even charitable nature renders authoritarian rule more appealing and endurable even while also more hegemonic. As a result, ideologies (or particular programs of governance) may grip (or interpellate) subjects effectively. As Grossberg writes:

> [A]ffect is the missing term in an adequate understanding of ideology, for it offers the possibility of a "psychology of belief" which would explain how and why ideologies are sometimes and only sometimes, effective, and always to varying degrees … It is the affective investment in particular ideological sites … that explain the power of the articulation which binds particular representations and realities. It is the affective investment which enables ideological relations to be internalized and, consequently, naturalized.
>
> (Grossberg 1992: 83)

Human beings embody not only ideas and beliefs, but also desires, hopes, fears and socio-political aspirations, and human beings and affects intertwine in various social programs, interventions and administrative projects. For example, the government-supported circulation of happiness and its attachment to workers who have been displaced and impoverished by economic restructuring in China offers an alternative to disappointment, depression and anger expressed against the state. A select few of the unemployed who have been mobilized and represented as "re-employment-star" entrepreneurs come to symbolize the positive potential of the marginalized (Yang 2007). This is a political process. Such affective investment through happiness therapy in subjects strengthens bonds between particular representations (say, of laid-off workers in China as budding entrepreneurs) and realities (the potential their marginal status offers for achieving entrepreneurial success), which downplays negative effects of economic restructuring and even defends and legitimates such economic restructuring (see Chapters 2, 6).

Affective labor, potentiality and biopolitical economy

As mentioned, East Asia scholars often focus on the role of culture or Confucianism in the region's economic growth (cf. Rohlen 1974; Brook and Luong 1997), while the affective dimension of capitalist development remains understudied. The role of affect in the capitalist economy is captured in Marx's comparison of the capitalist and the miser: "This boundless drive for enrichment, this passionate chase after value is common to the capitalist and the miser" (Marx 1976: vol. 1, 278). In recent years, scholars have explored the relationship between affect and business effectiveness. Beyond extracting value through the exploitation of its subjects as a workforce, economic power has increasingly capitalized on the lucrative regulation of people's ways of living, life dynamics and affective interactions (Prada 2010). The traditional notion of production, focused on goods, is now being extended to pleasure and entertainment, to the (computerized) production of intangible goods and information, and to the production of sociability itself (ibid.). Indeed, the entertainment and culture industries create and manipulate affects, while service industries rely heavily on caring and affective labor (Hardt 1999). Authors contributing to this volume examine affective labor as positioned within biopolitical economies (Chapters 4, 7, 8).

Affective labor refers to labor that produces affects (Hardt and Negri 2000), including a feeling of ease, well-being, satisfaction, excitement, passion, social networks, forms of community, or biopower (Hardt 1999: 96). Feminist analyses have long recognized the social value of affective labor (i.e. care labor, kin work and maternal activities). What is new is the extent to which such labor is directly productive of capital (Hardt 1999: 97). The role of affect in the neoliberal economy differs from the "emotion work" identified in earlier feminist studies by focusing on the circulation and formation of subjects through affect, rather than the circulation of emotions between subjects (Richard and Rudnyckyj 2009: 69). That is, affect forms a medium through which people act on others and are acted upon, creating new types of subjects and new relations among those subjects (see McElhinny 2010; Chapter 9, this volume).

Scholars who focus on the role of affect in capitalist modes of production (Hochschild 1983; Hardt 1999; Hardt and Negri 2000) suggest that production has become communicative, affective and de-industrialized, "elevated" to the level of human relations that are entirely dominated by and internal to capital (Hardt 1999: 96). In addition to the role of affect in capitalist production, contributions collected here demonstrate the way affect serves social and political objectives. Through an ethnographic analysis of both commercial and public TV production processes in Japan, White uses tears as a vehicle to understand how affect is utilized in strategies of capital gain and tempered by the ethics of public broadcasting. As he argues, tears as repositories of feelings and emotions, besides facilitating the drive for capital in commercial broadcasters' ratings competitions; tears also fulfill other social and political purposes, serving as tools of emotional education for Japan's public broadcaster, and defining democracy, responsibility and public engagement for Japanese citizens.

Combining power and affective labor, Hardt (1999: 99) defines biopower as the potential or product of affective labor. Similarly, Ben Anderson (2012) suggests that affective life can be an object of and condition for specific forms of biopower. Indeed, scholars have recently tracked changes in the workings of biopower (Rabinow and Rose 2006; Prada 2010; Anderson 2012). They argue that there is less emphasis today on direct control over the body and the biological condition of the population first identified by Foucault (1978). The focus now is on producing and regulating ways of living, enjoying and experiencing life. Prada (2010) suggests that a new economic dynamic privileges the individual-as-body much more than previous biopower regimes, in which individuals were simply political subjects. Now human beings are perceived as possessors of life and, therefore, as wealth in themselves.[7] Further, Venn (2007) looks at biopower as a mode of power that sees being (i.e. identities, relations) as harboring potentiality animated by desire, emotions, or spirit (ibid.: 111). Thus, while biopower still refers to governance over life itself, the operations of this governance are understood to occur within an economy of affective registers related to broad potentialities. Affective registers and energies are now required to work within the economic process, shifting from an imagination of the commodity alone to an economic process in which imagination of the social relations of production is made accessible and appropriate for the market.

Authors here consider the notion of affective excess in generating new values and new potentialities. The excess generated by affect or affective labor goes beyond the enclosed machine of economy. It constitutes a new vector for releasing potential and a resource for extracting value. Both Kuan and Satsuka engage such generative excess: one is a summer camp teacher using a moment within natural and historical landscape to invest in camp students' minds and hearts for them to imagine and to withdraw as a future resource. Satsuka discusses the excess produced by tour guides' affective interaction with tourists, the full-bodied enactment of the beauty and tranquility of the Rockies without expecting any return from their clients. Such excess, Satsuka argues, also constitutes a source of surplus value, which the tourist industry tries to encompass into the entangled moral and capitalist economies of Japanese tourism in the Canadian Rockies but is not always successful.

Adams *et al.* (2009) suggest that the recent fascination with affect can be understood as an intensification of regimes of anticipation (see Chapter 11, this volume). Like Hippler, they argue that hope and fear are increasingly prominent political factors that point toward possibility and potentiality, thereby opening up spaces for change or expansion. Indeed, scholars have begun to view potentiality as a parameter of (bio)politics (cf. Hardt 1999; Massumi 2007; Venn 2007; Anderson 2011; Svendsen 2011). Svendsen (2011), for example, has proposed an anthropological approach to potentiality in an analysis of health-optimizing strategies (such as those surrounding the use of "blank" stem cells). This approach "addresses the cultural context as well as the material conditions of that seen as incomplete yet with a power—a potency—to develop into something else" (ibid.: 416). Svendsen emphasizes the potency of potentiality in actualizing and transforming social networks and relations.

However, this anthropological approach fails to address the politics of potentiality—that is, the political process in which potentialities are defined, distributed, animated and actualized, or preempted. This volume fills that gap by offering contributions that examine a potential politics addressing potentiality in two dimensions: potentiality to and potentiality not to. The collected work sees potential as the capacity to do or be something whether by positive action or restraint. Opposing the claim that potentiality exists only in acting, Agamben (1998) endorses Aristotle's emphasis on the autonomous existence of potentiality. Potentiality does not always disappear immediately into actuality; it can be the potentiality *not* to (do or be). In other words, potentiality remains capable of the act in not realizing it (Agamben 1998: 45). Power (2010) critiques Agamben's notion of potentiality, which emphasizes inactivity or the power to suspend the passage of potentiality to actuality. Power argues that this notion of potentiality constructs reduced or promissory subjects. However, in the Chinese context, both notions of positive and negative potentiality maximize individual agency. In the case of promoting the happiness of the underprivileged in China, potentiality to (be actualized) encompasses positive potentials for entrepreneurship or the good life. However, these same groups of people also embody potentialities *not* to, for example, fulfilling potential threats such as alcohol abuse, physical violence, or social unrest, which marginalized workers are capable of actualizing although they may have not yet done so. To preempt the actualization of such potential threats or negative potentials (see Massumi 2007 and Anderson 2011 on potential politics of preemption), affect can be an effective tool. For example, re-employment counseling programs in China highlight the happiness of select laid-off workers and the positive potentialities released by such happiness (i.e. entrepreneurship) as a way of downplaying the manifestation of negative potentials such as alcoholism, physical violence or social unrest (see Chapter 2).

Notes

1 Other studies stress, for example, the politics or military/security dimension in East Asia.
2 In his latest work, Nye (2008b) puts forward another concept called "smart power," which is a mixture of soft and hard power.
3 While some argue that in its South China Seas policies, China has undercut its charm offensive, a recent analysis shows that through their 2013 tours of Southeast Asia, China's President Xi Jinping and Premier Li Keqiang had launched a new charm offensive by increasing its trade and infrastructure investment in Southeast Asia (Nguyen 2013).

4 This definition of affect is inspired by Yanhua Zhang's notion of emotion in her study of emotions through Chinese medicine, which is a "felt quality of culture that informs and gives styles and meanings to Chinese experience of pain and malaise" (Zhang 2007: 3). However, Zhang's definition of emotion is an embodied or psychological mode of affect.

5 I own this idea to Jane Whittington.

6 This psychological self-help literature and media focus on love, marriage and family issues, which are gendered, targeting women, who are seen as more capable than men of reorienting themselves through self-help.

7 Prada (2011) suggests that contemporary biopower is becoming much more closely associated with affective spaces and responses, for example, considerations of consumer satisfaction as a lucrative form of regulating ways of living.

References

Adams, Vincanne, Murphy, Michelle, and Clark, Adele E. 2009. "Anticipation: Technoscience, Life, Affect, Temporality." *Subjectivity* 28: 246–65.

Agamben, Giorgio. 1998. *Homa Sacer: Sovereign Power and Bare Life*. Stanford, CA: Stanford University Press.

Ahmed, Sara. 2004. *The Cultural Politics of Emotion*. London: Routledge.

——2010. *The Promise of Happiness*. Durham, NC and London: Duke University Press.

Allison, Anne. 1994. *Nightwork: Sexuality, Pleasure, and Corporate Masculinity in a Tokyo Hostess Club*. Chicago, IL: University of Chicago Press.

Althusser, Louis. 1971. "Ideology and Ideological State Apparatuses." In *Lenin and Philosophy*. New York: Monthly Review Press, 127–86.

Anderson, Ben. 2011. "Preemption, Precaution, Preparedness: Anticipatory Action and Future Geographies." *Progress in Human Geography* 34(6): 777–98.

——2012. "Affect and Biopower: Towards a Politics of Life." *Transactions of the British Institute of Geographers* 37(1): 28–43.

Bell, Daniel A. 2008. *China's New Confucianism: Politics and Everyday Life in a Changing Society*. Princeton, NJ: Princeton University Press.

Berlant, Lauren 2008. "Cruel Optimism: On Marx, Loss and the Senses." *New Formations* 63(1): 33–51.

——2011. *Cruel Optimism*. Durham, NC: Duke University Press.

Bottici, Chiara and Challand, Benoît, eds. 2011. *The Politics of Imagination*. New York: Birkbeck Law Press.

Brook, Timothy and Luong, Hy V. 1997. *Culture and Economy: The Shaping of Capitalism in Eastern Asia*. Ann Arbor: University of Michigan Press.

Bugliani, Adriano. 2011. "From Soul to Mind: Psychology and Political Imagination." In Chiara Bottici and Benoit Challand (eds), *The Politics of Imagination*. New York: Birkbeck Law Press, 73–85.

Chin-Dahler, Patrick. 2010. "Universal Human Rights, Cultural Relativism and the Asian Value Debate." *East Asia Forum*. October 9.

Clough, Patricia Ticineto. 2007. "Introduction." In Patricia Ticineto Clough with Jean Halley (eds), *The Affective Turn: Theorizing the Social*. Durham, NC: Duke University Press.

Fijiwara, Masahiko. 2006. *The Dignity of a State Democracy*. Tokyo: IBC Publishing.

Foucault, Michel. 1978. *The History of Sexuality: Volume I: An Introduction*. New York: Pantheon Books.

Gorton, Kristyn. 2007. "Theorizing Emotion and Affect: Feminist Engagements." *Feminist Theory* 8(3): 333–48.
Gregg, Melissa and Selgworth, Gregory J. 2010. *The Affect Theory Reader*. Durham, NC: Duke University Press.
Grossberg, Lawrence. 1992. "Mapping Popular Culture." In *We Gotta Get Out of this Place: Popular Conservatism and Postmodern Culture*. New York: Routledge, 69–87.
Haraway, Donna J. 1991. "Biopolitics of Postmodern Bodies." In *Simians, Cyborgs, and Women: The Reinvention of Women*. New York: Routledge.
Hardt, Michael. 1999. "Affective Labor." *Boundary 2* 26(2): 89–100.
Hardt, Michael and Negri, Antonio. 2000. *Empire*. Cambridge, MA: Harvard University Press.
Henriques, Julian, Holloway, Wendy, Urwin, Chathi, Venn, Couze and Warkerdine, Valerie, eds. 1984. *Changing the Subject: Psychology, Social Regulation, and Subjectivity*. New York: Methuen.
Hippler, Thomas. 2011. "The Politics of Imagination: Spinoza and the Origins of Critical Theory." In Chiara Bottici and Benoît Challand (eds), *The Politics of Imagination*. New York: Birkbeck Law Press, 55–72.
Hochschild, Arlie R. 1983. *The Managed Heart: Commercialization of Human Feeling*. Berkeley: University of California Press.
Jackson, Michael. 1983. "Knowledge of the Body." *Man* 18: 327–45.
Jaggar, Alison M. 1989. "Love and Knowledge: Emotion in Feminist Epistemology." In Ann Garry and Marilyn Pearsall (eds), *Women, Knowledge, and Reality: Explorations in Feminist Philosophy*. Boston, MA, London, Sydney and Wellington: Unwin Hyman, 129–56.
Kipnis, Andrew B. 1997. *Producing Guanxi: Sentiment, Self and Subculture in a North China Village*. Durham, NC: Duke University Press.
Kleinman, Arthur. 2010. "Remaking the Moral Person in China: Implications for Health." *The Lancet* 375: 1074–75.
Kurlantzick, Joshua. 2007. *Charm Offensive: How China's Soft Power is Transforming the World*. New Haven, CT and London: Yale University Press.
Lorde, Audre. 1978. *Sister Outsider. Essays & Speeches*. New York: The Crossing Press.
Lutz, Catherine A. 1988. *Unnatural Emotions: Everyday Sentiments on a Micronesian Atoll and their Challenge to Western Theory*. Chicago, IL: University of Chicago Press.
Lyon, Margot L. 1995. "Missing Emotion: the Limitations of Cultural Constructionism in the Study of Emotion." *Cultural Anthropology* 10(2): 244–63.
Mahoney, Maureen A. and Yngvesson, Barbara. 1992. "The Construction of Subjectivity and the Paradox of Resistance: Reintegrating Feminist Anthropology and Psychology." *Signs: Journal of Women in Culture and Society* 18(1): 44–73.
Marx, Karl. 1976. *Capital: A Critique of Political Economy*, vol. 1, trans. B. Fowkes. Harmondsworth: Penguin Books.
Massumi, Brian. 2002. *Parables for the Virtual*. Durham, NC: Duke University Press.
——2007. "Potential Politics and the Primacy of Preemption." *Theory and Event* 10(2).
McElhinny, Bonnie. 2007. *Words, Worlds, Material Girls: Language, Gender and Globalization*. Berlin: Mouton.
——2010. "The Audacity of Affect: Gender, Race, and History in Linguistic Account of Legitimacy and Belonging." *Annual Review of Anthropology* 39: 309–28.
Miyazaki, Hirokazu. 2004. *The Method of Hope: Anthropology, Philosophy, and Fijian Knowledge*. Stanford, CA: Stanford University Press.

Negri, Antonio. 1999. "Value and Affect." *Boundary 2* 26(2): 77–88.

Ness, Sally Ann. 2011 "Bouldering in Yosemite: Emergent Signs of Place and Landscape." *American Anthropologist* 113(1): 71–87.

Ngai, Sianne. 2005. *Ugly Feelings.* Cambridge, MA and London: Harvard University Press.

Nguyen, Phuong. 2013. "China's Charm Offensive Signals a New Strategic Era in Southeast Asia." csis.org/publication/chinas-charm-offensive-signals-new-strategic-era-southeast-asia (accessed on October 24, 2013).

Nolan, James L., Jr. 1998. *The Therapeutic State: Justifying Government at Century's End.* New York and London: New York University Press.

Nye, Josephe S. Jr. 2004. *Soft Power: The Means to Success in World Politics.* New York: Public Affairs.

——2008a. "Foreword." In Yasushi Watanabe and David McConnell (eds), *Soft Power Superpowers: Cultural and National Assets of Japan and the United States.* New York: M.E. Sharpe, ix–xiv.

——2008b. *The Powers to Lead.* Oxford: Oxford University Press.

Pomfret, Richard. 2011. *Regionalism in East Asia: Why Has it Flourished Since 2000 and How Far Will it Go?* Singapore: World Scientific.

Power, Nina. 2010. "Potentiality or Capacity?—Agamben's Missing Subjects." *Theory and Event* 13(1).

Prada, Juan Martin. 2010. "Economies of Affectivity." caringlabor.wordpress.com/?s=economies+of+affectivity (accessed on June 15, 2011).

——2011. "Affective Link, Policies of Affectivity, Aesthetics of Biopower." carin glabor.wordpress.com (accessed on June 15, 2011).

Protevi, John. 2009. *Political Affect: Connecting the Social and the Somatic.* Minneapolis: University of Minnesota Press.

Rabinow, Paul and Rose, Nikolas. 2006. "Biopower Today." *BioSocieties* (1): 195–217.

Richard, Analiese and Rudnyckyj, Daromir. 2009. "Economies of Affect." *Journal of the Royal Anthropological Institute* 15: 57–77.

Riley, Denise. 2005. *Impersonal Passion: Language as Affect.* Durham, NC and London: Duke University Press.

Rohlen, Thomas P. 1974. *For Harmony and Strength: Japanese White-Collar Organization in Anthropological Perspective.* Berkeley, Los Angeles and London: University of California Press.

Rose, Nikolas. 1996. *Inventing Our Selves: Psychology, Power and Personhood.* Cambridge: Cambridge University Press.

Sedgwick, Eve Kosofsky. 2003. *Touching Feeling: Affect, Pedagogy, Performativity.* Durham, NC: Duke University Press.

Smart, Alan. 1993. "Gifts, Bribes, and *Guanxi*: A Reconsideration of Bourdieu's Social Capital." *Cultural Anthropology* 8(3): 388–408.

Spelman, Elizabeth V. 1989. "Anger and Insubordination." In Ann Garry and Marilyn Pearsall (eds), *Women, Knowledge, and Reality: Explorations in Feminist Philosophy.* Boston, MA, London, Sydney and Wellington: Unwin Hyman, 263–74.

Stewart, Kathleen. 2007. *Ordinary Affects.* Durham, NC: Duke University Press.

Stiglitz, Joseph E. and Yusuf, Shahid. 2001. *Rethinking the East Asia Miracle.* New York: The World Bank and Oxford University Press.

Svendsen, Mette N. 2011. "Articulating Potentiality: Notes on the Delineation of the Blank Figure in Human Embryonic Stem Cell Research." *Cultural Anthropology* 26(3): 414–37.

Tai, Hung-chao. 1989. *Confucianism and Economic Development: An Oriental Alternative?* Washington, DC: The Washington Institute Press.

Thrift, Nigel. 2007. *Non-Representational Theory: Space, Politics, Affect*. New York: Routledge
Tie, Warwick. 2004. "The Psychic Life of Governmentality." *Culture, Theory, and Critique* 45(2): 161–76.
Venn, Couze. 2007. "Cultural Theory, Biopolitics and the Question of Power." *Theory, Culture and Society* 24(3): 111–24.
Williams, Raymond. 1977. *Marxism and Literature*. Oxford and New York: Oxford University Press.
Wissinger, Elizabeth. 2007. "Always on Display: Affective Production in the Modeling Industry." In Patricia Clough with Jean Halley (eds), *The Affective Turn: Theorising the Social*. Durham, NC: Duke University Press, 231–60.
Yan, Yunxiang. 1996. *The Flow of Gifts: Reciprocity and Social Networks in a Chinese Village*. Stanford, CA: Stanford University Press.
Yang, Jie. 2007. "'Re-employment Stars': Language, Gender and Neoliberal Restructuring in China." In Bonnie McElhinny (ed.), *Words, Worlds and Materials Girls: Language, Gender and Globalization*. Berlin: Mouton de Gruyter, 73–102.
Yang, Mayfair Meihui. 1984. *Gifts, Banquets, and the Art of Social Relationships in China*. Ithaca, NY: Cornell University Press.
——1988. "The Modernity of Power in the Chinese Socialist Order." *Cultural Anthropology* 3(4): 408–27.
Yao, Souchou. 2002. *Confucian Capitalism: Discourse, Practice and the Myth of Chinese Enterprise*. New York and London: RoutledgeCurzon.
Yasushi, Watanabe and McConnell, David. 2008. *Soft Power Superpowers: Cultural and National Assets of Japan and the United States*. New York: M.E. Sharpe.
Zhang, Yanhua. 2007. *Transforming Emotions through Chinese Medicine: An Ethnographic Account from Contemporary China*. Albany: State University of New York Press.

Part II

Happiness and psychologization

1 Crafting Confucian remedies for happiness in contemporary China

Unraveling the Yu Dan phenomenon

Yanhua Zhang

During the National Day celebration week in October 2006, China Central Television (CCTV) broadcast a series of lectures entitled "Lunyu Xinde" (Confucian Analects from the Heart) by Yu Dan, a media studies professor from Beijing Normal University. Yu's unconventional interpretation of *The Analects* in terms of Confucian wisdom to "happiness of the heart" was promoted enthusiastically by the state media and embraced eagerly by general viewers. The transcript of her lectures was immediately edited into a book and sold millions of copies,[1] and Yu Dan became an instant household name and a celebrity appearing in numerous television interviews. Yu appeals to the affective undertone of *The Analects* and packs her interpretations of the Confucian texts with inspirational stories and the language of popular psychology. She is widely praised for making Confucian teachings accessible to the masses unversed in Chinese classics and for forging an emotion-based cultural link between the Confucian tradition as a source of happiness and everyday life in the fast-paced market-oriented contemporary China. Yu's instant popularity is referred to as the Yu Dan phenomenon, a highlight of the recent "revival of national learning" (*guoxue re*) in China.

How can we make sense of the Yu Dan phenomenon? Many Confucian scholars refrain from commenting and dismiss it as one of many media sensations created by the entertainment industry. Others, as shown in the public protest letter signed by ten Confucian academics from elite universities, are indignant over Yu Dan's "vulgarization and trivialization" of Confucian teachings.[2] Nevertheless, the fact that Yu Dan, a relatively unknown college professor at the time, was given a prime time TV platform to lecture on Confucian *Analects* and that millions of Chinese not only eagerly tune in to be "entertained" by her lectures but also are willing to spend money to buy her lecture notes is extraordinary. Yu's quick rise to stardom itself is a remarkable sociocultural phenomenon, symptomatic of particular challenges, desires, and needs of Chinese modernity in the market era, which merits close ethnographic attention.

This chapter makes the Yu Dan phenomenon the site of an ethnographic investigation. It asks what makes Yu Dan's Confucian narrative particularly appealing to the contemporary Chinese populace, who, in one way or another, partake extensively in the global system of capitalism. Particularly, I examine how Yu Dan's affect-based Confucian message is interdiscursively produced through language use, embodied practices, and media strategies. The purpose of this inquiry is not so much to identify how Yu Dan's popularized version of Confucianism "deviates" from the authentic Confucian teachings and conventional Confucian scholarship, but rather to use Yu Dan's televised Confucian lectures and the interests and debates generated by them as an analytical gateway to understand the larger social and cultural context of the recent "revival of national learning" (*guoxue re*) as part of the Chinese efforts to negotiate an alternative narrative of modernity, which is able to accommodate Chinese cultural sensibilities and mediate the tensions between the existing social formations and the market-based neoliberal ideologies and practices in contemporary China. I show that Yu Dan's televised lectures on the Confucian heart for happiness can be approached as a series of meaning-making affective practices that are a response to the entangled needs of the state, the market, and the consumer subjects in contemporary China and the very product of their joint efforts.

I use Yu Dan's lectures and interviews as well as the relevant comments and debates that circulate on the web and in the print media as the primary data for analysis. This research draws on anthropological theorization on emotion, language and governmentality, and the analytical framework of critical discourse analysis, and is also informed by my own continuous research on the experience of emotion-related disorders in contemporary China (see Zhang 2007). It attends to the discursive construction of "the happiness of the heart" in Yu's narrative of Confucian wisdom and examines how the psychologization of the *Analects* is interdiscursively embedded in the larger ideological and material context that privileges a particular hybrid Confucian discourse, an indigenized addition to the emerging "psycho-boom" (Kleinman 2010) in China.[3] In this chapter, I will start with a discussion of the role of gendered voice in re-narrating the Confucian stories that projects how the audience should take meanings from the Confucian texts. I suggest that this popularized Confucian message in a maternal voice helps redefine the post-reform governance in China in affective terms. In so doing, I hope to shed light on the power of the state in the shaping of the Yu Dan phenomenon. I will then examine interdiscursive construction of "the Confucian wisdom for happiness" across different texts, genres and media, particularly on the strategic use of *xinde* (knowing from embodied learning of the heart) in creating a hybrid Confucian solution that articulates the social and economic conflicts and dis-eases in terms of psychological needs for happiness and of personal problems in adaptation. I conclude by considering how this particular Confucian remedy for the heart is appropriated as therapeutic resources and knowledge for self-care and self-strengthening. I argue that this popularized Confucian wisdom for happiness is surely ideological but also emotive, and is crafted, prescribed and appropriated to mediate between how to "feel" as a cultural subject of Chinese person and to "live" in everyday life as a modern neoliberal individual in the globalized market era in contemporary China.

Confucian message through a maternal voice

Daniel A. Bell, a professor of political philosophy at Qinghua University in Beijing, includes a commentary on the Yu Dan phenomenon in his recent book *China's New Confucianism* (2008). He points out that Yu Dan's gender may have played a role in her popularity. According to Bell, Confucianism has been branded by its gender prejudice against women, and "the best argument against the view that Confucianism justifies patriarchy, perhaps, is for an impressive female intellectual to show that she takes Confucianism seriously" (Bell 2008: 163). He argues that by presenting herself in the mass media as a serious advocate of the Confucian tradition, Yu Dan lends her voice to the de-gendered Confucianism that is compatible with modern life, which can be attractive to those who are turned away by its alleged gender bias. However, as I show in the following, Yu Dan's gender does play a role in her popularity, yet it is not so much due to her de-gendered universalization of Confucianism, but rather to her particular feminine image and voice through which Confucian stories are re-narrated and accorded an affective appeal, which Yu Dan refers to as "the temperature" (*wendu*) to move and warm the hearts of the ordinary people.

The issue of gender itself is not a voiced concern in Yu Dan's lectures. To her, "Confucius only has temperature but no color" (Yu 2006: 1), in that Confucius is not colored by any particular positions including gender and his teachings offer universal affective appeal, and therefore Confucius should not be approached from a gendered perspective. Yet, Yu Dan's status as a female and a mother has been a focus of media attention and a constant reference in the commentaries of her Confucian expositions. She is described as showing "the female softness" (*nvxing de rouruan*) and "the maternal tenderness" (*muqin de xini*),[4] and frequently referred to as "a cultural nanny (*wenhua naima*)." Her interviewers never hesitate to highlight her gender status and Yu Dan herself also readily displays her identity as a "happy woman."[5] In a way, both Yu Dan and her audience are oriented to her gender status and see it as constitutive to her Confucian message.

The Confucian texts and stories told and embodied by Yu Dan via mass media are in every way antithetical to the elitist academic Confucian discourse embodied by straight-faced male scholars, who expound Confucianism in terms of philosophic theories, moral and political principles, and personal cultivation and ethics in an academic context to a relatively specialized and sophisticated audience. When inviting Yu Dan to lecture on the *Analects of Confucius*, the CCTV Lecture Forum (*Baijia Jiangtan*), a popular TV platform for promoting traditional Chinese culture, envisioned a very different Confucius, who speaks the language of the masses to the ordinary people including those with limited education, and about their experience in contemporary everyday life. Yu Dan was selected to embody a Confucius that is not detached and intimidating but rather kind and personable, showing an "affinity" (*qinhe li*) with ordinary folks. The media attention on Yu Dan's gender plays out nicely in accordance with the process of popularization of Confucianism and also helps highlight the boundaries between her task as a popularizer of Confucian teachings and serious scholarly research on Confucian classics. Yi Zhongtian, another cultural celebrity created by the CCTV Lecture Forum, who introduces Yu Dan's book *Confucian Analects from the Heart,* unapologetically calls Yu Dan "a smart little woman" (*congming de xiao nizi*). Talking about Yu Dan's Confucius, he writes "I don't know if this is the scholars' Confucius, nor do I know if this is the historical Confucius, and less do I know if this is the real Confucius. However, I know this is our Confucius, Confucius of the masses, Confucius of the people, and Confucius forever" (Yu 2006: 2).

The Analects of Confucius from the Heart (*Lunyu Xinde*) definitely has Yu Dan's image, the image of a "cultural nanny." According to the article "Why is Yu Dan So Popular?" published in the *People's Daily* on February 7, 2007, Yu Dan's "feminine sensitivity of feelings" (*nvxing teyou de xini qinggan*) and "her voice of poetic charm" (*yinyong ban de yudiao*)[6] help bring a kind of privileged experience of engaging Confucian texts and wisdom from the ivory tower to the living rooms of ordinary people. She assures the audience that they do not have to "look up with reverence to Confucius as some divine figure high above," and the truth Confucius teaches is simple and relevant to us all—that is, "how we can live the kind of happy life that our heart desires." (Yu 2006). This combination of femininity and the happiness-oriented affective approach to Confucian teachings makes it particularly attractive to the ordinary Chinese in a time of rapid social change, as shown in a commentary published online:

> We live in an era of market economy and intense competition that values material gains over the spiritual pursuit. We have difficulty finding a home for our soul … We need a friend. We need comfort, self-understanding, and support … What we want beyond material possessions is something spiritual and affective. But looking around, we have nothing, and we need someone to show us directions when our lives do not go anywhere. We need someone to bring us courage when we are trapped in difficult situations. We need someone to cheer us up with a bright smile when we feel disappointed with our lives … *Like an understanding mother, Yu Dan came to our side … feeding the hungry crowd with sweet milk of our cultural tradition. She came at the right time and she deserves the title of "cultural nanny."*[7]

Here Confucius starts to assume a maternal image and voice—affectionate, nurturing and comforting. By viewing and listening to Yu Dan lecturing on the Confucian heart for happiness on TV, reflecting on Yu Dan's Confucian messages, and sharing their reflections with friends or strangers online, individual viewers and readers in private homes come to experience themselves as belonging to a public united through "the mass mediated communicative forms" (Wilce 2009: 21). This maternal transformation also projects how the audience and readers should take meaning from the *Analects*. If the transformation of the masculine Avalokiteśvara into the feminine Guan Yin, the goddess of compassion in popularized Buddhist practices in China, was a response to the particular spiritual and emotional need of the historical time (see Yu 2001), the Yu Dan phenomenon might also rise out of the popular need to balance the conventional masculine Confucianism that focuses on enlightenment through diligent learning (*jiaohua*) with the feminine version of affinity through affective projects (*ganhua*).

This "transformation" of Confucius is obviously supported ideologically and technologically by the state, and Yu Dan's interpretation of Confucius plays in tune with the goal of the Chinese state to build a "harmonious society" (*hexie shehui*), which with three decades of socialist market-oriented reforms and rapid social transformations, the existing political rhetoric of "socialism with Chinese character" is plagued with contradictions and practical difficulties. Yu Dan's affective reading of Confucianism helps re-imagine the role of governance and advocates a felt relationship of the citizens to the nation-state, which is a maternal emotive one rather than a paternalistic moral one.

Confucianism has been adopted as the source of political legitimacy and the official ideology in China's long history. In a Confucian world, family is "a governing metaphor" and is "conceived as the center of all order, social and cosmic" (Ames 2011: 97). The ruler assumes a paternalistic role as the head of a family who is expected to protect, provide for and redistribute resources fairly among the members of the family. The Chinese pre-reform socialist state, to a large extent, is also identified with this paternalistic model, which is a political and moral order with prescribed obligations, such that it has been naturalized and deeply internalized in the subconscious of Chinese political imagination. Recently, Zhang Mingshu (2013), a scholar of political science from the Chinese Academy of Social Science, published *What Democracy Do Chinese Want?* (*Zhongguo Ren Xiang Yao Shenmeyang de Minzhu*), based on his survey of "Chinese citizens' political qualities" (*Zhongguo gongmin de zhengzhi suzhi*). His findings show that the Confucian ethic-oriented political ideal still dominates Chinese political imagination that values exemplary personal virtues and a paternalistic benevolent government. The Confucian political thought embedded within the family metaphor for governing inevitably inherits a power of critique. The Chinese orientation to paternalistic governance in contemporary life is readily observable in the criticism of the government and the justification for political actions. An urban laid-off worker mentioned in Mun Young Cho's article "Dividing the Poor" (2012: 187) is a good example. While pointing to the phrase "Serve the People" posted outside a government office in Harbin, he claims "The government should not abandon us if it wants to display Mao's handwriting and if China is still to be called a socialist country!" A cab driver in Beijing with whom I interacted put it even more bluntly: "What is the use of the government who is unable to keep a bowl of water balanced [*yi wan shui duanping*] but allows one child to have everything and another to have nothing?"

Yu Dan's popularized Confucian narrative does not so much challenge the Chinese political imagination rooted in the Confucian family-centered tradition as it helps mediate its potential critical potency by conflating the nation-state as polity with nation-culture as a symbolic and affective source of identity. With the shift of attention from the paternalistic moral order to maternal affective affinity, the government is then not to be judged morally on obligations for providing health, work and livelihood, but to be embraced as the source of pride and affection—the object of love and loyalty, as well as the source for spiritual growth and psychological comfort. The 2008 Beijing Olympic Games Opening Ceremony, with a staggering parade of the cultural achievements in Chinese history, operated on similar discursive "cues." Many viewers and readers of Yu Dan's Confucius lectures comment that Yu Dan makes them feel proud of their cultural heritage and of being Chinese. Explaining a passage in the *Analects*—a conversation between Zigong and the Master on how to govern effectively, Yu (2006: 9–10) interprets "*min xin zhi*" as "the common people should have faith in the government" (*laobaixing yao dui guojia you xinyang*), and she further explains that it is Confucius' political conviction that faith in the government is the source of internal peace and a collective identity. The alternative interpretation embedded in the original text that the most important factor for governing effectively is for the government to fulfill its obligations and earn the people's trust has been downplayed.

Yu Dan's televised performance in promoting the Confucian teachings to the ordinary Chinese people can be seen as part of a larger effort to mold Chinese subjectivity or "the Chinese soul" in accordance with the cultural tradition of Confucianism against the background of globalization and "the changing moral landscape in contemporary China" (Yan 2011: 36). However, by emphasizing self-responsibility for happiness of the heart, Yu Dan's affect-based version of Confucianism coincides happily with the neoliberal market ideology, which translates the social and economic conflicts into the problems of psychology and personality and calls for the Confucian "secrets for happiness" (*kuaile de mijue*) as a Chinese way for what Nikolas Rose (1990) calls "governing the soul." However, if Rose's "soul" refers to the deep psychological interior as the locus for self regulation, Yu Dan's Confucian solution is more articulated within the Chinese sensibility of self—*xintai* (often translated as attitude), an affect-charged disposition of the heart amenable to internal and external persuasion.

The Confucian heart made for happiness

In her lectures on *Confucian Analects*, Yu Dan repeatedly reminds her audience of the relevance of Confucianism to contemporary life, centering on its affect-based wisdom for happiness (*xingfu*), and emphasizes that the true message of Confucian teachings is simply how one can live a happy life as one's heart desires. However, there has been no internal logic in the *Confucian Analects* that inevitably leads to this particular affective reading of the Confucian classic. In fact, the claim that Confucius is all about how to achieve inner happiness constitutes a bold revision of the mainstream narrative of Confucianism, since the quest for happiness has simply not been the focus of philosophical commentaries on Confucian scholarship both inside and outside of China. One can certainly find relevant vocabulary in the *Confucian Analects* such as "*yue*" (please, pleasure, pleasant) and "*le*" (joy, joyful, enjoy), yet they constitute a small number and are not the same as the modern concept of *xingfu*, a Chinese equivalent for happy or happiness. Actually the definition of *xingfu* as "feeling of the great pleasure and contentment derived from satisfaction with one's life"[8] is relatively recent. According to the earliest Chinese dictionary *Shuowen*, *xing* has the meaning of "luck, fortunate" and *fu* has the meaning of "bless, blessing." The combination of *xing* and *fu* can be traced to the phrase *xing fu er huo* (pray for blessing but receive a disaster), found in the historical book *Xin Tang Shu* (1045 AD). Even in the recent past of the Maoist collective era, *xingfu* was commonly understood as the experience of contentment attributable more to a stable and adequate collective life that provides its members with a sense of security and belonging.

Then teaching *Confucian Analects* in terms of how to be happy is rather a strategic choice made by the CCTV Lecture Forum as well as by Yu Dan herself. Since CCTV is the central government's official television station, the choice to focus on happiness as the lecture theme on Confucius is logically both a choice of ideology and a choice of business strategy. A commentator, talking about the media's role in creating the Yu Dan phenomenon, points out that "the public media can use its own power to direct the public's attention and create 'an agenda' for them to talk about. Although the media is not able to determine how the public thinks, it can influence what the public pays attention to within a period of time, thus exercising its influence over the society."[9] Since the beginning of the new century, *xingfu* or happiness has increasingly become a buzzword in the public media, and numerous publications and TV shows or programs have *xingfu* as the theme or topic. Quite a lot of government-supported research and projects focuses on "happiness" as the topic of investigation, such as the Annual Reports on *Chinese Family Happiness Investigation* led by the Chinese Academy of Social Science and the annual survey on Chinese people's happiness index conducted for the past seven years by the journal *Xiao Kang* (Well-Off), one of the Chinese Communist Party's (CCP) official publications.[10]

A proliferation of happiness discourse, to an extent, reflects an overflow of happiness practices—ways to enjoy simple pleasures, fulfill various desires, and to search for good life and fortune. Anthropologists working in contemporary China show that both discursive and embodied practices of happiness have been produced by China's recent history, especially by its transition economically and ideologically from the collective-oriented socialism to the post-reform market-driven post-socialism (see Farquhar 2002; Rofel 2007; Kleinman *et al.* 2011). As captured vividly in *Deep China* (Kleinman *et al.* 2011), the sea change brought about by the market-oriented reforms at the institutional and policy levels forced individuals to be on their own, which in turn released the potential of the individual and altered subjectivity. The result is "the rise of the new kind of enterprising and desiring self" (Kleinman *et al.* 2011: 11) which makes the quest for personal happiness and self-realization a marked story of post-socialist China.

It is understandable why the public media participates enthusiastically in the discursive production of happiness, but why Confucius? Why is it necessary and desirable to redefine Confucianism primarily as the wisdom for "happiness of the heart?" What is at stake in this "happiness turn," using Sarah Ahmed's (2010) words, in the promotion of Confucianism in contemporary China? Wu Jun, a business owner from Jiang Su province, in response to the reporter's inquiry about his view of happiness, says "the fact that *xingfu* (happiness) is talked about so much is already an indication of some *bu xingfu* (unhappiness)."[11] Surely individualization both as a strategy and a consequence of marketization engineered by the Chinese state produces happiness and unhappiness as well as differential access to resources and power. A neoliberal practice of governance through creating "desiring subjects" (see Rofel 2007) can also be destabilized by widely spread unhappiness resulting from assaulted desires for "being rich and glorious." Considering China's particular history and political culture, the perceived unhappiness can also be amplified by the spread of nostalgia for a relatively egalitarian past. Can neoliberalism be reconfigured to articulate a particular Chinese subjectivity that negotiates between an enterprising independent individual and a culturally informed member of collectivity to mitigate negative feelings of disappointment and regret? As Aihwa Ong (2006) argues, neoliberalism as a technology of governance is flexible and it engages and articulates other ethical systems in particular historical and cultural contexts. This process can also be seen as the process of neoliberal localization. Yu Dan's Confucian lectures on happiness could be understood as such a process that seeks to articulate neoliberal self-governance in terms of Confucian self-cultivation.

In her first Confucian lecture, Yu Dan cites the global GNH (gross national happiness) index to show that the Chinese happiness index has fallen in the recent survey while material conditions have being improved significantly. She then directs the audience to Confucius's favorite disciple, Yan Yuan, who was very poor but could find joy in what he had. Confucius praised him, "How admirable Hui is!" Yu Dan then formulates her Confucian view on happiness:

> Everybody hopes to live a happy life, but happiness is a feeling, which has nothing to do with being wealthy or poor but has everything to do with one's inner heart. *The Confucian Analects* teaches his students how

to look for happiness in life. This philosophy has been passed down over the ages and has influenced a great many scholars and poets in history.
(Yu 2006: 12)

Here, Yu Dan offers a Confucian solution that supplements the neoliberal technology of self by focusing on how to deal with ourselves if we are not happy. In a way, Yu Dan's Confucian technology for happiness is not meant so much to "produce social norms" but rather to teach how to "feel"—in other words, how to re-evaluate one's feelings in relation to one's existential world and to readjust them positively in accordance with the Confucian ideal that is perfectly in sync with the goal of the state to build a harmonious society. In short, Yu Dan's Confucius speaks to the Chinese national obsession with the quest for happiness, which is "one of the most important stories in China today" (Kleinman *et al.* 2011: 267), and subscribes to the dominant discourse on happiness that is value laden with the neoliberal ideology of the market,[12] and the affect-based Confucian nationalism in contemporary China. Happiness is then not only an important goal and a practical concern in everyday life, but is effectively employed as a neoliberal technology of governance.

Finally, how is this affective revision of Confucianism achieved and popularized? Can we trace in the textualization of Yu Dan's Confucian lectures how this "Confucius for happiness" is motivated and shaped by the wider social and political interests and practices? Specifically, how is this particular version of Confucian wisdom forged in Yu Dan's lectures to link Confucian moral ethics of "self-cultivation" to the post-socialist pursuit of personal happiness and a good life? How does her reading of Confucian classics, which is criticized by some as performing "quasi-psychological counseling" (*xinli yisheng shi de jiedu*),[13] manage to find a way into the hearts of millions of Chinese and thus help mold the moral Chinese self in the name of Confucian tradition?

Yu Dan's *Confucian Analects from the Heart* is presented as *xinde* (knowing from the heart, literally), a specific genre of writing in Chinese that can be more or less described as insights or knowledge gained through embodied learning or practice. The writing of *xinde* is highly personal and rooted in an individual's particular experience of engaging texts, emotions and practices, which is not amenable to the criteria of right or wrong but is read or heard for sensibility and inner experience. Normally *xinde* does not belong to the public media, but Yu Dan's public lectures take the genre of *xinde* mainly as a narrative strategy and a rhetoric technique. On the one hand, her interpretation of the *Analects* is presented as understanding only from her own heart (*yi xin zhi de*) and others may have different readings. On the other hand, she speaks for Confucius. She quotes a Confucian text, re-textualizes the original in plain modern Chinese, and interprets what the Confucian text means for contemporary living. What is remarkable is that *xinde* is used to create an inter-discursive space where texts from different genres, sources, contexts and historical times are transplanted, interceded and re-contextualized to produce a highly hybrid and ambiguous narrative in which the narrator's "voice of the heart" serves as an interpretive reference.

An example from Yu Dan's second lecture, "*Xinling Zhi Dao*" (the way of the heart) may shed light on how Confucian wisdom is crafted interdiscursively as a technique to find happiness in spite of negative life circumstances. The theme of the lecture is set with Yu Dan's own voice: "Everybody, moving through life, may inevitably experience regrets and disappointment. We may not be able to change the reality, but we can change our attitude toward these matters" (Yu 2006: 20). The example of the imperfection of life cited from the *Analects* is an interaction between two of Confucius's disciples. Sima Niu was sad that everybody else had brothers and he was the only one without a brother. Zixia consoled him saying "*sheng-si you ming, fu-gui zai tian*" (life and death are matters of fate, and wealth and honor rest with heaven), and a cultivated gentleman should not worry about having no brothers because people all over the world would love and respect him like a brother. This message by itself rings mundane and the actual quote of "*sheng-si you ming, fu-gui zai tian*" has long become a Chinese proverb, the value of which is very likely viewed by a majority of Chinese today as old fashioned and feudal. Yu Dan then summarizes for the audience what she takes as Confucian values from this interaction: first, since life and death, and wealth and honor are beyond one's control, it is important to learn to accept the reality and move on; and second, one should keep a positive attitude and do whatever one can to make up for the imperfection. Then she quotes from a poem by Tagore, an Indian poet, well known to Chinese readers, to the effect that if one cries over missing the light of the sun, one would also miss the shining of the stars, which balances the pragmatic Chinese wisdom with a pleasant aesthetic hue.

Following this, Yu Dan brings in a story from a newspaper report about a British tennis player, Gem Gilbert, who, as a little girl, witnessed her mother's sudden death in the dentist's chair. She could never get over this adverse life effect; when she absolutely had to receive dental treatment, she died before the procedure even started. Here Yu Dan, using popular psychological language, describes the death of the tennis player as caused by a strong psychological suggestion. She further employs scientific registers such as "lab instruments," "test" and "carbon dioxide" to make a point that it is healthy physically and emotionally to let go of regrets and negative emotions, and also to add some weight of "expert knowledge." Then Yu Dan inserts another story, selected from a fable that she encountered somewhere probably in the English readings from her early years as a student. The story is about a girl who lived a poor life with her mother and had never owned anything pretty in her life and suffered from feelings of inferiority. At Christmas when she was eighteen, she was given some money to buy gifts for herself. At the store she tried out a beautiful ornament in her hair and was amazed by her own beauty. She bought the ornament, attached it to her hair, and was transformed instantly into a confident and beautiful young woman, smiling and greeting people. On her way home she attracted a lot of attention and even got an invitation from the boy she secretly admired. She did not realize this whole time, her flowery ornament was not attached to her hair. What transformed her or what made up for her lack of social status and economic means? It is her confidence and her attitude. Here Yu Dan's *xinde* goes "A different attitude can result in completely different quality of life" (Yu 2006: 24). This process of crafting Confucian wisdom starts with a small quote from the *Confucian Analects* with Sima Niu's regret for not having a brother and brings in diverse discursive formations to create a mixture of culturally and ideologically appropriate common sense advice.

Through a discursive strategy, Yu Dan skillfully forges an imagined coherence between the Confucian wisdom centering on relational harmony and moralistic self-cultivation and the neoliberal modernity characterized by the competition of the market and the individualistic pursuit of happiness. This intertextual ambiguity and the affect-filled voice embedded in Yu Dan's Confucian message enables the Chinese audience from different existential situations to relate their everyday experience to Yu Dan's version of Confucian wisdom and to gain psychological and spiritual benefit from it. The fact that 14,000 copies of Yu Dan's book were sold in a single day at *Zhongguancun* bookstore in Beijing when it first came out in November 2006 was testimony to the success of her syncretic lectures in the form of *xinde* which integrate Confucian texts and cultural sensibilities with personal aspiration and positive psychology. Interestingly, at an interview with the reporter from *The South Morning Paper*, Yu Dan likens *Confucian Analects* to "a diagnostic spring" (*wen bing quan*), immersed in which, individuals with different problems and difficulties would all find their own desired answers.[14] This reference probably applies to Yu Dan's own Confucian stories.

Conclusion: making Confucianism therapeutic

Who is Yu Dan's audience? For whom are her lectures and books intended? The English translator of Yu's book says "The Chinese original of this book is easy to follow and has been intentionally made so by using a relatively small number of Chinese characters, ingeniously combined to form understandable concepts" (Yu 2009: 180). Many of Yu Dan's commentators make similar observations that Yu Dan makes Confucianism simple and easy to understand and even those with little education can benefit. Arguably, Yu Dan's version of Confucian wisdom is not intended for the social and economically privileged elites, although historically they were the groups of society schooled in Confucianism. Yu's Confucius is directed at the masses, who are very likely those displaced and left behind by China's fast economic growth and expansion, or for those who are deemed unfit for the fierce competition in the neoliberal market and are falling off the track, disheartened and bitter. In Yu Dan's words, they are the groups who have difficulty finding their *rensheng zuobiao* (personal bearing in society). For her audience, Yu Dan offers a promise of Confucian remedies that would help them "live more confidently and increase happiness."[15]

Like many self-help types of advice across cultural traditions and religions, Yu Dan's Confucian lectures do provide certain psychological insights and advice and encourage individuals to re-appraise their existential situations and exercise positive psychology. Yu Dan's *Confucian Analects from the Heart* has been recommended and used for therapeutic purposes. I came upon my first copy of Yu Dan's book when I visited a relative in 2007, who was suffering what the traditional Chinese medicine would call *qingzhi bing* (an emotion-related disorder), with depressed mood, insomnia and social difficulties. She was given a copy of Yu Dan's book as a gift by her sister-in-law and told it contained the wisdom of healing, which might help her "unravel the knots and tangles in the heart" (Yu 2009: 34). Interestingly, much advice attributed to Confucius by Yu Dan sounds exactly like the persuasions used by the doctor I used to work with in Beijing, such as "As we move through life, it is hard for us to avoid things that cause regret and disappointment. We may lack the strength to change this, but what we can change is the attitude with which we approach these setbacks" (Yu 2009: 34). It would not be surprising for a Chinese doctor to prescribe Yu Dan's book on Confucius to a patient suffering from social difficulties and psychological distress. In fact, Yu Dan's book is sometimes used for treating anti-social behavior. For example, Jinan Prison in Shandong province was reported in the news for having its 2,000 inmates read Yu Dan's *Confucian Analects from the Heart*.[16]

By making *Confucian Analects* therapeutic and available to the public through the mass media, readers and viewers are allowed access to expert knowledge and psychological insights without assuming a vulnerable patient role, particularly when mental illness is still culturally stigmatized and socially shunned in China. Indeed, reading or listening to Yu Dan's Confucian lectures makes individuals the consumers of a cultural tradition exercising their own free will, and helps them identify themselves as co-participants in a culturally sanctioned and valued practice of "reading the classics" (*du jing*), which can be personally empowering and elevating. For the Chinese state, the recourse to the re-engineering of the cultural legacy for governance is less costly and more sustainable, in a way, transforming "governmentality" into "governing mentality" or *xintai* (attitudes) in Yu Dan's own words.

Apparently, in today's China, Confucianism is being actively explored to resolve social problems and to maintain political stability. Yu Dan's hybrid Confucius, which may be depoliticized on the surface, becomes a preferred version for a politicized goal. In Yu's narrative, Confucius becomes less a subject of philosophical exposition and textual research and more an affective reference to Chinese cultural identity, which downplays the critical implications of Confucian political philosophy and incorporates the global neoliberalism disguised in affective terms of "searching for happiness." From the "heart-felt Confucius" to "the Confucian heart for happiness," Yu offers her Chinese compatriots a bowl of "chicken soup" that is culturally tasty, psychologically soothing and, most of all, politically and economically affordable for the entire social spectrum in the market-oriented contemporary China.

Notes

1 The China Publishing House published the collection of Yu Dan's lectures in November 2006, one month after her lectures were broadcast on CCTV. The English translation, *Confucius from the Heart*, by Esther Tyldesley, was published by ATRIA Books in 2009.
2 See "Why We Oppose Yu Dan and the Likes of her," signed by ten Confucian scholars. bbs.tianya.cn/post-free-870238-1.shtml (accessed on March 28, 2013).
3 According to Arthur Kleinman (2010), the emerging "psycho-boom" in China refers to an awakening interest in psychology books, psychometric terms and training in counseling, with an increasing use of psychology in governing social life. Some 90 percent of the psychological self-help publications in Chinese are translated from the psychology writings in Western languages.
4 See "于丹：做有幸福感的女人 要将中国文化洒遍世界." ent.sina.com.cn/v/h/2010-01-08/16122838206.shtml.
5 See "于丹：我宁可不创造历史也要做幸福的女人." www.360doc.com/content/10/0612/11/1647471_32658773.shtml (accessed on March 28, 2013). As a cultural celebrity, Yu Dan has been frequently invited to give lectures on "the way to become a happy woman" or "a woman with the sense of happiness" (*you xinfu gan de nv ren*).
6 See "Why is Yu Dan So Popular?" (*Yu Dan weishenme zheyang hong*), *People's Daily Online*, February 7, 2007. culture.people.com.cn/GB/27296/5375980.html (accessed on March 29, 2013).
7 See 黄权旺：博士们，于丹没有说你们是她的儿子！news.163.com/07/0305/10/38QHMF88000121EP.html (accessed on March 28, 2013). Translation is my own.
8 The information is from zdic.net. Translation is my own.
9 See "'*Yu Wan' weishenme ai Yu Dan*" (Why Yu Dan's Fans Love Her). *People's Daily*, February 12, 2007.
10 See "媒体梳理国人幸福指标 (Public Media Trace People's Happiness Index)." news.sina.com.cn/c/sd/2012-11-05/163125514046.shtml (accessed on September 28, 2013).
11 See news.sina.com.cn/c/sd/2012-11-05/163125514046_4.shtml (accessed on September 28, 2013).
12 In a recent interview on *xingfu guan* (view of happiness) by a reporter, the well-known Chinese economist Zhang Weiying said: "you achieve happiness by making others happy; this is the logic of the market." news.sina.com.cn/c/sd/2012-11-05/163125514046_4.shtml (accessed on September 28, 2013).
13 See "Why is Yu Dan So Popular?" (*Yu Dan weishenme zheyang hong*).
14 See "Yu Dan Interview." culture.people.com.cn/GB/40462/40463/5221205.html (accessed on March 19, 2013).
15 See "Why is Yu Dan So Popular?" (*Yu Dan weishenme zheyang hong*).
16 See legal.dbw.cn/system/2007/02/12/050703747.shtml (accessed on March 28, 2013).

References

Ahmed, Sara. 2010. *The Promise of Happiness.* Durham, NC and London: Duke University Press.

Ames, Roger T. 2011. *Confucian Role Ethics: A Vocabulary.* Honolulu: University of Hawai'i Press.

Ames, Roger and Rosemont, Henry. 1998. *The Analects of Confucius: A Philosophical Translation*. New York: The Random House Publishing Group.

Bell, Daniel A. 2008. *China's New Confucianism: Politics and Everyday Life in a Changing Society*. Princeton, NJ: Princeton University Press.

Brooks, Bruce and Brooks, Taeko. 1998. *The Original Analects—Sayings of Confucius and his Successors: A New Translation and Commentary*. New York: Columbia University Press.

Cho, Mun Young. 2012. "Dividing the Poor." *American Ethnologist* 39(1): 187–200.

Fairclough, Norman. 1995. *Critical Discourse Analysis: Papers in the Critical Study of Language*. London and New York: Longman.

Farquhar, Judith. 2002. *Appetites: Food and Sex in Post-Socialist China*. Durham, NC: Duke University Press.

Kleinman, Arthur. 2010. "Remaking the Moral Person in China: Implications for Health." *The Lancet* 375(9720).

Kleinman, Arthur, Yan, Yunxiang, Jun, Jing, Lee, Sing, Zhang, Everett, Tianshu, Pan, Fei, Wu and Guo, Jinhua. 2011. *Deep China: The Moral Life of the Person*. Berkeley: University of California Press.

Li, Ling. 2007. *Sang Jia Gou: Wo Du Lunyu* (A Homeless Dog: My Reading of *Confucian Analects*). Taiyuan: Shanxi People's Press.

Miller, Toby. 2007. *Cultural Citizenship: Cosmopolitanism, Consumerism, and Television in a Neoliberal Age*. Philadelphia, PA: Temple University Press.

Ong, Aihwa. 2006. *Neoliberalism as Exception: Mutations in Citizenship and Sovereignty*. Durham, NC and London: Duke University Press.

Rofel, Lisa. 2007. *Desiring China: Experiments in Neoliberalism, Sexuality, and Public Culture*. Durham, NC: Duke University Press.

Rose, Nikolas. 1990. *Governing the Soul: The Shaping of the Private Life*. London and New York: Routledge.

——2007. *The Politics of Life Itself: Biomedicine, Power, and Subjectivity in the Twenty-First Century*. Princeton, NJ: Princeton University Press.

Wilce, James M. 2009. *Language and Emotion*. Cambridge: Cambridge University Press.

Yan, Yunxiang. 2011. "The Changing Moral Landscape." In Arthur Kleinman *et al.* (eds), *Deep China*. Berkeley: University of California Press.

Yu, Chun-Fang. 2001. *Kuan-Yin: The Chinese Transformation of Avalokitesvara*. New York: Columbia University Press.

Yu, Dan. 2006. *Lunyu Xinde*. Beijing: Zhonghua Book Company.

——2009. *Confucius from the Heart*, trans. by Esther Tyldesley. New York: ARRIA Books.

Zhang, Mingshu, 2013. *Zhongguo Ren Xiang Yao Shenmeyang de Minzhu* (What Democracy Do Chinese Want?) Beijing: Shehui Kexue Wanxian Press.

Zhang, Yanhua. 2007. *Transforming Emotions with Chinese Medicine: An Ethnography from Contemporary China*. New York: SUNY Press.

2 The happiness of the marginalized

Affect, counseling and self-reflexivity in China

Jie Yang

China has recently witnessed the emergence of numerous counseling programs, self-help genres, self-reflexive projects and confessional TV talk shows that promote happiness and positive psychology (see Zhang, Chapter 1, this volume, on happiness promotions by psychologizing Confucianism). There are dozens of programs and series on the nationally viewed China Central Television (CCTV) and on local cable television channels using terms like *xingfu*, *kuaile*, *huanle* or *kaixin*, which are roughly translated as happiness in Chinese. However, the use of happiness here is commodified, part of a larger marketing strategy by the party-governed media—that is, using happiness as the ultimate goal to stimulate consumption, for example, Coca Cola's 2009 Open Happiness Campaign in China. Also, since 2006, happiness has been adopted as an index to evaluate economic growth and governing efficiency (Liu 2006), particularly in relation to the new political project of constructing "a harmonious society," which claims to be people-centered and socially and economically sustainable.[1] Happiness then becomes a governing technology to sustain social harmony.

These instances seem to demonstrate that the "happiness turn" (Ahmed 2008) has taken place in China.[2] However, to understand better this turn in China, we need to examine *what* we turn towards when we turn to happiness (Ahmed 2010), and *which* notion of happiness is most appealing (to the ruling party). Lisa Blackman (2008) suggests that the happiness turn is a way of turning to psychology and its various traditions for thinking through affect, life and power over life. Indeed, a psycho-boom has recently emerged in China, including the awakening interest in psychological books, psychometrical terms, self-help literature, and training in counseling and psychotherapy (Kleinman 2010). The promotion of happiness in China through counseling and media campaigns is directed to all of China's citizens, but is particularly associated with one group: the newly marginalized, such as workers laid off from state-owned enterprises since the mid-1990s.[3] Up to early 2000, over 35 million workers had been laid off from state-owned enterprises in China (Wang and Zheng 2008); these newly displaced and impoverished workers as the once prestigious proletariat, the founding class of the communist party, have experienced drastic downward mobility in status. They are *not* happy.

The widespread happiness campaigns show precisely the lack of happiness and harmony in today's China (Sun Wanning, personal communication).

In this social context, precepts loosely identified with positive psychology have been invoked to instill happiness and optimism in people (especially the unemployed and urban poor) to help them endure poverty and despair. In this sense, instead of seeing happiness as part of the broad cultural turn, happiness promotion that is particularly targeting the underprivileged in China represents a governing technology, which delivers "therapy," for example, to the unemployed to reconstruct their happiness that has been compromised or destroyed by recent economic restructuring. Such happiness promotion also aims to preempt potential threats posed by this same group because they are widely perceived to harbor *yinhuan*, hidden dangers and risks, or negative potentiality that may pose a potential threat to social and political stability. In this sense, promoting the happiness of the underprivileged is part of the emerging psychologization trend in China, which manages social, economic and political issues in psychological modes of thinking.

Like the kind of self-absorbed individual happiness promoted by American self-help, happiness promotion in China also encourages people to focus on the self, adjusting oneself to realize one's self. Indeed, one of the real political effects of such happiness campaigns is the inculcation of new values such as self-care, self-realization and self-enterprise.[4] However, diverging from such self-absorbed happiness that stops at the self, the goal of state-sponsored happiness campaigns targeting the unemployed is to tie individual desire for happiness and their self-realization to broader social, economic and political objectives, for example, to advance entrepreneurial capital and sustain stability. Of course, this does not mean these nationalist goals of wealth and power entirely subsume current happiness promotion; as shown below, there are spiritual and idealistic aspects of happiness and enjoyment derived from such re-employment counseling programs.

While psychologization is often associated with Western advanced liberal societies (cf. Rose 1996; Gordo and De Vos 2010), Greg Eghigian (2004: 183) points out that psychological sciences also flourished in societies such as Nazi Germany and the former Soviet Union. Such a development is not a departure from authoritarian rule, but "an extension of the socialist utopian project" (ibid.: 184). In China, we can argue that at the most general level, psychologization legitimates and facilitates current socialist projects, for example, the harmonious society. Happiness is invoked as a promise and as something that gives meaning and order to life, mesmerizing people to have faith that adjustment to certain forms of living and thinking will secure their happiness (Berlant 2008). In other words, the goals and purposes that psychology claims to achieve are in line with the ideals or utopias promised by socialism or communism. On the other hand, since happiness putatively promises freedom, autonomy and fulfillment, it constructs entrepreneurial subjects for market development.

This chapter zeroes in on one set of practices where we can study this psychologization trend: state-led re-employment counseling programs for those who have been laid off from state-owned enterprises since the mid-1980s. These programs, imbued with psychologically infused ideologies and practices, have taught the unemployed how to pursue happiness and positive thinking even in the most difficult and unfair situations caused by retrenchment or unemployment as a result of economic restructuring. One way of achieving such happiness, according to these programs, is to turn inward and manage one's relationship with one's self through "proper" self-reflexivity. By tapping into the individual's desire for happiness and fulfillment, these programs have attempted to provide affective and psychological solutions to social issues (i.e. unemployment and mental illness). Indeed, to echo Ahmed (2010), how better to legitimate crippling economic restructuring and intensified social stratification than to deploy programs that suggest that these processes are actually an opening that could lead to happiness? In this sense, class-based socioeconomic inequality is displaced onto individual emotions and psychology. Although appeals to happiness and positive psychology appear to diffuse the role of class struggle for the disadvantaged in collective radical politics, such psychologization has not gone without contestation. In other words, despite its potential for depoliticizing social struggle (cf. Gordo and De Vos 2010), psychologization in China constitutes a new political arena for the marginalized to challenge the ruling party. Workers' critiques demonstrate that the discourse of happiness in China is not firmly hegemonic or totalizing.

The focus of the analysis is how happiness and self-reflection are promoted as a therapeutic strategy to encourage the unemployed to reposition or adapt themselves to the market economy, which, in turn, sustains stability and advances market development. The chapter first lays out the sociopolitical background of the use of psychology and happiness, highlighting state-promoted happiness as an affect that taps into and optimizes individual desire for happiness and fulfillment and implicitly ties them to political and economic ends. The chapter goes on to discuss the promotion of happiness through self-reflexivity that attempts to transcend, enhance and realize the self. The final section of the chapter focuses on workers' contestation against the happiness promotion and psychologization trend. This chapter contributes to the growing anthropological literature on happiness (cf. Mathews 2006; Thin 2008; Johnston 2012) by engaging with this emotion as it is embedded within a governing technology based on psychologization and as a force for both the government and underprivileged people to rally resources to their respective causes.

The reflections in this chapter arise out of both ethnographic research and readings of current intellectual and popular discourse. The time span of my field experience in China (2002–03) coincides approximately with two parallel processes: the gradual collapse of the socialist work-unit system as the institutional basis for ideological control due to urban economic restructuring, and the emerging psycho-boom and gradual commercialization of psychological counseling; this parallel appears to be a planned development. The data used in this chapter were mainly collected during my field research into the privatization of state-owned enterprises between 2002 and 2003 and complemented by further field work into psychological intervention programs in Beijing in the summers of 2007–11.

Happiness and positive psychology

Without a truism in its meaning, happiness becomes a floating signifier without fixed referents. The power of this term does not derive from its capacity to describe adequately or comprehensively a political or social reality that already exists, but from its semantic volatility, which enables it to become a site where investments may accrue and, thus, wields the power to rally, mobilize and produce the political contingency it appears to represent (see Butler 1993: 199, for a fuller account of this dynamic). However, the promotion of happiness among the underprivileged by the government seems mainly to address two broad issues: people's low self-reported happiness and the so-called "mental health crisis." Either of these issues could pose a threat to both social stability and the political legitimacy of the party. In the case of the first, the post-Mao eudemonic politics diverted the public interest to tangible gains and led people to linking their assessment of the government to their personal material advancement—exchanging material goods for public support (Chen 1997: 423). However, in recent years, the government's capacity to deliver goods and services has paled in the face of people's increased expectations, resulting in widespread dissatisfaction in society. For example, workers have expressed their resentment against the government's casting off of millions of them from the state sector since the mid-1980s through various forms of unrest. Indeed, urban economic restructuring up to the mid-1990s has transformed at least 12–15 million into the new urban poor (Rocca 2003). The unemployed and urban poor often report lower levels of happiness (Dolan *et al.* 2008; Smyth and Qian 2008).

Also, despite the massive improvement in living standards in China since the 1990s, people's self-reported happiness and life satisfaction have declined in general (Brockmann *et al.* 2009). The growing commodification of a number of areas of life, including housing, education, etc. has resulted in greater financial dissatisfaction, which affects people's overall feeling of well-being. In a moment when happiness is monetized, money means happiness (Brockmann *et al.* 2009). The prioritization of market expansion over people's welfare in China, combined with competitive consumption that predominates in a growth-oriented market economy, further intensifies economic inequality. This has led some to conclude that people's sense of happiness will inevitably continue to deteriorate (Ng and Ho 2006). Therefore, besides offering socioeconomic solutions (though inefficient), the government has also turned to psychological or affective intervention, which promotes (false) happiness and positive psychology to downplay economic inequalities.

The "mental health crisis" also contributes to the happiness promotion and psychologization trend. The so-called mental health crisis, which includes people experiencing depression, anxiety, schizophrenia and suicidal tendencies, currently impacts over 100 million people (Han and Zhang 2007).[5] Yet, China's public support for mental health has been inadequate: mental ailments, which account for about one-fifth of China's public health burden, receive only 2 percent of the health budget (WHO 2001 survey). Formal counseling training was initiated in 2002 (Higgins *et al.* 2008: 102). Private counseling is available but targets mainly the well-to-do middle class. In this context, government-sponsored (job) counseling was implemented in re-employment programs to assist the unemployed.

Instead of focusing on job supply, these programs have adopted an individualized and psychologized approach to un/re-employment. As famous psychologist Shi Kan (1999) points out, the key to re-employment is psychology. Indeed, since the mid-1990s, counseling has been integrated into re-employment and poverty-relief programs for laid-off workers. Rather than being sensitive to the trauma experienced by many state workers during mass unemployment (see Kong, Chapter 6, this volume),[6] this approach focuses on modeling workers' behavior, attitudes and motivation; it promotes self-reliance and self-governance.[7] The counseling programs often adopt methods loosely identified with rational emotive behavior therapy (REBT), which helps people overcome "unrealistic" and "irrational" feelings or actions and allows them to put these in perspective (Ellis 1973). REBT works on specific problems and is easily adapted to the fragmented format of such programs. The therapeutic ideals of such counseling programs are happiness, harmony and growth. As the following section details, belief in the adoption of a positive attitude and the routines of self-reflection is supposed to guarantee personal happiness and success over adverse circumstances. Counseling provides a therapeutic approach for programs and agencies to manage a newly marginalized group made up of laid-off workers (see also Polsky 1991).

Affect, happiness and potentiality

To challenge the rationalist readings of power and governance in political and social sciences, Judith Butler (1997) suggests that political rationalities possess a psychic dimension. Further, Warwick Tie (2004: 169) develops a framework to understand the psychic life of governmentality by arguing that governments design programs utilizing their awareness of affective or psychic aspects to assist in their hold on subjects. These programs resonate, often at the level of the unconscious, with popular, pleasurable fantasies (for example, happiness and hope). Similarly, Slavoj Žižek (1994: 56–57) examines the unconscious supplement of power, which, he claims, provides enjoyment to serve as the unacknowledged support of meaning. Subjects, who are in the making, for example, in their interactions with state programs, can be interpellated, that is, called forth as the appropriate recipients for a given program, when they are seduced by meanings that resonate with their own particular economies of pleasure, as in the case of individuals' aspirations for happiness. By maximizing the potential impact of positive feelings for individuals, happiness produces *jouissance* (meaningful enjoyment); once such happiness infuses in social norms or ideals, it would enable these norms or ideals to grip the minds of masses affectively. Similarly, in purveying happiness, Chinese counseling programs for the unemployed connect to a real desire in people and place it in service of state goals, such as that of a harmonious society. Such pleasurable fantasies enable subjects to be interpellated at an emotional level, rendering power more affective and hegemonic (Tie 2004: 163).

However, such an affective strategy (of promoting happiness) is a unity of contradictory practices: reconstructing happiness or harmony after economic restructuring has dismantled the socialist job security and public welfare and destroyed the social balance that sustained people's happiness. Simply put, it is a reconstruction of happiness after its destruction. Therefore, such happiness promoted by those re-employment projects, in addition to releasing positive potentialities (entrepreneurship, positive feelings), preempts negative potentialities. It is important to understand both facets of potentiality (potentiality to and potentiality not to). Here I define potential as the capacity to do or be something. Opposing the claim that potentiality exists only in acts, Agamben (1998) endorses Aristotle's emphasis on the autonomous existence of potentiality. Potentiality does not simply disappear into actuality; it can be the potentiality *not* to (do or be). In other words, potentiality remains sovereignly capable of the act in not realizing it (Agamben 1998: 45). For example, a builder keeps his ability to build even when he does not build. In the case of happiness promotion, for the unemployed, potentiality to (be actualized) encompasses (positive) potential for entrepreneurship, the adoption of new morals, or the enjoyment of life. However, these same groups of people also embody potentialities *not* to: for example, potential threats posed by the unemployed including alcohol abuse, physical violence, or social unrest, which they are capable of actualizing but may have not done so yet. The emphasis on the happiness of the unemployed aims to preempt these future threats and to make them the cause of the self-propelling movement of current government (happiness promotion). Indeed, preemption of this kind is a form of potential politics; it operates in the present on a future threat.

Self-reflexivity and the regime of the self

Psychological counseling constructs self-cultivating and self-reflective subjects. Self-reflexivity is often considered a mode of self-making and of subjection, as self-reflexivity is predicated on the fact that individuals have been initiated into the process of self-concern and self-regulation. As Anthony Giddens (1991: 36) states, "Reflexivity is a defining characteristic of all human action. All human beings routinely 'keep in touch' with the grounds of what they do as an integral element of doing it." The trade union leader of the watch factory in Changping, where I have conducted field research since 2002, once commented on the trauma of layoffs: "If there is ever to be healing, there must be reflecting. People are trying to sweep things under the carpet, but they have to face what has happened [layoffs is traumatic to many workers in Changping] in order to move on completely." The adoption of a positive attitude and routines of self-reflection is assumed to be therapeutic and to guarantee personal success over adverse circumstances. Self-reflexivity is key to establishing a "correct" self-image. According to the director of the Re-employment Service Center at the Changping factory,[8] the self-image within one's heart is the core of one's self. To discover that self-image requires a mirror. Self-reflection creates that mirror. Through it, the individual sees his or herself, then transcends, enhances and realizes his or her "correct" self.

I want to focus on three modes of self-reflexivity that were promoted by the watch factory in order to nurture personal happiness and growth. These modes of reflexivity did not render individuals passive or docile. Rather, they endowed them with new competencies and qualities. However, in exercising such officially promoted self-scrutiny, the subject unwittingly reproduced the same systems of limitation and exclusion through which the subject came into being in the first place. The three modes are also therapeutic, in the sense that they were designed to make people feel better by enhancing their self-confidence and bringing them immediate relief to get through life more easily. All posit a self that is responsive; each responds to different types of stimulus. In general, self-reflexivity orients people to turn away from the sociopolitical structure and turn toward their inner selves for happiness and salvation.

The first mode of self-reflexivity is a form of self-transcendence. At the Changping factory in January 2003, the trade union leader used this mode of reflexivity to pacify workers who demanded a salary raise:

> When I started to work at the factory, we only made 41.10 *yuan*. We had this salary for many years. We were content then. [Because people were equally poor—communizing poverty—but now workers suffer relative poverty.] Now we make one hundred times more than this, and we're not happy. But we should be satisfied and grateful. Don't compare yourself with other people, and compare yourself with yourself, with your own past—what you ate, where you lived twenty years ago. Look at what we eat and where we live now! Then you feel grateful and at peace with life.

This is a kind of transcendental happiness (Ho 2006: 63), the result of considering the totality of life experience. This transcendental attitude seems to be in direct conflict with economic principles of maximization, but is explained as a natural development as one becomes more spiritual over time (Ho 2006: 48). To enhance happiness, one needs to resolve conflicts, both internally within one's mind, and externally in terms of relating harmoniously to other individuals (Ho 2006). Such self-transcendence can also be realized through a strategic comparison with those who are less fortunate and less able than oneself. Bi Shumin, the famous Chinese writer and counselor, who celebrates the happiness of everyday life through her television lecture entitled *tixing xingfu* "Reminding Happiness,"[9] uses an example of her own life experience to explain that her happiness and satisfaction are derived from her reflections on her own life as a soldier for 16 years in Tibet, where she witnessed many of her comrades sacrifice their lives.[10] Indeed, according to Mikhail Bakhtin, one gains an identity only across a boundary; it takes a minimum of two consciousnesses to guarantee an authentic image of any given self (cited in Emerson 2006: 27).

When we do as Bi does and compare ourselves to those who are less fortunate than us, a feeling of gratitude can result. In fact, the notion of gratitude (towards life or society) has been invoked by enterprise management to promote happiness and optimism among downtrodden workers and lead them to act in a virtuous way. However, as Arlie R. Hochschild (2003: 104–18) suggests, gratitude involves not only feelings of appreciation, warmth and a desire to return the favor, but also the structured position of indebtedness. In this case, nurturing such attitudes of gratitude suggests indebtedness to the life and society offered (or ruled) by the party.

The second mode of self-reflection is a process of self-affirmation: affirming one's existence and one's power to affect the environment through strategically selecting a sounding board. In this mode, the self is seen as a reflected object existing primarily in others. Nature is one such sounding board and provides psychological relief, for example, through the practice of eco-psychology. Seemingly depoliticized and neutral, the practice of eco-psychology temporarily detaches people from socioeconomic structures. At the watch factory in spring 2003, the trade union leader claimed that many workers felt distressed and had lost their consciousness of their true selves in the privatization process. To help workers relieve their anxiety about layoffs and rediscover their identities, he organized a series of mountain-climbing contests as both a physical and psychological exercise. One component of the competition was "shouting at mountains" (*hanshan*). The union leader encouraged workers to shout as loud as possible, shouting out whatever was on their minds:

> Simply shout at the top of your lungs and shout out all your anxiety and concerns, cursing and name-calling. When you hear your echo resounding, you realize the very existence of yourself, your voice and your strength. You come back, refreshed and energized.

According to the trade union leader, mountain shouting has significant implications for workers' identities. The echo aggrandized or enhanced the self; the self became the source of power and strength. This is an acoustic, proprioceptive self derived from bodily sensations and perception (Vitz 1994: xxii). It is the reduced or subdued self, aware of its basic existence, and to feel one's aggrandized existence in one's echo is a way of counteracting the process of restructuring in state enterprises that has been reducing (the number and confidence of) workers and the cause of a drop in their social status. Moreover, the affective and energetic transmission between nature and human beings has a long tradition of being seen as therapeutic, assisting in the production of happy and healthy subjects; according to the trade union leader, such an exercise was good for health. Besides, it was more enjoyable than taking medicine.

However, these mountain-climbing contests involved prizes such as soap, towels, mugs, soft drinks and cookies. Many of the workers who joined the mountain climbing were there only for the prizes. One worker told me that after working at the factory during the day and riding a pedicab at night, he was not in the mood and did not have the energy to climb mountains. This was a luxury for the elite (factory management) who do not need to labor hard to make a living. There was nothing new about mountain climbing or mountain shouting, but promoting such practices in the rhetoric of the therapeutics of the body and soul and in terms of eco-psychology was unprecedented: it signified the emergence of a therapeutic ethos of governance in China.[11]

The third mode of self-reflexivity is performed through an official narrative structure, which implies that conforming to dominant ideologies can achieve entrepreneurship and self-realization. A salient example is the media discourse of re-employment. Since the mid-1990s, the Chinese media have been saturated with images and stories of "re-employment stars." These are predominantly female, formerly laid-off workers who have been re-employed in the service industry. To be designated a re-employment star, an official government designation, is considered an honor. The women are then "invited" to reflect upon and narrate their re-employment experiences in official media outlets. The narrative line of these self-reflections is usually a three-stage flashback: first, unemployment and its negative impact on the narrator's life and psychology—anxiety, depression and frustration; second, empowerment through job training and psychotherapeutic counseling offered by state enterprises, social programs, or women's organizations; and third, the marked improvement in quality of life and psychology after re-employment. This constitutes more than a happiness campaign (Yang 2007). It becomes a site for subject formation: the re-employment stars' happiness and success demonstrate their sense of fulfillment from having overcome the crippling effects of unemployment; they are happy, psychologically "healthy" subjects. More than normalization, this discourse glorifies and glamorizes those unemployed women. As both ideological and affective subjects, they speak for the state and defend the neoliberal market economy.

For example, in December 2002, on the China Central TV program *Contemporary Workers*, a woman, beaming with confidence, narrated her re-employment story. She had been laid off from a fabric factory and then re-employed at a laundry stall. She then became an entrepreneur and managed several laundries in Beijing. She described her work trajectory and emotional transformation:

> I was very depressed after layoff. I didn't want to see people, and sometimes I felt ashamed. I remember one day I bumped into a neighbor at a market, I pretended not to see her. But she saw me, and I told her I was on holiday ... Then I started to attend re-employment training sessions, job counseling, and finally got hired at a laundry ... They noticed how hard I worked and trusted me. The next year, they allowed me to contract the laundry stall. Then I had more confidence and contracted all the laundry for a nearby hospital ... Now I wished I had come out earlier and embraced the change earlier rather than feeling so bitter and depressed for so long. Nothing can really beat you if you don't beat yourself.

Watching this woman on TV, it was easy to see the affective charge of this discourse and its capacity to move people at emotional and sensorial levels. There may be some real happiness derived from her reemployment experiences. However, in such official representation, the notion of happiness is constructed mainly through conforming to dominant ideologies and state mobilization—through re-employment, a state call to manage "gendered layoffs" (Wang 2003; Kong, Chapter 6, this volume).[12] Here happiness is achieved through efforts that demand patience, diligence and perseverance. In the context of intensified inequality in China, happiness or optimism involves thinking that in exchange for these virtues, one can achieve recognition—that is, in essence, recognition of one's ability to adapt to social change and endure the crippling effects of economic restructuring.

This new laundry entrepreneur realized her potential through re-employment. She experienced a process of self-actualization and an affirmation of her true self. The self previously repressed under the planned economy was actualized in the market economy. The woman described herself as becoming better integrated, more productive and more confident. Re-employment is celebrated as a therapeutic process of renegotiating one's emotional state and reconstructing one's selfhood—a process for changing and growing the self so as to create ideal affective and ideological subjects authorized by both the state and psychological professionals to promote the psychotherapy industry and advance market development. However, such re-employment stars are ideal subjects and role models for state propaganda, which renders their own subjectivities invisible (see Yoshimizu, Chapter 7, this volume). The emphasis on this discourse of "re-employment stars" also illustrates the role that (subaltern) women play in the psychological intervention—how they are targeted and mobilized to play the role of the vanguard in promoting psychotherapy.

In the discourse of re-employment, happiness and optimism are emotions "more valuable" and "more suitable" to the "liberating" market economy than depression or anxiety. Emotionality is dependent on relations of power, which endows some emotions with more value than others; the hierarchy of emotions can thus be translated into, and reinforced by, a given social hierarchy (Ahmed 2008: 10–11). In this sense within the culture of psychology, the market economy is preferred over the planned economy.

Counseling and happiness promotion as *huyou*

The factory in Changping had a special connection with the famous Chinese psychologist Shi Kan, who conducted a psychological research project to improve efficiency there in the late 1980s. Because of this, management paid special attention to Shi's work on positive psychology and his TV counseling to unemployed workers. For example, in interviews with me, the director of the Re-employment Service Center at the factory (who is now a licensed counselor) emphasized the importance of optimism in re-employment for instilling in workers an alternative interpretation of layoffs:

> If you think of unemployment as a crisis, crisis (in Chinese, *wei ji*) has two characters and two meanings: *wei* means "in danger"; *ji* means "opportunity." Unemployment is a crisis but it also offers opportunities to start something new. Those who beam with optimism and smile will get hired first. That's why you need to be optimistic. No employer likes a person who is bitter or grumpy.

This director taught unemployed workers how to present themselves for job interviews—how to dress, smile, shake hands and so forth, to create a plastic and transient self that would impress employers. Indeed, optimism has been advocated as a key strategy for re-employment. One worker who attended a training session considered this teaching useless. "Most jobs we can apply for are dirty labor work. No one wants to shake hands with you or see how big your smile is. It's hard to smile, considering the way we have been treated [laid off]. It's like 'killing the mule immediately after it finishes work' (*xie mo sha lu*)." Despite this kind of doubt and real pain, workers' misery is seen not only as an opportunity for the individual to start anew but also as providing abundant opportunities for management to transform themselves into therapeutic practitioners. Indeed, several managers at this former factory have become community counselors or social workers since 2006. Because their training was largely based on Western counseling and social work, its application was not always culturally appropriate.[13] At a job counseling session, this same director once gave an example of how happiness and optimism can impress people to the benefit of both the giver and receiver. The story had to do with Johnny, an American beggar at a grocery store. After hearing a life counselor preach the power of optimism and of encouragement, Johnny began searching for encouraging phrases in books and typing them onto small pieces of paper. When he begged outside a grocery store, he would place a piece of paper with the uplifting words into his potential beneficiary's shopping bag. Much to the surprise of the grocery store owner, the checkout line where Johnny situated himself was always full of customers; people would wait longer to check out to get Johnny's nice saying. Johnny's optimism benefited other people too. After finishing the story, the director said, "Johnny is a beggar, but we are only temporarily laid off." A worker interrupted him: "I want to beg but no grocery store would allow me in here. We want to go to America."

This kind of critique, however, is not always welcome. For workers for whom psychological strategies fail, the discourse of mental illness is often evoked. The factory of my study was located close to two mental hospitals at Hui Long Guan, making it easy to invoke the language of mental illness to stigmatize and regulate unemployed individuals who made trouble. A worker whose wife committed suicide because of her layoff kept telling people that he would use a chef's knife to cut management into 1,000 pieces, but the factory director said that the wife was hysterical and the husband probably needed to go to Hui Long Guan as well. Management, in general, labeled laid-off workers who refused to sever their relationship with a state enterprise, or who constantly returned to "make a fuss," as "crazy." However, the discourse of psychology and mental illness is also a site of contestation. Workers appropriate this discourse for their own interests, as in acting "mentally ill" to show resistance (see Yang 2010).

Workers have other forms of resistance to government-proffered happiness and counseling as well. In my field work, they often criticized counseling as a kind of *huyou* (roughly, trick or hoodwink). For many workers in Changping, *huyou* is about psychology or counseling; the person counseled is lured into pleasantly and willingly accepting the ideologies or concepts offered by counselors. *Huyou* is not a neologism but has recently acquired new significance after comedian Zhao Benshan's successful TV skits in 2001 and 2003. In the comedy of *maiguai* (selling crutches) at CCTV's Chinese New Year Gala of 2001, Zhao Benshan successfully convinced Fan Wei that Fan would get a serious illness if he did not purchase a pair of crutches for his leg; actually he is perfectly healthy but a little stupid. Fan is lured into buying the crutches. Fan is so convinced that he is even grateful to Zhao for helping him identify his potential health problem and preventing it from getting worse. These comedies were such a success that *huyou* has become a household term in China. *Huyou* creates a scheme that makes the target feel appreciated and cared for and thus easily and pleasantly fall into the trap—a folk understanding of Žižek's unconscious supplement. Counseling works the same way, tapping into one's desire for happiness and a good life and tying them to sociopolitical objectives; people then have to rely on themselves to solve "their own" problems. Both counseling and *huyou* identify personal problems, diagnose them and then prescribe solutions. Like *huyou*, which is premised on the tactic of creating and imposing a problem on a target in order to achieve certain purpose (often to cheat), counseling uses the language of psychology to identify or impose a psychological problem and encourage people to rely on themselves for solutions or adapt themselves to social change. By tapping into individuals' concerns for their well-being (health, safety and other interests), the practice of *huyou* is often affective (to affect and to be affected)—the person who is "*huyou*ed" (*bei huyou*) goes as far as to express gratitude to the person who practices *huyou*, like in Zhao's skits.

Conclusion

The recent turn to happiness in China, then, is a turn towards psychology and affective life. Unlike Zhang's (Chapter 1, this volume) notion of psychologization, which popularizes and internalizes psychologically infused Confucian doctrines, state-led re-employment counseling programs, by promoting happiness and self-reflexivity, manage socioeconomic issues (i.e. unemployment) in psychological terms. Like communism or socialism, happiness points to a hope and a promise, creating a personal and political horizon that allows people to envision a good life (Ahmed 2008: 12). However, the real control that occurs through happiness promotion or therapeutic governance is often unconscious as they optimize the individual's pleasurable fantasies and ally them to political and economic objectives. Promoting happiness for the underprivileged to make them happy while they have nothing to be happy about, aims to preempt potential threats posed by the same group and alleviate the crippling effects of socioeconomic dislocation caused by recent economic restructuring. By turning economic stratification into the personal, emotional and psychological, such happiness promotion downplays structural inequalities. In this context, unemployment is constructed not as a result of economic restructuring but as an opportunity for entrepreneurship and self-realization.

The rise of psychology in the form of self-help and happiness campaigns in China ushers in a new body of therapeutic expertise, with new sites for the practice of therapy and new ways of construing, evaluating and actualizing relations. The government not only uses psychology to provide a language or framework for people to interpret change in China, but also integrates psychological forces—for example, the emphasis on the self: self-adjustment, self-responsibility and self-enterprising—into socioeconomic processes. Such psychologization in China apparently satisfies the contingent needs, interests and aspirations of a certain class (i.e. entrepreneurs, psychotherapists, the state). However, as the above ethnographic data demonstrate, the happiness promotion and psychologization trend also attract contestation. The contestation occurs even as China continues to promote happiness as the measure of a good life; such a parallel demonstrates that happiness has become both a nexus for contending with social and political change, and an analytical tool for social critique.

Acknowledgements

An earlier version of this chapter was delivered on a panel organized by Jesook Song and Jie Yang at AES/CASCA at the University of British Columbia in May 2009; at a workshop on Affects and Markets in East Asia organized by Jie Yang on May 18, 2009; and at a conference "China Inside Out: Modernity and the Individual Psyche" organized by Andrew Kipnis and Tamara Jacka at the Australian National University on August 16–17, 2010. I thank the participants for their comments and questions. I am especially grateful to Andrew Kipnis and Tamara Jacka for inviting me to their conference, and for their insightful, penetrating comments on an earlier draft of this chapter. Thanks also go to Marguerite Pigeon and Janet Keller for their excellent comments and editorial suggestions.

Notes

1 Key features of the harmonious society, as proposed by Hu Jintao and Wen Jiabao in 2004, include democracy, the rule of law, equity, justice, sincerity, amity and vitality.

2 Sara Ahmed (2008) suggests that there is a happiness turn not only in academic disciplines such as history, psychology, architecture and economics, but also in governance and international arenas (in anthropology, see Gordon Mathews 2006).

3 TV series such as *pinzu Zhangdamin de xingfu shenghuo* (The happy life of talkative Zhangdamin), *Yangguang de Kuaile Shenghuo* (Yangguang's happy life), and *laoda de xingfu* (Happiness of the eldest brother), and movies like *Gaoxing*, all treat underprivileged characters and settings (see Yang 2013).

4 This is different from Mao's time, when happiness was derived from politics and from the elevation of the collective over the self (McGrath 2009).

5 The crisis is real, directly linked as it must be with the socioeconomic dislocation described above. However, it is also a state and expert discursive construct that supports the use of psychology (via counseling, psychiatry, or social work) as a solution to social problems.

6 State workers, who had been promised life-long employment in state enterprises but were laid off due to privatization, often experienced their layoffs as traumatic events. Many workers I spoke to in Changping conveyed, with extraordinary acuity, stories of this trauma and its psychological and physical impact.

7 Leaders of state enterprises also suggest that there is no efficient way to deal with the problem of unemployment other than encouraging workers to be self-reliant. The government's message is that workers' problems come not from the state but from their own failure to adapt to the market, and that workers ought to accept market-based logic when examining their own lives (Blecher 2002: 298–99).

8 Re-employment Service Centers as part of the national re-employment project were implemented at state enterprises between 1998 and 2003 to help laid-off workers to get re-employed.

9 Bi Shumin's bestselling books like *Zhengjiu Lufang* (Saving the Breasts) or *Nv Xinli Shi* (Female Counselors) focus on women and promote psychological introspection and emotional management.

10 Similarly, a movie called *Gao Xing*, which describes the life of Liu Gaoxing, a garbage collector in Xi'an City, promotes a notion of gratitude as a way of enhancing optimism, energy and happiness and of leading people to act virtuously. Liu thanks each of his organs every day for keeping him healthy and productive. The emphasis on optimism and happiness romanticizes the poverty and suffering of a marginalized group.

11 Basic precepts of eco-psychology are often invoked in advertisements for eco-tourism and counseling in Beijing. For example, in a television counseling program in Beijing TV, a "forest shower" (*senlin yu*), walking in the forest, is considered therapeutic because it enables nature's energy and self-correcting balance to flow through the heart (psyche) to support well-being.

12 Women have suffered both unemployment and the new urban poverty to a greater extent than men. For example, according to one official statistic, of the 11.51 million laid-off workers in China's cities at the end of 1997, more than half (59.2 percent, or 6.8 million) were female. However, women only took up 39 percent of the workforce (Wang 2003: 161).

13 Many Chinese psychologists have only a general college degree and some on-the-job experience (Clay 2002). There is a national certification program for both counselors and psychologists, but most professionals are not certified, as it is not always required for employment. Social work was established as an academic discipline in China in 1987; to date, there are fifty-eight master programs and two hundred and fifty bachelor programs of social work in Chinese universities. There are about 45,000 licensed social workers in China (personal communication, Professor Zhang Mo, July 2011).

References

Agamben, Giorgio. 1998. *Homa Sacer: Sovereign Power and Bare Life*. Stanford, CA: Stanford University Press.

Ahmed, Sara. 2008. "The Happiness Turn." *New Formations* 63: 7–14.

——2010. *The Promise of Happiness*. Durham, NC: Duke University Press.

Berlant, Lauren. 2008. "Cruel Optimism: On Marx, Loss and the Senses." *New Formations* 63: 33–51.

Blackman, Lisa. 2008. "Is Happiness Contagious?" *New Formations* 63: 15–32.

Blecher, Marc J. 2002. "Hegemony and Workers' Politics in China." *The China Quarterly* 170: 283–303.

Brockmann, Hilke, Delhey, Jan, Welzel, Christian and Hao Yuan. 2009. "The China Puzzle: Falling Happiness in a Rising Economy." *Journal of Happiness Studies* 10(4): 387–405.

Butler, Judith. 1993. *Bodies That Matter: On the Discursive Limits of "Sex"*. London and New York: Routledge.

——1997. *The Psychic Life of Power: Theories in Subjection*. Stanford, CA: Stanford University Press.

Chen, Feng. 1997. "The Dilemma of Eudaemonic Legitimacy in Post-Mao China." *Polity* XXIX(3): 422–35.

China Digital Times. 2006. "'Happiness Index' into regional development system—An Bei." chinadigitaltimes.net/2006/02/happiness-index-into-regional-development.

Clay, Rebecca A. 2002. "Chinese Psychology." *Monitor on Psychology* 33(3): 64.

Dolan, Paul, Peasgood, Tessa and White, Matthew. 2008. "Do We Really Know What Makes Us Happy? A Review of the Economics Literature on the Factors Associated with Subjective Well-being." *Journal of Economic Psychology* 29: 94–122.

Eghigian, Greg. 2004. "The Psychologization of the Socialist Self: East German Forensic Psychology and its Deviants, 1945–75." *German History* 22(2): 181–205.

Ehrenreich, Barbara. *RSA: Smile or Die*. www.youtube.com/watch?v=u5um8QWRvo&feature=channel.

Ellis, Albert. 1973. *Humanistic Psychotherapy: The Rational-emotive Approach*. New York: Julian Press.

Emerson, Caryl. 2006. "Building a Responsive Self in a Post-Relativistic World: The Contribution of Mikhail Bakhtin." In Paul C. Vitz and Susan M. Felch (eds), *The Self: Beyond the Postmodern Crisis*. Wilmington, DE: ISI Books.

Giddens, Anthony. 1991. *Modernity and Self-Identity: Self and Society in the Late Modern Age*. Cambridge: Polity Press.

Gordo, Angel and De Vos, Jan. 2010 "Psychologism, Psychologising and Depsychologisation." *Annual Review of Critical Psychology* 8: 3–7.

Han, Buxin and Zhang, Kan. 2007. "Psychology in China." *The Psychologist* 20: 734–36.

Higgins, Louise T., Davey, Gareth, Xiang Gao, Richang Zheng, Zijun Ni and Lijun Lang. 2008. "Counselling in China: Past, Present and Future." *Psychology and Developing Societies* 20(1): 99–109.

Ho, Sang Lok. 2006. "The 'Three Happinesses' and Public Policy." In Yew-Kwang Ng and Lok Sang Ho (eds), *Happiness and Public Policy: Theory, Case Studies and Implications.* Hampshire: Palgrave Macmillan.

Hochschild, Arlie. R. 2003. *The Commercialization of Intimate Life: Notes from Home and Work*. Berkeley: University of California Press.

Johnston, Barbara Rose. 2012. "Introduction to Happiness." *American Anthropologist* 114(1): 6–7.

Kernan, Antoine and Rocca, Jean-Louis. 2000. "Social Responses to Unemployment and the 'New Urban Poor': Case Study in Shenyang City and Liaoning Province." *China Perspectives* 27: 35–51.

Kleinman, Arthur. 2010. "Remaking the Moral Person in China: Implications for Health." *The Lancet* 375: 1074–75.

Lee, Ching Kwan. 2007. *Against the Law: Labor Protests in China's Rustbelt and Sunbelt*. Berkeley: University of California Press.

Lee, Haiyan. 2006. "*Nannies for Foreigners*: The Enchantment of Chinese Womanhood in the Age of Millennial Capitalism." *Public Culture* 18(3): 507–29.

Liu, Yu. 2006. "Can Society's Happiness Be Measured by a Set of Figures?" www.bjreview.com.cn/forum/txt/2006-12/18/content_51268.htm (accessed on March 22, 2012).

Massumi, Brian. 2002. *Parables for the Virtual: Movement, Affect, Sensation*. Durham, NC: Duke University Press.

——2007. "Potential Politics and the Primacy of Preemption." *Theory and Event* 10(2).

Mathews, Gordon. 2006. "Happiness and the Pursuit of a Life Worth Living: An Anthropological Approach." In Yew-Kwang Ng and Lok Sang Ho (eds), *Happiness and Public Policy*. Hampshire: Palgrave Macmillan, 147–68.

McGrath, Jason. 2009. "Communists Have More Fun! The Dialectics of Fulfillment in Cinema of the People's Republic of China." *World Picture* 3.

Miller, Peter and Rose, Nikolas. 2008. *Governing the Present: Administering Economic, Social and Personal Life*. Cambridge: Polity Press.

Ng, Yew-Kwang and Ho, Lok Sang, eds. 2006. *Happiness and Public Policy: Theory, Case Studies and Implications*. New York: Palgrave Macmillan.

Phillips, Michael R., Xianyun Li, and Yanping Zhang. 2002. "Suicide Rates in China, 1995–99." *The Lancet* 359: 835–40.

Polsky, Andrew J. 1991. *The Rise of the Therapeutic State*. Princeton, NJ: Princeton University Press.

Richard, Analiese and Rudnyckyj, Daromir. 2009. "Economies of Affect." *Journal of Royal Anthropological Institute* 15: 57–77.

Rimke, Heidi Marie. 2000. "Governing Citizens through Self-Help Literature." *Cultural Studies* 14(1): 61–78.

Rocca, Jean-Louis. 2003. "Old Working Class, New Working Class: Reforms, Labor Crisis and the Two Faces of Conflicts in Chinese Urban Areas." In Taciana Fisac and Leila Fernandez-Stembridge (eds), *China Today: Economic Reforms, Social Cohesion and Collective Identities*. London and New York: RoutledgeCurzon, 77–104.

Rose, Nikolas. 1996. *Inventing Our Selves: Psychology, Power and Personhood*. Cambridge: Cambridge University Press.

Rosen, Stanley. 1994. "Chinese Women in the 1990s: Images and Roles in Contention." In Maurice Brosseau and Lo Chi Kin (eds), *China Review 1994*. Hong Kong: Chinese University of Hong Kong Press.
Shi Kan. 1999. *Zhiye zhidao de lilun and yingyong* (Job Guidance: Theories and Practices). Beijing: Beijing Xicheng Qu Zhiye Zhidao Shiyan Jidi.
Smyth, Russell and Xiaolei Qian. 2008. "Inequality and Happiness in Urban China." *Economics Bulletin* 4(24): 1–10.
Thin, Neil. 2008. "Why Anthropology Can Ill Afford to Ignore Well-Being." In Gordon Mathews and Carolina Izquierdo (eds), *Pursuits of Happiness: Well-being in Anthropological Perspective*. New York: Berghahn, 23–44.
Tie, Warwick. 2004. "The Psychic Life of Governmentality." *Culture, Theory, and Critique* 45(2): 161–76.
Vitz, Paul C. 1994. *Psychology as Religion: The Cult of Self-Worship*. Grand Rapids, MI: William B. Eerdmans Publishing Company.
Wang Gungwu and Zheng Yongnian. 2008. *China and the New International Order*. London and New York: Routledge.
Wang, Zheng. 2003. "Gender, Employment and Women's Resistance." In Elizabeth J. Perry and Mark Selden (eds), *Chinese Society: Change, Conflict and Resistance*, 158–82. London and New York: RoutledgeCurzon.
WHO. 2001. *Survey on Mental Health in China*.
Yang, Jie. 2007. "'Reemployment Stars': Language, Gender and Neoliberal Restructuring in China." In Bonnie McElhinny (ed.), *Words, Worlds, and Material Girls: Language, Gender and Globalization*. Berlin: Mouton de Gruyter, 73–102.
——2010. "The Crisis of Masculinity: Class, Gender, and Kindly Power in Post-Mao China." *American Ethnologist* 37(3): 550–62.
——2013. "Fake Happiness: Counseling, Potentiality and Psycho-politics in China." *Ethos* 41(3): 291–311.
Yu, Dan. 2006. *Yu Dan's Reflections on Analects*. Beijing: Zhonghua Shuju.
Žižek, Slavoj. 1994. *The Metastases of Enjoyment: Six Essays on Woman and Causality*. London and New York: Verso.

Part III

Body, affect and subjectivity

3 Banking in affects

The child, a landscape and the performance of a canonical view

Teresa Kuan

> Impersonal affect is the connecting thread of experience. It is the invisible glue that holds the world together. In event.
>
> (Massumi 2002: 217)

> The production of normalization is no longer simply entrusted to the family, kin groups, or other institutions of civil society; it also involves the investment in and regulation of a market-driven circulation of affect and attention.
>
> (Clough 2007: 19)

The phrase "banking in affects" expresses this double life of affect: as a new domain of capital accumulation and as a world-connecting thread of experience. The conjoining of the economic with the non-economic in this phrase, however, is not only meant to suggest an argument to be developed. Instead, this chapter is written in the spirit of assemblage, a get-together in which affect theory and a friend's creative expression—the source of this phrase—can productively mingle. For the whole point of the affective turn is to open up new possibilities for moving out of, as Brown and Tucker (2010: 248) put it, "the semiotic and post-Foucauldian slough of despondency into which millennial social science lurched." Banking in affects is an idea that addresses China's socioeconomic transition, while at the same time making visible the vibrant presence of what we are calling "affect."

On affect

The concept of affect is traced to Baruch Spinoza, whose *Ethics* concerned the question of what a body can do. Here, the body is defined not so much by its physical boundaries, but rather, by its power to affect and its capacity to be affected. This is not a body to be grasped in terms of its form, substance, nor taxonomic name, but rather by the relations that it enters into (Deleuze 1992). For this reason, relations can also be called affects. For Deleuze and Guattari an affect can be a composition or assemblage of rather unlikely things: "For example, the Tick, attracted by the light, hoists itself up to the tip of a branch; it is sensitive to the smell of mammals, and lets itself fall when one passes beneath the branch; it digs into its skin, at the least hairy place it can find" (Deleuze and Guattari 1987: 257). The light and the tick, the tick and a smell, and finally, the tick nestled close to the body of a hairy terrestrial animal; these are "just three affects" (ibid.). The body is defined by what it is capable of relative to what it assembles with, thus always "becoming" something else. Because a body could potentially enter into a relation with any number of things, it is hard to predict what a body can do.

Affect is understood to be a kind of "preindividual" energy or vitality that circulates between bodies and environments (Clough 2007; Wissinger 2007); it is always on the move and never in residence (Ahmed 2004). If this sounds vague, it is because affect theory concerns something rather indeterminate and ineffable. This is not because the life of affect leaves too few traces, but rather, because it leaves *too many*. For this reason, affect is simply a kind of intensity. As Brian Massumi (2002: 13) points out, "sensation is never simple." Something as seemingly plain as an echo arises out of the complex patterning that forms by virtue of the movement of sound between surfaces, thus transforming surface distances into "intensity." Such an intensity constitutes a reserve of potential, a "pressing crowd of incipiencies and tendencies" (Massumi 2002: 30), from which the will and conscious thinking may selectively recognize in navigating the phenomenal world. Because conscious life involves differentiating what is otherwise continuous and integrated, the uninterrupted flow of matter and energy remains a virtual phenomenon. What the body is capable of, meanwhile, is the "infolding" of impinging stimuli as affect.

This relates directly to the core definition of affect, i.e. the body's power to affect and its capacity to be affected. Here I would like to quote Massumi's discussion of tactility at length:

> Tactility is the sensibility of the skin as surface of contact between the perceiving subject and the perceived object. Proprioception folds tactility into the body, enveloping the skin's contact with the external world in a dimension of medium depth: between epidermis and viscera … Proprioception translates the exertions and ease of the body's encounters with objects into a muscular memory of relationality. This is the cumulative memory of skill, habit, posture. At the same time as proprioception folds tactility in, it draws out the subject's reactions to the qualities of the objects it perceives through all five senses, bringing them into the motor realm of externalizable response.
>
> (Massumi 2002: 58–59)

A body is best defined by its capacity to be affected—by its responsiveness to the sensation of touch and movement, which is converted, by way of an accumulation of experience internalized as muscular memory, into a habit or a skill. What Massumi does not mention between these pages is how the capacity to be affected might be mobilized into a power to affect in a given historical context. A skill, a habit, a posture, can have tremendous social and political significance, where a body's capacity to act, and to affect, may constitute a major focus of discursive concern and pedagogical intervention.

This chapter discusses how the body of the child has come to be seen as a site where affective forces could be put into play in the changing of a country's future. My ethnographic case is drawn from research I conducted in the mid-2000s on the *suzhi jiaoyu* (quality education) reform movement in China, which grew out of a concern over whether or not Chinese educational practices produce the kind of citizen-subject who can contribute to economic development and national strength. Its antithesis, the stubbornly entrenched system of education for exam taking or *yingshi jiaoyu*, is understood as "stuffing" children like ducks and producing "test-taking machines," with its emphasis on rote memorization and rigorous discipline. If China is successfully to "link tracks with the rest of the world" (*yu shijie jiegui*), that is to say, compete on the global stage, the cultivation of a certain kind of affective subject would be in order. In response, both official policies and popular discourses concerning the education reform call for an augmentation and expansion of affect (Clough 2007). To speak in more emic terms, the importance of an educational strategy that nurtures "creative thinking habits" and a "spirit for innovation" is reiterated.

Although formulations of *suzhi jiaoyu* vary between the institutional and family domains, all of its advocates could agree on one thing: Chinese children are bereft of direct experience. Their bodies do not encounter much sensory stimulus, nor do they move much, for they sit for many consecutive hours behind a study desk, day after day. This state of affairs had even become a cause for concern for Jiang Zemin, who urged in a 2000 speech, "[We] must not confine our youth in rooms and in books all day, [and we] must let them participate in some social practice, open their field of vision, and enlarge their social experience" (Jiang 2001: 4). This desire to transform China's education system from one that emphasizes test taking to one that emphasizes direct experience could be understood as a call to "unharden" a system that has become too rigid. It is a call to set energies in motion, so as to initiate some kind of qualitative change. Because the child's body enters into too few relations, its capacity to act is diminished. This has implications not only for the national economy and China's quest for global strength, but also for a child's moral development and his or her capacity to connect with his or her social, cultural and natural environments.

Producing value in in-between spaces

That affect could have implications for a nation's economy and its quest for strength should come as no surprise given the recent shift toward neoliberal governmentality across the globe. In its paradigmatic rejection of the interventionist policies of the welfare state, which have come to be seen as producing inactive citizens, neoliberal theory proposes that human well-being and economic development is best advanced by encouraging individual responsibility and entrepreneurial skills while minimizing the direct presence of the state (Harvey 2005). This global economic shift has involved a conjoining of economic and non-economic domains to an unprecedented degree.

In China, the transition from centralized economic planning to "socialist market economy" has involved not only an apparent diminishing of administrative interventions on the part of the central government (Sigley 2006), but also the emergence of a generalized discourse around the notion of human quality, or *suzhi*—a discourse that constructs the problem of national strength and economic development in terms of personal improvement (Yan 2003; Woronov 2003, 2009; Anagnost 2004; Kuan 2012). Individual efforts to better oneself simultaneously advance the goals of economic development by transferring, to a significant degree, the responsibility for economic planning and well-being from the state to the individual (see also Hoffman 2006).

While governmentality theorists demonstrate how economic restructuring has involved the human capacity to act upon oneself, affect theory sheds a different kind of light. For one, affect allows us to think about the pre-individual and virtual dimensions of the contemporary economic order, and about the in-between spaces in which value is produced. In other words, there is more than an intensification of human subjectivity involved here (Rose 1996, 1999). To start, the post-Fordist economy involves communication systems characterized by feedback and unpredictability. For instance, under "Toyotism," the relationship between the producer and consumer becomes a "rapid feedback loop," where factory communications with the market are constant and immediate. Unlike Fordist modes of production, Toyotism maintains "zero stock," producing goods only after a market demand has been communicated (Hardt 1999: 93–94). Richard and Rudnyckyj show how a certain kind of affective feedback helps to sustain the viability of nongovernmental organizations (NGOs) as mediators of neoliberal transitions. Employing the phrase "economy of affect," they describe how staffers at a Mexican NGO invest affective labor in "binding" representatives from the global North to their cause and to local villages during site visits, creating a sense of solidarity despite large geographic distances (Richard and Rudnyckyj 2009: 65–66). Here, affect is understood as a milieu, an in-between space that must be facilitated, through the management of fragile social relationships. Wissinger's work on the modeling industry finds the circulation and modulation of energy—between a model and environmental stimuli—to be more important than finding pretty girls and manufacturing beautiful images; what turns out to be most productive in the competition for consumers' attention is difficult to define, measure and name. For this reason, models "work to be sensitive to the flow of affect by broadening their affective capacity so that stimulus easily produces affects in their bodies that might then translate into an external change" (Wissinger 2007: 243). It is also the job of the assembled professionals to create an atmosphere in which the model could "get into the flow" (ibid.: 242), with music, food, some coddling and coaxing. The more relaxed a model, the more responsive she may be; the more variable her responses, the greater the potential for impact in a saturated marketplace.

Taken together, these cases illustrate the role of indeterminacy in neoliberal or information-based economies in the production of value. Whether understood as an economy of affect or an affective economy, late capitalism involves putting "unformed and unstructured potential" into play (Shouse 2005: 5). What goes into and comes out of the current economic paradigm is not easy to measure or quantify (Negri 1999), yet the logic of the affective economy reverberates throughout the late capitalist world. Speaking for the *suzhi jiaoyu* reform movement in China, one education minister located value-producing spontaneity in the human person: "Humans are the most positive (*jiji*) and lively element in productivity, [they are] the subject of its liberation and development" (Chen 2001: 4). What productive human capacities might be, however, is not always well articulated. In fact, advocates repudiate hard definitions, invoking, instead, the idea of potential (see Yang, Chapter 2, this volume).

In theory, *suzhi jiaoyu* is not oriented toward cultivating the ideal child, as has been the case in other pedagogical traditions in Chinese cultural history (Bai 2005). Rather, it aims to stimulate and modulate a child's vitality and affective flow (cf. Wissinger 2007). As bestselling author Huang Quanyu puts it:

> The purpose of *suzhi jiaoyu* is to tap a person's potential to the greatest limit, so as to let a person's *suzhi* fully develop. Therefore, we should tell our children with the assumption that justice is on our side (*lizhi qizhuang di*): "As long as your potential has been released to its greatest limit, [and] your *suzhi* has been able to develop fully, then you have succeeded!"
>
> (Huang 2001: 14)

Theoretically, *suzhi jiaoyu* rejects utilitarian goals and narrow definitions of success, despite its connection to national revitalization and economic development plans. Not dissimilar to American professionals working in the modeling industry, who are vague about "what it is that gets a model work" (Wissinger 2007: 237), most experts and some parents insist on broad definitions. A father, in explaining how he understands the meaning of being "outstanding" (*youxiu*), said that in Chinese society today, one does not necessarily have to become the best-in-a-field (*jia*) to be an outstanding person. "As long as you have an acquired specialty," he told me, "And then, you find a position that suits you, something you find interesting, something you are willing to do, and something that allows you to contribute to society, then you are a successful person. That is good enough."

Reform advocates see *yingshi jiaoyu* (test-taking education) as a system with few winners and many losers, while *suzhi jiaoyu* offers to liberate the potential of each and every child with its emphasis on "well-roundedness" and "whole development." It is my contention that because *suzhi jiaoyu* concerns the liberation of potential, the movement does not so much prioritize subject making as it does the creation of an appropriate environment in which the power to affect and the capacity to be affected can be put into play in as many ways as possible. This is the reason why the idea of *tiaojian*, which can be translated as "condition" or "circumstance," comes up so often in popular and official formulations of human development. Policy documents are littered with calls for creating or providing *tiaojian* that would facilitate the implementation of state directives. Parents, meanwhile, often say that their only responsibility is to create *tiaojian*, and that what happens thereafter is out of their control. The more that children are exposed to, and the more opportunities given, the more likely latent potential may be expressed and value produced.

What is at stake in bringing affect theory to bear?

As the preceding discussion shows, affect theory sheds light on the underlying logic of the contemporary economic order in general, and China's economic transition in particular, where the economic and the non-economic have been conjoined to an unprecedented degree. Moreover, affect theory moves us beyond the more obvious, though important, reading of the *suzhi jiaoyu* movement as a biopolitical project that sets up subject positions to occupy—the "high-quality child" and the "good mother"—linking the micro-level pole of individual bodies to the macro-level pole of population government (Greenhalgh and Winckler 2005). This is crucial for thinking about how the indeterminate and the undefined can in fact be "functional" in the context at hand, but I would like to use affect theory to do more than critique market logic and new regimes of normalization, however, and to ponder instead the notion of affect as world-connecting thread of pure experience (Massumi 2002).

To start: how well-roundedness and whole development are understood and cultivated by educators is as variable as the shapes and colors of a handful of pebbles. This is not merely because "the state has its limits" (Woronov 2009). In fact, the reform movement took shape well before the Ministry of Education issued a resolution for moving *suzhi jiaoyu* forward in 1999. Moreover, the variety of formulations constitutes creative responses to the question of how to balance economic ambitions and pedagogical ideals against the weight of a hardened system that attempts to quantify and measure human capacities. Different experts have come to ask this question in different professional and personal situations, thereby generating slightly variant responses. The notion of "creativity" here is not meant to suggest a psychological property belonging to intentional individuals. Rather, creativity is a property of process—something that arises by virtue of an infolding of multiple lines of force, rather than some history-making capacity unique to humankind alone. Creativity arises by virtue of the singularity of events. Nothing ever happens in exactly the same way twice (cf. McLean 2009).[1]

There is much at stake in using affect theory to interpret ethnographic material. Bruno Latour (2005: 102) has pointed out that sociological explanation "starts only after a profound *suspicion* has been introduced about the very existence of the objects to be accounted for." Rather than look for hidden forces, i.e. false consciousness, fetishism, the making of social distinctions, etc., he makes a plea for attending to the concrete. Indeed, a social explanation seems necessary in the context of a political economy that has instrumentalized affect itself in the production of value, but is this not yet another expression of the very "despondency" affect theory invites us to challenge? What can the people we follow teach us?

Qinggan jiaoyu: cultivating the affective child

For Zhou Ting, a popular expert based in Kunming, the education system in China is deeply worrisome. In the brochure advertising a mothering class she offered on Saturday nights, she states: "if the education of a child only stresses academic achievement, then the child will inevitably lose many developmental opportunities because this age saves a secure and happy life environment for children who have received education of the heart-spirit (*xinling*) and sensory-emotions (*qinggan*)."[2] When I met her in 2004, Zhou was trying to make sense of a multiple homicide that had taken place at Yunnan University, where she also teaches. Earlier that year, four students were found dead in a campus dormitory. They had been beaten with a blunt object, wrapped in newspaper and stuffed into separate closets. The culprit, Ma Jiajue, a biotechnology student, was a classmate and friend of the victims whom everyone else knew as a bit odd. The case stimulated a flurry of public discussions over what drove him to crime: most commentators sympathized with Ma, a poor student from the countryside, while others argued that he should have taken more personal responsibility for his own mental health. For Zhou, however, Ma Jiajue was emblematic of an education system that continues to focus too much on academic achievement, despite ongoing efforts at reform. He was highly developed intellectually and earned good marks, but tragically underdeveloped with respect to his sensory-emotions (*qinggan*).

Shortly after the murder, the State Council issued an official document entitled "Regarding suggestions for another step toward the construction of strengthening and improving young persons' morals" (2004). Zhou Ting was already engaged in school-based research projects on character development at the time, but had been feeling dissatisfied with the scope of her efforts and thought she could easily get financial support for a more immersive research project with this official call to action. Her request was denied, however, so she took matters into her own hands. In an interview with a newspaper reporter, she stated, "There's going to be another murder for all we know. The upper levels want you to carry out [moral education work], but people at the lower levels don't support you. How many people can I affect just teaching a mothering class?"

While she does not identify herself as a *suzhi jiaoyu* advocate, per se, Zhou's approach to child education introduces something new to the ongoing "soccer game" of education reform in China. I borrow Brian Massumi's soccer game analogy to de-emphasize the role of the state in directing change in post-Mao China, because this analogy emphasizes reform as the collective activity that it is, involving the individual actions of many players. In soccer, every move introduces a change to the field of potential, the ever-changing conditions of emergence. In the case of *suzhi jiaoyu*, those who care to speak about it or act in its name continually modify the discourse with new ideas, stories and experiments. The idea of *suzhi jiaoyu* is like the soccer ball, catalyzing responses from the players involved. I have written elsewhere about another popular expert who brands his approach as *shangshi jiaoyu*, or educating by appreciating (Kuan 2012). Zhou Ting, on the other hand, advocates something called *qinggan jiaoyu*, or the education of sensory-emotions, which she understands as filling the gap left behind by a school system too intent on training test takers and too utilitarian in its objectives. If *suzhi jiaoyu* advocates have the general concern that *yingshi jiaoyu* fails to liberate the potential of every child, Zhou Ting is especially worried that children in China have too few opportunities for accumulating sensory experiences. This has implications for a child's capacity to relate to others.

In a fieldtrip Zhou Ting organized, the question of how sensory experience contributes to moral development was explored in the practical context of guiding a group of children in a tour of Beijing. What I will describe belongs to the larger context of the *suzhi jiaoyu* reform movement, in that Zhou has been inspired by certain well-known experts and advocates in China, while also developing her own approach. Although I have used the phrase "citizen-subject" up until this point—to refer to the subject who embodies a potential to transform the fate of a nation—I will use the phrase "affective subject" to refer more specifically to what Zhou Ting has in mind, in a kind of theoretical translation.

The affective subject has a porous body characterized and shaped by its responsiveness to external stimuli. This is a body characterized by affectivity: the capacity to infold the energy or vitality in an environment, and the power to convert intensity into externalized action. This is also a body that can be assembled into as many combinations as possible: the more relations an affective subject can enter into, the more relational capacities it will accumulate. As such, an affective subject is also a moral subject, in the sense that he or she can relate to others; his or her moral emotions—for example, empathy and enthusiasm—take form through the accumulation of sensory engagements with the material world.

A trip to Beijing: assembling with cultural accumulation

Early in July 2004, Zhou Ting signed up twenty-five children through her mothering class for a trip she would lead to Beijing. This trip would be a convergence of her own research agenda with the willingness of many middle-class Kunming parents to broaden their child's breadth of experience (*jianshi*).[3] While the top of the registration form read: "A trip to Beijing for 'children's *qinggan* experience of China's accumulated cultural achievements'," Zhou verbally described the trip as something that would allow participants to "read" Chinese history "right on site." For Zhou, two kinds of experiences can educate *qinggan*: one is reading, the other is nature—loosely defined. The two are interrelated in that reading constitutes a kind of experience, and only individuals who know how to sense, observe and engage with the world have the capacity to write.

The trip to Beijing promised to expand the affective capacities of children by exposing them to "China's accumulated cultural achievements," which themselves are affective. "Chinese culture is of the *qinggan*," Zhou explained on the day of registration, suggesting that China's historical and cultural monuments embody a certain energy and vitality. Foreshadowing Patricia Clough's characterization of affective economies as augmenting and expanding affect, Zhou advertised the trip as an opportunity for expanding the participants' range of *qinggan* in the experience of Beijing, where she will "adjust," "expand" and "guide" *qinggan*s along the way. What she promised parents was most explicitly realized the day the group visited the Summer Palace. The text below is a rendition in prose of what my video camera recorded.

Banking in affects

It was the end of a muggy day in mid-July and the weather had been stiflingly hot. The Summer Palace, former retreat of Empress Dowager Ci Xi, had been packed with visitors. Teacher Zhou spontaneously stopped the children at the side of Kunming Lake on their way toward the exit. She wanted everyone to appreciate the view and the dramatic change in weather. It was suddenly much cooler as the sun had retreated behind a blanket of clouds and a wind had begun to blow. Zhou asked the children if they could describe the kind of wind in the air. She suggests "gentle breeze." One child jokingly answers with "typhoon."

She instructed them to pay focused attention on their feeling (*ganshou*), and then directed their attention across the lake. "Please look at the little island and then at Seventeen-Arch Bridge from this angle," she said to them. There was a pause. Children gazed obediently, while a few others goofed off. Zhou continued, "At this moment, all of the natural conditions, weather, view, color, etc., how is this affecting your state of mind? Especially the things that teacher wants you to do. It isn't that you cannot understand, it isn't that you cannot accept [my instructions]. Compare your state of mind at the time with what you are feeling now. If I were to ask you to do something now, would you be willing to do it, or would you be unwilling?"

A sixth-grade boy answered in a perfunctory and sing-song fashion, "Willing!" (*Yuanyi!*), poking fun at her exercise. Zhou stated that she did not need an answer and began to give an improvised monologue. She spontaneously invented a novel idea:

> This kind of beautiful, calm, and peaceful state of mind (*xinjing*), I'll tell you, you can't buy this with money, [we] only have these few minutes, here and now. If it were noon, under a scorching sun, [and] you were being drenched [with sweat], you wouldn't even be in the mood for experiencing this nature. You'd be wiping sweat, drinking water, replacing water. How would your attention be on your state of mind? How would you have a good state of mind? That's why you are making deposits into your state-of-mind-bank (*xinqing yinhang*) right now.

Addressing the kids who were not paying attention, Zhou reproved, "Some people have their doors open and can deposit bundles and bundles, but they're not willing, still busy with other business."

Zhou instructed the children to store the moment in their banks because it was something that would influence them for the rest of their lives. She told them that Empress Dowager Ci Xi did not like to live in the Forbidden City, and preferred to spend her time here for good reason. The empress came here to nourish her state of mind.

At this point, the just mentioned "state-of-mind-bank" (*xinqing yinhang*) evolved into "*qinggan* bank." Teacher Zhou continued to say, "Open up your *qinggan* bank right now. The view right now is giving you bundles of *qinggan* banknotes to store in your bank. The *renminbi* [China's currency] that you can really see is not valuable. What's valuable are your *qinggan* banknotes. Such a beautiful view, this is what you call valuable. Take it if you want it. But you have to use your heart, your *qinggan*s to make deposits."

A large crowd had gathered around us by now. One mother-son pair not belonging to our group followed Teacher Zhou's instructions diligently, more so than some of the children in our group. Integrating the moment at hand and what she knew about the Chinese curriculum in schools, Zhou instructed her kids to, "Take a broad view. Look at how the water in front of you twinkles like jade. 'Ripples on the surface of the water,' those phrases, this is it, the image before your eyes. What's in your books, what you learned in your textbooks, still have to pass a [inaudible]. I'm telling you, why is it that some people cannot experience the most beautiful things described when they're learning literature? It's because they don't have this image in their *qinggan* bank." Toward the end of her monologue, Teacher Zhou explained that deposits were made by opening the seven channels. Putting what the children were supposed to do in concrete terms, she explained, "Your *qinggan* channels are your eyes, ears, nose, mouth, skin, your sense of movement. Including your sense of your insides. Most ordinary people rarely use these channels for making deposits into their *qinggan* banks." Before concluding the lesson with a blow of the whistle and a waving of her yellow flag, Zhou instructed the group to remember this very moment, to store the moment in their "*qinggan* bank" so as to have a good state of mind in the face of daily tasks and difficulties.

The "*qinggan* banknote" that Zhou invented at the side of Kunming Lake seems to be a perfect crystallization of the relationship between affect and market in post-Mao China, but I am wary of reading this lesson as evidence that capital accumulation has completely and successfully shifted to the domain of life itself. Indeed, there are good reasons for understanding Zhou's lesson in such a way. The trip to Beijing likely contributed to the well-rounded development of its participants in some way, shaping them as citizen-subjects that embody the potential to deliver China to its destiny as a strong nation. The expansion of their affective capacity raises their *suzhi*, one could say, actualizing national agendas for a kind of economic development that is dependent on turning China's population burden into a resource. Moreover, because mobility for leisure and cultural capital are highly correlated, the children at the side of Kunming Lake are quite literally acquiring or accumulating a non-economic form of capital. The exercise legitimates parents' financial investments in the trip.

I think there was more going on here, simultaneously. This lakeside exercise could be further understood as expressing a conception of the child's body as a composition of sensory surfaces that could convert distances into intensity—i.e. unformed and unstructured potential (Shouse 2005: 5), the felt flow of energy between bodies and environments (Wissinger 2007), or, "the pressing crowd of incipiencies" (Massumi 2002: 30). When she encouraged her participants to take note of the breeze, their feeling, the view and the general "color" of the "natural" environment, she was effectively leading an exercise in the infolding of the external conditions so as to create a resonance (an echo, or a complex pattern, to borrow from Massumi) that could possibly become something else. In fact, Massumi might call the child's body as she conceived it a transducer of qualitatively different forms of matter, "Like electricity into sound waves. Or heat into pain. Or light waves into vision. Or vision into imagination. Or noise in the ear into music in the heart. *Or outside coming in*" (Massumi 2002: 135). Or, breeze, view and color into compliance with a teacher, a good state of mind, and the capacity to appreciate literary phrases such as "ripples on the surface of the water." The issue of compliance here should not be understood in terms of power. That is to say, I am not interested in reducing the circulation of affect to the order of normalization. This is not simply about making pliable citizen-subjects who will obey the wishes of their teacher and ultimately the nation. Instead, I see these conversions as articulating with the same creative processes that animate change and transformation in the non-organic, non-human world (DeLanda 1992).

Importantly, the lakeside exercise was also a creative response to difficulties belonging to an irreducibly singular situation. This visit to the Summer Palace took place just a few days into the trip when Teacher Zhou was already feeling overwhelmed. She had not prepared herself for all the heterogeneity that she would face. The day they departed Kunming for Beijing by train, Zhou suddenly found herself responsible for twenty-five children, more than she had planned to register, and many of whom she had never met before. In addition to narrating the trip (guiding, expanding, adjusting *qinggans*), managing her three assistants and thinking about her research questions, she also made sure that each child ate enough, brushed their teeth, made their bed and so on. Moreover, the trip was filled with unexpected hardship. Lacking the kind of facilities and means of transportation available to commercial summer camps, Zhou, her assistants and the twenty-five children stayed in a tiny bungalow, took cold showers, used a public toilet and traveled by public bus. Some children developed bloody blisters on their feet from walking; others had heat rashes from the humidity—something Kunming people are not used to. It was in preparation for a long bus ride back that Zhou asked her participants to take the moment seriously. At the very end of her monologue by the lake, Zhou promised that this kind of view, if stored properly, could treat hurt, hunger, thirst and, most importantly, one's state of mind. Before concluding the lesson Zhou proclaimed, "Having seen all this, the next time you're in pain, think a little, and go into your *qinggan* bank right away and move these things out. Your state of mind will immediately return to the feeling you now have."

Garden technology

Zhou Ting's life project—"molding character" (*suzao renge*) by way of stimulating the seven sensory channels—is affect theory applied. Zhou worries that China's children have been de-capacitated. One of the biggest challenges for educators in China today is the ever-present possibility of a condition called "*yanxue*", or sickness of/hatred toward school, which is an effect of a system that rewards students who "study to death and study dead books" (*si du shu, du si shu*). To speak in the language of affect theory, the current education system has come to be seen as devoid of vitality. Something like *qinggan jiaoyu*, on the other hand, circulates affective flows, such that even "dead books" might be brought to life.

The exercise by Kunming Lake not only addressed the participants' capacity for enduring hardship but also their attitude toward learning. For many of them, the trip to Beijing was their first time encountering the national monuments described in textbooks. I would add that it was also their first time encountering the affectivity of sites such as the Summer Palace and Kunming Lake, which have inspired, it seems, phrases like "twinkling pieces of jade" and "ripples on the surface of the water." Terry Woronov observes that set phrases linked to specific places are commonly used in language instruction, for example, schoolchildren learn to memorize the phrase "burning hot" for Gobi desert sand and "a sea of trees" for the Manchurian forest (Woronov 2003: 246). Such instruction serves to insert schoolchildren into a language community rooted in classical Chinese. As Nyíri points out with respect to promotional tourism literature, set phrases such as "lofty and awe-inspiring," "grand and fantastic," and "splendid and imposing," "are chosen to describe certain kinds of sites not at random but following an established standard with which all writers are familiar" (Nyíri 2006: 53).

While Woronov rightly notes that we might consider such phrases as clichés, I would add that they are rooted in a much deeper cultural history of circulating affective flows. Perhaps this is the reason why Zhou Ting asserts that Chinese culture is "of the *qinggan*." Both affect theory and indigenous Chinese thought posit a dynamic universe composed of fluid and transformative forces. Both can be characterized as immanent modes of thought that perceive an "ontological affinity and compatibility of things and categories" (Yeh 1987: 252). In this context, natural features brim with an affective quality the premodern Chinese captured and circulated in language, art and architecture. When Zhou referred to such phrases as "those phrases," and stated, "this is it, the image before your eyes," she simultaneously pointed to their canonical status and to the affectivity of the surface of the lake—its intensity—in the shortness of her language. Unlike Western travel traditions that emphasize the journey, adventure, and spontaneous encounters with "nature" and its wilderness, the premodern Chinese tradition—which never conceived of any nature/culture binary—emphasized affinity within a ritually enclosed and ordered nature (Nyíri 2006: 67). Ritual enclosure is effected in language—in the use of canonical phrases in travel writing and in literary inscriptions on rocks, and also in the performance of canonical views (Strassberg 1993; Brook 1998; Nyíri 2006).

Zhou's instructions on how to take in a view ("take a broad view"), what to look at ("the little island and then at Seventeen-Arch Bridge"), and from what angle ("this angle"), encouraged her participants to plug in to the virtual, namely, to history, and ultimately, to a larger language community that includes modern and premodern persons, and historically significant landscapes. If media technologies aid in the circulation of affective flows in the case of Wissinger's modeling industry, achieving human contact in the space of the virtual, then it is the technology of architecture, and garden design in particular, that puts affect into circulation in this case. Unlike media technologies, however, garden technology is quite old. The Summer Palace, an Imperial garden, plugs schoolchildren (and other tourists) into a virtuality that spans time rather than space. The performance of a canonical view connects them to the Empress Dowager Ci Xi, to whom this garden once belonged. It connects them to late Ming literati, who gazed at landscapes in ritualized sets of eight, ten, or more views (Brook 1998: 182). The enclosing and ordering of nature in ritualized language and performance could be considered an indigenous technology for assembling the human person by way of non-human agencies.

Just as travel in the neo-Confucian tradition became linked to self-cultivation, travel in the post-Mao period also constitutes a kind of moral pedagogy. Both involve plugging the human person into a larger order. For premodern literati, "The comprehension of universal principles in the world and in the mind through a combination of empirical inquiry and self-scrutiny," best achieved in nature, "was the key to perfecting the Noble Man and his ability to create social and political order" (Strassberg 1993: 46). For the twenty-first-century child, exposing oneself to the circulation of affects, best achieved in direct experiences beyond the desk, is key to enabling a citizen-subject who might contribute to the strengthening of the nation, by first becoming an affective subject. For Zhou, such a project might begin in encounters with non-human agencies, like the lake, which could treat hurt, hunger, thirst and one's state of mind if viewed correctly, in the right weather conditions. If her participants could allow themselves to be affected, they might develop moral emotions. If they develop moral emotions, they might be able to bear the hardship of their trip. If they could bear the hardship of the trip, they would be able to bear the burden of learning. If they could bear the burden of learning, China as a nation just might have some hope after all—a hope that, for Zhou, had dimmed temporarily with the news of Ma Jiajue's crime.

The affectivity of national monuments—in being of the *qinggan*, as Zhou puts it—addresses China's wish for a smooth, non-violent transition toward free market social organization. If this is, in the end, still a form of governmentality, i.e. the conduct of conduct, then it is an art of government that China had figured out long ago—one that does not conceive of the state and of society as distinct categories (the former always regarded with suspicion). Instead, this relationship is understood as one of mutual correspondence, with every social domain having the power to affect and the capacity to be affected by another.

Context versus situation: a conclusion

In the final chapter of *Parables for the Virtual*, Brian Massumi makes a distinction between context and situation: a context is determinate and regularized, while a situation is singular and irreproducible. A situation, as event, is composed of "contingent ingredients," which "give it its uniqueness, its stubbornness in remaining perceptibly itself… The event retains a quality of 'this-ness'" (Massumi 2002: 222). A context, on the other hand, creates objects to manipulate and reproduce. A scientific laboratory, for example, is a context, marked by asymmetrical language use and power differentials (ibid.: 228). For Massumi, there is no metaphysical difference between context and situation; they coexist within a "processual rhythm" (ibid.: 217). With this in mind, I argue that the "*qinggan* banknote" indexes both context and situation, two co-existing dimensions. The context here is market development and China's quest for global strength; it has involved not only an intensification of subjectivity but also the deployment of an affective economy that puts indeterminacy into play in the production of value.

Simultaneously, the lakeside exercise was irreducibly singular. Zhou's novel and spontaneous invention of the *qinggan* banknote feeds off one of capitalism's greatest inventions. It is a poaching of the medium that helped to establish equivalence between dissimilar things, thereby making total subsumption possible, for a situation marked with singular qualities: this teacher, this hot day, these children, those blisters, that return bus ride. Playing on the children's familiarity with monetary value, Zhou effectively led an exercise in producing another kind of surplus value by encouraging an accumulation of affects that, one day, will amount to good habits such as caring for people and for things.[4] Today, the metaphor is the banknote; tomorrow it will be something different.

On a different occasion during this trip, Teacher Zhou circulated the affectivity of the Roman Coliseum to manage the problem of too-many-shoes-everywhere in the tiny bungalow where the group stayed, an image she encountered virtually by way of media technology. Setting out plastic washbasins, she asked the participants to stack their shoes in a circular fashion with the toe-side pointing downward, modeling how affectivity could be deployed in the management of life's many challenges. This example demonstrates that well-roundedness is more than a discursive ideal: it concerns becoming. The more one allows oneself to be affected, the more one can affect and therefore transform, and not merely struggle against, difficult situations.

My point here is that the relationship between markets and affects is a complicated one. As much as the deployment of affect has become central to economic restructuring in China, and as much as one could read the lakeside exercise as a conversion of monetary wealth into cultural capital, I wonder if we could ponder the affective side of the phrase "affective economy" a bit more. Affect has a sense of humor, capital does not. Affect plays hide-and-seek. Capital only knows to seek; it barely knows how to play. The way of the world is play, a dynamic affect theory celebrates in its presentation style, or its "style of being present" (Seigworth and Gregg 2010: 14). The *qinggan* banknote will likely continue to foster economic development in China, but the *qinggan* banknote was also, simultaneously and irreducibly, a creative response to the ever-present problem of balance in a dynamic, ever-changing world. It is the "becoming" of affect.

Notes

1 It is important to note that Chinese understandings of whole development and well-roundedness have a much deeper history that I cannot go into, due to space limitations.

2 Zhou Ting's conception of *qinggan* could be translated as affect, because for her, non-human agents can embody *qinggan*, and because her conception is sensitive to the materiality of the sensed world and of the sensing body.

3 Zhou Ting is not a pseudonym. Teacher Zhou consented to my using her real name, in the hope that I could help to circulate her ideas.

4 In his discussant comments on a shorter version of this chapter, presented at the 2011 American Anthropological Association meeting in Montreal, Massumi noted a surplus of effect over cause, and the surplus value of life.

References

Ahmed, Sara. 2004. "Affective Economies." *Social Text* 22(2): 117–39.

Anagnost, Ann. 2004. "The Corporeal Politics of Quality (suzhi)." *Public Culture* 16 (2): 189–208.

Bai, Limin. 2005. *Shaping the Ideal Child: Children and their Primers in Late Imperial China*. Hong Kong: The Chinese University Press.

Brook, Timothy. 1998. *The Confusions of Pleasure: Commerce and Culture in Ming China*. Berkeley: University of California Press.

Brown, Steven D. and Tucker, Ian. 2010. "Eff the Ineffable: Affect, Somatic Management, and Mental Health Service Users." In Melissa Gregg and Gregory J. Seigworth (eds), *The Affect Theory Reader*. Durham, NC: Duke University Press, 229–49.

Chen, Zhili. 2001. "Yi Jiang Zeming tongzhi 'tanhua' jingshen wei zhidao nuli kaichuang 'shiwu' qijian jiaoyu gongzuo xin jumian" (Under the Guidance of the Spirit of Comrade Jiang Zemin's "Discussion," Initiate with Effort a New Phase in Education Work [in the] "10 5" Period). In Peng Li and Li Chen (eds), *Suzhi jiaoyu de huhuan: shuo "jianfu", tan gaige* (The Call for Education for Quality: Say "Reduce," Discuss Reform). Beijing: Xinhua chubanshe.

Clough, Patricia Ticineto. 2007. "Introduction." In Patricia Ticineto Clough with Jean Halley (eds), *The Affective Turn: Theorizing the Social*. Durham, NC: Duke University Press, 1–33.

DeLanda, Manuel. 1992. "Nonorganic Life." In Jonathan Crary and Sanford Kwinter (eds), *Incorporations*. New York: Zone, 129–67.

Deleuze, Gilles. 1992. "Ethology: Spinoza and Us." In Jonathan Crary and Sanford Kwinter (eds), *Incorporations*. New York: Zone, 129–67.

Deleuze, Gilles and Guattari, Félix. 1987 [1980]. *A Thousand Plateaus: Capitalism and Schizophrenia*, trans. Brian Massumi. Minneapolis: University of Minnesota Press.

Greenhalgh, Susan and Winckler, Edwin A. 2005. *Governing China's Population: From Leninist to Neoliberal Biopolitics*. Stanford, CA: Stanford University Press.

Hardt, Michael. 1999. "Affective Labor." *Boundary 2* 26(2): 89–100.

Harvey, David. 2005. *A Brief History of Neoliberalism*. Oxford and New York: Oxford University Press.

Hoffman, Lisa. 2006. "Autonomous Choices and Patriotic Professionalism: On Governmentality in Late-Socialist China." *Economy and Society* 35(4): 550–70.

Huang Quanyu. 2001. *Jiating Jiaoyu zai Meiguo* (Family Education in America). Guangzhou: Guangdong Jiaoyu Chubanshe.

Jiang Zemin. 2001. "Guanyu jiaoyu wenti de tanhua" (A Talk Regarding the Education Problem). In Peng Li and Li Chen (eds), *Suzhi jiaoyu de huhuan: shuo "jianfu", tan gaige* (The Call for Education for Quality: Say "Reduce," Discuss Reform). Beijing: Xinhua chubanshe.

Kipnis, Andrew. 2006. "*Suzhi*: A Keyword Approach." *The China Quarterly* 186.

Kuan, Teresa. 2012. "The Horrific and the Exemplary: Public Stories and Education Reform in Late Socialist China." *Positions: Asia Critique* 20(4): 1095–125.

Latour, Bruno. 2005. *Reassembling the Social: An Introduction to Actor-Network Theory*. Oxford: Oxford University Press.

Massumi, Brian. 2002. *Parables for the Virtual: Movement, Affect, Sensation*. Durham, NC: Duke University Press.

McLean, Stuart. 2009. "Stories and Cosmogonies: Imagining Creativity Beyond 'Nature' and 'Culture.'" *Cultural Anthropology* 24(2): 213–245.

Negri, Antonio. 1999. "Value and Affect," trans. Michael Hardt. *Boundary 2* 26(2): 77–88.

Nyíri, Pál. 2006. *Scenic Spots: Chinese Tourism, the State, and Cultural Authority*. Seattle and London: University of Washington Press.

Richard, Analiese and Rudnyckyj, Daromir. 2009. "Economies of Affect." *Journal of the Royal Anthropological Institute* 15: 57–77.
Rose, Nikolas. 1996. *Inventing Our Selves: Psychology, Power, and Personhood.* Cambridge: Cambridge University Press.
——1999. *Powers of Freedom: Reframing Political Thought*. Cambridge: Cambridge University Press.
Seigworth, Gregory J. and Gregg, Melissa. 2010. "An Inventory of Shimmers." In Melissa Gregg and Gregory J. Seigworth (eds), *The Affect Theory Reader*. Durham, NC: Duke University Press, 1–25.
Shouse, Eric. 2005. "Feeling, Emotion, Affect." *M/C Journal* 8(6).
Sigley, Gary. 2006. "Chinese Governmentalities: Government, Governance and the Social Market Economy." *Economy and Society* 35(4): 487–508.
Strassberg, Richard E. 1993. *Inscribed Landscapes: Travel Writing from Imperial China*. Berkeley: University of California Press.
Wissinger, Elizabeth. 2007. "Always on Display: Affective Production in the Modeling Industry." In Patricia Ticineto Clough with Jean Halley (eds), *The Affective Turn: Theorizing the Social*. Durham, NC: Duke University Press.
Woronov, Terry. 2003. "Transforming the Future: 'Quality' Children and the Chinese Nation." PhD dissertation, Department of Anthropology, University of Chicago.
——2009. "Governing China's Children: Governmentality and 'Education for Quality'." *Positions: East Asia Cultures Critique* 17(3): 567–89.
Yan, Hairong. 2003. "Neoliberal Governmentality and Neohumanism: Organizing Suzhi/Value Flow through Labor Recruitment Networks." *Cultural Anthropology* 18 (4): 493–523.
Yeh, Michelle. 1987. "Metaphor and *Bi*: Western and Chinese Poetics." *Comparative Literature* 39(3): 237–54.

4 Hospitality and detachment

Japanese tour guides' affective labor in Canada

Shiho Satsuka

Introduction: economy of hospitality

Tourism is often categorized as part of the "hospitality industry"; however, this seems an oxymoronic constitution. How can hospitality, the generous reception of a stranger, fit into a profit-making capitalist industry? How do workers make sense of this contradictory entanglement of unselfish openhandedness and invested trade? How do they negotiate their positions in this economy? By exploring these questions, I examine the politics of "affective labor" in the tourist economy. In particular, I focus on the work practices of Japanese tour guides in the Canadian Rockies based on fieldwork I did with a Japanese guide company, which I call Rocky Mountain Tours (hereafter RMT), from 2000 to 2001, and follow-up research in Japan and Canada from 2002 to 2012.[1] The guides play an integral part of value production in tourism because their labor is central to shaping tourist experiences of enjoyment. Therefore the work practices of the guides allow us to analyze the dynamics of affective labor. I use "affective labor" following Michael Hardt, as a form of labor that produces intangible and immaterial effects through human contacts and communication, such as "a feeling of ease, well-being, satisfaction, excitement, passion—even a sense of connectedness or community," and involves "the creation and manipulation of affect" (Hardt 1999: 96). Adding to the recent critical inquiries of "hospitality" in the tourist industry (e.g. Lashley and Morrison 2000; Molz and Gibson 2007), this chapter highlights the importance of affective labor in the hospitality industry.[2]

In the subcontract system of the tourist industry, tour guides were expected to provide a travel agency with the specific services of giving tourists local information. The travel agency would then assemble it alongside other services, such as transportation, accommodation and meals, to produce a whole tour. Yet, in actual practice, instead of offering segmented services, the guides provided hospitality in a holistic manner. Compared to other workers, such as bus drivers, hotel employees or restaurant workers, the guides would spend long periods of time with tourists in various tour settings and place their bodies in the same space with their customers. They would have more opportunities to communicate and cooperate directly with the tourists to create the tour experiences.[3] The guides affected tourists by literally guiding the tourists' bodily conducts and sensory receptions through instructions of where to walk, and what to see, listen and taste, thereby affecting the tourists' feelings via the body. In turn, the guides were also affected by tourists as they responded, adjusted and reshaped their conduct, reflecting the tourists' reactions. Through these constant interactions, the guides constructed their subjectivities as active agents of the tourist economy, or the affective economies of enjoyment that circulate the experiences of pleasure, fulfillment and the sense of well-being. In this economy, the guides' labor power was used not only to provide information and knowledge, but also to affect the tourists and to be affected by them in order to produce enjoyable travel experiences. The guides' subjectivities were constituted in this affective cooperation. This process of affective economy makes a good contrast to Sara Ahmed's (2004) description of the affective economies of fear. In her discussion of the aftermath of post-September 11, 2001, the feeling of fear was attached to the particular bodies of Arab and Asians, and circulated to amplify the emotional reactions among self-identified "ordinary" white citizens to defend their collectivity and national borders by excluding asylum seekers. The affective economy of enjoyment in Japanese overseas tourism looks almost like a mirror image of Ahmed's economies of fear. The admired figure of emancipation from the constraining national community is attached to the bodies of Japanese guides in Canada, and in turn, the "ordinary Japanese" are imagined to be victims who had sacrificed their personal enjoyment for the sake of the national and corporate communities. Thus, the fantasy of experiencing personal enjoyment, pleasure and amusement is imagined to be located "elsewhere" outside Japan, and circulated and amplified by the circulation of liberating images of the Japanese living overseas.

In this process, the guides' personalities were constructed as products of these intersubjective experiences with the tourists,[4] and, as such, become important commodities. Therefore, in addition to the obvious commercial aspects, the guides' interactions with the tourists also entailed the characteristics of what anthropologists have described as "gift" exchange—reciprocal practices of giving goods and hospitalities that are inalienable from the personality of givers and receivers (e.g. Mauss 2000; Gregory 1982; Carrier 1995).[5]

In contrast to the existing analyses of the service industry that set gift exchange and commodity economy as contradictory oppositional poles, I argue that gift and commodity mutually amplify the circular logic of exchange. In contemporary capitalism, human affective capacity has become an important source of value production in the entangled circular logic of gift and commodity production. The parallel economies of the gift and capitalism subsume the worker's affective labor power and use it for the production of value, both in the form of economic surplus as well as the moral value of individual experiences of happiness, pleasure, enjoyment and well-being that are treasured in "late liberalism" (Povinelli 2011).[6]

However, in actual practice, I observed that the guides were sometimes indifferent to engaging in these circles of reciprocity. Often, the guides insisted on the "here-ness" and "now-ness" of their services. They were forgetful of their own actions of generosity to tourists, creating a tension in their entanglements with systems of reciprocity and economic transaction. What created the tension in the guides' work was not the gift and commodity in opposition; rather, it was the conflicts between the entangled circular logic of gift/commodity on one side, and the guides' actions of detachment from the assumed reciprocity both in gift and commodity exchanges on the other side. Drawing from Derrida's (1992) provocative account on the impossibility of "pure gift"—giving without any expectations of any return—I argue that the guides' forgetfulness and detachment were an unintentional challenge to capitalism's subsumption of their affective labor power. The process of guides' subjectivity construction suggests that the subject is a constant "battlefield" (Virno 2004) between the generative human capacity of producing affect and attempts by the economic machine to subsume the excess into the circular exchange.

In order to analyze the dynamics of this struggle, I first examine how some young Japanese migrate to Canada, transform themselves into local tour guides, and become active agents of affective economies of enjoyment by acting as "commodities" in the tourist industry. Because guides' personalities were the result of intersubjective production between the guides and the tourists, it is necessary to pay attention to the particular historical conjuncture that shaped the encounter between the guides and the tourists. Central to shaping this Japanese tourist encounter in Canada were the discourses of emancipation from the company prevalent at the turn of the twentieth century in Japan. In the affective economies of enjoyment, the pure, clear and refreshing images attached to the natural landscape of the Canadian Rockies have been associated with the social landscape of Canada, imagined as a place where one can be true to oneself without being constrained by traditional communal ties and duties in a Japanese workplace. This imaginary has been further extended to the guides' bodies, becoming an embodiment of Japanese cosmopolitan desire free from Japanese social pressures and communal obligations. As such, the guides caught the attention of the tourists, and in turn, the interactions with tourists were an integral part of the guides' subjectivity construction. I examine how the guides performatively constructed their subjectivities responding to these discourses of emancipation from the company (*kaisha kara no kaihō*) and self-search (*jibun sagashi*).

Second, I provide examples of the guides' detachment. The guides were often indifferent to cultivating long-time reciprocal relationships with tourists beyond the present moment in tours despite the management's interest in gaining repeat customers. I discuss how the guides' forgetfulness of their own generous acts resisted the entangled circles of moral and capitalist economy. In particular, I explain the case in which a guide was upset when she found that her generous act to her customers was placed in the reciprocal cycle. The guides' affect, the generative excess, indicates an elusive potential of the human relations deterritorialized from the enclosed machine of economy (Deleuze and Guattari 1987), but remains a central resource for the affective economy.

The generative power of affective workers is a source of surplus value, thus there is a strong interest in the industry to reterritorialize this excess into the entangled moral and capitalist economies.

Embodiment of cosmopolitan desire

Canada as dreamland

The way Japanese tourism promoted the Canadian Rockies has provided a site of collaboration between tourists and guides that facilitated the guides' enactment as Japanese cosmopolitans. Canada was developed as a "clean" destination for Japanese tourism in the 1970s when the growing Japanese overseas travel was associated with social problems, in particular, increased sex tourism in neighboring Asian countries. The tourism industry was concerned with the latter's negative impact on perceptions of overseas tourism in general. Travel agencies looked for a new destination where family and female travelers would feel safe and comfortable. Promoters played up Canada's vast natural landscape and the imagined pure air in a way that stimulated a clean image, and catered to desires to escape Japan's rapid urbanization and associated problems.

Canada has been often depicted as an alternative to the United States, the most influential country in the formation of post-World War II Japanese consumer capitalism and the mobilization of the mass population into the self-identified "middle class" (Ivy 1993). Often, this vision was expressed as freedom of personal expression through consumption, leisure and travel. The US–Japan coalition during the Cold War period initiated this socioeconomic transition in an effort to stabilize the Japanese economy and stimulate domestic industrial production and consumption under the vision of "democracy." In such a vision, every citizen would be entitled to the product of their hard work by consuming goods and leisure time. Sociologist Shunya Yoshimi (2001) points out that this conflation of democracy and economic affluence helped turn Japan into a poster child of the capitalist economy when Asia was a heated battleground between communism and capitalism. However, although the desire for the democratic consumer "America" gained hegemony in post-World War II Japan, the process was not smooth. In the 1960s and 1970s, radical students and labor movements challenged the alliance between the US and Japanese governments as a sign of neo-imperialism. In this context, Canada gained particular significance in the Japanese travel imagination as an alternative to "America." Canada, an English-speaking country in North America, is geographically and culturally close to the United States yet is a different nation. The vast natural landscape of Canada also helped contribute to imaginings of an alternative space away from the social problems in Japan.

The image of Canada as a safe and comfortable place with a relaxed lifestyle and harmonious relationships between human and nature has been widely circulated throughout popular media and literature.[7] In 2000, when I started my fieldwork, Canada was particularly popular with honeymooners, middle-aged baby boomers who were starting to think of a relaxed life after retirement, and those who wanted to take their parents on overseas travel. The actual number of Japanese tourists going to Canada was not exceptionally high due to high travel costs and distance;[8] however, these "obstacles" helped boost the prestige of Canada as a "dream" destination. Canada has often been listed as the most desired destination in tour industry surveys in Japan. The Canadian Rockies, in particular, have taken center stage in this imagination.

The center of tourism in the Canadian Rockies is the town of Banff, located in Banff National Park, the nation's oldest and most popular national park, established in 1885. Banff and the surrounding national and provincial parks are conglomerated into the Canadian Rocky Mountain Parks World Heritage Site for its large-scale wilderness. The population of the town of Banff was about 7,000. The residency was restricted to those who "need to reside" in the park for environmental protection purposes. Many of the residents were young travelers and outdoor enthusiasts who found work in tourist industries. Some of these transient workers would eventually become permanent residents. The town was small, but often characterized as both multicultural and multinational.

Emancipation from the company

The imaginary of Canada as a dreamlike place has been further extended to the bodies of the RMT guides in the tourist imagination. During the tour, many tourists said to a guide "I envy you that you are living in such a dreamlike place" (*Iidesune, konna yume mitai na tokoro ni sunde*). The guides as residents of these exclusive cosmopolitan mountain resorts often attracted tourists' curiosity. As the RMT guide trainer said to the trainees, the most common tourist questions did not concern specific information about the area, such as the name of the highest peaks or the number of bears in the park, but about the guides themselves. The guides were frequently asked how long they had been living in Canada, where in Japan they were from, why they moved to Canada, and how they found Canadian life. In these conversations, influenced by the images circulated in tourism discourse and popular media, the guides became an embodiment of liberation from the constraining society in Japan. When I interviewed tourists upon their return to Japan, some of them told me that encountering a unique tour guide was the most remarkable experience of their tour. The tourists often sent the guides letters and photographs of the tour as well as gifts, such as Japanese sweets, books and magazines, as tokens of appreciation.

The way tour guides attracted the tourists' attention resonates with the discourse of "emancipation" from the company-as-community model proliferating in the late twentieth century. Around 2000, Japanese companies and workers were caught in a debate between two conflicting views of the company: whether to maintain the community model of "welfare capitalism," foundational to post-World War II Japanese economic development, or to transform the company into a shareholder model suitable for "stock market capitalism" under the strong pressure of corporate restructuring as a part of financial globalization (Dore 2000).[9] The work situation in Japan, from which the tour guides were compelled to escape, was influenced by tension within the workplaces as these two conflicting notions of the company co-existed and competed. In this debate, the so-called "Japanese-style" community model was accused of depriving employees' freedom; in exchange for stable, long-term employment, employees were urged to sacrifice their personal enjoyment for the benefit of workplace community. In popular discourse, the dream of emancipation from the company was often articulated alongside cosmopolitan desire; in order to free oneself from the Japanese-style corporate community, one needed to transcend national boundaries and become a global citizen.

Many of the older generation of guides who started work before the mid-1990s had had secure jobs with full employee benefits. They were voluntary drop-outs from the Japanese corporate system and the normalized middle-class *sararīman* (salary men) lifestyle. They expressed their intention of fleeing from the strong social obligations that required employees to commit closely to workplace community. In contrast, the younger guides who entered into the job market after the mid-1990s experienced the so-called "job seeker's ice age" (*Shūshoku hyōgaki*). With a reduction of long-term full-time positions, young people were thrown into insecure labor relations and were unable to develop strong ties with the company-as-community. Ironically, the younger ones were already given "freedom" from allegiance to any company. Despite being unable to enter the company-as-community, they refused to become Japan's disposable labor force.[10]

Although the specific social contexts differ, both generations of guides tried to "get free" from corporate communities in Japan. The notion of "freedom" from the company has been associated with the proliferating discourse of *jibun sagashi* (finding self). In search of an imagined "authentic" self (*hontō no jibun*) outside the communities of company and nation, a number of young Japanese ventured overseas by using the "working holiday" visa system, which allowed youth to work while traveling in countries where Japan had working holiday exchange agreements. In order to find the location of the self, they turned themselves into flexible overseas workers.

The guides were complicit with the tourists in embodying the fantasy of Japanese cosmopolitanism, or of being Japanese yet also global citizens and thus able to move freely between different worlds. They performatively constructed their subjectivities as residents of this "dreamlike place." Even though they had anxieties about their short-term visa status, seasonal and irregular income, and little sense of their future security, through interaction with the tourists, they convince the tourists and themselves that there were more valuable things in life—that is, their lives were financially modest but personally fulfilling.

Enchanting commodity

Although seemingly contradictory, central to the guides' construction of subjectivities as free individuals was the process of the commodification of self. Immediately after being hired, the guides in the RMT were required to go through the company's training sessions. In the training they were told to remind themselves that they were "commodities" (*shōhin*) in the tourism industry. The trainer used the word "commodity" to indicate a polished, high-quality product that the company could offer the tourists with pride. This product should be attractive or even admirable for tourists so that they would be willing to pay for the tour.

In the trainer's instructions, the guides' affective capacity to "move" tourists' feelings was conflated with their practical ability physically to direct the bodily movements of the tourists. He repeatedly emphasized that if a guide was attractive, they would generate the feeling of enjoyment and create the sense of amazement and amusement in tourists. He also said that the tourist would listen to the words of such a guide carefully, and obediently follow the guide's instructions and suggestions of where to look, where to go and what to buy. On the contrary, if the guide was not attractive to tourists, they would be treated as servant-like service providers merely following the clients' demands, or worse, the trainers and managers warned, they would not be able to work as tour guides. The trainees were cautioned that they could perform this job only when they had "polished themselves" (*jibun o migaku*) and become attractive persons. They were instructed that their ability to achieve the status of commodity was dependent on their quality as honest and sincere persons (*shōjiki de seijitsu na hito*), who were true to their own feelings of being attracted by the Canadian Rockies, sharing the joy of being in this landscape and willing to help others enjoy their experience during the tour.

These instructions matched with the guides' own aspirations of finding their "true" selves, vaguely imagined, and of polishing themselves to be better persons. The interaction with tourists on the tour was considered to be a prime opportunity to find their true selves and to sincerely enact their personalities. The tourists' responses and appreciation of the guides' work affirmed the guides' sense of achievement in this attempt. Thus, unlike the common understanding of commodification as a process of self-alienation, Japanese tour guides in the RMT interpreted being a guide-as-commodity as an opportunity to construct performatively their subjectivities as unique and independent individuals emancipated from the old workplace communities in Japan.[11]

Detachment

Here-ness and now-ness

Although the interaction with tourists was integral to the guides' construction of self and, moreover, ostensibly the fun part of the work, once the tours were over, many guides were indifferent to making connections with the tourists. I was puzzled by the guides' indifference. This disengagement with the customers was contrary to the management's interests. The company's managers wanted to develop a long-term relationship with their clients so that they would become repeat customers. Some guides, especially those who were more business inclined, did reply to the tourists, but quite a number of the guides were disengaged in the exchange of letters and gifts with the tourists.

Some tourists wanted to cultivate their relationship with the guides. For example, Mr and Mrs Oda, a couple in their late forties who hiked with Eri and me, sent us a thank you letter with several discs of digital photos and a large box of Japanese snacks. After the summer tourist season, I visited the Odas at their home in Yokohama for an interview. They entertained me with generous hospitality as if I were their relative living overseas. Before the interview, they took me to an amusement park, put me on a rollercoaster, and fed me good-quality sushi. Upon returning to Banff, I told Eri how they had entertained me and that they also asked Eri to stop by when she came to Japan. She said, "Oh, you are so lucky! I'd love to eat sushi in Japan, too! By the way, who are the Odas? (*Oda-san te daredakke?*)" She soon remembered who they were when I explained to her which hiking route we had taken, how we pushed them to climb up to the top of the mountain, how they enjoyed the landscape, and the chemistry between the husband and the wife. The details of the tour were easily recovered with my cue. She vividly remembered the efforts she made to loosen up the reserved husband, and the feeling of joy when she saw him eventually open up and smile. If they returned as customers, she would enjoy touring with them again. The guides' post-tour indifference did not mean that they were not paying attention to the tourists. Rather, during the tour, the guides were intensively attentive to the tourists; however, once the tour was over, they did not register the customers as someone with whom to cultivate long-term reciprocal relationships.

Yukio was one of the popular guides who had repeat customers. He had two regular female customers from Tokyo who came to Banff every year for over ten years. These women worked in offices in Tokyo and had limited vacation time. I interviewed them and asked why they chose to come to Banff and requested Yukio as their guide every year. Their answer was that in their first tour with Yukio, they immediately felt they connected with him as if he were "an uncle in Canada." Although Yukio was in his mid-thirties, just several years older than them, his laid-back attitude, cheerful personality and his passion for outdoor activities charmed them. They said that walking in the mountains with him gave them a combination of relaxing feelings and refreshing change as if they were visiting a relative in Canada. However, Yukio did not seem enthusiastic to do the extra work of cultivating the long-term relationship with these customers. He said that that kind of work was something the administrative office should do, not him. Even though Yukio enjoyed the tour with these women, he insisted on the here-ness and now-ness (*ima konoba de*) of his service. Once the tour was over, he wanted to spend his time improving his outdoor guide skills and learning more about the environment, so that he could enjoy every moment of the tour not only with these regular customers but also other future customers.

The guides' disengagement in reciprocal exchange with the tourists can be analyzed as a sign of boundary maintenance between the realms of the public and private, work and personal, or gift and commodity. Existing literature on the service industry highlights the predicament of emotional workers who are asked to sell their "selves" as commodity and how they try to protect themselves from emotional drain (e.g. Hochschild 1983; Russ 2005). However, protecting their "selves" cannot fully explain the RMT guides' practices and feelings.

Entangled economies

Kiyoko's predicament is a telling example of this complex engagement of gift and commodity. One night in the staff accommodation she told another apprentice guide and me about her ambivalent and frustrated feelings toward the company administration. She was in her late twenties with five years of experience and was considered one of the most reliable bus guides in the company. The previous fall, the RMT had had a contract organizing an incentive tour with a Japanese corporation. The corporation made a good profit that year and invited their business partners and employees to share the rewards. They chartered several large buses for their one-week tour, and held special events in the most expensive hotels in the area. All the guides in the RMT were called up to assist on the tour. Kiyoko was a main guide and worked closely with the tourists. At the end of the tour, a group of tourists asked Kiyoko to come to karaoke with them that night. Kiyoko agreed to go. When the manager, Atsuko-san, heard of this plan, she repeatedly apologized to Kiyoko for this extra work. Atsuko-san was also concerned about sending Kiyoko alone with a group of middle-aged men at night. She told Kiyoko that she should leave the group whenever she wanted, and handed Kiyoko the company's cell phone, instructing Kiyoko to call her in the case of an emergency.

When Kiyoko started to tell this story, I initially thought that her frustration derived from the extra work or an overtime wage, but she was not concerned about these issues at all. Rather, Kiyoko was delighted to see the tourists, who still had some energy and curiosity, venture out to town by themselves. Throughout the week, she accompanied the extremely tight schedule of their tour. On top of the notorious Japanese-style tour that crams too many sightseeing spots into a short trip, this incentive tour was packed with company ceremonies and events. She felt pity for her customers. She worried that they did not have a chance to relax and enjoy their experience in the Canadian Rockies. Kiyoko said, "the customers must stretch out their wings freely (*hane o nobasanakya*) after all these crazy schedules." Kiyoko was confident that her customers were "good men" (*ii ojisan tachi*), and that she did not need to worry about sexual harassment or other inappropriate behavior as Atsuko-san had cautioned. Kiyoko understood that the customers wanted her to come with them because they would feel more comfortable going out in a foreign town with a local and also they considered her as a part of the group after spending nearly a week together. She simply wanted to see her customers fully enjoy their trip.

After the karaoke singing ended past midnight, Kiyoko "was shocked" to see Atsuko-san standing at the exit of the karaoke bar. Atsuko-san waited for Kiyoko in order to drive her home. On the one hand, Kiyoko was impressed by Atsuko-san's strong sense of responsibility as a manager. Kiyoko liked Atsuko-san as she constantly gave her staff care and affection as if she were their surrogate mother or elder sister in Canada. Kiyoko appreciated her compassion, and she interpreted that Atsuko-san had come to the bar concerned about Kiyoko's well-being. On the other hand, for Kiyoko, Atsuko-san's presence ruined the evening. Kiyoko felt sorry for her customers. Atsuko-san's paternalistic protection made Kiyoko feel that she was sent to the outing with the customers as a part of the tourist economy. Even though Kiyoko voluntarily joined the outing to help her customers and did not count on the after-hour wage nor any other monetary transaction, still, Atsuko-san's presence enclosed the event in this moral economy.

When Kiyoko agreed to go out for karaoke with the customers, she forgot that her presence at the karaoke bar could be interpreted as a "gift." However, seeing Atsuko-san made her realize that what she was doing was an act of giving her presence as a gift to the customers, which could easily become an extra service. Because Kiyoko gave her hospitality to the customers, the customers were indebted. They were obliged to appreciate Kiyoko's work and to be well behaved, pleasant customers to make the rest of the tour easy for her. The customers were also expected to use the company's service again, or to spread the reputation of the guide and the company. This moral economy can be easily merged into the tourism business economy in the logic of reciprocity (cf. Rus 2008).

Politics of hospitality

The gift given within this formula inevitably leads to "patterns of real and symbolic investment" (Wortham 1997: 410). A future return is expected. As Simon Wortham points out, this economism reinforces the idea of possessive individualism and property rights, the relations that ruin the gift *qua* gift (ibid.). If we see the tourist business as operating in tandem with a parallel of a reciprocal moral economy, the notion of a "hospitality industry" does not seem to be so oxymoronic. Giving a gift, generosity and hospitality are conveyed and circulated in the entangled circular trajectory of expected reciprocity, or what Derrida (1992) calls the "madness of economic reason." In contrast to this madness of economy, Derrida urges us to think of the absolute notion of the gift that does not expect any return. He asks, "is not the gift, if there is any, also that which interrupts economy? That which, in suspending economic calculation, no longer gives rise to exchange" (ibid.: 7). In order for the gift to exist as present (literally as a "present" that appears at this moment only), the principle of exchange, such as reciprocity, obligation, debt, "must be absolutely dispensed with or forgotten" (Wortham 1997: 409). This corollary is because the recognition of a gift as a gift implicitly binds the actors into the logic of exchange, future investment and the debt in account.

In a strict sense, Kiyoko's action might not be an absolute gift as she received a sense of satisfaction in return for her presence at the bar, thus gaining something as a consequence of her action. Nevertheless, her forgetfulness of her presence as giving herself and her time potentially comes close to a non-economy—just giving without return, no expectation of reciprocity. Kiyoko's predicament was not that of being an agent of moralistically conflicting economies of gift and commodity; it was her realization that everything is enclosed in the circle of reciprocity. The slim chance of fleeing from the circular logic of economy was ironically shattered by Atsuko-san's benevolent care of her staff.

The conundrum that creates this dynamic field of negotiation is not the oppositional poles of gift and commodity. It is the entangled existence of gift/commodity economy and the non-economy, the excess or supplement produced from the guides' affect, the generative capacity of the human to experience affect. In this case, it was Kiyoko's capacity to be affected by sharing time and space with her customers, empathetically feeling their experiences of the tightly scheduled tour, and her ability to affect others by her action of helping the tourists to "stretch out their wings" in Canada. What is contested is the company's business interest in retrieving this excess into the system of reciprocity (whether it is monetary or non-monetary, moralistic or capitalist value production), and the guide's practice of letting it loose, irretrievable in the machine of exchange (whether the motor of the machine is moral achievement or capitalist profit making).

Due to the elusive nature of affective labor, the issue of who has control over the excess produced by the guides' labor was constantly contested. The guides and the company always negotiate how much extra service the guides give the tourists. Accepting the customers' invitations to go out for dinner or drinks was considered acceptable at the RMT, but going out for a short walk with them was not because the company offered a mini-hike as an optional tour. Making a detour and showing tourists extra sight-seeing spots was a tricky issue. The guides were often urged to please customers by responding to the tourists' specific personal interests and desires and giving them extra service. The company convinced the guides not to show extra sights if the sights were listed in an optional tour itinerary they could sell to the customer. If the sight was not listed on any of the available tours, the company often turned a blind eye, but this practice had ambivalent meaning for the business. On the one hand, the extra service as a "gift" from the guide to the customers could enhance the customer satisfaction and help establish the company's long-term relationship with the customers. On the other hand, visiting the site could be sold as a customized optional tour which would bring revenue directly to the company.

The guides' subjectivities were constructed not simply within the "phenomenology of exchange" (Russ 2005). The guide's subjectivity-as-commodity in the hospitality industry suggests that the subject is a constant "battlefield" (Virno 2004: 78). In this field, the guides' generative power to give excessive affect constantly fought with the economic machine to subsume this excess into circular exchange.

Conclusion: forgetfulness and indeterminacy

The tour guides' detachment seems to exemplify their unintentional critique of the economic machine. Their forgetfulness of their own capacity of giving affect suggests a human potential that cannot be easily channeled into the capitalist circuit of exchange. I asked the guides why they did not reply to the tourists' letters even though the management encouraged them to get repeat customers and the guides themselves committed to maintaining good relations with the tourists during the tours. Some of the guides even disengaged with my question. Eri said "I don't know. Maybe I simply forget." Another popular hiking guide, Yoshiko told me "Maybe I'm just lazy. I receive and read [the letters] with great appreciation. That's all." (*Totemo arigataku yomasete itadakimasu. Soredake.*) Yet, it is misleading to interpret their replies as signs that the guides did not care for the tourists. Rather, it is deeply connected to their sense of sincere care and hospitality to the customers. The guides often used the expression of "*ichigo ichie*" (one time, one meeting), when they explained their commitment to the customers. This expression has its roots in *sadō*, the Japanese tea ceremony, where its meaning derives from the notions that this meeting was once a lifetime and the host and the guest could not expect to meet each other again, thus one should fully appreciate each moment of the encounter and "give oneself to it with utter sincerity" (Murai 1989: 29).

The guides' detachment, or the forgetfulness of reciprocity, has the potential to cut the line of the entangled circulation of moral and capitalist economies, the double circulation of liberal economy based both on the morality of reciprocity and the exchange of value equivalence. The guides' actions keep the possibility of the non-reciprocal gift open at least conceptually, even though it may be impossible to activate it in reality. Their disengagement at least prolonged the conclusion of impossibility, extended the moment of indecisiveness, delayed the closure, and dawdled over the completion of the economic machine. They left the end loose and open.

Acknowledgements

This chapter is based on research funded by the Social Sciences and Humanities Council of Canada and the University of California Pacific Rim Research

Fund. The first version was presented on the panel at the American Anthropological Association meeting in 2009 organized by Gabriella Lukacs and Akiko Takeyama. I thank the organizers and the discussant, Hirokazu Miyazaki. My thanks also go to Akiko Takesue, Lena Mortensen, Sasha Welland and Anna Tsing, who made helpful comments.

Notes

1 All the names in this chapter are pseudonyms. The RMT was one of several subcontracting companies in Banff that provided guides for major Japanese travel agencies. Most of the fifty tour guides in the company were Japanese transient workers. The characteristic feature of Japanese tourism in Banff was that unlike other foreign tours led by tour escorts coming from somewhere else, Japanese tours depended on local Japanese residents for guiding. Several guide companies run by Japanese immigrants provided Japanese-speaking local guides to major Japanese travel agencies.

2 For further discussion on affective labor in this approach, see also Hardt and Negri (2000, 2004).

3 I do not intend to argue that other service workers do not share the holistic characteristics of affective labor, but simply point out that it is easily observable in tour guides' work.

4 See Clough (2007) for the significance of affect in intersubjective co-constitution of self and other. See in particular Wissinger (2007) for the discussion on model industry workers' intersubjective formation of self.

5 Marcel Mauss's seminal work, *The Gift* (2000 [1950]), inspired this genre of literature. Gregory's (1982) work is influential in analyzing the contrast between gift reciprocity in which the personalities of givers and receivers are inseparable from the exchange, and commodity economy in which personality is detached from exchange. See Carrier (1995), Parry and Bloch (1989), and Weiner (1992) for further development of anthropological discussions of gift and commodity that complicates this distinction. More recently, Keane (2008), Richard and Rudnyckyj (2009) and Venkatesan (2011) discuss how gift and commodity modes of exchanges are entangled, and the morality and sociality in contemporary capitalism.

6 See Ahmed (2010) for how "happiness" has been mobilized for the central moral economy of self-worth in contemporary capitalism.

7 See, for example, the influential work of Ohashi Kyosen, the popular television entertainer and one-time member of the House of Councilors (Satsuka 2009).

8 According to Japan's Ministry of Land, Infrastructure, Transport and Tourism statistics, Canada was the thirteenth most visited country after Britain and France, with about 374,000 Japanese visitors in 2000 (Ministry of Land, Infrastructure, Transport and Tourism 2001).

9 See also Iwai (2002, 2003) for more discussion on corporate restructuring.

10 See Allison (2012) for the discussion of precariousness, especially among the youth in Japan since the 1990s.

11 See Satsuka (n.d., forthcoming) about the guide training process and the construction of guides as commodities.

References

Ahmed, Sara. 2004. "Affective Economies." *Social Text* 79(2): 117–39.

——2010. *The Promise of Happiness.* Durham, NC: Duke University Press.

Allison, Anne. 2012. "Ordinary Refugees: Social Precarity and Soul in 21st Century Japan." *Anthropological Quarterly* 85(2): 345–70.
Carrier, James G. 1995. *Gifts and Commodities: Exchange and Western Capitalism since 1700*. London and New York: Routledge.
Clough, Patricia Ticineto, ed. 2007. *The Affective Turn: Theorizing the Social*. Durham, NC: Duke University Press.
Deleuze, Gilles and Guattari, Felix. 1987. *A Thousand Plateaus: Capitalism and Schizophrenia*. Minneapolis: University of Minnesota Press.
Derrida, Jacques. 1992. *Given Time I. Counterfeit Money*. Chicago, IL and London: University of Chicago Press.
Dore, Ronald. 2000. *Stock Market Capitalism: Welfare Capitalism. Japan and Germany versus the Anglo-Saxons*. Oxford: Oxford University Press.
Gregory, Chris A. 1982. *Gifts and Commodities*. London: Academic Press.
Hardt, Michael. 1999. "Affective Labor." *Boundary 2* 26(2): 89–100.
Hardt, Michael and Negri, Antonio. 2000. *Empire*. Cambridge, MA: Harvard University Press.
——2004. *Multitude: War and Democracy in the Age of Empire*. New York: Penguin.
Hochschild, Arlie Russell. 1983. *The Managed Heart: Commercialization of Human Feeling*. Berkeley: University of California Press.
Ivy, Marilyn. 1993. "Formation of Mass Culture." In Andrew Gordon (ed.), *Postwar Japan as History*. Berkeley: University of California Press, 239–58.
Iwai, Katsuhito. 2002. "The Nature of the Business Corporation: Its Legal Structure and Economic Functions." *Japanese Economic Review* 53(3): 243–73.
——2003. *Kaisha wa Korekara Donarunoka* (What Will Happen to Corporations?) Tokyo: Heibonsha.
Ministry of Land, Infrastructure, Transport and Tourism (Japan). 2001. *Kanko Hakusho* (White Paper on Tourism).
Keane, Webb. 2008. "Market, Materiality and Moral Metalanguage." *Anthropological Theory* 8(1): 27–42.
Lashley, Conrad and Morrison, Alison, eds. 2000. *In Search of Hospitality: Theoretical Perspectives and Debates*. Oxford: Butterworth-Heinemann.
Mauss, Marcel. 2000 [1950]. *The Gift: The Form and Reason for Exchange in Archaic Societies*. New York: W.W. Norton.
Molz, Jennie Germann and Gibson, Sarah, eds. 2007. *Mobilizing Hospitality: The Ethics of Social Relations in a Mobile World*. Aldershot and Burlington, VT: Ashgate.
Murai, Yoshihiko. 1989. "The Development of Chanoyu: Before Rikyu." In Paul Varley and Isao Kumakura (eds), *Tea in Japan: Essays on the History of Chanoyu*. Honolulu: University of Hawaii Press, 3–32.
Parry, Jonathan and Bloch, Maurice, eds. 1989. *Money and the Morality of Exchange*. Cambridge and New York: Cambridge University Press.
Povinelli, Elizabeth A. 2011. *Economies of Abandonment: Social Belonging and Endurance in Late Liberalism*. Durham, NC: Duke University Press.
Richard, Analiese and Rudnyckyj, Daromir. 2009. "Economies of Affect." *Journal of the Royal Anthropological Institute* 15: 57–77.
Rus, Andrej. 2008. "'Gifts vs. Commodity' Rebate Revisited." *Anthropological Notebooks* 14(1): 81–102.
Russ, Ann Julienne. 2005. "Love's Labor Paid for: Gift and Commodity at the Threshold of Death." *Cultural Anthropology* 20(1): 128–55.

Satsuka, Shiho. 2009. "Populist Cosmopolitanism: The Predicament of Subjectivity and the Japanese Fascination with Overseas." *Inter-Asia Cultural Studies* 10(1): 67–82.

——n.d., forthcoming. *Nature in Translation: Freedom, Subjectivity, Japanese Tourist Encounters in Canada*. Durham, NC: Duke University Press.

Venkatesan, Soumhya. 2011. "The Social Life of a 'Free' Gift." *American Ethnologist* 38(1): 47–57.

Virno, Paolo. 2004. *A Grammar of the Multitude: For an Analysis of Contemporary Forms of Life*. New York: Semiotext(s).

Weiner, Annette. 1992. *Inalienable Possessions: The Paradox of Keeping While Giving*. Berkeley: University of California Press.

Wissinger, Elizabeth. 2007. "Always on Display: Affective Production in the Modeling Industry." In *The Affective Turn: Theorizing the Social*, ed. Patricia Ticineto Clough, 231–60. Durham, NC: Duke University Press.

Wortham, Simon. 1997. "Bringing Criticism to Account: Economy, Exchange and Cultural Theory." *Economy and Society* 26(3): 400–18.

Yoshimi, Shunya. 2001. "'Amerika' wo Yokubo/Bokyaku Suru Sengo: 'Kichi' to 'Shōhi' no Kussetsu wo Megutte" (The Post-war that Desires/Forgets 'America': On 'Military Bases' and 'Consumption'). *Gendai Shiso Special Edition* 29(2): 44–63.

Part IV

Tears, media and affective articulation

5 Tears, capital, ethics

Television and the public sphere in Japan

Daniel White

Tears flood Japanese television. From the enormously popular TV dramas and variety shows of Japan's commercial broadcasters to the documentary specials of its public broadcaster, tears mark a media sphere thick with affective bodies and sentimental timbre. Early theorists of the public sphere such as John Dewey (1991) and Walter Lippmann (1993, 1997) argued that the media in modern society—in their scope, influence and private interests—play a fundamental role in the realization or inhibition of the public sphere. Today, assessing the public sphere's legitimacy is a matter often determined by the degree to which rational debate is established free and independent of both state and home, an approach based heavily on the reading—or for some, misreading (Warner 2005: 46)—of Jürgen Habermas's (1989) model of the public sphere as it evolved in seventeenth- and eighteenth-century Western Europe. The enduring influence of this model has sustained a perception of emotion as reason's other, inimical to the ideal conditions for making "good citizens" (Pantti and van Zoonen 2006). Given this understanding of emotion, should the amount of tears appearing on Japanese TV trouble us? If the media play a major role in affecting the shape of the public sphere, and if that effect is highly emotionally charged, is the legitimacy of the public sphere then under threat?

In the wake of critique of what many see as Habermas's overly idealized model (Fraser 1992; Hanada 1997; Hayashi 2006), scholars have begun to pay increased attention to the relationship between emotion and the public sphere. Many have attempted to reformulate emotion not as an element in opposition or threatening to the public sphere, but as one important if not indispensable to its realization (see Fraser 1992; Madsen 1993; Schlesinger 1997, 1999; Yang 1999; Marcus *et al.* 2000; Ahmed 2004; Richards 2004). Approaching questions of affect and emotion from an ethnographic perspective, I want to situate this relationship between emotion and the public sphere in its local settings. Rather than discuss the political question of whether a legitimate public sphere is possible in Japan, I examine how those invested in the possibilities of the public sphere argue for its legitimacy, and in doing so, variously appropriate, contextualize and problematize emotion. Specifically, I pay attention to the ways tears are represented in Japanese media. One reason for doing this is because tears mark highly affective sites of consumption in

Japanese TV, places where one finds overt and often melodramatic ethical claims. Moreover, tears also serve as an important visual symbol in TV production that producers objectify, rationalize and operationalize toward varying ends, whether on the part of commercial broadcasters in the race for ratings or by Japan's public broadcaster in the aim of educating citizens, cultivating responsibility and even defining democracy. Observing tears in sites of both media consumption and production, then, serves as a methodological tool to trace a moral economy of emotion in Japanese TV.

This chapter looks at a number of ways Japanese television producers manage tears. By contrasting examples of commercial and public television productions, it describes representations of crying on TV appropriated toward varying ethical ends. Ultimately, the discussion aims to draw attention to the ways producers and the institutions within which they work shape the meanings of two contingent categories: emotion and the public sphere. The chapter proceeds through three parts. First, it situates a case study on feeling in Japanese television within recent theoretical considerations of affect, both clarifying terms and highlighting some of the inevitable problems in the ethnographic description of affect. Second, it presents a typical example of how tears are appropriated toward ratings among commercial TV producers, focusing on a TV Asahi broadcast of a nationwide, elementary school sporting contest. Third, the chapter contrasts this commercial broadcast with a public one, a documentary on early-onset Alzheimer's, illustrating how similar melodramatic narratives are leveraged not only for commercial but also for educational ends. The chapter concludes by exploring some theories of the public sphere that in moving away from Habermas's model may better shed light on the role of tears in Japanese TV and serve future studies of the relationship between emotion and public spheres more generally. Together, these sections present ethnographic scenes of how the experience, imagination, construction and, most importantly, feelings of the public sphere are negotiated in the virtual TV realities of real-life Japan.

Definitions and problems for an anthropology of affect

Any investigation of affective forms of life begs for a clarification of terms. The affective turn in the social sciences (Clough 2007: ix)—or what might better be called the affective "return"—has both represented and inspired a collection of important work on the relationship between culture and feeling.[1] However, these works have also been characterized by a rather messy and confusing proliferation of definitions. In particular, theorists have yet to reach a consensus on the distinctions between the term affect and its kindred keywords ("feeling," "emotion," "passion," "sentiment," "structure of feeling"), most of which had already been seriously discussed long before this most recent wave of interest in affect.[2] Rather than offering yet another theoretical genealogy of affect in order to justify its application to analyses of feeling in contemporary media culture, however, I want to build a case for affect by making the simple argument that to the degree that the term "affect" can elucidate more or different forms of feeling in culture than the term "emotion" can alone, it is a tool worth adding to the anthropologist's evolving, contemporary toolkit (Rabinow 2003).

In part due to his expert readings (1992) of Deleuze and in part to his early and rigorous theoretical inquiry into affect as a key term (2002), Brian Massumi has become the dominant reference in these new inquiries into affect. His distinction between emotion and affect attributes the former to the conscious field of narrative and socially represented feelings and the latter to the nonconscious field of bodily intensities and capacities to both move and be moved. The distinction is productive, affording anthropologists new ways to engage with the more technical elements of embodiment and nonconscious aspects of cultural life outside the domain of psychoanalytic theory. As nonconscious physiological responses of the body reacting to outside, culturally conditioned stimuli, tears serve as an excellent example of this. Traditionally, anthropologists have often taken the physiological for granted, struggling to find a language to talk about the cultural constituents of biological life that does not also incorporate a somewhat begrudging political critique of the dominance of scientific over cultural knowledge. Rooted securely in literary theory and philosophy, Massumi's exploration of affect offers a critical theory of the physiological in language that anthropologists find more settling.

Despite the productivity of his critique, however, Massumi's theory is not without some limitations that have specific consequences for the ethnographic description of affect. Although his critical theory allows for new ways of engaging with the hard materiality of biological life, his distinction between affect and emotion creates an irreconcilable epistemological gap between the two that forecloses the possibility for a dynamic theory of culture to challenge classic models of the nature-nurture divide. For Massumi, affect is defined by its absolute impossibility of narrative capture: it is implicit, autonomous, and can only be perceived as escape (Massumi 2002: 35–36). A definition of affect that holds this rigorously to the inability of its narration creates methodological challenges for the ethnographer whose primary task remains the recording of cultural life in text. Anthropologists like Kathleen Stewart have recognized this problem. In her work *Ordinary Affects* (2007), Stewart bridges what I have come to call the *affect-emotion gap* through the form of vignettes: short glimpses into middle American life that point to moments of affective intensity but stop short of narrative capture. As we might expect from such an expert stylist, this experimental writing strategy is effective; however, analyses of affect that depend on formal virtuosity cannot, unfortunately, sustain the kind of unified field of inquiry that would most benefit anthropologists of affect working across multiple and divergent sites.

The literary critic Sianne Ngai offers a different, more practical solution. Where Massumi and Stewart would maintain the ontological distinction between affect and emotion, thus rendering their descriptive attempts into either theoretical abstraction or formal experimentation, Ngai (2005) provides an alternative approach that allows culture to play a more fundamental role in guiding empirical analysis. She accomplishes this by presenting her examination of affects, or "ugly feelings," in Western literature as a "modal" rather than "formal" critique—a distinction of *degree* rather than *kind*. She explains, "What the switch from formal to modal difference enables is an analysis of the transitions from one pole to the other: the passages whereby affects acquire the semantic density and narrative complexity of emotions, and emotions conversely denature into affects" (ibid.: 27). She bases her hypothesis on the understanding that affects, although rooted in the body, are thoroughly culturally conditioned; however, rather than leave the question of this distinction between the physiology of affect and the sociality of emotion to philosophy, she offers something more pragmatic. Effectively suspending the irreconcilability of the two for what she calls "aesthetic productivity" (ibid.: 28), she explains: "My assumption is that affects are less formed and structured than emotions, but not lacking form or structure altogether; less 'sociolinguistically fixed,' but by no means code-free or meaningless" (ibid.: 27). Proposing that affect and emotion are constituted in relation to each other on a continuous scale between physical manifestations of affect and social categories of emotion allows for the possibility of bridging the epistemological gap between what we feel and what we know about what we feel—between affect and emotion.

Tears in Japanese TV are affective rather than emotional things. They are nonconscious, physiological responses to stimuli. However, they are entirely cultural things as well—bodily capacities developed over a long history in which experiences are paired with learned behavior that is culturally conditioned, regulated and disciplined. In engaging with emotion in media spheres in Japan, my strategy is not only to pay equal attention to the physical manifestations of tears as well as to the cultural meanings of them (e.g. shame, loss, sadness, happiness, satisfaction, bliss), but also to analyze how each shapes the other. Just as our capacity for crying infuses our social narratives with affective energy, those narratives construct our physiological capacity to produce tears. Relying on Ngai's dynamic theory of affect, the rest of this chapter analyses how these two elements of feeling and story are uniquely coupled in Japanese TV, illustrating how affective intensity functions as integral rather than injurious to a flourishing public sphere.

Commercial broadcasting and ratings

"Thirty People, Thirty-one Legs" (*Sanjūnin sanjūikkyaku*) is one of numerous commercial programs on Japanese TV heavily saturated with tears. Sponsored by the newspaper *Asahi Shimbun*, the show is a two-hour special broadcast from its affiliated station, TV Asahi. The program features a nationwide tournament of grammar school students competing to test which school has the fastest "thirty-one-legged team." Most North Americans having experienced grammar school recesses, summer camps, or neighborhood parties are

Figure 5.1 Screenshot from *Sanjūnin sanjūikkyaku*, TV Asahi, December 6, 2008

familiar with the "three-legged race," where two participants lash each of their legs together by a chord or rope and cooperate by coordinating their steps to move the most quickly and efficiently from the start to finish line. The Japanese thirty-one-legged race version of this is the same idea writ large, involving the fixing together of the legs of thirty grade school students who must, in careful synchronization, coordinate their steps in a timed race to the finish line. Teams, the winning schools from each of Japan's forty-seven prefectures, cover the distance of 50 meters marking times between 9 and 11 seconds in a gait that is likely to shock observers familiar with only the two-person version (Figure 5.1). Although viewers unfamiliar with this exercise tend to interpret the program comically, one quickly realizes that the event is serious business. In the course of the race, teams rarely fall, laugh, or exhibit any other comical elements. In fact, falling becomes a severe, emotionally painful (*kuyashii*) event, one that demands tears rather than laughter.

Tears suffuse the program, marking a highly affective environment. The students, along with the cheering parents in the stands, cry at the elimination of their team; coaches of the team either fight back tears or openly cry along with team members as evidence of their emotional investment; and the four commentators watching the event from TV Asahi's studio cry copiously throughout the show. Indeed, the program aims purposefully to evoke such

Figure 5.2 Screenshot from *Sanjūnin sanjūikkyaku*, TV Asahi, December 6, 2008

sentiment. Between races the show features personal stories of individuals who have been filmed periodically during the year's preparation for the event.[3] Further, announcers offer commentary throughout the entire program. One of them continually solicits impressions (*kansō*) from students and coaches before the race, highlighting their enthusiasm and determination, and again after the race, focusing in particular on the losing team. The student selected for an interview inevitably appears alongside the rest of his or her peers in tears, the emotional sign of a bitter end to a long process of individual sacrifice (*gaman*) and group effort (*kyōryoku*).

In fact, the specific appearance of tears in the program serves as one of the most convincing examples of evidence for the claim made by Teresa Brennan (2004) that affects are regularly transmitted from one body to another. Tears are contagious. Participants on the show demonstrate this by crying in groups (see Figure 5.2), revealing not only that affects can be transmitted and shared among subjects, but also that those shared affects intensify the emotional experience as, through the show's narration, they are fixed to cultural values of effort and sacrifice. Further, repeated interviews with students, coaches and parents, coupled with the comments from the hosts, facilitate the translation of affect into narrated emotion. The direction of this process is important. As articulated in William James's classic model of emotion, we do not cry because we are sad; rather, we become sad because we cry (James 1884: 190). Interviewers push the participants and crowd members to give explanations for their tears. Example responses to interviewers' questions reveal sentiments like disappointment at the loss in the face of months and months of effort (*dōryoku*) and sacrifice (*gaman*), shame at letting down one's team members, and pride on the part of coaches and parents as they watch the students struggle. These scenes show how affective capacities—the capacity to be affected by disappointment, shame and pride—have been built into the body through particular cultural narratives of these emotions, of which the television show serves as only the most formulaic representation. Consistent with Ngai's account, the show illustrates how culture codes affect as much as affects are coded in emotion.

One might call this process of inscribing sentimental capacities into the body a kind of "affective socialization," if only to draw attention to the fact that all socialization, from the most Dionysian to the most Apollonian, entails an ethical component. The various responses I received from the American viewers to whom I showed the program compared to those of Japanese viewers illustrate this cultural particularity. Where Japanese viewers are, for the most part, inclined to cry, American ones tend to laugh. However, such dispositions are in no way immutable, as is demonstrated by one American informant who confessed to me that when she first came to Japan she thought Japanese TV dramas were predictable and silly; now, while they are still predictable, she cannot stop crying. Tears exhibit the flow and form of affect: they move between bodies and intensities but they are also fixed in flesh, coded by culture's ability to reengineer capacities to respond to sentimental stimuli immediately but not indefinitely outside conscious awareness.

Television producers have a sense for the important role narrative plays in this process, and for what kinds of stories elicit strong affective reactions. Media producers aim to secure this relationship between affect, emotion and narration through reflexive practices (Ong and Collier 2005: 7; Caldwell 2008) of program evaluation without explicitly referencing formal theories of emotion. Through the tracking technologies of ratings and a more generalized genre system, the rationalization of informal narrative formulas that repeatedly and reliably elicit tears establishes a connection between emotional life and the circulation of capital. Rationalizing the relationship between narration and tears, in fact, has manifested in a massive industry. Publishers frequently offer workbooks on scenario writing that teach aspiring writers how to recreate scenes thick with emotion, expensive schools host classes for aspiring TV drama writers, and the entire genre of tearjerker TV programs constitutes a huge market share of TV ratings (Lukács 2010: 105–9). *Sanjūnin sanjūik-kyaku* proves representative of a number of these tearjerker programs that attract viewers through sentimental storylines.[4] Other versions include melodramatic narratives of love or incurable disease, documentaries on the trials of public education, and the vast array of variety shows focusing on sentimental themes like the relationship between humans and animals.[5] This genre of the sentimental tearjerker (*onamida chōdai*), literally, "receiving tears" or "consuming tears," is a product of a largely insulated and domestically oriented production process. Although popular Japanese media today circulate transnationally (an important topic beyond the scope of this chapter, but see Iwabuchi 2002; Allison 2006; Condry 2006; Lukács 2010; and Yano 2013), TV production processes remain based on business models that imagine and target a domestic viewership. Since 1970, Iwabuchi (2004: 22) explains, over 90 percent of Japanese television has been domestically produced. In Japan's competitive commercial television market, tears in these *onamida chōdai* programs are indispensible resources for generating capital.

Important to understanding this economically productive use of tears, though, is its rootedness in a culturally situated ethics—in a particular relationship individuals establish with mainstream morality.[6] In *Sanjūnin sanjūikkyaku* it is the conventional values of effort (*dōryoku*), cooperation (*kyōryoku*), and sacrifice (*gaman*) around which the program is organized. In order to guarantee emotional evocations these moral scripts must be both fixed and obvious. This is the logic of melodrama. Melodrama secures its sentimental appeal in the clear juxtaposition of victory and defeat, good and evil. As Peter Brooks explains, "Melodrama is indeed, typically, not only a moralistic drama but the drama of morality: it strives to find, to articulate, to demonstrate, to 'prove' the existence of a moral universe" (Brooks 1976: 20). The intensity of emotion found in melodrama is guaranteed by what Brooks calls these "most fundamental psychic relations and cosmic ethical forces" (ibid.: 13). The emotional satisfaction one feels in either victory or defeat comes not from the fact that the world is an obviously and fundamentally moral place, but that it so often is not. The space of the program, however, carves out in clear narrative form the world as it should be—a space where the winners are rewarded for their effort in victory and the losers commended for courage in the face of defeat. Emotion in *Sanjūnin*, then, is not simply the manipulation of viewers' emotion for ratings, it is the performance of a moral sensibility that at once conditions and operationalizes affective responses to particular cultural scripts. It is in these performative sites where affect and emotion are mutually constructed and embodied.

While commercial broadcasters ultimately measure success in terms of ratings, Japan's public broadcaster must consider not only ratings but also responsibility. This ethical distinction underlies the discourse of *kōkyōsei* (公共性)—what we would refer to in English as the "public sphere" (more often designated as *kōkyōken*) but in Japanese means something closer to "publicness"—and problematizes emotion, raising the question: what are the responsible uses and narrations of emotion for a public broadcaster?

Public broadcasting and ethics

In early November 2008, I sat in a small audience at *Nippon Hōsō Kyōkai*'s (NHK) public archives in Kawaguchi, about an hour outside the center of Tokyo, for a public showing of a documentary on early-onset Alzheimer's (*jakunensei ninchishō*). The audience being composed almost exclusively of elderly Japanese, the only thing I seemed to share with the group was that we were all wiping plentiful tears from our eyes. I was attending a public showing (*mirukai*) of various productions from Japan's public broadcaster, NHK. Such showings at the archives are organized about once a month, and on that occasion featured a documentary from 2005, entitled, "Etching our Time into the Heart" (*Futari no toki o kokoro ni kizamu*). The opening scene shows the central character, Ochi-san, at a podium in front of a large audience. His movements are slow, his hands somewhat shaky. He is reading a prepared statement, a short memoir of his experience and ongoing battle with Alzheimer's. A young woman stands next to him, whispering in his ear at points where he stumbles over his words. Ochi-san comes to the climactic conclusion of his speech, where, tearing up himself, he expresses gratitude to his wife, the most important person in his life without whom he would be unable to carry on. As the camera zooms in on the face of his wife in the audience, smiling proudly, the faces of the audience both in the documentary and in the archives are streamed with tears.

In a conversation shortly following the showing, the primary organizer of the showing at NHK, whom I call Takada-san, cited the importance of this depiction of Ochi-san's speech. The scene, he suggested, along with being a powerfully emotional one, demonstrates how far the public understanding of Alzheimer's has come among Japanese people. In the past, he explained, Japanese people did not understand anything about Alzheimer's. They misunderstood the condition, saying that things were fine so long as the patient seemed happy with his life. However, with great progress and effort among professionals, family members and patients themselves, Japanese people have come to reconcile that misunderstanding. This shift in thought and feeling toward Alzheimer's patients represents for Takada-san a mark of progress for Japanese people. The tearful reaction of the audience is evidence, from his perspective, of a development in social maturity.

Futari no toki demonstrates how emotion and ethics develop in relation to each other in Japanese media spheres. Emotional evocation is dependent on the ethical consensus that what is happening is tragic and, in fact, *should* evoke tears. Tears, then, are indicators of healthy affects. The documentary goes to significant lengths in drawing out sympathy not only for Ochi-san but also for his wife, Sumiko. It explores two themes in particular: the suffering of Ochi-san and the determination and efforts of his wife in the face of both his and her suffering. Sumiko sacrifices, cares, works and, above all, cries over her husband's condition. In fact, the program's point of empathy is directed less toward the husband, who is often depicted in moments of quiet content, and more toward Sumiko, whose suffering the viewer observes through scenes of "private" displays of pain and tears.[7] This focus on strength in the face of suffering not only appeals to familiar cultural values such as perseverance (*gaman*), also featured prominently in TV Asahi's "Thirty People, Thirty-one Legs," but it also represents a common script employed in NHK documentaries that typically feature emotionally evocative, sentimental themes such as struggle, determination and sacrifice.

These heavily melodramatic styles of documentary depiction point to what John Caldwell (2008) and Ian Condry (2013) have called "collaborative creativity," a style of production rooted not in the idealism of the auteur but rather in the institutional practices of production pedagogy. As I learned through discussions with documentary directors, prior to entering NHK, few have any experience with documentary production—let alone with TV, film, or media in general.[8] Consequently, NHK teaches styles of documentary narration and production through a form of professional apprenticeship. Aesthetic forms of documentary become, then, rooted in collective organization, NHK being one of the largest in Japanese media.[9] Directors learn what Christine Yano refers to in her analysis of sentimental song in Japan as the *kata*, "forms" or "patterns," of sentimental narration (Yano 2002: 24–26). These fixed storytelling *kata* create an intimate relationship between producers and viewers who have learned what kinds of messages to expect through the medium of documentary. In fact, for Japanese audiences, intense sentimental affects become the very medium of documentary communication. Where early-onset Alzheimer's as an at one time stigmatized illness in Japan may be an ambiguous and slippery theme to narrate, melodramatic stories of struggle and determination in the face of suffering are NHK staples.

Indeed, melodrama as a genre serves as an ideal form through which to introduce difficult, complex topics into the public sphere. One can find structural affinities between the history of Alzheimer's and that of other sensitive conditions in Japan that Western medicine would identify under the category of "mental illness" (see Ohnuki-Tierney 1984; Traphagan 2000; Lock 2013; Nakamura 2013). Characteristic of these forms of suffering in Japan is the lack of a public discourse in which to root a normative understanding of the appropriate ethical and emotional reactions to abnormal bodies. Suffering in these circumstances remains a private affair, susceptible to anxiety over public shame and the unpredictable reactions of others. For a public broadcaster with a responsibility to represent public views as well as to inform them, constructing a public narrative for a stereotypically private and multivalent experience of sickness is challenging; in short, few precedents for its narration exist, causing a sense of unease for producers. One strategy for negotiating this discomfort is to translate ethically unclear situations into typical melodramatic scripts of suffering and strength.

NHK directors and producers are not unreflexive about the ethical implications of highly-emotional productions. For them, emotion serves as an effective communication device. Miyata-san, the producer of *Futari no toki*, described to me the difference between British and Japanese narrative styles of documentary, explaining that while British documentaries aim for the viewer's "head" (*atama*), Japanese documentaries aim for the viewer's "stomach" (*hara*). It is his job, he said, to "drop the story in the viewer's stomach" (*hara ni otosu*). In Japan, as elsewhere in East and Southeast Asia, the stomach as an alternative locus of understanding to the head is a common theme. "*Fu ni ochinai*" (腑に落ちない) is a Japanese phrase often used to refer to someone who does not understand what he or she is being told. Although in English one might talk about knowing in one's gut, the more equivalent phrase in English would be when one says, in an entirely cerebral metaphor, that one's words went "in one ear and out the other." In contrast to the head, the imagery of the stomach is visceral. Positing the stomach as the symbolic seat of understanding suggests a form of knowing that—much like in theories of affect—is rooted in the body. It imagines knowledge in the form of a hearty substance that settles in the stomach, slowly becoming part of the person as its nutrients are digested and chemically transform the body and its affective capacities. "*Fu ni ochinai*" refers to one who does not "get it," and that what one is attempting to communicate passes straight through the person, leaving him or her unaffected, unmoved and, thus, ignorant. Emotional evocation thus becomes necessary to communicate the meaning of the story, and tears among viewers serve as affective evidence that the story has, indeed, hit its mark.[10]

In Japan, such an emotional theory of documentary production and audience reception underlies television production in general, indicating that the difference between the varying ethical ends of capital and public responsibility that typically distinguish commercial from public broadcasting is less clear in practice. One producer at NHK told me that Japanese audiences *require* the sentimental narrative styles and overt narration that has come to characterize NHK documentary production: "It is what Japanese audiences are used to," he explained. His comment expresses a theory of emotion sensitive to cultural differences, if overly objectified. Here the producer and anthropologist share similar styles of theorizing emotion. In our mutual considerations of the operation of sentiment among Japanese audiences, we similarly take into consideration the variety of patterns the body learns over a period of time that are dependent upon cultural scripts of what it means to be an ethical, caring, or productive member of society in Japan—values that as an anthropologist I am interested in articulating, and as a public broadcaster he is obliged to communicate. Where I might question NHK's explicit and, from my perspective, rather heavy-handed appeals to emotion, for producers they constitute a communicative necessity rooted in repeated forms of learned communication styles in Japanese culture—what Suzuki (2006) calls forms of "emotive communication." For the producer of *Futari no toki*, such sentimental narrations are ethical not in spite of their emotional evocations but precisely because of them. In contrast to traditional theorizations of the public sphere in much of Western scholarship, highly emotional responses serve as a confirmation of ethical and public legitimacy in Japan. For a producer or director to diverge too far from these forms—for example, in following certain "rational argumentative" patterns exemplified by the BBC, with which producers are very familiar—would be an insensitive and irresponsible response to the needs of the Japanese public as producers imagine them.

Emotion and public responsibility become mutually constitutive in feedback loops of Japanese production culture: as NHK experts imagine the emotional needs of their audience, constructing narrative devices to communicate both affectively and effectively, audience members cultivate the capacity to be more or less affected, communicating that information back to producers in various communication technologies such as viewer comments, surveys and, most importantly, ratings.

These highly affective sentimental scripts in Japanese public broadcasting, however, do not go uncontested. More than a few Japanese viewers of NHK whom I interviewed commented on what they see as narratives that "push" (*oshitsukeru*) one narrow understanding over another and employ emotion, unfairly, to do so. The recognition that subjects' bodies are susceptible to affect even when their minds are not—an informal theory of the difference between affect and emotion resembling Massumi's—makes this objection to melodramatic narration possible. Critics who oppose NHK's sentimentalism do so precisely because they have recognized the ability to be affected despite a desire to be. As any reflective viewer might admit, one can be easily surprised or even confused at one's tears as affect bubbles up to catch the consciousness off guard. For these critics, such emotional narrations are unethical and unbefitting of a public broadcaster. However, as such stylizations are tied to the culture of TV production more generally and sustained in the daily practices of large, bureaucratic apparatuses like NHK, producers cannot so easily reform them. Moreover, rarely is television problematized in this way and made public enough to stimulate debate. Such a complicated relationship between ethical positions, institutions and power reveals the uneven terrain of the public sphere and the need from the perspective of public broadcasters for well-crafted, popular narratives to bring issues to public attention.

Conclusions on public sphere theory, media and method

Before Habermas articulated his structural and communicative theory of the public sphere as a space of emancipatory potential in which the rational, free and democratic exchange of ideas could take place independent of the authority of the state, John Dewey in 1927 developed a different definition of the public—simply put, as that community which organizes around specific problems. Such problems, says Dewey, are indivisible from the forms of their communication. Resonating with current distinctions between affect and emotion among affect theorists today, Dewey suggests that a public cannot emerge unless "indirect consequences" (Dewey 1991: 131) can be consciously perceived rather than simply felt. He explains, "At present, many consequences are felt rather than perceived; they are suffered, but they cannot be said to be known" (ibid.: 131). In other words, a public comes into being—thereby distinguishing itself from those agents of political manipulation that threaten it—when it becomes self-conscious of itself through the perception of indirect consequences, or what Bruno Latour (2005: 19) would later identify as "matters of concern." The formalization of indirect consequences in "presentation" serves as an indispensable part of this process of realization, and presentation, says Dewey, is always a matter of art:

> The function of art has always been to break through the crust of conventionalized and routine consciousness. Common things, a flower, a gleam of moonlight, the song of a bird, not things rare and remote, are means with which the deeper levels of life are touched so that they spring up as desire and thought. This process is art … Artists have always been the real purveyors of news, for it is not the outward happening in itself which is new, but the kindling by it of emotion, perception and appreciation.
>
> (Dewey 1991: 184)

Dewey's theorization of the public sphere, of its potential to realize itself, places it squarely within the domain of media production. Media and its artists—the "real purveyors of news"—are the ones who present those narratives and other aesthetic forms on which the public depends to think, feel and actualize problems. This actualization may take the shape, in one instance, of matters of personal identity upon which we choose to work in various technologies of self-fashioning, or, in another instance, of political contests for the procurement of individual rights, protection, or collective entitlements. Media is double-edged: for better or worse, the public's potential to realize itself is left largely in the media's hands, a fact that in the eyes of many public broadcasters and their supporters reaffirms their indispensability for modern democracies.

Although Dewey might be surprised at the degree to which private media has inundated our daily lives in the contemporary, the possibility was never beyond his purview. In fact, as one of the thinkers observing the media's increasing role in public issues during the 1920s, he predicted the relevance and responsibility it would bear in the future. Today, in what in a rather liberal interpretation of history (Schudson 2008) we call a "debate," we juxtapose Dewey with journalist and public intellectual Walter Lippmann in articulating precisely this problem of the relationship between media and the public (Marres 2005).[11] While Dewey and Lippmann indeed differed in their assessments of what mechanisms would be most conducive to the responsible engendering of the public sphere, they both agreed that the present state of the media harmed rather than served its constituents. Whether or not Dewey would approve of the emotional form through which NHK narrates problems for its audience today, his theory of the public sphere proves effective for anthropologists interested in empirically locating and identifying its local patterns of emergence. Mobilizing his theory methodologically would require shifting from a realist to an instrumentalist view, asking not how well structures of communication and debate resemble an idealized model of a rational public sphere, but rather, asking how well particular media represent the interests and feelings of those invested in local problems.

From Dewey's perspective, the role of public media professionals like Takada-san and Miyata-san as artistic purveyors of news is to narrate matters of common concern—to turn social consequences into public problems through artistic stylizations. When I questioned Takada-san about NHK's public responsibility, he responded, "It is NHK's mission to contribute to society. It is a virtue to be able to use such programs as this one [*Futari no toki*] to increase public understanding of issues such as early-onset Alzheimer's." For Takada-san, the public showing of *Futari no toki* demonstrates the successful contribution of NHK to public education. Although Takada-san would judge the kind of education to which NHK contributes as one of building public awareness, observers can see how such a program does much more than that: it also confirms and secures a particular connection between emotion and ethics. That NHK programs often elicit tears suggests that affects play a fundamental role in this process, highlighting the need to further develop critical theories and methodologies for an anthropology of affect.

Notes

1 Lawrence Grossberg 1992, 2005; Michael Hardt and Antonio Negri 2000, 2004, 2009; Lauren Berlant 2000, 2011; Rei Terada 2001; Philip Fisher 2002; Eve Sedgwick 2002; Sara Ahmed 2004; Theresa Brennan 2004; Manuel De Landa 2006; Patricia Clough 2007; Kathleen Stewart 2007; Melissa Gregg and Gregory Seigworth 2010.
2 See in particular the anthropological and sociological work on emotion by Levy 1973; Rosaldo 1980; Hochschild 1983; Lutz 1988; Lutz and Abu-Lughod 1990; Schieffelin 1990; and Katz 2001.
3 One segment tells the story of a girl, the captain of her team, who injured her leg during one practice and recovered only a few weeks prior to the event—just in time, needless to say, to provide the anticipated, emotionally dramatic resolution to the story.
4 Also see Andrew Painter's (1994) work on representations of adolescence (*seishun*).
5 See NTV's "Genius Shimura Zoo" (*Tensai! Shimura dōbutsuen*), broadcast since 2004.
6 The rigidity of mainstream ethics performed in both this program and *Nippon Hōsō Kyōkai*'s (NHK) documentary, discussed later, contributes to the often-observed homogeneity of Japanese media representations. Although beyond the scope of this chapter, it is important to draw attention to the power imbalances such representations engender as they at once enable and marginalize what Michael Warner (2005) has called "counterpublics"—social groupings formed in large part around their difference to and exclusion from mainstream moral virtues (see also Fraser 1992; and Xing 2012).
7 The sense of privacy in this case is visually constructed through a variety of different cinematographic techniques, such as showing doorframes in the picture to create a conceptual border between the camera's public space and Sumiko's "private" space.
8 One director with whom I spoke majored in modern Japanese literature. He joked that one day he was writing a thesis on Dazai Osamu and the next day he was directing documentaries.
9 NHK has roughly 10,500 employees, well over three times the number of employees for any of Japan's commercial broadcasters: www.nhk.or.jp/faq-corner/01nhk/05/01-05-05.htm (accessed on September 10, 2013).

10 Although these ideas were directly expressed by the NHK producer of *Futari no toki*, I hesitate to push such a potentially essentialist dichotomy between British and Japanese theories of documentary narration too far. The objectification and exaggeration of cultural differences is a common conversation topic between Japanese and their perceived ethnic others, like myself. However, the producer's distinction does point to an alternative ethos of documentary production that becomes institutionalized in NHK's production practices. For more on NHK production practices see Krauss (2000). For a more nuanced, first-hand account of British public broadcasting practices, see Georgina Born (2004), or for an Australian example, Ang *et al.* (2008).

11 I thank Christopher Kelty for drawing my attention to Schudson's critique.

References

Ahmed, Sara. 2004. *The Cultural Politics of Emotion*. Edinburgh: Edinburgh University Press.

Allison, Anne. 2006. *Millennial Monsters: Japanese Toys and the Global Imagination*. Berkeley: University of California Press.

Ang, Ien, Hawkins, Gay and Dabboussy, Lamia. 2008. *The SBS Story: The Challenge of Cultural Diversity*. New South Wales: UNSW Press.

Berlant, Lauren. 2000. *Intimacy: A Critical Inquiry Book*. Chicago, IL: University of Chicago Press.

——2011. *Cruel Optimism*. Durham, NC: Duke University Press.

Born, Georgina. 2004. *Uncertain Vision: Birt, Dyke and the Reinvention of the BBC*. London: Secker & Warburg.

Brennan, Teresa. 2004. *The Transmission of Affect*. Ithaca, NY: Cornell University Press.

Brooks, Peter. 1976. *The Melodramatic Imagination: Balzac, Henry James, Melodrama, and the Mode of Excess*. New Haven, CT: Yale University Press.

Caldwell, John Thornton. 2008. *Production Culture: Industrial Reflexivity and Critical Practice in Film and Television*. Durham, NC: Duke University Press.

Clough, Patricia, with Jean Halley. 2007. *The Affective Turn: Theorizing the Social*. Durham, NC: Duke University Press.

Condry, Ian. 2006. *Hip-Hop Japan: Rap and the Paths of Cultural Globalization*. Durham, NC: Duke University Press.

——2013. *The Soul of Anime. Collaborative Creativity and Japan's Media Success Story*. Durham, NC: Duke University Press.

De Landa, Manuel. 2006. *A New Philosophy of Society: Assemblage Theory and Social Complexity*. New York: Continuum.

Dewey, John. 1991. *The Public and its Problems*. Athens, OH: Swallow Press.

Fisher, Philip. 2002. *The Vehement Passions*. Princeton, NJ: Princeton University Press.

Fraser, Nancy. 1992. "Rethinking the Public Sphere: A Contribution to the Critique of Actually Existing Democracy." In Craig Calhoun (ed.), *Habermas and the Public Sphere*, 109–42. Cambridge, MA: MIT Press.

Gregg, Melissa and Seigworth, Gregory J., eds. 2010. *The Affect Theory Reader*. Durham, NC: Duke University Press.

Grossberg, Lawrence. 1992. *We Gotta Get Out of this Place: Popular Conservatism and Postmodern Culture*. New York: Routledge.

——2005. *Caught in the Crossfire: Kids, Politics, and America's Future*. Boulder, CO: Paradigm Publishers.

Habermas, Jürgen. 1989. *The Structural Transformation of the Public Sphere: An Inquiry into a Category of Bourgeois Society.* Cambridge, MA: MIT Press.
Hanada Tatsuro. 1997. "Can There Be a Public Sphere in Japan?" *Review of Media, Information and Society* 2: 1–23.
Hardt, Michael and Negri, Antonio. 2000. *Empire.* Cambridge, MA: Harvard University Press.
——2004. *Multitude: War and Democracy in the Age of Empire.* New York: The Penguin Press.
——2009. *Commonwealth.* Cambridge, MA: Belknap Press of Harvard University Press.
Hayashi, Kaori. 2006. "Reflections on Japan's Public Sphere and Journalism from a Historical Perspective." *Review of Media, Information and Society* 4: 89–114.
Hochschild, Arlie Russell. 1983. *The Managed Heart: Commercialization of Human Feeling.* Berkeley: University of California Press.
Iwabuchi, Kōichi. 2002. *Recentering Globalization: Popular Culture and Japanese Transnationalism.* Durham, NC: Duke University Press.
——2004. "Feeling Glocal: Japan in the Global Format Television Business." In Albert Moran and Michael Keane (eds), *Television Across Asia: Television Industries, Programme Formats and Globalisation.* Oxford: Routledge, 21–35.
James, William. 1884. "What is an Emotion." *Mind* 9(34): 188–205.
Katz, Jack. 2001. *How Emotions Work.* Chicago, IL: Chicago University Press.
Krauss, Ellis S. 2000. *Broadcasting Politics in Japan: NHK and Television News.* Ithaca, NY: Cornell University Press.
Latour, Bruno. 2005. "From Realpolitik to Dingpolitik or How to Make Things Public." In Bruno Latour and Peter Weibel (eds), *Making Things Public: Atmospheres of Democracy.* Cambridge, MA: The MIT Press, 14–43.
Levy, Robert I. 1973. *Tahitians: Mind and Experience in the Society Islands.* Chicago, IL: University of Chicago Press.
Lippmann, Walter. 1993. *The Phantom Public.* Piscataway, NJ: Transaction Publishers.
——1997. *Public Opinion.* New York: Free Press Paperbacks.
Lock, Margaret. 2013. *The Alzheimer Conundrum: Entanglements of Dementia and Aging.* Princeton, NJ: Princeton University Press.
Lukács, Gabriella. 2010. *Scripted Affects, Branded Selves: Television, Subjectivity, and Capitalism in 1990s Japan.* Durham, NC: Duke University Press.
Lutz, Catherine. 1988. *Unnatural Emotions: Everyday Sentiments on a Micronesian Atoll & their Challenge to Western Theory.* Chicago, IL: University of Chicago Press.
Lutz, Catherine and Abu-Lughod, Lila. 1990. *Language and the Politics of Emotion: Studies in Emotion and Social Interaction.* Cambridge: Cambridge University Press.
Madsen, Richard. 1993. "The Public Sphere, Civil Society, and Moral Community: A Research Agenda for Contemporary Chinese Studies." *Modern China* 19(2): 183–98.
Marcus, George E., Neuman, W. Russell and MacKuen, Michael. 2000. *Affective Intelligence and Political Judgment.* Chicago, IL: University of Chicago Press.
Marres, Noortje. 2005. "Issues Spark a Public into Being: A Key but Often Forgotten Point of the Lippmann-Dewey Debate." In Bruno Latour and Peter Weibel (eds), *Making Things Public: Atmospheres of Democracy.* Cambridge, MA: The MIT Press, 208–17.
Massumi, Brian. 1992. *A User's Guide to Capitalism and Schizophrenia: Deviations from Deleuze and Guattari.* Cambridge, MA: The MIT Press.
——2002. *Parables for the Virtual: Movement, Affect, Sensation.* Durham, NC: Duke University Press.

Nakamura, Karen. 2013. *A Disability of the Soul: An Ethnography of Schizophrenia and Mental Illness in Contemporary Japan*. Ithaca, NY: Cornell University Press.
Ngai, Sianne. 2005. *Ugly Feelings*. Cambridge, MA: Harvard University Press.
NHK. 2005. "Futari no toki o kokoro ni kizamu" (Etching our Time into the Heart). *Ningen Document*. March 4.
NTV. n.d. "Tensai! Shimura dōbutsuen" (Genius! Shimura's Zoo). www.ntv.co.jp/zoo (accessed March 5, 2010).
Ohnuki-Tierney, Emiko. 1984. *Illness and Culture in Contemporary Japan: An Anthropological View*. Cambridge: Cambridge University Press.
Ong, Aihwa and Collier, Steven. 2005. *Global Assemblages: Technology, Politics, and Ethics as Anthropological Problems*. Malden, MA: Blackwell Publishing.
Painter, Andrew A. 1994. "On the Anthropology of Television: A Perspective from Japan." *Visual Anthropology Review* 10(1): 70–84.
Pantti, Mervi and van Zoonen, Liesbet. 2006. "Do Crying Citizens Make Good Citizens?" *Social Semiotics* 16(2): 205–24.
Rabinow, Paul. 2003. *Anthropos Today: Reflections on Modern Equipment*. Princeton, NJ: Princeton University Press.
Richards, Barry. 2004. "The Emotional Deficit in Political Communication." *Political Communication* 21(3): 339–52.
Rosaldo, Michelle Zimbalist. 1980. *Knowledge and Passion: Ilongot Notions of Self and Social Life*. Cambridge: Cambridge University Press.
Schieffelin, Bambi B. 1990. *The Give and Take of Everyday Life: Language Socialization of Kaluli Children*. Cambridge: Cambridge University Press.
Schlesinger, Philip. 1997. "From Cultural Defence to Political Culture: Media, Politics and Collective Identity in the European Union." *Media, Culture and Society* 19(3): 369–91.
——1999. "Changing Spaces of Political Communication: The Case of the European Union." *Political Communication* 16(3): 263–79.
Schudson, Michael. 2008. "The 'Lippmann-Dewey Debate' and the Invention of Walter Lippmann as an Anti-Democrat." *International Journal of Communication* 2: 1–20.
Sedgwick, Eve Kosofsky. 2002. *Touching Feeling: Affect, Pedagogy, Performativity*. Durham, NC: Duke University Press.
Stewart, Kathleen. 2007. *Ordinary Affects*. Durham, NC: Duke University Press.
Suzuki Satoko, ed. 2006. *Emotive Communication in Japanese*. Philadelphia, PA: John Benjamins Publishing Co.
Terada, Rei. 2001. *Feeling in Theory: Emotion After the "Death of the Subject"*. Cambridge, MA: Harvard University Press.
Traphagan, John. 2000. *Taming Oblivion: Aging Bodies and the Fear of Senility in Japan*. New York: State University of New York Press.
TV Asahi. 2008. "Shōgakusei kurasu taikō—sanjūnin sanjūikkyaku" (Elementary School Class Battle: Thirty People, Thirty-one Legs). December 6.
Warner, Michael. 2005. *Publics and Counterpublics*. Cambridge: Zone Books.
Xing, Guoxin. 2012. "Online Activism and Counter-Public Spheres: A Case Study of Migrant Labour Resistance." *Javnost-the Public* 19(2): 63–82.
Yang, Mayfair Mei-Hui. 1999. *Spaces of their Own: Women's Public Sphere in Transnational China*. Minneapolis: University of Minnesota Press.
Yano, Christine. 2002. *Tears of Longing: Nostalgia and the Nation in Japanese Popular Song*. Cambridge, MA: Harvard University Asia Center.
——2013. *Pink Globalization: Hello Kitty's Trek Across the Pacific*. Durham, NC: Duke University Press.

6 Melodrama for change

Gender, *kuqing xi* and the affective articulation of Chinese TV drama

Shuyu Kong

In the last three decades, the TV serial drama (*dianshi lianxuju*) has developed into one of the most popular narrative forms in Mainland China and has spawned a huge cultural industry. According to industry statistics, by 2002 there were over seven hundred television production companies in China with over 200 million yuan invested in producing 10,381 annual episodes of television drama. Some 70 percent of commercial revenues for television stations came from advertising slots broadcast during television dramas (Shanghai TV Festival and CVSC Sofres Media 2004: 20, 25). Chinese television drama has also gained pre-eminence in terms of TV programming and television audiences. Often first shown at prime time and subsequently repeated in the late evening and daytime, popular TV dramas maintain average viewing figures of over 100 million people, with the average Chinese person spending over 50 minutes per day watching them (Shanghai TV Festival and CVSC Sofres Media 2004: 35). TV drama has outgrown film and literature to become the principal form of storytelling in contemporary China, exerting a profound influence in shaping the social imagination and in mediating the contemporary experience of social change.

The last three decades also marked an historic transition in China from a planned socialist to a market economy. Accompanying this rapid economic growth, urbanization and technological revolution, serious social problems, emotional conflicts and contentious moral debates have emerged in Chinese society. Like soap operas and telenovelas in other countries, the meanings and significance of Chinese TV drama are generated against the backdrop of this social process of modernization, and its formal conventions and discursive nature as a cultural forum have been determined by various evolving formative forces. On the one hand, the Party-state still keeps a firm grip on this popular media form through various control mechanisms, from content censorship to broadcasting regulations, and TV drama, like Chinese mass media as a whole, still maintains its role as a vehicle for the party-state to disseminate its official line and new policies (cf. Zhao 2008; Bai 2005). Yet on the other hand, with the Chinese media industry undergoing rapid commercialization, restructuring and market competition, television has become increasingly attuned to the demands of its mass audience and preoccupied with the pursuit of higher viewing rates (Bai 2005). Besides satisfying viewers' entertainment needs, television must also seek to address their social concerns and emotional requirements, something that TV drama is especially well suited to do.

To understand fully the complex social functions and operating mechanisms of Chinese TV drama, it is important to draw from the recent scholarship on "the affective turn" that has emerged in various disciplines in the humanities and social sciences (cf. Clough 2007; Seigworth and Gregg 2010), especially studies of visual media. This conceptual turn recognizes "the primacy of the affective in image reception" (Massumi 2002: 24), and offers a new way of thinking about the meaning of popular media that goes beyond purely ideological concerns. As Lawrence Grossberg (1992: 85) points out, "The terrain of commercial popular culture is the primary space where affective relationships are articulated; the consumer industries increasingly appeal not only to ideological consensus, but to the contemporary structures of affective needs and investments."

In the case of Chinese TV dramas, this means we need to pay attention to the emotional content as well as the whole social practice of producing and consuming TV drama as an affective "articulation." Here I use articulation as both a theoretical concept and methodological strategy mainly as developed in the works of Grossberg (1992, 1996, 1997), which are themselves built on Stuart Hall's theory of articulation. Utilizing the double meanings of the original word—one being utterance and expression, the other connection and linkage—Stuart and Grossberg's theory of articulation emphasizes the specific agencies of affective individuals in social formations. This concept is thus crucial in understanding how ideological elements "become articulated, in specific conjunctures, to a political subject" (Grossberg 1996: 142), especially through affective investment (Grossberg 1997: 150).

By shifting our critical focus from purely representational and ideological aspects to dimensions that include the expressive and affective aspects of Chinese television drama, this chapter will address the often neglected area of emotional communication and its various expressive forms in contemporary China. In the process, I will provide a more nuanced account of the multi-layered and complex contents, contours and functions of TV drama, a genre which exerts such power over the Chinese popular imagination and has become the most active and productive form of social discourse in contemporary China.

Specifically, I will use recent TV serial dramas about laid-off female workers, in particular, the 2004 drama *Crying Your Heart Out* (*youlei jinqing liu*) as an example of this "affective articulation," to demonstrate the multi-layered discursive space of Chinese TV drama and its ambivalent televisual discourse on economic reforms and the new dominance of capital in Chinese society. The chapter engages close generic analysis of the melodramatic features of the settings, characters and plotlines of selected TV dramas, supplemented by audiences' viewing experiences. I will examine three dimensions: first, the affective dimension and emotional meanings of these dramas; second, the various narrative techniques and audio/visual devices employed to elicit these social emotions; and, finally, the social implications and emotional impact of these melodramatic narratives in the context of the public discourse on retrenchment (*xiagang*), which has been one of the most divisive and painful consequences of China's economic reforms. I argue that the plight and potential salvation of laid-off women, and by extension, of other less privileged social groups, has been used as a powerfully affective form by various social agents with their own agendas. Such agendas include promoting the government's re-employment project, voicing social discontent and emotional distress, and attempting to make sense of the enormous changes taking place in China today.

Before I proceed to detailed discussion of the emotional contents of this TV drama and the various devices employed to elicit these emotions, I will briefly recount the media's rewriting of the unemployment issue into an aspirational story of neoliberalism, since this ideological practice of "masking" and "whitewashing" a huge social scar provides the precise context for the social emotions that I will discuss in the rest of the chapter.

From female laid-off workers to "re-employment stars": women in Chinese media discourse

Since the late 1980s, the increasing number of workers laid off by China's restructured state-owned industrial sector has come to represent the dark side of China's transition from a planned socialist to a free-wheeling capitalist economy. According to official statistics, by the end of 1997 there were 11.51 million laid-off workers in China's cities (of whom 7.87 million were from state-owned enterprises), and 6.8 million (or 59.2 percent) of these were female workers (Wang 2003: 161). These "gendered layoffs" (Wang 2003), in other words, the disproportionate laying off of middle-aged female workers and, more crucially, their subsequent difficulties finding new jobs in a competitive capitalist employment market, have been one of the most controversial consequences of China's economic reforms (see Appleton *et al.* 2002: 252–75). These unemployed women are not only fighting a losing battle in the job market against younger and better-educated generations, due to their age and lack of up-to-date skills, but in many cases have also encountered serious disruption in their family lives. Many have been forced by their circumstances to work on the bottom rungs of the expanding service sector, especially in roles such as domestic workers.

As laid-off workers and their survival turned into "one of the most explosive issues in China and a highly contentious subject ideologically" (Zhao 2002: 121), the party-state thus established a nationwide re-employment program in the mid 1990s, mainly consisting of the establishment of re-employment service centers at state enterprises and attempts to create a re-employment market. The core spirit of this project, however, as Jaeyoun Won (2004) points out, is not so much helping laid-off workers find stable jobs but rather instilling in them the principles of survival in a market economy and advocating "self-reliant" employment. As Won puts it, the government unemployment policy is "a hybrid of socialist and new-market rationalities; an ethic of self-reliance is drawn from the market economy, but the ethical work (thought work) is taken from socialism" (ibid.: 73). In other words, "thought work is being re-deployed to create a new set of social beings for the market economy" (ibid.: 72) by transforming laid-off workers' old thinking and their habitual dependency on the state and work-units for job security. In this "subject reforming" approach to the unemployment issue, the media and related cultural forms had an important role to play, "managing media discourse on this issue [became] the party's top propaganda priority" (Zhao 2002: 121).

Prior to the mid-1990s, the media tended to ignore this problem of "retrenchment" and its impact on laid-off workers and their families. While the official media often explained the official line about the necessity for systemic reform and increased efficiency in state enterprises, rarely could one find any discussion of the human costs of economic reform: the material difficulties and emotional plight of laid-off workers, and their sense of betrayal by the state (Yu 1999).

By the late 1990s, however, media coverage of the retrenchment issue took a different turn: "Official guidelines emphasized the need to acknowledge the problem, to promote non-sensational and constructive reporting, and to supply the media with information about government re-employment efforts" (Zhao 2002: 121). Laid-off workers' stories started to appear in great numbers on television and in the press: while the media interpreted the difficulties of some unemployed workers finding work "as due to 'lack of skills', 'lack of training', and 'lack of flexibility'" (Dai 2002: 228), they also featured other laid-off workers as "re-employment stars" (Yang 2007), people who had managed to turn their lives around and achieve new success in the job market.

For example, in 1996, Chinese Central Television (CCTV) aired a special program called "The Story of Autumn," featuring a former textile worker, Zhuang Hongwei, from Shanghai. After completing a re-employment training program organized by the local government, Zhuang borrowed 30,000 yuan to set up Mother Zhuang's Vegetable Cleaning Service with four other laid-off workers. This eventually expanded into a successful business with over a hundred and forty employees. Zhuang's transformation story and others like it inspired a new model for media accounts of female laid-off workers. National and provincial state-controlled newspapers, radio and television stations poured out heartwarming stories of laid-off workers who had bravely taken unemployment as a new opportunity to realize their dreams of owning their own businesses, and eventually turned themselves into self-reliant employees and even entrepreneurs. In these media stories, laid-off middle-aged women were often featured as heroic protagonists as well as eloquent narrators, creating a positive image of model workers who had adopted the spirit of capitalism (Dai 2002; Yang 2007). They generally focus on triumph and success after an initial period of hardship and suffering. The lesson of these stories is that only self-reliance can survive in the market economy and that economically rational behavior is also morally laudable (Won 2004: 82).

In this way, the discourse of women's re-employment is a new transitional narrative to facilitate China's current socialist transformation (Yang 2007: 78). It has used former laid-off women workers to promote the officially approved concept of economically rational individuals who succeed through their competitive and entrepreneurial spirit, a concept that is diametrically opposed to the old socialist model of worker cooperation and egalitarianism. Through this "re-employment star discourse," the massive failure of socialism is thus transformed into an inspirational story of self-salvation, and painful retrenchment is welcomed as an opportunity for regeneration and new life. Female laid-off workers, far from becoming victims of the dismantling of socialist relations of production and the welfare state, are now seen as the "cultural vanguard of millennial capitalism" (Lee 2006: 515).

While the official media have extolled the stories of laid-off workers turned re-employment stars, the bleak reality is that the "majority of unemployed workers have become desolate and degraded, as probationary part-time workers in the informal service economies or jobless non-workers" (Won 2005: 85).[1] Indeed, there have emerged contesting voices in the popular media, literature and other cultural forms that have given powerful critiques of the social stratification, injustice and moral corruption caused by the "broken socialist promise." As Dai notes, "Realist works are beginning to find ways of addressing the reality of class division" (Dai 2002: 229). For example, one popular rhyming saying (*shunkouliu*) pithily expressed the reality of many laid-off women's experience: "Laid off women, stop your cries! Bravely advance into night clubs and dives. There you can eat, drink and make lots of money. That's the way to break free from relying on the Party!" (see also Link and Zhou 2002). Here the socialist discourse of women's liberation and the Party as the savior of common people are mocked by the predicament of female laid-off workers who become sex workers just to make ends meet.

More serious and sustained criticism of the human price of retrenchment can be found in some realist literary works of the past decade. The novella "Na'er" ("International," 2004), by Cao Zhenglu, is a moving account of the collapse of the state factory system. Cao describes the powerful few making illicit profits from selling off state assets under the cover of economic restructuring, while ordinary workers are completely stripped of their jobs and of the ownership of the factory where they have worked all their lives. The novella gives a bleak depiction of the prospects of this sacrificed social group, especially through the story of one female worker. To support her family, and to pay for the medical costs of her disabled child, this middle aged woman has to sell food at a street stall during the day and sell her body to occasional customers at night. It is the predicament and fallen state of this woman that motivates the hero, a union leader who once loved this woman in her youth, to expose the corruption of the factory leaders, ultimately at the cost of his life. Contrasting sharply with the female heroes of CCTV news reports, in the critical realist tradition of socially engaged literature, a woman and her suffering become an indictment of social injustice as well as a call for political action.

Female laid-off workers and "main melody" drama

Since the late 1990s, female laid-off workers and their stories of survival have become a major subject of many TV dramas. The first drama of this type was *Women Through Winter* (*Zouguo dongtian de nuren*), which was initially shown in 1997. Produced and broadcast by Shanghai Oriental Television Station, this six-episode TV drama was based on the difficulties faced by many Shanghainese in the late 1990s following the closure of large numbers of state-owned textile factories. Most female workers remained unemployed for an extended period due to their poor educational background and age disadvantage. At the same time, this TV drama was also related to the local media's promotion of "the Shanghai experience" (Won 2004: 75), which provided a model for the subsequent nationwide re-employment project, and especially its method of solving the unemployment problem through promoting the domestic service industry.

The female protagonist in this drama, Ah Zhen, who not only loses her job at a textile factory but also loses her husband to an extramarital affair, seems to express a common bitter experience of many textile workers as they have had to shoulder various problems brought about by privatization and economic restructuring. To survive, Ah Zhen tries different odd jobs and endures tremendous difficulties, including an emotional resignation from a Taiwanese clothing factory to protest against its overt exploitation of the workers. Through this process, however, Ah Zhen learns that she can rely on no one but herself. Eventually, she sets up a modest but successful handicraft business with her former boss, a Taiwanese businesswoman, and hires her former co-workers to work for her.

Similar to Mother Zhuang's story on CCTV, *Women Through Winter* set the tone for TV dramas to promote the orthodox version of laid-off workers' struggles as a journey of self-growth and self-reinvention. Since then, the retrenched female worker story has featured in numerous other TV dramas, especially those intended to promote "leitmotif," or main melody, themes as part of the propaganda campaigns. Particularly since 2003, when new guidelines for propaganda work issued under Hu Jintao's leadership emphasized the "three closenesses" (close to reality, close to life and close to the masses) and building a "harmonious society," TV dramas on contemporary life and socially disadvantaged groups became a niche genre. Among the most prominent TV dramas exclusively dealing with retrenchment and re-employment of laid-off women workers were *Crying Your Heart Out* (*Youlei jinqing liu*, 2004), *Women Factory Workers* (*Nugong*, 2007) and *Start All Over Again* (*Congtou zailai*, 2009). If we look purely at the generic formulas of these dramas—their settings, characters and basic plotlines—they all seem to imitate closely the media stories of re-employment stars that we discussed above, and present a story of aspiration with a happy ending.

The 2004 drama *Crying Your Heart Out* clearly illustrates this point: a thirty-something woman, Ma Xiaoshuang, is initially over-dependent and immature, spoiled by her husband's "unconditional" love and her job as a saleswoman in a state-owned grocery store. However, her luck runs out soon after the TV drama starts. First, she loses her job after the city government closes down this unprofitable retail business; then her husband dies in a work-related accident. Despite receiving some help and consolation from former colleagues, from good friends and from her neighbor, Qiu Yiping, who was a co-worker of her late husband, Xiaoshuang is left in a desperate situation. She must try to look after her helpless young daughter and her hostile old mother-in-law with virtually no money. Even the 60,000 yuan in compensation from her husband's death is grabbed by her mother-in-law, on the pretext of keeping it for her granddaughter's future tuition fees. Lacking skills and connections, Xiaoshuang tries many different menial jobs, including waitressing, hourly cleaning for an intellectual family, saleswoman for adult toys and even illegal matchmaking services, for which she is arrested. She finally finds work in a food service business that specializes in lunch takeouts and is owned by her capable sister-in-law Bai Yuping. When Bai decides to leave the business to work in the civil service, Xiaoshuang steps up to buy the business using her 60,000 yuan compensation (over which she has now gained control) plus loans from family and friends. With guidance and encouragement from Bai and a charming businessman, Xu Linfeng, she overcomes fierce competition in the food service industry and the resentment of her former friends and colleagues (now her employees), and not only survives but also expands the business into a thriving chain providing food services for numerous white-collar professionals. During this transformation, Xiaoshuang also grows into a confident and mature businesswoman who finishes continuing her studies at college and finally becomes a truly independent woman and a model for her young daughter to emulate. The final episode sees the self-confident and assured Xiaoshuang telling her daughter, "Now I have grown up!"

Ma Xiaoshuang is not the only female character in these TV dramas who finds her melodramatic salvation through reinventing herself by investing in a service industry. It is a familiar choice for many other characters too. For example, in *Crying Your Heart Out*, Ma's much older girlfriend (and former co-worker), Sister Zhou, ends up managing an old people's home after attending her disabled husband for many years. There, her female virtues of patience and compassion finally find their market value. Likewise, Pu Xiaoti, the heroine in *Women Factory Workers*, who is laid off despite being a model worker in a state machinery factory, also finds a new career helping others by becoming a nanny. With the help of her US-educated daughter, she then builds this into a domestic service company, applying modern methods of business administration. Indeed, there is a whole subgenre of TV dramas on nannies or maids featuring retrenched female workers, including *Professor*

Tian and his Twenty-eight Maids (*Tianjiaoshou jia de ershiba ge baomu*, 2001), *Chinese Maids in Foreign Families* (*Shewai baomu*, 2002), and *Maid* (*Baomu*, 2007).

In these television dramas, the female private entrepreneurs with their domestic service businesses thus seem designed to represent the ideal transformation of former state workers in China's new economic order. While preserving traditional female virtues such as hard work, motherly care, and patience, they combine these virtues with some modern professional training in organizing domestic work, thus developing the "personal quality" (*suzhi*) that is required for women to take up their new positions in contemporary Chinese society. Moreover, because of their successful transformation into "enterprise selves," these female characters are "charged with the responsibility of thought work" (Sun 2008: 98), educating and inspiring others to change their mindsets too. Thus, in *Women Factory Workers*, Pu Xiaoti with her motherly love shows her daughter that being a nanny is not degrading but an opportunity to help others and at the same time make a successful business out of it. Similarly, in *Professor Tian and his Twenty-eight Maids*, Huijuan's patient guidance and encouragement help Yiwen change her hostile attitude and happily become the "twenty-eighth maid." As Sun Wanning observes, these popular TV dramas "not only articulate an adjusted subject position of national women, they also present a powerful discursive space to educate national subjects and turn them into useful citizens" (Sun 2008: 97). It is in this sense that these TV dramas function as vehicles for remodeling female subjects for the new social order—in other words, as an agent for change.

Yet while the above understanding of the social and ideological function of TV drama is valid up to a point, a closer reading of these TV dramas reveals a deeper level of sense-making that has remained largely unexplored by scholars. This is the emotional experience and affective impact of TV drama in mediating the contemporary experience of change. As I will show in the following, despite the positive message of aspiration and happy endings on the surface of these narratives, there is a prominent theme of suffering and salvation that is expressed in a melodramatic style, and a deep-seated emotional antagonism grounded in popular discontent and resentment constantly finds its expression through the characterization of laid-off female workers as crying subjects.

Women's tears and the affective space of *Crying Your Heart Out*

Crying Your Heart Out was directed by Kang Honglei, a veteran director famous for his many sentimental TV serials, including the hit *Passionate Years* (*Jiqing ranshao de suiyue*, 2001) and *Soldiers' Sortie* (*Shibing tuji*, 2007). *Crying Your Heart Out* received very high ratings (8.4 percent of the viewing audience) when first broadcast on Beijing TV4 in 2004, and it was rerun on various provincial TV stations. Both official critics and ordinary viewers enthusiastically praised it, though for different reasons. Critics and cultural officials held it up as a model of the latest government cultural policy ("close to reality, close to life and close to the masses") and as an inspirational story for those needing to adjust their mindsets to the new economy (Ni 2005; Zhong 2005; Dai 2005). By contrast, many ordinary viewers focused much more on the deep emotions aroused by this serial drama.

According to the scriptwriter, Ni Xueli, when it was still at the approval stage, many ordinary people, including laid-off workers, were invited to the screening by the review committee, and they all wept profusely as they shared the experiences of the heroine Ma Xiaoshuang (Ni 2005). This account is corroborated by a survey of posts on the sites of online fan clubs.[2] The predominant reason they give for the drama's popularity is that "it gives me a good cry." Some claimed that they watched the drama while crying into paper tissues all the way through, especially when hearing the theme song; that their weeping helped them release the tensions, frustrations or sadness in their own lives. Many viewers were equally moved despite not having experienced unemployment themselves. The drama seemed to resonate with these viewers' own job situations, their family lives, and their general outlook on life and survival in contemporary China. Many viewers in their posts make themselves the subject of their own life stories in a melodramatic way fashioned by *Crying Your Heart Out*. For example, one "netizen" (internet citizen) related Xiaoshuang's struggles to her own difficult experience of helping her old-aged parents to find medical services in Beijing, including dealing with the high cost of medical treatments, finding personal connections to get them into a decent hospital, and even just finding a place to live for herself. Clearly, for these people, watching this TV drama is much more a form of catharsis or emotional release or involvement than an inspiring educational or ideological learning exercise.

Though a quantitative survey would be required for a more nuanced audience analysis, something that is beyond the scope of this chapter, it is not difficult to see that, based on observed audience responses, there is a "sentimental" or emotional dimension to Chinese television drama in mediating the social experience of change. In particular, we see the constructing and performing of "*ku*" (crying or weeping) through a highly melodramatic form, which is in turn transmitted to the audience (Wu and Wang 2008: 427).

A quick illustration of this performativity of emotion can be found in the title sequence of *Crying Your Heart Out*. In less than two minutes of the title sequence, shots of highlights from different episodes display the emotional facial expressions of different characters, many of them weeping or crying, with close-up shots of the main character Xiaoshuang's weeping face from several different angles leading the sequence. This visual treatment of emotion is further strengthened by the theme music, a haunting melody with the following lyrics:

> Because you are still with me, Seeing everything that I see:
> But it's too late to be happy, because it's just a past memory.

Because you are still with me, Sighing whenever I sigh:
But there's no time to be heartbroken, because the dawn lights up the sky.
Only in my dreams can my tears fully flow,
No need to hide them as they fall onto your clothes,
That is the most beautiful cry I've had in my whole life.
How much happiness is in my heart? If I try to express it, I cannot make it clear,
But your strong support gives me the strength to go on here …
Because you are still with me: In my dreams I can embrace you,
And I know that I still live within your heart too …

Sung by Sandy Lam (Lin Yilian), a Cantopop singer famous for expressing the loss, sorrow and self-pity that women experience in their romantic lives and marriages, the melancholy tune and lyrics, which are supposed to be the heroine's ode to her dead husband, convey a "sentimental longing" and "pathos of the age" common to many songs composed for Chinese TV dramas (Zhong 2010: 144): broken dreams, lost love, anxiety about the uncertain future and a "yearning" for genuine care and lasting relationships. This theme song, repeated at the start of every episode and frequently replayed at moments of extreme emotion, functions as an affective marker throughout the serial. It powerfully conveys the melancholic tone and unsettled mood that run through the whole twenty-one episodes of the drama, and establishes an affective space where sentimental engagements between the viewers and the characters come into play.

To demonstrate further how such television dramas communicate social moods and feelings against the backdrop of social changes, I will examine the melodramatic treatment of female laid-off workers in *Crying Your Heart Out* and the emotional content of this drama in more detail through analysis of its narrative form and audio/visual language.

Melodrama in literature, film and TV shows often uses aesthetic techniques and characteristics such as exaggerated plots and characters to appeal to the emotions of audiences. Through the emotional pathos that it creates, melodrama also frequently explores psychological and sexual repression as a way of "responding to a time of historical transition and social crisis" (Pickowicz 1993: 320). This melodramatic narrative mode is manifested in *Crying Your Heart Out* through its narrative situation and characterization, as well as through its acting and visual style.

To start with, *Crying Your Heart Out* quickly sets up a melodramatic context through a series of traumatic incidents in the first five episodes: a situation of loss, of mourning, and of pain. We see the naive and apparently incapable Xiaoshuang unexpectedly hit by unemployment, and while she is still trying to recover from the shock, a further crushing blow comes with her husband's sudden death in an accident. Here, personal loss is unambiguously entangled with the collective experience of retrenchment or social change. The emotional tension and psychological stress continue to accumulate in the following episodes when this single mother has to deal with various difficult situations in her struggle to survive: the physical exhaustion of begging for work and being constantly humiliated; the everyday chaos of looking after her young daughter and difficult mother-in-law, punctuated by conflicts with her sisters-in-law; especially the mental challenges of her changing identity from a "paid laborer" to a "ruthless boss" when moving upward in a world dominated by capital and competition.

In this TV drama, Ma Xiaoshuang's misfortunes, suffering and emotional upheaval are by no means isolated examples, but are echoed in the lives of almost all the women characters in this drama, especially those of her three former colleagues who all endured terrible difficulties of their own. The collapse of domestic order and the breakdown of intimate relationships seem to be the common experiences of these women and frequently lead to the characters' emotional outbursts throughout the serial.

This emotional mobilization is also manifested in the audio or visual language of the drama. Director Kang Honglei employs many stylistic devices to elicit emotions, and to ensure an emotional connection between the audience and characters in the drama, in particular through edited "scenes of empathy." One such scene frequently mentioned by fans depicts the morning after Xiaoshuang's husband dies. Xiaoshuang, while brushing her teeth in front of the mirror, recalls that just a couple of days earlier the two of them were teasing each other and playing together, a flashback shot cuts in to indicate the mental state of Xiaoshuang back then, and then it cuts to a lengthy close-up shot of Xiaoshuang's weeping face reflected in the mirror.

Such subjective shots that deliberately set up the performativity of emotion occur frequently in the drama. Another "scene of empathy," where we see a whole group sobbing and crying at length, is the closure of the state-owned grocery store, which is extensively played out throughout episode four. First we see the administrator coldly announcing that the store is shutting; then under the anxious gaze of the staff, a truck arrives to take away the inventory in the store. With emotional theme music playing in the background, we see a series of shots of the four main female characters trying in vain to stop the truck drivers, their twisted faces shouting and crying, and then their bodies lying on the ground in front of the truck's wheels, all displayed lyrically in slow motion. The expressive technique of slow motion and the melodramatic tour de force of weeping lasts over three minutes, and conveys a sense of the catastrophe and trauma as experienced by these women.

Thus despite their intended propaganda function and ideological closure, TV dramas on laid-off women present a "tragic structure of feeling" (Ang 1985), which emerges from the melodramatic situation and emotional displays by the characters, whose constant crying and weeping (*ku*) evoke an emotional experience and overall mood of extensive mourning and sadness induced by their present uncertainty, anxiety, hardship and suffering. Such symptomatic crying thus not only constitutes the core experience of the characters, but also functions as a major channel for the audience's emotional identification with the characters.

The content of this "crying" includes many emotional elements: besides mourning the loss of loved ones and of the reassuring security of a past life, it also contains fear and anxiety as these women characters face being laid off and must deal with unbearable pressure. Furthermore, there is also anger and resentment arising from the growing social injustice and class divisions in society, as well as tension and confusion about the changing values resulting from the social transition from an egalitarian socialism to survival-of-the-fittest capitalism.

This last point is illustrated clearly in episode six, which depicts the four women wandering through the bustling streets desperately looking for jobs. Through their eyes, we see the increasing social inequality, extreme consumerism and snobbery (when Xiaoshuang looks for work in a luxurious boutique and is intimidated by the shop assistants); we also see moral corruption and abuse of power (when Sister Zhou is beaten and fired from her janitor position for reporting a prostitute, and when the director of one government office takes a bribe from Tian Lichun but refuses to give her a job). When finally these still unemployed women sit in a crowded restaurant, using their last cents to buy beer and release their frustration, they comment on how they used to be young and desirable, but are now abandoned by both their husbands and society, and they wonder out loud "how are we going to survive the change?" The scene ends with the half-drunk Sister Zhou making an ironic and daring toast: "We have just achieved two things: one is anti-corruption, the other is sweeping away immorality. These are supposed to be the government's responsibility, but it is we retrenched workers who did it for them!" The bitter emotions voiced by laid-off female workers, be it sorrow, pain, resentment or anger, arise out of a sense of powerlessness among the characters, and reveal a frustration of a more lasting kind. They are direct emotional expressions of their strong judgment about unfairness and injustice, which are also closely bound up with the lived experiences of Chinese mass audiences, who themselves must deal with corrupt government officials, social degeneration, and an increasing gap between the haves and have nots.

Crying Your Heart Out also depicts the moral conflicts and changes in human relationships that result from economic reform, and cause tension, frustration and confusion, especially among friends, family members and other intimate relationships. This is particularly manifested in the conflict between Xiaoshuang's aspirations for upward mobility and her attempt to maintain her prior relationships with her "sisters" (her former work colleagues). At first, the members of this sisterhood are bound together by their common experiences and past, and the group serves as an emotional shelter for Xiaoshuang. They stand beside her as she deals with the pain of losing her husband, and they come to her when she needs help to cope with her many daily struggles. However, later we see this relationship endure severe trials when Xiaoshuang acquires the food service business from Bai, and her "sisters" now become her "employees." Misunderstandings, jealousy and even resentment develop among them, and they frequently run into conflicts due to their differing economic interests and changing social status. One of the telling dramatic scenes is in episode twenty, when Xiaoshuang tries to discuss the profits that the business is making with her former close friends (now employees) and encounters coldness and ridicule. After this awkward episode, her three friends decide to leave the business, and Xiaoshuang, while moving on with her new life, somehow feels a deep loneliness and deplores the loss of intimacy and friendship.

Similarly, Xiaoshuang's romantic relationships with two male characters, Qiu Yiping and Xu Linfeng, are also permeated with complex ethical judgments and closely related with her mobility. Qiu is the conventional "kind" guy: he is a co-worker and close friend of Xiaoshuang's ex-husband and quietly helps Xiaoshuang with household chores after Chen dies. He is patient, considerate, hardworking, and has secretly loved Xiaoshuang for years. Yet his conservative attitudes, mediocrity and even his thrifty habits mean that he is inadequately qualified with the kind of masculinity that Xiaoshuang is seeking. Instead, Xiaoshuang, while acting as matchmaker for Qiu with her "sister" Zhou, who is much older and less qualified for upward mobility, develops feelings for Xu, a capable and successful businessman who is not easily committed but does provide useful financial aid and management tips to Xiaoshuang to assist with her newly acquired business. Like many other melodramas, Xiaoshuang's situation and final choice represent a moral dilemma inextricably related to her potential mobility in the process of social stratification.

Kuqing xi and the ambivalent televisual discourse of change

From a generic perspective, these TV dramas about laid-off women also share many thematic and stylistic characteristics, especially in terms of their *ku* (crying) as a central emotional marker, with *Kuqing xi*, "dramas of bitter emotion," a subgenre of family melodrama which has recently seen a revival in popularity on Chinese TV screens. These dramas often focus on the everyday struggles of urban poor, laid-off workers, retirees, maids and rural migrant workers. Dwelling on the hardships and emotional turbulence of their everyday lives—financial difficulties, inadequate housing, psychological problems and physical illnesses, aged parents and strained family relationships—these dramas present a world of victims and losers buffeted by dramatic social changes. They are punctuated by an incessant series of unfortunate events, illnesses and deaths, and their characters are suffused with the feeling of being abandoned by their times. Some commentators have summarized this subgenre as "three brokennesses and one suffering" (broken families, broken feelings, broken marriages, and suffering at home).[3]

The direct generic influence of *Kuqing xi* is Taiwan in the 1980s and early 1990s. Taiwanese TV dramas and films such as *The Stars Understand My Heart* (*Xingxing zhi woxin*) and *Love Me Again, Mom* (*Mama, zai ai wo yici*) often present a moral dilemma through the form of family melodrama and traditional themes of filial piety and compassion. These works not only offered Mainland Chinese TV drama producers a practical model to work with—the famous

Yearning (*Kewang*, 1990) is a direct result of such influence (Zha 1995)—but also coached popular media producers on how to "reconstruct the victimized voice/self/nation of *ku*" (Wu and Wang 2008: 425) in a post-1989 Chinese society. In the last two decades, more and more *Kuqing xi* with local and contemporary relevance have dominated Chinese television screens, from *Our Dad and Mom* (*Zanba zanma*, 1996), to *Family Tree* (*Qinqing shu*, 2003), *My Beloved Brothers* (*Qinxiong redi*, 2007), and *My Ugly Mother* (*Wo de chou niang*, 2008).

The popularity of *Kuqing xi* has to do with a longstanding and important melodramatic narrative tradition in Chinese operatic art as well as in earlier Chinese films, where women's suffering and tears are often used as a significant device for social criticism. *Kuqing xi*'s conception of human suffering has to be understood within both the Chinese folklore tradition and the Confucian interpretation of the political implications of *ku*: as Wu and Wang (2008: 416–17) argue, "women's performance of *ku* in expressing condolence offers a primary vehicle to present the struggle between political ideals and emotional frustrations in a patriarchal society."

However, more importantly, as one TV drama producer, Hai Yan, has observed, the proliferation of *Kuqing xi* "speaks to a collective unconscious and social mood that are not addressed in historical costume dramas (the dominant genre of Chinese TV drama)" (Liu 2005). This collective unconsciousness and social mood is exactly the foundation for the kind of affective articulation in which TV drama and its audiences are engaged. Despite their highly melodramatic and occasionally unbelievable plots, viewers do find "melodramatic identification" (Ang 1996) and "emotional realism" in these dramas through their tears. In Ien Ang's words, there is a "close collaboration of the dramatic situation with social reality" (Ang 1985: 46), something that is especially meaningful considering the fact that TV audiences in China "primarily comprise viewers of lower educational levels, females, the upper middle aged and elderly, and the economically less affluent" (Kong 2008: 82). In other words, these are the lower ranks in society and those who have lost out in economic reforms.

As our discussion of *Crying Your Heart Out* suggests, the melodramatic presentation of social and personal experiences of laid-off workers clearly seeks to exaggerate and draw out the emotions of suffering, sorrow, grief and anger to an extreme degree, directly in the tradition of *Kuqing xi*. In this way, it highlights the psychological and emotional plight of laid-off women and reshapes a reality that is much darker and more ambivalent than the typical presentations of cheery and inspirational media reports. Precisely through this kind of "pedestrian form of suffering" (Ang 1985: 78), embodied in individual experiences and everyday life, an emotional antagonism and subtle critique come into play. Such emotional antagonism generates a different conception of social changes from the ideological optimism that characterizes media stories on the same theme.

The affective space and emotional realism that we see in *Crying Your Heart Out* and other such examples of *Kuqing xi* call our attention to the complexity and the polysemic nature of TV drama in contemporary China. In other words, there are "subtle layers of controversial meanings" that lie beneath the apparently harmonious ideological surface, "layers of meanings that are arranged on different levels of explicitness" (Ma 1999: 113) to deal with the differing, sometimes contradictory, demands of their audiences. On the one hand, we see a neoliberal message of inspiration and upward mobility in a new market economy, and a living example of what a changed mindset can do to improve the lives of laid-off women. Yet on the other hand, we also see contentious voices from the victims' point of view, which tend to complicate the ideological messages and open up a subtle critique of heightened social inequality and the new dominance of capital over all other values.

Another social context for the proliferation of *Kuqing xi* is, ironically, the censorship and regulations imposed on the production and broadcasting of TV drama. Chinese TV practitioners must constantly look over their shoulders to avoid the undesirable result of their work being "censored." This is particularly true for those who work on contemporary subjects which are sensitive and have many constraints: the nationwide ban on the popular genre of anti-corruption police dramas in 2004 is just such an example of sudden disruption through censorship. One consequence of this situation has been the proliferation of costume dramas and martial arts films on both TV and cinematic screens, due to their less controversial, non-contemporary settings.

Seen in this light, we can see that family melodrama, which cloaks the contemporary reality of class division and the suffering of working people with the veil of "traditional" ethical and emotional themes relating to the Chinese family (Dai 2002: 229), avoids directly running afoul of the censors, but at the same time mediates the social experiences and fulfils the emotional needs of contemporary viewers in a more subtle way. Working within the affective space opened up by everyday scenes and individual experiences, Chinese TV drama on laid-off women and other *Kuqing xi* refracts the historical forces and social crises that have emerged in a time of transition. The weeping and crying on and off Chinese TV screens is thus both symptomatic of powerful underlying social emotions and at the same time provides a productive means for communicating and sharing those emotions, and we can find its political implications in the following observation: "The last twenty years has witnessed alternatives in the cultural domain of *ku* that represent a growing autonomy of the common people and emphasize a return of emotions and feelings to disperse the political atmosphere, discipline, hierarchy, and homogeneity" (Wu and Wang 2008: 427).

Conclusion

This discussion of the emotional quality and affective dimension of TV dramas about laid-off women workers has identified a polysemic or ambivalent meaning in many of these dramas. The emergence of TV dramas about laid-off women workers clearly had its roots in the state's re-employment project and economic reform discourse, something that is clear from the profusion of reports on laid-off workers that emerged in the official media from the mid-to-late 1990s onwards. TV dramas on this theme produced by the state-controlled TV stations also first appeared at that time—not surprisingly, since the official cultural bureaucracy has long viewed TV drama as one more popular form that must be mobilized to deliver the policy messages of the party-state in an easy-to-swallow format. In fact, many of these dramas have been produced by TV production centers in association with central and local government propaganda departments. Clearly, therefore, their producers intended them to be main melody TV dramas promoting the new official re-employment project.

Yet more often than not, the broadcast versions of these dramas are actually more complex and ambivalent than one would expect from their production context, raising various controversial social issues and presenting a range of voices and emotions, some of which appear to be at variance with the positive official message. As we have shown, the use of melodramatic forms in these TV dramas in mediating social issues and emotions produces emotional meanings far beyond their superficial ideological content. In these TV dramas, just as in some of their cinematic and literary precedents, "the personalization of historical and social forces, the privileged site of the family as the microcosm of historical crisis, the portrayal of a beautiful, piteous woman as the victim of injustice, the clear-cut moral polarization of good and evil, the dramatically inflated scenes and sounds—all these work together to play on the senses and the hearts of the audience and to produce catharsis" (Wang 2004: 144).

While this is not necessarily a subversive function of these TV dramas, at the very least it strongly suggests that for many people in China, being laid off from their jobs, or simply struggling to survive in today's neoliberal world where capital is king, is not a new beginning but an ongoing, painful and heart-wrenching reality. It is in this sense that these TV dramas address the emotional complexities in a post-socialist society like China today, and dramatize the essential conflicts of an historical transition to a new economic order.

Notes

1 According to the *Blue Book of Chinese Society* (2003), the re-employment rate was only 15 percent in 2002.
2 See tieba.baidu.com/f?kw=%D3%D0%C0%E1%BE%A1%C7%E9%C1%F7.
3 Cultural officials have recently decided that the emotions of *Kuqing xi* are disturbing, and such works should be discouraged (Anonymous 2009).

References

Ang, Ien. 1985. *Watching Dallas: Soap Opera and the Melodramatic Imagination*. New York: Methuen & Co.

——1996. "Melodramatic Identifications: Television Fiction and Women's Fantasy." In *Living Room Wars: Rethinking Media Audiences for Postmodern World*. London; New York: Routledge.

Anonymous. 2009. "Guangdianzongju jiang zhaoshou zhendun kuqingxi, fandui sanpoyiku" (SARFT Starts to Rectify TV Dramas of Emotional Hardship, Opposing "Three Brokennesses and One Suffering). *Zhejiang zaixian* (Zhejiang online), May 19. news.163.com/09/0519/06/59LIRNVH0001124J.html (accessed on October 16, 2010).

Appleton, Simon, Knight, John, Song, Lina and Qingjie Xia. 2002. "Labour Retrenchment in China: Determinants and Consequences." *China Economic Review* 13(2/3): 252–75.

Bai, Ruoyun. 2005. "Media Commercialization, Entertainment, and the Party-State: The Political Economy of Contemporary Chinese Television Entertainment Culture." *Global Media Journal* 4(6), American Edition.

Cao Zhenglu. 2004. "Na'er" (International). *Dangdai* (Contemporary) 5.

Clough, Patricia T. 2007. *The Affective Turn: Theorizing the Social*. Durham, NC: Duke University Press.

Dai, Jinhua. 2002. "Invisible Writing: The Politics of Mass Culture in the 1990s." In Jing Wang and Tani E. Barlow (eds), *Cinema and Desire: Feminist Marxism and Cultural Politics in the Work of Dai Jinhua*. London and New York: Verso, 213–34.

Dai, Qing. 2005. "Guojia jubian xia de nuxing jingshen chengzhang" (Women's Spiritual Growth Under the Dramatic Changes Taking Place in China). *Zhongguo dianshi* (Chinese Television) 8.

Grossberg, Lawrence. 1992. *We Gotta Get Out of this Place: Popular Conservatism and Post Modern Culture*. London and New York: Routledge.

——ed. 1996. "On Postmodernism and Articulation: An Interview with Stuart Hall." In David Morley and Kuan-hsing Chen (eds), *Stuart Hall: Critical Dialogues in Cultural Studies*. London and New York: Routledge, 131–50.

——1997. *Dancing in Spite of Myself: Essays on Popular Culture*. Durham, NC: Duke University Press.

Kong, Shuyu. 2008. "Family Matters: Reconstructing the Family on the Chinese TV Screen." In *TV Drama in China*, eds. Ying Zhu, Michael Keane and Ruoyun Bai. Hong Kong: Hong Kong University Press, 75–88.

Lee, Haiyan. 2006. "Nannies for Foreigners: The Enchantment of Chinese Womanhood in the Age of Millenial Capitalism." *Public Culture* 18(3): 507–529.

Link, Perry and Zhou, Kate. 2002. "Shunkouliu: Popular Satirical Sayings and Popular Thought." In Perry Link, Paul G. Pickowicz and Richard P. Madsen (eds), *Popular China: Unofficial Culture in a Globalizing Society*. Lanham, MD: Rowman and Littlefield Publishers, 89–110.

Liu, Wei. 2005. "Cuoai yisheng shoushilu duoguan, kuqing xi zai xian gaofeng" ("A Life of Mistaken Love" Gets Top Spot in Ratings, Another Surge of Interest in Drama of Bitter Emotion). *Xin Jingbao*, July 23.

Ma, Eric Kit-wai. 1999. *Culture, Politics, and Television in Hong Kong*. London and New York: Routledge.

Massumi, Brian. 2002. *The Parables for the Virtual: Movement, Affect, Sensation*. Durham, NC: Duke University Press.

Ni, Xueli. 2005. "Zhenxing dianshiju shizi shandai bianju" (Revitalization of TV Drama Starting from Script Writers). *Xiandai Chuanbo* (Modern Communications) 3: 67–72.

Pickowicz, Paul G. 1993. "Melodramatic Representation and the 'May Fourth' Tradition of Chinese Cinema." In Ellen Widmer and David Der-wei Wang (eds), *From May Fourth to June Fourth*. Cambridge, MA: Harvard University Press, 295–326.

Rofel, Lisa. 1994. "*Yearnings*: Televisual Love and Melodramatic Politics in Contemporary China." *American Ethnologist* 21(4): 700–22.
Seigworth, Gregory J. and Gregg, Melissa, eds. 2010. *The Affect Theory Reader*. Durham, NC: Duke University Press.
Shanghai TV Festival and CVSC Sofres Media. 2004. *Zhongguo dianshiju shichangbaogao* (China TV Drama Report 2003–04). Beijing: Huaxia Publishing House.
Sun, Wanning. 2008. "Maids in the Televisual City: Competing Tales of Post-Socialist Modernity." In Ying Zhu, Michael Keane and Ruoyun Bai (eds), *TV Drama in China*. Hong Kong: Hong Kong University Press, 89–102.
Wang, Ban. 2004. *Illuminations from the Past: Trauma, Memory, and History in Modern China*. Stanford, CA: Stanford University Press.
Wang, Zheng. 2003. "Gender, Employment and Women's Resistance." In Elizabeth J. Perry and Mark Sheldon (eds), *Chinese Society: Change Conflict and Resistance*, 158–82 (2nd edn). London and New York: Routledge.
Won, Jaeyoun. 2004. "Withering Away of the Iron Rice Bowl? The Re-Employment Project of Post-Socialist China." *Studies in Comparative International Development (SCID)* 39(2): 71–93.
Wu, Weihua and Wang Xiying. 2008. "Cultural Performance and Ethnography of Ku in China." *Positions: East Asian Cultural Critiques* 16(2): 409–33.
Yang Jie. 2007. "Reemployment Stars: Language, Gender and Neoliberal Restructuring in China." In Bonnie S. McElhinny (ed.), *Words, Worlds, and Material Girls: Language, Gender, Globalization*, 73–102. Berlin: Mouton De Gruyter.
Yu, Hongmei. 1999. "Zhebi yu kejian: Xinwen he wenxue zhong de xiagang nugong xingxiang fenxi" (Disguise and Exposure: Analysis of the Representation of Laid-off-female Workers in Media Stories and Literature), unpublished conference paper.
Zha, Jiaying. 1995. *China Pop: How Soap Operas, Tabloids, and Bestsellers are Transforming a Culture*. New York: The New Press.
Zhao, Yuezhi. 2002. "The Rich, the Laid-off, and the Criminal in Tabloid Tales: Read All about It." In Perry Link, Paul G. Pickowicz and Richard P. Madsen (eds), *Popular China: Unofficial Culture in a Globalizing Society*, 111–36. Lanham, MD: Rowman and Littlefield Publishers.
——2008. *Communication in China: Political Economy, Power and Conflict*. Lanham, MD: Rowman and Littlefield Publishers.
Zhong, Chengxiang. 2005. "Youlei jinqingliu guanhousuixiang" (Thoughts on *Crying Your Heart Out*). *Zhongguo dianshi* (Chinese Television) 8.
Zhong, Xueping. 2010. *Mainstream Culture Refocused: Television Drama, Society and the Production of Meaning in Reform-era China*. Honolulu: University of Hawaii Press.

Part V

Gender, affective labor and biopolitical economy

7 “Affective foreigners save our elder citizens”

Gender, affective labor and biopolitics in Japan

Ayaka Yoshimizu

A young woman smiles in a newspaper photograph (Figure 7.1). She looks at her hands gently holding the right hand of a Japanese elder; in response to her smile, the elder bows and shyly covers part of her face with her other hand. This photograph, published in the national edition of *Asahi Shimbun* (2009c), accompanies an article with the headline, “Indonesian Candidates for Care Workers Arrive at Fifty-one Nursing Homes Across Japan.” The caption of the photograph proclaims that the woman “greets a resident with a smile.” In all press photographs that capture Indonesian workers interacting with Japanese elders, care workers are smiling and gently touching those elders. These Indonesian care workers become “affective subjects” who bring “love,” “happiness” and “family bond” to nursing homes—now the last resort for Japanese elders. Such representations open up a new discursive space that welcomes foreign workers as saviors of Japan’s “care crisis” and potential preservers of its old family values.

In 2008, to handle the national nursing-home worker shortage in the face of a rapidly aging population, Japan strategically accepted its first group of Indonesian candidates for nurses and care workers under the Japan-Indonesia Economic Partnership Agreement (JIEPA) (see Tsujimoto, Chapter 8, this volume, on the South Korea situation). Upon their arrival in August 2008, these Indonesian candidates took a six-month Japanese-language training program offered either by the Association for Overseas Technical Scholarship (AOTS) or the Japan Foundation. After completing the program, one hundred and one Indonesian care worker candidates began working in fifty-one Japanese nursing homes on January 29, 2009, and one hundred and four nurse candidates did the same at forty-seven nursing homes on February 13, 2009. The Japanese government expects the Indonesians to work at these facilities as assistants for three years (care workers) or four years (nurses) while preparing for the national examination, the successful completion of which will allow them to obtain the formal qualifications necessary for working as care workers or nurses in Japan. Only those who pass the examination may extend their visas.

One cannot ignore the social and political significance of Japan’s deployment of foreign workers in the care labor market. It marks a new phase in the

Figure 7.1 "Ema Yuliana greets a resident with a smile." A photograph taken by Mari Endo at Hodogaya-ku, Yokohama-shi

nation's biopolitics that legitimates the neoliberal restructuring of Japan's welfare state by utilizing its half century-old, neo-colonial relationship with its World War II-era colonies. These recent biopolitical measures rely on existing sexual and racial stereotypes of the ex-colonized and reinforce sexist and racist structures by mobilizing these subordinate bodies. Discursively re-shaped into feminized and affective subjects in the care labor market, foreign workers become affective subjects who provide both physical and emotional labor in caring others without having their own quality of life assured (Foucault 1978: 139).

This chapter focuses on specific media outlets as sites through which discourses of emotions produce, circulate and marginalize such affective subjects. While the representations of Indonesian workers as "lovable" and "happy" show that people radically subvert negative portrayals of non-Western foreign residents in Japan, who are often reported as "criminals," "invaders" or "victims" and the "uneducated poor," they still deserve critical attention. I stress the importance of examining the roles that the discourses of emotions play, because these discourses justify the fixing of them in the marginalized, dead-end and low-paying care labor market by evoking emotions such as happiness and love. This marginalization process occurs simultaneously with the feminization of care labor. Indeed, while one third of the care worker candidates who participated in the AOTS language training were male, most press reports only show female workers in photographs and only represent female workers' voices in quotes.[1] Such gendered representation not only feminizes the entire group of foreign care worker candidates who arrived in Japan in 2009, but also perpetuates the stereotype of care work as women's work. In this chapter, I draw on Sara Ahmed's (2004) notion of "affective economy" and examine dominant representations of Indonesian migrant workers as concrete sites for producing racially and sexually marginal subjectivities.

In this context, I do not sharply distinguish between the terms "affect" and "emotion."[2] I follow Sianne Ngai's position that the difference between the two is a matter of degree:

> affects are *less* formed and structured than emotions, but not lacking form or structure altogether; *less* 'sociolinguistically fixed,' but by no means code-free or meaningless; *less* 'organized in response to our interpretations of situations,' but no means entirely devoid of organization or diagnostic powers.
>
> (Ngai 2005: 27, emphasis in the original)

Ngai's theorization proves useful because it allows us to discuss the "*transitions* from one pole to the other," rather than view them as two "qualitatively" different kinds of phenomena (Ngai 2005: 27, emphasis in the original). In this discussion, emotions refer to feelings of happiness and love, which are discursively more "fixable" forms of migrant workers' affective experiences, circulated by dominant institutions and likely to evoke a sharable state of mind among people. The term of affective subject expresses the process through which migrant care workers become subjects whose bodies and minds are "affected" by discourses of these institutions, including nursing homes, and who have "power to affect" bodies and minds of others (Hardt 2007: ix). In this sense, unlike "emotional labor" in earlier feminist studies, in which emotions circulate between subjects, in the neoliberal economy, affect forms a medium through which people act on others and are acted upon, creating new types of subjects and new relations among those subjects; in other words, subjects circulate within and are formed through affect (Richard and Rudnyckyj 2009). Note that I do not intend to establish a linear causal relationship between the institutional discourse as an affecting subject and the migrant worker as an affected object. On the contrary, these workers are subjects who actively, though not solely, participate in the discursive production of emotions, which may or may not offer a source by which they make sense of their own bodily and cognitive experiences of migration and work at nursing homes. However, questions about how migrant workers feel and articulate these experiences in their terms are beyond this chapter's scope.

With this in mind, I analyze several AOTS publications and one major daily Japanese newspaper, *Asahi Shimbun*, as powerful media outlets that shape public understanding of the foreign candidates. Before examining media representations of Indonesian migrant workers, I first discuss the recent acceptance of migrant workers under bilateral EPAs as one of Japan's neoliberal politico-economic strategies. I examine how the biopolitics around care work involves (re)production of gender and racial hierarchies.

Biopolitics, neoliberalism and affective labor

Michel Foucault described the modern period as "an era of 'biopower'," characterized by "an explosion of numerous and diverse techniques for achieving the subjugation of bodies and the control of populations" (Foucault 1978: 140). Foucault's notion of biopower proves useful because it defines power not in terms of its ability "to kill, but to invest life through and through" (ibid.: 139). What is at stake is not death but the quality of life (Stoler 1995: 83; Anagnost 2004). In such an era, human bodies become central to the state politics; the state apparatus transforms individuals into a collective "species body" whose propagation, births, mortality, level of health, life expectancy and longevity must be scrutinized and controlled. This allows one to consider the nursing home as one of the modern sites where others control and manage the material bodies of elders via the professionalized discipline of care and nursing. Capitalism necessarily links to the biopolitical realm of care. In the modern era, "care of the body becomes an obsessive focus of bourgeois consumption" (Anagnost 2004: 200), while unprivileged bodies become sites of exploitation for (social) production (ibid.: 201).

Two trends characterize Japan's biopolitics of care today: the introduction of the neoliberal framework to control foreign care laborers and the racist restructuring of the care labor market that has been infected by sexism and classism. The JIEPA, established in July 2008, and the Japan-Philippine Economic Partnership Agreement (JPEPA) of September 2007, are Japan's first, official large-scale attempts to accept migrant workers into the care labor market. One can understand this as a strategic politico-economic measure to address the labor shortage while keeping care laborers' wages low. Rather than a human-centered framework to protect migrant laborers' rights and improve their status in Japan, the market-driven neoliberal framework of bilateral EPAs legitimizes the acceptance of Indonesian workers (Yu-Jose 2005: 19). These bilateral, sub-regional EPAs complement the World Trade Organization (WTO) and create a more flexible environment in which the "neoliberal state" of Japan can pursue its economic interests and capital accumulation (Harvey 2005: 7). Along with various types of commodities, both the JIEPA and JPEPA specifically create a category governing the entrance of nurse and care worker "candidates." At the same time, Japan's immigration control continues to regulate the inflow of people, strictly limiting the number of incoming candidates and their length of stay. Few will be able to extend their visas by passing the national examination conducted in Japanese within a specific number of years after their arrival (three years for care workers, four years for nurses). This system, therefore, only allows "elites" to stay longer for their language proficiency, which serves as the measure of their qualifications to adapt to the Japanese culture.

This neoliberal strategy to invite workers from overseas exemplifies a selective adoption of neoliberal forms, which Aihwa Ong (2006) calls "neoliberalism as exception" and "exceptions to neoliberalism." At one level, Japan employs neoliberalism "exceptionally" as part of a biopolitical strategy for the "management of populations and the administration of special spaces" (Ong 2006: 3–4). The new economic agreement responded specifically to the recent "care crisis," requiring workers to manage the increasing numbers of elderly. At another level, the government reserves welfare benefits for Japanese citizens and excludes noncitizens from the benefits of capitalist development, which constitutes an "exception to neoliberalism" (ibid.: 4). The agreements ensure that Japan welcomes newcomers only as care workers or nurses and only as non-citizens, and creates a means separate from immigration, settlement, or development of multicultural communities to allow the workers to live permanently in Japan. Furthermore, this "exception" only applies to a few Southeast Asian developing countries to which Japan maintains a superior political, economic and cultural position. While facilitating migrants' transnational border crossing and increasing their mobility, these exceptions simultaneously and paradoxically preserve the state's power to control their movements by maximizing the flexibility of migrant workers as disposable laborers.

Japan's deployment of migrant workers in the care labor market marks a new phase in the nation's biopolitics in the field of elder care while continuously perpetuating the economically lowered status of care work. In Japan, elder care was traditionally performed by family members, usually daughters-in-law, to fulfill the social ideal of filial piety or to respond to the social pressure to meet such an ideal (Maeda 1983; Lechner and Sasaki 1995). No home care services existed before 1962 (Maeda 1983: 579); even facing the rapidly aging nation in the 1980s, the government promoted keeping "frail elders in the community [and home], not in institutions" (Lechner and Sasaki 1995: 109). Since the late 1970s, however, the number of care services has increased in response to the combination of major demographic shifts: the increase of childless old people, the migration of young people from rural to urban areas, the increase of working women and the decrease of children. These factors have rendered some families incapable of caring for aged parents (Maeda 1983: 579–81). A combination of different social problems both in domestic and institutional realms of elder care, which affect both elders and caregivers, characterize this "care crisis." The most pronounced domestic problems include "care homicide" and elder abuse, while institutional problems include the lowering of care-worker wages due to the privatization of nursing homes and the decrease in the number of Japanese willing to work for lower wages (Yuki 2009: 78).[3] Among all Japanese with official care-worker qualifications, only 57 percent actually work in the capacity of care workers due to the low status and low salary (Ueno and Tateiwa 2009: 39). Although care work is supposedly a skilled profession that requires both practical experience and government certification, most Japanese avoid these positions even during economic recessions.

The low status of care laborers reaches beyond the shores of Japan. Scholars from different disciplines have studied the marginalization of care labor at the global level. For example, Michael Hardt and Antonio Negri identify care labor as a type of "affective labor," that is, "labor that produces or manipulates affects such as a feeling of ease, well-being, satisfaction, excitement, or passion" (Hardt and Negri 2004: 108). They define affective labor as immaterial labor that creates "immaterial products, such as knowledge, information, communication, a relationship, or an emotional response" (ibid.). One characteristic of these productive activities is that they are not normally recognized as work (Lazzarato 1996: 132). While it does involve both material and intellectual work in its productive processes—care labor involves manual work such as lifting elders as well as intellectual work through required medical knowledge and the need for knowledge about individual elders—their products remain invisible and difficult to measure. As a result, bodily, emotional and intellectual labor involved in care work remains unrecognized and underpaid.

In addition, scholars of emotional labor argue that care work proves an extremely gendered practice based on "the image of the ideal emotional labourer [to be] female, as the work is assumed to require attributes and capabilities which are stereotypically defined as feminine and believed to be 'naturally' possessed by women" (Lewis 2008: 131; James 1989: 22). When institutional establishments began offering care outside the domestic sphere, women were progressively deployed in the care labor market (Morini 2007: 41). As a result, care labor is still considered "women's work," which, in the eyes of dominant males, does not deserve high wages or a high social status (Ueno and Tateiwa 2009: 67).

Care labor maintains its low status, performed by such marginalized groups as women, immigrants and racial minorities (Ida 2009: 243). Many developed countries have recruited women from developing countries to fill the void created by the economic mobility of women in their own countries who leave these positions (Morini 2007: 42). Among Southeast Asian countries, the Philippines is a major country that exports care laborers including domestic workers and nurses (Cheng 1996; Tyner 1996; Lan 2002; Parrenas 2003; Asato 2009; Tsujimoto, this volume). While Japan has not yet imported a large number of domestic workers (Ball and Piper 2002: 1025), the current deployment of care workers from Indonesia follows the same process of substituting Japanese people who are privileged enough to avoid such jobs with female migrants willing to accept those jobs at the prevailing wage. Ehrenreich and Hochschild (2002) see this as a new form of imperialism which extracts not only natural resources but also women and their emotions, or "love," from the developing countries.

Thus, the operation of biopolitics in managing the increasing population of elders is inflected by gender and race in addition to class (Chow 2002: 9). Racism intervenes in assuring the quality of lives of citizens, while exploiting subordinate migrant workers as affective subjects who provide both physical and emotional labor without having their own quality of life assured (Foucault 1978: 139). Nonetheless, both paradoxical and important, biopower transforms such racially discriminatory treatment into a "*generative* activity undertaken *for* the life of the entire human species," including the migrants and their nations, which makes the racist practice invisible (Chow 2002: 9, emphasis in the original). This generative form of biopower is, as Rey Chow defines, "liberally intended, discourse bound, culturally produced and transmitted" (ibid.: 15). For example, the Japanese government discursively defines Indonesian care workers as candidates. It explains the current acceptance of these workers as a way of *enabling* them to acquire required knowledge and skills in order to obtain the national qualification that allows them to become a nurse or a care worker in Japan. This suggests a liberal idea that workers use free will to make their decisions to work in Japan rather than become victims of the coercive power of government authority. Importing care workers and nurses, therefore, would be translated by the Japanese government as a way to *help* the development of unprivileged countries' economies and human resources.

Media discourse and the production of affective subjects

The big smiles of Indonesian care workers and nurses captured by press photographs give viewers an impression that these workers are happy. Newspaper descriptions of these migrant workers as kind, gentle, or affable generate assumptions that workers always possess and express positive emotions and, therefore, are "appropriate" for care-giving jobs. However, following Sara Ahmed's (2004) notion of affective economy, I argue that these feelings do not reside in subjects or objects, in this case, the migrant care workers or nurses, but are produced as effects of circulation of the migrant workers (see also Richard and Rudnyckyj 2009). The dominant institutions produce these positive emotions in the context of workers' circulation and contact with the Japanese. I will next examine institutional discourses and stereotypes of migrant care workers and nurses to explore how an affective subject is discursively generated through them, focusing on one of the major daily newspapers in Japan, *Asahi Shimbun*, press releases, and a magazine published by the AOTS, one of the two organizations that offered a Japanese-language training program for the first group of Indonesian workers.

Applying Ahmed's theoretical and methodological approaches, I focus on the cultural politics of emotions. Three aspects of emotions Ahmed discusses are particularly useful here. First, emotions are political: emotionality as a claim *about* a subject or a collective is dependent on relations of power, which endow "others" with meaning and value (Ahmed 2004: 4). As it can be understood from the fact that affective labor has historically related to marginalized groups in the social and economic hierarchies, emotions become attributes of bodies as a way of transforming what is "lower" or "higher" into bodily traits. These traits are often stereotyped and considered to be naturally given.

Second, emotions are intentional in the sense that they are "about" something and this "aboutness" of emotions means they involve a stance on the world, or a way of apprehending the world (Ahmed 2004: 7). In particular, such positive emotions as happiness, love and care are often oriented toward objects as being good or the social ideal (Ahmed 2007: 126). Based on this view, the representations of Indonesian care workers do not depict happy people, but instead are supposed to be happy to be fulfilling the social ideal, or presented as happy by the dominant discourse for fulfilling such an ideal.

Third, emotions, or how we respond to objects and others, create surfaces that define a distinctive characteristic of particular collective bodies (Ahmed 2004: 10). Ahmed provides an example of the United Kingdom as a collective body wherein the dominant political narratives often represent the nation as having a soft-touch barrier through which others "try and 'get into'" (ibid.: 2). Here the implicit demand is for a nation that is less emotional, less open, less easily moved, one that is hard or tough so that the nation will not be invaded by others. Indeed, not only do emotions become attributes of a collective body, but they also produce the very surfaces and boundaries that allow the individual and the social to be delineated as if they are objects (ibid.: 10). I argue that the dominant discourse around Indonesian care workers and nurses produce affective subjects who constitute a soft collective body characterized as emotional, easily moved and shaped by the demands of others. The inclusion of them into the care labor market further softens its boundary, making it easily controllable by state policy, creating a new system of inclusion and exclusion that determines who belongs to the realm of care work based on emotional attributes.

Unlike the bureaucratic, inhuman language of the Ministry of Health, Labor and Welfare which treats Indonesian care workers and nurses as faceless foreign candidates, both AOTS and *Asahi* create a set of individual personal characters by portraying them in emotive terms such as cheerful, kind, pure, or affable. Rather than constructing them as threatening foreigners, both AOTS and *Asahi* generally describe workers in a welcoming tone, evoking the reader's sympathetic feelings and making the foreign workers more *acceptable* to the Japanese.

For example, AOTS' press release announcing its six-month Japanese-language training program for the Indonesian workers states:

> The [program] participants are all wonderful young persons, cheerful, polite, and always considerate to Japanese people. Just when they were getting accustomed to the environment in Japan after arriving on August 7, Ramadan began [with] the program on September 1. So the first two months [sic] seemed difficult for Muslim participants to go through

> mentally and physically. But under such hard conditions, the participants have been encouraging each other to continue their training and the atmosphere of the group has been very good. Although there is an uneven progress in Japanese language skills among individuals, over all they keep a positive attitude and are eager to speak to Japanese people in Japanese. (AOTS 2008)

The winter 2009 issue of AOTS' organizational magazine also describes them as young, cheerful, serious and pure (AOTS 2009b: 316). From these positive comments about Indonesian trainees one can summarize three points: these Indonesians are hardworking; they respect Japanese people and try to learn their culture; and they feel positive about their current circumstances and, therefore, are positive people. The comments present Indonesian workers as ideal care laborers by establishing an image of them being at once productive, respectful, traditional and, furthermore, happy about this state of being. This renders invisible their actual tasks of learning Japanese language and culture, of showing respect, and of expressing positive feelings because the document suggests that they are *naturally* such people.

Asahi echoes the AOTS' discourse in its news reports on the candidates' completion of AOTS language training and their arrival at and working experience in nursing homes. An additional layer of discourse gets embedded in *Asahi*'s news reports—they are hardworking but *never perfect* due to their lack of language proficiency. For example, a feature article on five nurse candidates published in the national edition on March 2, 2009, is entitled, "Nursing Spirit, Language Barrier but [they say] 'I Will Work Hard'" (*Asahi Shimbun* 2009g). The article covers their struggle with Japanese while highlighting their positive attitudes about studying the language and learning about the newest medical technology in Japan. A Japanese teacher responsible for their language training commented, "Their only problem is Japanese," implying that they are otherwise great workers while still placing an emphasis on the significance of improving the language. Furthermore, the title emphasizes the workers' characteristics of being positive and hardworking by quoting them: "I will work hard."

Multiple news reports between January and March 2009, from different regions of Japan, emphasize these care laborers' lack of language proficiency over their actual intellectual capacity and professional qualification to be nurses or care workers back in their own country. Such comments as "Japanese is difficult" but "I will work hard [to make improvements]" become almost cliché. These comments construct an image of the Japanese as sophisticated and complex (see also Nakamura, Chapter 9, this volume), while fixing a subordinate image of migrant workers as *simply cheerful*. A local report from the Kansai region notes the laborer's interest in Japanese culture and highlights three Indonesian workers who enjoy Japanese culture as they interact with elderly residents in the annual traditional event *setsubun*, celebrating the close of winter (*Asahi Shimbun* 2009h). The report positively portrays their openness to Japanese culture yet does not ensure their acquisition of the culture because it shows only their superficial level of engagement with the culture. As a result, this constructs workers as friendly outsiders who accept Japanese culture yet will never be able to practice it because of its complexities.

Meanwhile, these news reports highlight these foreign workers' adaptability to the nursing home environment through the sympathetic voices of either Japanese workers or the elderly residents who warmly welcome workers from overseas. The stories represent the positive feelings of not only Indonesian candidates but also other members of the nursing home communities, ultimately projecting positive and happy feelings to the reader. For example, in an *Asahi* story from Kagawa Prefecture, an elderly resident commented on two Indonesian care workers who just started to work at the nursing home: "They look cheerful and kind. It must be difficult to come from abroad. I have to appreciate them" (*Asahi Shimbun* 2009b). In a story from Kanagawa Prefecture, a Japanese care worker compliments two newly arrived Indonesian workers for their professionalism, including their ability to manage their intonation and tone of voice, and to adjust their eye level depending on the height of each elder; "Even Japanese are often not able to talk to elders well. These two are excellent," he says (*Asahi Shimbun* 2009f).

These reports produce the image that the Indonesian workers are caring and accommodating. In addition to the actual smiles captured in the photographs, the articles repeatedly use the term smile, gentle, kind, or affable, thereby creating a soft image of the candidates. Moreover, the workers are depicted as gently *touching* elders, further enhancing the image of their softness. In one photograph, a female candidate gently holds elders' hands and touches their bodies when introducing herself (*Asahi Shimbun* 2009b). In another photo, a female worker places her hand on the arm of a resident and talks to her with a smile (*Asahi Shimbun* 2009f). "Touch," another key word used in these news reports, demonstrates the affective capacity of Indonesian care workers.

These affective images did not emerge accidentally; they are tied to stereotypes of Southeast Asian women prevalent in other, related spatio-temporal contexts. Some of these Indonesian-worker images produced via the Japanese media discourse share similarities with stereotypes of Filipinas in care-giving jobs in other parts of the globe today. Major institutions in both host countries and the Philippines produce stereotypes of Filipinas by promoting them in terms of their reliability, docility, competence and low cost (Tyner 1996). They also market Filipinas as loyal, disciplined and obedient. Foreign employers, in turn, request Filipina maids because they are considered to be better at cooking, cleaning and child rearing.[4]

These stereotypes overlap with the images of Indonesian care workers and nurses as hardworking, gentle, kind and affable, yet subordinate due to the lack of language proficiency and their status as candidates. In fact, an historical basis exists in Japan that roots the discourse of Asian women as suited to care giving. One can link such images with Japan's exploitation of so-called "comfort women" during the period of Japan's colonial invasion of East and Southeast Asian countries, which serves as a ghostly grounding for the creation of Asian women's images as providers of sex, love and care. One reason that Indonesian care workers are constructed as affective bodies rather than professional nurses and care workers could be due to the sexualized images of the ancestors who connect them on a symbolic level to the sphere of *mere* body and simultaneously disconnect them from the sphere of intellectual capacity.

Another historical context has led to the current popular discourse about foreign Asian women. In the 1980s, a number of women from Asian countries entered Japan with so-called entertainers' visas. These visas allowed them to work in theatrical and musical performances and other forms of show business often associated with sex-related work (Komai 2000; Ball and Piper 2002). The largest group that obtained these visas were Filipina, later followed by women from South Korea, Taiwan and Thailand. There were also women who entered Japan on tourist visas and then engaged in entertainment-related jobs illegally. Indeed, care worker agencies in Japan reproduce this image of Asian women in the entertainment industry. These agencies promote Filipina residents for their communication skills (kind and cheerful) and hospitality (dedicated), perpetuating a discourse that Filipino national characteristics are suited for care-giving jobs (Takahata 2009: 114–15). One may imagine that such discourse has been extended to Indonesian candidates, from another former colony in Southeast Asia with which Japan maintains a neo-colonial relationship as a legacy of the past invasion.

In the news reports, Indonesian candidates seem to bring not only comfort and care but also happiness to the nursing homes. Following Ahmed's argument that happiness is good to think in terms of how it mediates between individual and social, private and public, affective and evaluative, mind and body, as well as norms, rules and ideals, and ways of being in the world (Ahmed 2007: 124), the representations of happy migrant workers and nursing homes involve public evaluations of social ideals. In other words, they are not simply happy people—they are (presented as) happy *about* fulfilling the social ideal. In a similar manner, nursing homes are not happy places from their inception, but such an atmosphere is created upon achievement of the social ideal based on the circulation of Indonesian workers with ideal characteristics in nursing homes, thereby obscuring problems associated with the working conditions of the nursing homes—including low wages and overwork.

In all the examined articles, I found, on one hand, that the Japanese seemed nostalgic for the traditional family that supposedly still exists in Indonesia and about the presence of daughters-in-law who took care of elderly family members. On the other hand, I saw a positive evaluation of Japanese nursing homes as contemporary sites where feminized care workers—performing the role of daughters or daughters-in-law—create an affective, family-like bond, one that is diminishing in contemporary Japanese families. Such a discourse transforms those elders from a burden on Japanese society into objects of love. This discourse establishes a *natural* relationship between migrant workers as loving subjects and elders as objects of love with multiple ideological functions.

First, such affective representation constructs a family-like bond in nursing homes, which further strengthens the social ideal of family (Ahmed 2003: 5). Cultural proximity further assures this artificial family bond. Positive representations of Indonesian candidates highlight their strong work ethic, cultural adaptability and family values that resemble those of an older Japan, reviving the *lost* Japanese tradition (see Nakamura, this volume, on the revitalization of Japanese tradition through the so-called Japanese women's language). At the same time, the representation of elders as objects of love not only results in an affirmation of the traditional ideal that elders are worthy people for whom one (or society) should care, but such representation *protects* the traditional ideal from the contemporary marginalization of elders as unproductive bodies incapable of participating in the capitalist economy. This, in turn, assures Japan's future productivity since it frees younger citizens of burdens such as caring for parents.

Second, the discourse of love these articles produce renders invisible the dislocation of the migrant workers' love and care from their own family in Indonesia. In an ironic twist, although the articles highlight Indonesian workers' traditional values in taking care of their new Japanese family and their contributions to maintaining Japanese family values, these media representations ignore the fact that the deployment of migrant workers to Japanese nursing homes *disables* their ability to fulfill their gender roles for their own families in Indonesia (see Tsujimoto, this volume, on a different scenario where Filipino care workers in South Korea see their transnational emotional labor as fulfilling their gender roles). These news reports never mention workers' actual families back home.

As discussed, these dominant discourses produce what Ahmed theorizes as new boundaries of collective bodies of migrant workers and of the care labor market. The media representations of kind, gentle and affable images of Indonesian candidates feminize and construct a soft surface of this collective body of Indonesian care workers (Ahmed 2004: 2). The collective body is emotional, easily moved, and shaped by the demands of others; therefore, society can easily manage and control it. The production of the image of the soft bodily surface encourages an integration of "foreign" migrants into the intimate space of care, a space that was once highly domestic. Furthermore, the integration of the soft body softens the boundary of the care labor market itself, making it easily penetrated and controlled by the state's policy. While Japan's care labor market was already highly feminized, the deployment of migrant workers and the reproduction of stereotypical feminized images of women from Southeast Asia has explicitly racialized and increasingly feminized it. The market's new boundary generates particular "affective subjects," creating a new system of inclusion and exclusion. Of importance, the deployment of both male and female migrant workers does not liberate the market from its gendered stereotypes and sexist structure. On the contrary, the dominant discourse justifies the feminization of labor by emphasizing the feminized characteristics of migrant workers and excluding Japanese men from the caregiving work (Ehrenreich and Hochschild 2002: 9). The idealization of Indonesian candidates further justifies the government's deployment of them exclusively to nursing homes, while prohibiting them from working in other capacities.

Conclusion: Japan's new marginal subjectivity

Geraldine Pratt argues that domestic workers are produced as subjects through stereotypes; it is important to chart these stereotypes because employment agents act upon them and workers' agency is severely constrained by the subject positions offered through them (Pratt 1997: 166). In a similar manner, I argue that no pool of affective subjects sits waiting to be deployed to the care labor market; rather, the discourses of the dominant institutions produce them. One must examine these discourses because the production of such subjectivity has material consequences, which are tied directly to the system of inclusion and exclusion of the particular labor market. As Foucault would point out, however, I acknowledge and emphasize that such discursive production of affective subjectivity does not entirely constitute subjectivities of migrant workers. They have agency to resist the dominant discourse and make sense of and articulate their experiences in their terms. To further analyze dynamic processes through which their subjectivities are constructed in a local context one needs to work closely with individual migrant workers, but that is beyond the scope of my analysis.

Although the experiment of recruiting Southeast Asian women as caregivers in Japan is not as successful as planned—many of these foreign care workers ended up being sent back on grounds of their failure to pass the national examination and there is a held perception at nursing homes that foreign workers are a burden due to their lack of sufficient Japanese—the deployment of foreign care workers to solve the caregiver crisis reflects the trend of Japan's recent biopolitics.[5] I argue that the deployment of migrant workers to the care labor market has at least two consequences in the production of marginal subjectivity in contemporary Japan, which is made completely invisible in the positive representations that highlight happy and peaceful encounters between Indonesian workers and Japanese elders. First, it marginalizes these migrant workers by reproducing the neocolonial relationship and treating them as flexible labor forces that can be purchased with a low price to fill the labor shortage in the domestic worker market in Japan. These marginal subjects are constructed in an ambivalent manner in the dominant discourse. On the one hand, they are marginalized, subordinate foreigners without legitimate citizenship status in Japan. In addition, even though they are highly educated as nurses or care workers in their own countries, the media often infantilize them because of their lack of Japanese language proficiency. On the other hand, they are strategically idealized as "good daughters" who are affectionate and suited for care-giving tasks. They are positively represented as having characteristics of ideal Japanese women that have disappeared. Nonetheless, however idealized they are, this still renders them subordinate as they are both feminized and projected as the nation's past, as they are both preservers of its old values and receivers of its aged burden.

Second, the deployment of migrant workers to the care labor market reproduces the marginal position that existed in Japan *prior* to the arrival of migrant workers. This position, once begins to be occupied by racialized subjects, is further marginalized or stigmatized. In other words, the marginalized subjectivity is not created for the first time as an effect of inclusion of *a priori* marginal subjects. The marginal position of the care labor market had already existed within Japan, and it is also the imposition of such a position upon Southeast Asian migrants that marginalizes them. Rey Chow's argument about the relation between marginalized identity (ethnicity) and labor is useful to clarify this point:

> The point to note about the relation between ethnicity and labor is therefore not the oft-reiterated one of the existential uprooting of the migrant worker from home … but rather that the ethnic as such stands in modernity as the site of a foreignness that is produced from within privileged societies and is at once defined by and constitutive of that society's hierarchical divisions of labor. A laborer becomes ethnicized because she is commodified in specific ways, because she has to pay for her living by performing certain kinds of work, while these kinds of work, despite being generated from within that society, continue to reduce the one who performs them to the position of the outsider, the ethnic.
>
> (Chow 2002: 34)

As Japan will continue to recruit workers from developing countries to its care labor market, it is important to make further inquiries into its consequences over the individual lives of these migrant workers and their relationships with their own families back in their countries, as well as Japanese policy on the care system and the continuing marginalization of the care labor market.

Acknowledgments

I am greatly indebted to Jie Yang and Kirsten McAllister for valuable advice, feedback and comments which helped me develop my ideas and write this chapter. Many thanks to Robert Prey and Seonok Lee for suggesting background literature on transnational migration in Asia. I would also like to acknowledge the Japanese Government Support for Long-Term Studying-Abroad program and the C.D. Nelson Memorial Graduate Scholarship which have supported my studies throughout the past several years.

Notes

1 One hundred and forty-nine candidates participated in AOTS language training at this time, of whom forty-eight were male and one hundred and one were female (AOTS 2009a).
2 However, I still acknowledge previous works that have emphasized the importance of distinguishing the notion of "affect" and that of "emotion." See Massumi (2002: 28) and Hardt and Negri (2004: 108), for examples.
3 Ueno and Tateiwa (2009: 41) estimate the average monthly salary for fully employed care workers in nursing homes to be 220,000 yen (approx. US$2,200; $1 = 100 yen).
4 See also Pratt (1997) for her study of the stereotyping regime deployed by nanny agents in Vancouver.
5 Between 2009 and 2013 a total of eight hundred and ninety-two Indonesian candidates were accepted under JIEPA, and between 2010 and 2013 a total of six hundred and seventy Filipino candidates were accepted under JPEPA (Ministry of Health, Labor and Welfare 2013a, 2013b). In March 2012, thirty-six out of ninety-five foreign examinees (37.9 percent) passed the National Examination for Care Workers, and in March 2013, one hundred and twenty-eight out of three hundred and twenty-two (39.8 percent) passed the same examination (Ministry of Health, Labor and Welfare 2013c). The percentage of successful foreign examinees is significantly lower than that of all successful examinees, which was 63.9 percent in 2012 and 64.4 percent in 2013.

References

Ahmed, Sara. 2003. "In the Name of Love." *Borderlands* 2(3).

——2004. *The Cultural Politics of Emotion*. Edinburgh: Edinburgh University Press.

——2007. "Multiculturalism and the Promise of Happiness." *New Formations* 63(1): 121–37.

Anagnost, Ann. 2004. "The Corporeal Politics of Quality (*suzhi*)." *Public Culture* 16 (2): 189–208.

AOTS (Association for Overseas Technical Scholarship). 2008. "Training Programs Implemented by AOTS for Candidates for Nurses and Care Workers Invited based on the Economic Partnership Agreement between Japan and Indonesia." Press Release, November 27.

——2009a. "Nichi-Indoneshia keizai renkei kyotei ni motozuku kangoshi, kaigofukushishi kohosha no ukeire ni saishi AOTS ga tantosuru nihongo-to kensyu no shuryo nit suite." Press Release, January 20.

——2009b. "News Topic." *Kenshu* (Winter): 18–19.

Asahi Shimbun. 2009a. "Indoneshia kara kaigoshi koho." *Asahi Shimbun (Mie)*, January 31.

——2009b. "Indoneshia kara no 4 nin kennai no tokuyo de." *Asahi Shimbun (Kagawa)*, January 30.

——2009c. "Indoneshia-jin kaigo fukushi-shi kohosha ga chakunin zenkoku 51-kasho de." *Asahi Shimbun*, January 29.

——2009d. "Indoneshia-jin kaigoshi no tamago, fukushi genba e—nihongo kenshu shuryo." *Asahi Shimbun*, January 28.

——2009e. "Kaigo no genba gaikokujin shokuin ukeire." *Asahi Shimbun (Hiroshima)*, March 20.

——2009f. "Kaigo no puro e, ikokude funto." *Asahi Shimbun (Kanagawa)*, February 12.

——2009g. "Kango no kokorozashi, kotobano kabe demo 'ganbarimasu'." *Asahi Shimbun*, March 2.
——2009h. "Setsubun, indoneshia-jin no 3 nin mo otoshiyori to mamemaki, maikata." *Asahi Shimbun (Kansai)*, February 3.
Asato, Wako. 2009. "Kea no kakuho wo megutte hikiokosareru hito no kokusai ido" (International Migration Caused by the Security of Care). *Gendai Shiso* 37(2): 91–105.
Ball, Rochelle and Piper, Nicola. 2002. "Globalisation and Regulation of Citizenship: Filipino Migrant Workers in Japan." *Political Geography* 21: 1013–34.
Cheng, Shu-Ju Ada. 1996. "Migrant Women Domestic Workers in Hong Kong, Singapore and Taiwan: A Comparative Analysis." *Asian Pacific Migration Journal* 5(1): 139–52.
Chow, Rey. 2002. *The Protestant Ethnic and the Spirit of Capitalism*. New York: Columbia University Press.
Ehrenreich, Barbara and Hochschild, Arlie Russell. 2002. "Introduction." In Barbara Ehrenreich and Arlie Russell Hochschild (eds), *Global Woman*. New York: Metropolitan Books, 1–14.
Foucault, Michel. 1978. *The History of Sexuality*, trans. R. Hurley. New York: Vintage Books.
Hardt, Michael. 2007. "Foreword: What Affects are Good for." In Patricia Ticineto Clough and Jean Halley (eds), *The Affective Turn: Theorizing the Social*, viiii–xiii. Durham, NC: Duke University Press.
Hardt, Michael and Negri, Antonio. 2004. *Multitude: War and Democracy in the Age of Empire*. New York: The Penguin Press.
Harvey, David. 2005. *A Brief History of Neoliberalism*. Oxford and New York: Oxford University Press.
He, Mei, Ohrui, Takashi and Arai, Hiroyuki. 2009. "Homicides of Frail Older Persons by their Caregivers in Japan." *Journal of the American Geriatrics Society* 57(1): 173–74.
Hochschild, Arlie Russell. 1983/2003. *The Managed Heart: Commercialization of Human Feeling*, 20th anniversary edn. Berkeley: University of California Press.
Ida, Kumiko. 2009. "Rodoryoku no jyoseika' kara 'rodo no jyoseika' e" (From Feminization of Laborer to Feminization of Labor). *Gendai Shiso* 37(2): 236–45.
James, Nicky. 1989. "Emotional Labour: Skill and Work in the Social Regulation of Feeling." *Sociological Review* 37(1): 15–42.
Komai, Hiroshi. 2000. "Immigrants in Japan." *Asian and Pacific Migration Journal* 9 (3): 310–26.
Lan, Pei-Chia. 2002. "Among Women: Migrant Domestics and their Taiwanese Employers across Generations." In Barbara Ehrenreich and Arlie Russell Hochschild (eds), *Global Woman*. New York: Metropolitan Books, 169–89.
Lazzarato, Maurizio. 1996. "Immaterial Labor." In Paolo Virno and Michael Hardt (eds), *Radical Thought in Italy: A Potential Politics*. Minneapolis and London: University of Minnesota Press, 132–46.
Lechner, Viola. M. and Sasaki, Masahito. 1995. "Japan and the United States Struggle with Who Will Care for Our Aging Parents When Caregivers are Employed." *Journal of Gerontological Social Work* 24(1/2): 97–114.
Lewis, Patricia. 2008. "Emotion Work and Emotion Space: Using a Spatial Perspective to Explore the Challenging of Masculine Emotion Management Practices." *British Journal of Management* 19: S130–S140.
Maeda, Daisaku. 1983. "Family Care in Japan." *The Gerontologist* 23(6): 579–83.

Massumi, Brian. 2002. *Parables for the Virtual: Movement, Affect, Sensation.* Durham, NC: Duke University Press.

Ministry of Health, Labor and Welfare. 2013a. *Acceptance of Indonesian Nurse and Care Worker Candidates.* www.mhlw.go.jp/bunya/koyou/other21/index.html.

——2013b. *Acceptance of Filipino Nurse and Care Worker Candidates.* www.mhlw.go.jp/bunya/koyou/other07/index.html.

——2013c. *128 EPA Care Work Candidates Passed the 25th Care Work National Examination.* www.mhlw.go.jp/stf/houdou/2r9852000002ycsb.html.

Mitchell, Katharyne. 2004. *Crossing the Neoliberal Line: Pacific Rim Migration and the Metropolis.* Philadelphia, PA: Temple University Press.

Morini, Cristina. 2007. "The Feminization of Labour in Cognitive Capitalism." *Feminist Review* 87: 40–59.

Motohashi, Tetsuya. 2005. *Postcolonialism.* Tokyo: Iwanami Shoten.

Ngai, Sianne. 2005. *Ugly Feelings.* Cambridge, MA: Harvard University Press.

Ong, Aihwa. 2006. *Neoliberalism as Exception: Mutations in Citizenship and Sovereignty.* Durham, NC: Duke University Press.

Parrenas, Rhacel Salazar. 2003. "The Care Crisis in the Philippines: Children and Transnational Families in the New Global Economy." In Barbara Ehrenreich and Arlie Russell Hochschild (eds), *Global Woman*, 39–54. New York: Metropolitan Books.

Pratt, Geraldine. 1997. "Stereotypes and Ambivalence: The Construction of Domestic Workers in Vancouver, British Columbia." *Gender, Place and Culture* 4(2): 159–77.

——1999. "From Registered Nurse to Registered Nanny: Discursive Geographies of Filipina Domestic Workers in Vancouver, B.C." *Economic Geography* 75(3): 215–36.

Richard, Analiese and Rudnyckyj, Daromir. 2009. "Economies of Affect." *Journal of the Royal Anthropological Institute* 15(1): 57–77.

Said, Edward. 1972. *Orientalism.* New York: Vintage.

Stoler, Ann L. 1995. *Race and the Education of Desire: Foucault's History of Sexuality and the Colonial Order of Things.* Durham, NC: Duke University Press.

Takahata, Sachi. 2009. "Zainichi firipin-jin kaigosha" (Filipino Caregivers in Japan). *Gendai Shiso* 37(2): 106–18.

Tyner, James A. 1996. "The Gendering of Philippine International Labor Migration." *Professional Geographer* 48(4): 405–16.

Ueno, Chizuko and Tateiwa, Shinya. 2009. "Rodo to shiteno kea" (Care as Labor). *Gendai Shiso* 37(2): 38–77.

Yu-Jose, Lydia N. 2005. "Japan and the Philippines: The Politics of an Economic Partnership." In Ateneo Center for Asian Studies (eds), *Asian Cooperation: Problems and Challenges in the New Century.* Quezon City: Ateneo Center for Asian Studies, 19–46.

Yuki, Yasuhiro. 2009. "Shakai-hosho seido ni okeru kaigo hoken sedo no igi" (The Significance of Care Insurance Program Offered Under the Social Security System). *Gendai Shiso* 37(2): 78–90.

8 Fulfilling the self and transnational intimacy through emotional labor

The experiences of migrant Filipino domestic workers in South Korea

Toshiko Tsujimoto

> It isn't much difficult to get a [domestic work] job for Filipinas here. Do you know why? Because I think that Filipinas are "*marunong kumayod, maalaga*" [diligent and caring].
>
> (Mel, emphasis added a Filipino domestic worker in South Korea)

The above quotation shows that migrant Filipino domestic workers in South Korea (hereafter, Korea) themselves highlight their talent to care for someone tenderly as one of the important job qualifications for domestic work.[1] The Philippines, as one of the major exporters of labor in the world and a country dependent on overseas remittance of these workers, has propagated an image of mostly Filipino women as "good carers" as a means for enhancing their competitiveness in the global labor market (Parreñas 2005; Ito *et al.* 2008). However, the government's and individual Filipino women's representation of what is a good carer may have different purposes and meanings (Suzuki 2007: 376; see also Yoshimizu, Chapter 7, this volume, for the making of female migrant workers as new "caring" subjects in Japan). The implications associated with such a divide draw our attention to a specific question: what are the tactics of migrant Filipino women when they profess to be "good carers"?

Most studies on migration in Asia have focused on domestic work as the primary legal entry point for most women (see Yeoh and Huang 1999; Asis *et al.* 2004; Cheng 2004; Chan 2005). However, fewer studies have analyzed the unique position of domestic work in other low-skilled jobs, such as factory work, undertaken by migrant women (Romero 1992; Tenegra 2006). As a result, the focus of this study will be how migrant female domestic workers, originally from the Philippines, chose their occupation voluntarily after they had entered Korea and experienced working in the factory environment. By focusing on the social dimensions of emotions in the transnational experiences of migrant Filipino women in Korea (Anderson and Smith 2001; Ahmed 2004; Bosco 2007; McKay 2007; Mai and King 2009), I argue that migrant women fulfill their selves, family obligations and intimacy by strategically mobilizing emotional labor in the comprehensive transnational situations, not only as their profession of domestic work, but also as part of their everyday lives and voluntary activities in a Catholic Church. With emotional labor as the tactical tool for Filipino women to juggle the roles of worker, mother, breadwinner and community volunteer (leader), this chapter rethinks the normative linkage of emotional labor with femininity, domesticity and victimhood of migrant women (Romero 1992; Hochschild 2000, 2003; Parreñas 2005) by highlighting various social domains and relationships that the emotional labor of migrant women brings about.

Domestic work has been discussed as being highly segmented by race, gender and class, involving insufficient remuneration, and as providing less legal protection or social benefit than other types of work; what tends to result from such discriminatory and precarious conditions is often the diminution and devaluing of domestic work and laborers (Glenn 1986; Romero 1992; Hondagneu-Sotelo 1994; Parreñas 2001). Specifically, migrant female domestic workers have been disproportionately exploited when they are fitted into a false "one of the family" relationship that compels them to engage in unrecognized and typically under- or unpaid emotional labor (Romero 1992: 123–26).

Historically, women have been pressured to provide paid and unpaid care in the reproductive sphere on the gendered ideology that women have "innate affinities" (Morokvasic 2007: 70) for performing such tasks out of their "affection" (Hochschild 1983; Parreñas 2001; Ahmed 2004; Suzuki 2007). Arlie R. Hochschild (1983) elaborates on the origin of this ideological link between emotional labor and femininity, suggesting that the exclusion of women from power and "status in society" compels them to "make a resource out of feeling" for compensating the deficient access to better employment and money (ibid.: 163). Based on an empirical study of the practices of female flight attendants, Hochschild (1983) defines this emotional labor as the "management" and suppression of "private" feelings "to sustain the outward countenance" and "to create a publicly observable facial and bodily display," such as smiling and behaving attentively to customers (ibid.: 7). In this way, the emotional labor of a flight attendant cannot be simply understood as an individual effort to perform tasks efficiently; the emotional status of workers is managed "from above," by profit-making corporations, in order to sell the products (e.g. smiling) of workers and "exchange" that value for "profit" (Hochschild 1983: 185–89). She cautions that emotional labor eventually causes a sense of "estrangement" for these workers, as they lose the sense of their own feelings by detaching their "private selves" from the "official feeling" they have to display in their work (ibid.: 186–89).

However, unlike the emotional labor presented in Hochschild's (1983: 148) study, which "[produces] a desired emotional state in others" or to suppress the private feelings of laborers, emotional labor in domestic work aims to develop a relationship with those in their care, such as young children, in order to attain the work of caring for the children through promoting their physical and emotional well-being (Himmelweit 1999: 35; Uttal and Tuominen 1999). While the emotional labor of female flight attendants is usually "transitory"—an interaction between workers and customers occurs in a limited amount of time and is almost entirely "one-sided"—emotional labor in domestic and care work generally occurs throughout the development of a relatively "long-term" human interaction between workers and their clients (Aronson and Neysmith 1996: 67; Himmelweit 1999: 35), and emotional bonds with the client become unavoidable if the worker aims to provide good care for the client (Aronson and Neysmith 1996; Himmelweit 1999; Uttal and Tuominen 1999). Moreover, while economic gain is usually the "motivation" for emotional labor in those aforementioned transitory types of service (Hochschild 1983; Himmelweit 1999: 36), emotional labor in domestic work is sometimes motivated by the feelings of satisfaction that come from establishing emotional intimacy with their young children (Himmelweit 1999: 32–33; Uttal and Tuominen 1999). For example, migrant domestic workers demonstrate feelings of love for the children of their employers as a compensation for and to assuage the guilt they feel as a result of their inability to care directly for their own children (Hondagneu-Sotelo and Avila 1997; Yeoh and Huang 1999; Parreñas 2001). Moreover, Rhacel S. Parreñas (2001: 179–88) suggests that emotional labor occasionally forms a strategic site for migrant women to protect themselves from derogatory treatment of their employers and to increase the benefit that they can obtain through domestic work.

Nonetheless, the emotional labor of migrant female domestic workers has been the center of an emergent discourse on victimhood (McKay 2007: 177), in which households in developed countries exploit the emotional and caring labor of migrant women from developing countries (Romero 1992; Hondagneu-Sotelo and Avila 1997; Hochschild 2000; Parreñas 2001, 2005). Based on Parreñas's (2001) study on migrant Filipino domestic workers, Hochschild (2000) has developed the concept of the "global care chains—a series of personal links between people across the globe based on the paid or unpaid work of caring" (ibid.: 131), in which migrant female domestic workers take the place of women in wealthier countries through undertaking housekeeping and child rearing, but can do so only by shifting the responsibility of care giving to their children onto female relatives or other impoverished women in home countries (Parreñas 2005: 23). These studies imply that migrant and non-migrant women, alike, are placed at the bottom of global stratification that coerces them to provide care for others and neglect their own socio-reproductive needs and desires (Hochschild 2000, 2003; Parreñas 2001, 2005; see also Yoshimizu, this volume).

Parreñas (2005) suggests, moreover, that the positions of these women in both paid domestic work and as transnational mothers for their own children only perpetuate their traditional gendered role as care giver; paid domestic work abroad, while providing alternative economic resources, never actually liberates these women from an obligation to nurture their own children and even forces them constantly to perform emotional labor—for example, providing guidance for their children and worrying about their well-being—from a distance (Parreñas 2005; see also Hondagneu-Sotelo and Avila 1997). However, a review of these studies may raise the following question: does emotional labor necessarily reinforce the subordination of migrant women to race, class and gender hierarchies that relegate them to occupy traditional positions and roles? (For more discussion of "global care chains" see Yeates 2004.)

While emotional labor has been predominantly discussed in the paid-work experiences of migrant domestic workers in terms of economic and political aspects of migration (Romero 1992; Hondagneu-Sotelo and Avila 1997; Hochschild 2000, 2003; Parreñas 2001), other emotional dimensions of a migrant's "decision to migrate and to continue living and working abroad" (Mai and King 2009: 297), and take a particular role in a certain context has only received cursory scholarly attention (ibid.). Although international labor migration requires one to detach from a familiar place and relationship and to adjust emotionally to new social conditions, emotional labor potentially plays a critical role in helping migrant workers to cope with such processes and proactively organize their transnational lives to achieve certain socioeconomic goals (McKay 2007). Thus, considering emotion entirely as a source of exploitation and subordination in terms of race, class and gender may neglect the multifunctionality of emotion in shaping the transnational life of a(n) (im) migrant woman, in particular (McKay 2007).

Sara Ahmed (2004) states that emotions are not limited to the "cognitive" or "psychological" sphere of an individual; rather, by creating the "effect of the surfaces and boundaries" (ibid.: 10) between the self and others, emotions carry out the function of "sociality" (ibid.: 8). Ahmed further states that emotion entails movement as "the word 'emotion' comes from the Latin, *emovere,* referring to 'to move, to move out'" (ibid.: 11), explaining that "[t]he intensity of pain sensations makes us aware of our bodily surfaces, and points to the *dynamic nature of surfacing itself*" (ibid.: 26, emphasis in original): for example, pain does not fix the one in the state of helplessness, but it rather motivates her/him to strive for "moving away from the pain" (Ahmed 2004: 24). Thus, emotion is not entirely reducible to a "private" category that separates from public social domains, but it opens up unprecedented spheres and relationships to the one (Anderson and Smith 2001). Fernando J. Bosco (2007) defines emotional labor as one's management of emotions to elevate "reactive emotions such as pain and anger" to "reciprocal emotional bonds" with others (ibid.: 551). He also explains that emotional labor is strategically mobilized by people "to create feelings of proximity, solidarity, and shared identities, often in spite of social distance and territorial separation" (ibid.: 546). Thus, emotions manifest into "a form of social presence rather than self-presence" (Ahmed 2004: 10); in this way, international labor migration may provide the best opportunity for migrants to bear various forms of emotional interaction with migrant and non-migrant members. For example, Deirdre McKay (2007) has suggested that migration can reconfigure various forms of "emotional connections within transnational families" (ibid.: 180) by allowing one to develop emotional management that accommodates "long-distance relationships" through remittances and communication technologies (ibid.: 178). Thus, emotional labor comes to be structured through the various everyday practices of individuals that are developed in the "transnational experiences" of migrant workers (McKay 2007: 181).

In what follows I will examine emotional labor in terms of the latter conceptualizations. I argue that rather than as something structured from above in an organizational manner and exclusive of the "private" self (Hochschild 1983; McElhinny 1994), emotional labor is strategically employed by migrant women, not only as their profession, but also as part of their comprehensive transnational experience, including voluntary activities in a Catholic Church. Besides, emotional labor involves the development of emotional closeness with clients or families back home as well as the management of migrants' emotions (i.e. pain and sadness) (Bosco 2007) through working for socioeconomic advancement and transnational intimacy with their children (McKay 2007). Emotional labor also involves the elevation of the "reactive emotions" to the "reciprocal emotional bonds" (Bosco 2007) with fellow migrant Filipinos, which provides the inner strength for migrant Filipino women to propel their transnational endeavors. Through this approach, I argue that emotional labor is not necessarily the site of subordination of migrant women to the hierarchies by race, class and gender (Romero 1992; Hochschild 2000, 2003; Parreñas 2001, 2005), but provides migrant women with the channel of self-fulfillment that comes with socioeconomic advancement and familial intimacy through effectively integrating their emotional labor into multiple roles of worker, mother, breadwinner and community volunteer (leader). Drawing on the study of Bonnie McElhinny (1994) discussing that female police officers rework the notions of femininity and masculinity in the highly masculine work environment, this chapter demonstrates how migrant Filipino women relativize the ideologies of femininity that have been normalized in emotional labor, particularly through their subjective reinterpretation.

Out of the data collected through in-depth interviews from 2004 to 2005, this chapter mainly draws upon the experiences of five migrant Filipino women who were domestic workers in the households of foreign diplomats, business persons and Korean families, four of whom worked as live-out laborers under multiple employers, and one of whom was a live-in laborer.[2] This study was completed as part of my doctoral project of ethnography via in-depth interviews with thirty-one migrant Filipino women living in Seoul and its suburbs between 2003 and 2005.

The experiences of emotional labor of Filipino domestic workers in Korea

Since the late 1980s, the rapid growth of the capitalist economy has caused severe labor shortages in Korea, especially in small and medium-sized manufacturing corporations, which has led to an increase in the migration of foreign workers from South and Southeast Asia (Seol 1999). To solve the problems of increasing labor shortages and undocumented migration, in 2004 the Korean government commenced the migrant import program—i.e. the employment permit system (EPS).[3] The bulk of the firms covered by the EPS belong to labor-intensive industries that create more job vacancies for men than women (Lee 2008: 223). On the other hand, migrant female workers have been almost "invisible" in Korea (Shin 2009: 94): first, migrant female workers constitute only 30 to 35 percent of the entire migrant workforce in the country (Lee 2003: 128);[4] and second, studies on foreign migrant women in Korea since the early 2000s have concentrated on those women who came to Korea by marrying Korean men, while few have investigated the experience of migrant female workers who engage in factory work or domestic work (Kim 2009).

Domestic work in Korea exhibits different modes and characteristics than domestic work in other Asian countries. As of 2002, the number of migrant domestic workers in Korea was estimated at fewer than 10,000 (Lee 2005: 354), whereas Hong Kong, Singapore and Taiwan hosted approximately 100,000–200,000 migrant domestic workers (Yeoh and Huang 1999; Cheng 2004; Chan 2005). Furthermore, the demand for domestic services in Korea is not very high because the country has depended heavily on the unpaid labor of married women to fulfill household and care-providing tasks (Lee 2005: 342–44). Thus, the traditional gender ideology that defines reproductive jobs as the responsibility of female family members has worked to hamper the market in domestic service, which made domestic work an unpopular option for migrant women (ibid.: 344). The employment of domestic workers is, thus, limited to a small number of Korean upper-middle or middle-class households (ibid.).

Migrant Filipino women, in this socio-economic context, represent barely 1 percent of the entire migrant domestic worker population (Lee 2003: 136; 2005: 354); the majority of migrant domestic workers are Korean–Chinese women. Currently, only migrant Korean–Chinese women are legally permitted to work in the domestic services industry (Lee 2005: 349; Shin 2009).[5] However, the domestic work labor market that absorbs migrant Filipino women and migrant Korean–Chinese women keeps them somewhat separate, for those migrant Filipino women who can find employment as domestic workers do so either on live-in or live-out bases, mostly for Western foreign diplomats and business persons sent by multinational corporations to branch offices in Seoul (Lee 2005: 351), and some work for Korean households. Foreign expatriates who frequently move from one country to another tend rarely to understand or speak the Korean language. Therefore, it is much more practical for them to employ Filipino women who are more likely to be able to communicate in English and are also more accustomed to foreign cultures (especially a Western way of living that includes food preparation and cleaning a house) than Korean–Chinese women. Filipino domestic workers tend to get jobs in diplomats' or business persons' households in an informal manner through the introduction of fellow migrant Filipinos. Although in principle the Korean government prohibits all foreign migrant women, except Korean–Chinese, to work in Korean households (Lee 2005: 349), foreign diplomats or business persons who have invested more than US$500,000 in the country are entitled to sponsor foreign domestic workers (Korea Immigration Service, Ministry of Justice 2013:

184–85). Filipino women find employment in this category of domestic work with undocumented status or using the F-1 (Visiting and Living Together) visa: it caters to both the people who visit or live with their families and work in private households of foreign expatriates (Korea Immigration Service, Ministry of Justice 2013: 180). The contract of employment between a Filipino domestic worker and her employer stipulating the minimum wage, working hours and free days must be approved by the Philippines Embassy in Korea prior to her beginning employment (Asato 2003: 99), and the official status she receives is unstable as these contracts, once approved, automatically end when their foreign sponsors leave Korea (a similar situation to Japan; see Tenegra 2006).

Nonetheless, some migrant Filipino women take domestic work as an alternative to factory work as it offers advantages such as higher payment and a more flexible work schedule. The basic monthly wage of a domestic worker is about ₩1,000,000 or more ($800 to $900); in contrast, factory workers earn between ₩800,000 and ₩900,000 ($650 to $750). This wage scale of domestic workers in Korea is higher than that in other migrant host countries in Asia (e.g. approximately $300 in Singapore, and $600 in Hong Kong; cited in Asato 2003: 100). Also, many Filipino domestic workers try to get sponsorship from their foreign expatriate employers to secure, at least, their legal status, and sometimes work under multiple employers after receiving official sponsorship from one foreign diplomat employer. Although domestic work never guarantees migrant Filipino women authentic legal status as workers, their ambivalent position in the niches of the Korean labor market defines their unconventional domestic work experiences (see also Tenegra 2006).

Switching jobs from factory work to domestic work

Switching from factory work to domestic work is a primary strategy of migrant Filipino women in order to achieve greater socioeconomic advantages. In fact, many respondents who had switched from factory to domestic work mentioned that they did not enjoy the long working hours (approximately twelve or more hours per day) and intensive working conditions in the manufacturing sector—these working conditions tend to demand quick movements and rigorous production requirements within short periods of time (see Romero 1992: 143–47); as Mel, formerly a factory worker, mentioned, "You have to move quickly always in factories, and you are always pressured not to produce inferior[-quality] goods." These conditions not only exhausted them physically but pressured them psychologically as a result of the demands to keep up with the high speed of production lines. Domestic work was therefore appealing because it would often allow laborers to work independently, without employer supervision (Romero 1992; Hondagneu-Sotelo 1994). For instance, Corazon, in her late forties, explained her reason for leaving her former factory work for domestic work as the flexibility that enables her to organize her own work schedule:

> I worked in the T-shirt factory, and I needed to increase output. For example, you work from 8:30 am until 8:30 pm. Besides, you have overtime, sometimes until 11 o'clock in the evening. If you work in the [night] shift, you need to work until 2 o'clock in the early morning. So you only have four or five hours to sleep before you go to work again … Domestic helper is, so to speak, a manager of the house … Our time is ours (means no need to work overtime), and we are less mentally pressured. Unlike in factories, employers are not there to watch us [inside a house].
>
> (Corazon)

As Corazon above describes a domestic worker as a "manager of the house," the work enabled her to organize her work schedule as she seldom had overtime work, unlike in factories. An additional advantage to domestic labor is the common presence of regular payment scheduling. Delayed and unpaid salaries were the most frequent type of exploitation endured by migrant factory workers in Korea at the time of the interviews, for the wages of migrant factory workers can occasionally be delayed or even intentionally neglected because of the "illegal" status of the factory workers themselves; it was known that undocumented migrants rarely take legal action in order to receive unpaid salary, for fear of deportation, and so opportunistic factory owners may exploit this unequal power relation and withhold salary payments. Therefore some decided to move to domestic labor jobs as a means of protecting themselves from an exploitative working environment. Moreover, the flexible and informal nature of domestic work allows migrants to earn extra income (Hondagneu-Sotelo 1994; Tenegra 2006). Mel, in her early forties, had been working for foreign families as a live-out domestic worker since 1997. She described that she worked independently for shorter hours and earned more than factory workers (see also Romero 1992: 143–48):

> When I look after [the employer's] children at night, they pay me an additional allowance. For example, when they [the employer couple] go to a party at night, I look after their children. Then, they pay me for it.
>
> (Mel)

Unlike factories where their overtime work is not properly paid, domestic work is generally based on hourly payment if migrants can secure a contract with their employers as Mel did. The greater security that comes with regular payment and extra income helps migrant Filipino women soothe their sadness due to the separation from their children, such as in Corazon's case, below. As a single parent, Corazon left two young children in the care of her brother when she migrated to Korea in 1991:

> Sometimes, I am not happy because [my children] are far from me … But at least here, I have the means to earn money. If you don't have an income, you end up quarrelling with your children all the time. It is more

> painful to see that your children can't eat three times a day ... Anyway, you can earn a lot with this job. But you need to make arrangements with your employer. When you take a job outside of your contracted working hours, you should ask them for extra payment.
>
> (Corazon)

Corazon managed her sadness by creating the rationale for being away from her children, a rationale which is also underpinned by a practical judgment of "the alternative [to] a life of poverty" (McKay 2007: 188); in itself such an alternative livelihood would also cause discord within the family and create additional hardship for Corazon (see also Parreñas 2001: 125). Moreover, her sadness caused by the separation from her young children rather motivated her to move forward (Ahmed 2004) to establish better economic conditions for her children through negotiating with her employers on her work contract. As Corazon's case indicates, migrant women's separation from their children not only accentuates or perpetuates their emotional suffering, but such emotion motivates them to pursue a better work environment and economic gain. In what follows, I specifically delineate the tactic of migrant Filipino women to develop "professionalism" in domestic work, which is closely connected with their engagement in emotional labor.

Developing the "professionalism" in domestic work through emotional labor

Mary Romero (1992) describes that Chicana workers in the United States elevate the racialized and gendered domestic work to "expert" labor through specializing their task such as cleaning and settling payment with employers (143–62; see also Hondagneu-Sotelo 1994; Cheng 2004; Tenegra 2006). She points out that such professionalism of Chicana domestic workers is accompanied by their practices of avoiding personal contact or refusing to develop "emotional closeness" with their employers so that they can protect themselves from the exploitation of unpaid emotional labor (Romero 1992: 136, 152–55). However, researchers (Glenn 1986: 156; Romero 1992; Parreñas 2001) also point out that the so-called "one of the family" relationships sometimes bring emotional "rewards" to migrant domestic workers. Parreñas (2001) delineates this ambivalent effect of emotional labor of Filipino domestic workers by explaining that these laborers negotiate their underprivileged conditions through developing intimacy with their employers (ibid.: 179–88; see also Romero 1992: 125–26). Such a contradictory linkage between professionalism and emotional labor tells us that they are not always mutually incompatible when we look closely at the experiences of Filipino domestic workers. As McElhinny's (1994: 167) study reveals, as emotional labor is linked with workers' professionalism, Filipino migrant women's efforts to elevate their domestic work to a career-oriented job come with emotional labor through establishing intimacy with their employers.

For example, Mel underscored the importance of the "family-like relationship" that she established with her foreign expatriate employers (see also Asis *et al.* 2004: 210–11):

> I prefer employers who treat me as one of their families. I treat them [her younger employer couple] as my younger sister and brother. I work for them because I think they are my family. I sometimes give them advice how to raise a child. Sometimes, they extend my working time, but it's OK. Because they also drive me to places where I want to go [during her days off]. It's better if our relationship is based on the "give and take." But if their treatment for me is like a slave or servant, of course, I don't feel easy and can't do the work that I want to do.
>
> (Mel; cited partially in Tsujimoto 2013: 179)

According to Mel's narrative—the establishment of a family-like and equal relationship with her employers—her strategy is to behave like a surrogate sibling of her employers and provide a form of emotional labor (such as giving child-rearing advice). The reciprocal relationship that Mel has attempted to develop and hold in high regard is indicated through her expression of "give and take," which demonstrates an equal need to perform dutifully for her employers.

Mel's narrative reveals that she has established a family-like relationship through emotional labor not only for the sake of the feeling of satisfaction (see Himmelweit 1999), but also in order to represent a certain level of "professionalism." In order to promote domestic work under a career-oriented status Mel had to assure that any devaluation by her employers—for instance, being treated as a "servant"—was eliminated (see also Parreñas 2001: 181). Establishing a family-like relationship was a first step toward realizing this professionalism, as revealed by her suggestion that her employment involves "the work that I want to do." Thus, emotional labor is strategically adopted by migrant Filipino women to transform domestic work from a socially devalued job to a career-oriented position, with a level of significance that allows them to navigate their transnational lives. Returning to the example of Corazon, it was also explained how the meaning of domestic work could be re-conceptualized, particularly by referring to the trust one could earn with foreign expatriate employers:

> We clean their houses, put their things in order, set up their bedding. It's big help for them. Therefore, they trust me. Even if people say that this kind of job has a low status, I don't mind. With this job, we can earn a lot, we can make a living, and we can send our children to schools … Our many employers respect us because we can speak English even though our English is not very fluent, but Koreans [Korean domestic workers] can't do that.
>
> (Corazon; cited partially in Tsujimoto 2013: 178)

Corazon's narrative indicates that she has tried to raise the socially devalued status of domestic work by developing trust relationships with her employers through a sincere attitude in her work and personal contact with her employers in English that develops familiarity between them. Thus, an emotional connection that is forged between workers and their employers does not entail the outcome of domesticity or "something apart from the economic" (Anderson and Smith 2001: 7), but extracts the trust-relationships that potentially produce steady economic opportunities (ibid.), such as "ongoing employment" status (McKay 2007: 187) and a higher likelihood of extra part-time work.

Converting domestic work into socially and economically rewarding jobs by availing personal contact with their employers and winning their trust suggests a way in which these women enhance their own control over the structure of working conditions and the realization of personal aspirations, such as the education of their children in the Philippines. As in the excerpt of Mel in the introduction to the chapter, Corazon added the value of the efficiency of Filipino women to their "caring" nature which supports their housekeeping and child-rearing abilities, which appeal to many employers. To this, their engagement in emotional labor is connected to their project of socioeconomic advancement and self-fulfillment.

Juggling the breadwinner and motherhood through emotional labor

As I have discussed above, the link between the emotional labor and the sense of professionalism (McElhinny 1994) of migrant Filipino women shows that these women appropriate the emotional labor, which has been discussed in the notions of femininity and victimhood (Hochschild 2000, 2003), in order to fit it into their private concern. On the other hand, migrant women strategically integrate emotional labor into the effort to juggle the roles of breadwinner and mother in a transnational situation. This is particularly fulfilled by availing themselves of the relatively higher wage scale of domestic work in Korea, and drawing men into the responsibility of mothering (Pe-Pua 2003; Asis *et al.* 2004).

The following example of a married couple in their mid-thirties, Diana and Ray, best describes how this couple has effectively fulfilled the economic needs and transnational intimacy with their children through Diana's domestic work: Ray became the primary care provider for their two children when Diana became a domestic worker in Korea. They were both undocumented migrant workers when they met and got married in Korea in 2002, and they sent their first daughter back to the Philippines in 2003—a result of the couple's undocumented status.[6] Ray eventually returned with their youngest to live in the Philippines in 2005. As an undocumented migrant, Ray could not easily find a factory job[7] and the couple decided that while Diana would remain in Korea to earn the family's income, Ray would take care of their two children in the Philippines. Beyond economic needs, Diana's anxiety about her young children being left without the care of their mother motivated her to come to this arrangement. In fact, Diana had suffered from emotional pain and sadness after sending the eldest back home. She explained how Ray caring for the children in the Philippines helped her to manage her uneasiness and responsibility as breadwinner:

> We agreed that we would be able to earn a lot of money if both of us continued to work here. But, on the other hand, we were afraid that we might later regret our decision if our children did not feel close to us … After he returned home, our children's attitude changed. Earlier, they would refuse to talk to us on the phone if they didn't feel like it. But now, he tries to make them talk with me on the phone. They have gradually started talking to me on the phone … After Ray returned to the Philippines, *gumaan ang loob ko* [literally means "my mind became lighter," and an indirect translation is "I feel relieved"] because I believe that he can properly explain [my absence] to our children.
>
> (Diana, emphasis added)

The couple achieved their goals of fulfilling the economic needs of the family and strengthening ties with their children through restructuring Diana's and Ray's roles. Thus, Diana's engagement in domestic work in Korea does not necessarily cause estrangement from her children because of Ray's care giving and transmitting of Diana's affection to the children in the Philippines (see Pribilsky 2004: 331). Sharing the duty of child care with her husband has not only lessened her anxiety over the possibility of emotional detachment because of the geographical distance, but has provided Diana with the ground to relieve her emotional burden through the emotional labor of managing her anxiety as her testimony: "*gumaan ang loob ko*" (I felt relieved) is evidence of this.

Moreover, Diana and Ray's case indicates that the gender division of labor is not always prioritized by migrants. As Jason Pribilsky (2004: 316) argues, migrant women and men adapt to the new arrangement and "priorities of maintaining a transnational livelihood"; Filipino migrants flexibly accept these role changes in order to conform to necessary employment conditions and constraints. Thus, emotional labor that aims to maintain familial intimacy does not always lead to strict gender role adherence or femininity, but can rather motivate a renegotiation of those roles. This is also demonstrated by the fact that the emotional labor of migrant mothers caring for their children from a distance does not perpetuate these women's care-providing role (Parreñas 2005), but encourages them to take the role of breadwinner. This is also evident in Nancy's experience below, as she performs as breadwinner and transnational mother for her children (see Pe-Pua 2003).

Nancy, in her early forties and a mother of three, had been working in the household of a foreign expatriate since 2004. While she came to Korea with her husband in 1995, he returned alone to the Philippines in 2003 as he had—like Ray in the above example—experienced, as an undocumented individual, a hard time finding employment. Therefore, Nancy's role as breadwinner was the natural course of the family decision although her greater responsibility for the family and tensions with her husband resulting from the increase in Nancy's economic ability and power in the family had occasionally distressed her (see Pe-Pua 2003). As scholars argue, becoming breadwinner does not necessarily free migrant women from the duty of care giving to their own children (Hondagneu-Sotelo and Avila 1997; Pe-Pua 2003; Parreñas 2005), and Nancy continued her mothering role by talking to her children regularly on the phone about their school life and daily events. However, she explained that such practice of "transnational mothering" (Hondagneu-Sotelo and Avila 1997; Parreñas 2005) gave her strength to perform the breadwinning role amidst the homesickness and challenges she had faced in Korea:

> This is what I have thought. The important thing is the way in which you leave your children behind. You can raise your children in the same way as if you're beside them … I know some parents here that they don't pay much attention to their children [left behind]. They just feed their children, but they don't offer any parental guidance. They don't even call their children so that their children can hear their voices. You know, even a telephone call makes difference. It gives me strength, too.
>
> (Nancy)

As Nancy suggests, her practice of transnational mothering has the effect of motivating her to continue the breadwinning role. This is another aspect of mothering and emotional labor; contrary to the accounts of "global care chains" that relegate migrant women to being the victims of emotional distress (Hochschild 2000, 2003) or a traditional gendered role (Parreñas 2005), emotional labor is strategically incorporated into the family strategy for survival and intimacy (McKay 2007). Therefore, emotional labor rather supports their transnational endeavor as mother and breadwinner while mitigating their emotional distress due to the separation from their families (Bosco 2007). In order further to advance the argument for the functions of emotional labor as the channel of supporting the transnational lives of migrant women, I shall next discuss religious beliefs and voluntary activities of migrant Filipinos.

Managing emotion through religious beliefs and voluntary activities

Roman Catholicism has been the magnet for Filipino (im)migrant communities, as well as for associated social networks abroad (Parreñas 2001; Tsujimoto 2003; Asis *et al.* 2004; Huang and Douglass 2009). Moreover, Christianity in general accounts for nearly 30 percent of the population in Korea, as "either Protestant or Catholic," which appears quite conspicuous in comparison to neighboring countries such as China and Japan (Kim 2007: 6). As many Filipinos are Catholics, Korean Catholic Churches have provided a great deal of support; for instance, they have supported Filipino Sunday mass celebrated by Filipino priests, and the Archdiocese of Seoul has provided a community center for Filipino migrants; the community center, then, which is mainly run by Filipino clergy and migrant Filipino volunteers, provides counseling for migrants' work-related and other pressing issues, shelter and various services (Tsujimoto 2003).

Aside from the secular functions of the Catholic Church, many Filipino migrants strategically incorporate Catholic beliefs into their experience in order to boost their transnational aspirations and regain emotional strength (see Parreñas 2001: 125); the motivations of emotional labor help them and give physical or emotional assistance to fellow migrants. In addition, a relationship of mutual trust between migrant Filipino women and their employers is occasionally strengthened on the basis of a shared religious affiliation, and some respondents mentioned that they had come to know their employers through referrals from clergy at a Catholic or Protestant church. The sharing of religious beliefs and practices, at the least, constitutes an already-present familiarity in workers' relationships with employers. Thus, emotion that inflicts pain on migrant Filipino women is managed by them through creating another emotional state within them in combination with religious beliefs so that they can sooth their pain (Bosco 2007).

Janet, in her mid-forties, who was a single parent with four children in the Philippines, had been working as a domestic worker in both Korean and foreign diplomats' households since 2003, through a referral from a Korean pastor in the Protestant Church (Janet is a born again Christian). She mentioned that her born again Christian employers treated her quite well and that she also regarded them as members of her own family. Initially, she said, she felt difficulty in taking care of other people's children but not her own; however, she gradually developed affection for her employers' children—similar to her feelings toward her own children (see also Asis *et al.* 2004: 210–11)—because she came to realize that her employers were "good-natured" and helpful Christians. While religious beliefs helped her to connect emotionally with her employers and employers' children, it also provided her with a site to rework her sense of transnational intimacy with her own children (see also Hondagneu-Sotelo and Avila 1997). The development of a religious-based love for her employers' children gave Janet the impetus to forge an alternative emotional tie with her own children. She explained how she reinterpreted her role as domestic worker and mother:

> I treat them [the employer's children] as my own children. I think they are innocent and they need me. I can't treat them insincerely because of the reason that they are not my children … Because I have strong faith in God that He will never abandon my children as long as I take good care of them [the employer's children]. My love toward them [her own children] is always there.
>
> (Janet)

As indicated in Janet's words, taking care of employers' children does not deprive a working mother of the affection she feels toward her own children; rather, it enables her to forge multiple bundles of affection by adopting alternative practices through religious belief and forms of emotional connection. Thus, emotional labor does not always mean "extracting" love for migrant women (Hochschild 2003: 26), but also provides an opportunity to develop various accounts of affection through different subjective language. The multiplicity of affection can therefore be a result of manipulating the accounts of care and emotional dedication to employers' children as a reinterpretation of a working mother's love toward her own children.

Direct participation in the church activities as a volunteer can also have a meaningful impact on the emotional integrity of migrant Filipino women, offering a way to overcome loneliness, and achieving a feeling of self-fulfillment by extending assistance to fellow Filipino migrants who are in need (see Asis *et al.* 2004: 210). As emotions are not merely cognitive events, but can create the effects of "sociality" (Ahmed 2004) through the forms of "solidarity" (Bosco 2007), thus one's loneliness and emotional predicament can be elevated to "reciprocal emotional bonds" (ibid.) among migrants through various activities in the Catholic Church.

Corazon, who spent most of her time in volunteering in the Catholic Church, explained how her involvement as a volunteer had supported her life in Korea—she volunteered as a visitor of sick Filipino migrants in hospitals, an assistant during weekly novenas and Sunday masses, and a fundraiser for hospitalization fees of sick migrants. Corazon had also been elected president of the Catholic migrant Filipino community several times because her fellow migrant Filipinos recognized her devotion to religious and other voluntary activities. On a practical level, the flexible schedule of domestic work made her engagement in such activities possible, but, at an emotional level, her involvement was largely motivated by the emotional distress that resulted from the separation from her children. Her involvement in voluntary work gave her the strength to continue supporting her family from afar and to become a leader, as she explained:

> The leader must establish *rapport* with people and always moves first so that other people will follow you. In short, the leader *kailangang may puso ka rin* [you must have a heart, too], and know how to build good relationships with people ... Maybe, the purpose of my devotion to the Church is that it makes me stronger and I'm inspired by such [religious and voluntary] activities.
>
> (Corazon, emphasis added)

Corazon emphasized interpersonal skills and an affectionate nature as the qualifications of a good leader, as indicated by her words "rapport" and "*puso* (heart)". Her physical and emotional labor to establish "reciprocal emotional bonds" (Bosco 2007) with people in the community convinced fellow migrant Filipinos to support her as president of the community. In return, the support she was able to earn from her fellow migrants encouraged her to continue her roles of transnational mother and breadwinner. This suggests that emotional labor brings about non-traditional gendered roles such as volunteer and leader in religious activities while reworking the notions of gendered subjugation in emotional labor.

Conclusion

In the above discussion, the emotional labor of the women effectively broadens the scope of their individual lives, as they are able to elevate their individual pain and emotional suffering to strength and empathy for others (Bosco 2007). The worlds to which these women relate are therefore exceedingly complex and not constituted as a singularly and necessarily static space in which traditional roles of mother and caretaker are imposed. This empirical study has demonstrated the role of emotional labor in promoting socio-economic status and transnational intimacy of migrant domestic workers. Contrary to previous studies that suggest how emotional labor subjugates migrant women within gender, class and racial hierarchies, this chapter has shown the ways in which emotional labor is also a tactical tool for fulfilling personal goals and familial concerns. Specifically, it has elucidated the modes of emotional labor that are structured by various practices of Filipino migrant women in the realms of both paid and unpaid work, such as through shared religious beliefs and voluntary activities. Filipino migrant women strive to develop optimism, even in a variety of social constraints, by adopting emotional labor practices that allow them to negotiate the impacts of those constraints and forge multiple bundles of affection toward both employers' and their own children in order to overcome emotional predicaments. Moreover, rather than viewing emotion as a source of victimization and gendered subjugation, it has been suggested that emotion is multifaceted in its functionality, and that it motivates migrant Filipino women to tread new paths and venture into spheres that form their different social roles and identities (Anderson and Smith 2001; McKay 2007). The cases illustrated in this chapter, such as emotional labor that supports migrant women to perform as breadwinner and active leader in the Filipino migrant community, are proof of this impact. While McElhinny (1994) raises a critical view of the normalized and gendered way of conceptualizing emotional labor because the boundary of femininity and masculinity is more flexible and not clear-cut in the actual experience of individuals, migrant Filipino women themselves do not see their emotional labor as a key site of exploitation or domesticity, but rather as a way of fulfilling the self, family obligations and familial intimacy.

In this chapter I suggest that the delimitation of emotional labor to the discourses of femininity and gendered subjugation may result in neglecting its dynamic functions that shape one's manifold experiences and roles that are concurrent with contemporary transnational migration. Further studies need to delve into the impact of the emotional labor of migrants upon their formation and reformation of social meanings held in domestic and care labor vis-à-vis government policies and the globalizing market of care.

Acknowledgements

I express my sincere appreciation to the Filipino migrant women who shared their stories and gave me a valuable opportunity to learn from them. I would also like to thank Jie Yang for her insightful suggestions and comments on earlier drafts of this chapter, Ayaka Yoshimizu for kindly sharing her earlier draft of this volume with me, and the editors for their helpful assessment to strengthen my analysis. The research in South Korea between 2003 and 2005 was funded by the Matsushita Asia Scholarship of the Matsushita International Foundation (Konosuke Matsushita International Scholarship of the Konosuke Matsushita Memorial Foundation), and the author received a fellowship of the government of Canada (Canadian Post-Doctoral Research Fellowship Programme—PDRF) while writing this chapter. I deeply thank these two organizations for their generous funds.

Notes

1 Nobue Suzuki (2007: 375) also points out this tendency of Filipino care laborers in Japan, representing themselves as "suited for caregiving."

2 I conducted the in-depth interviews in a semi-structured manner, in the respondents' residences and at a meeting room of the Catholic Church—wherever they felt comfortable. I translated all quotations in this chapter from Filipino to English. For privacy and security of the respondents, I have withheld their names and any information by which they can be identified.

3 Under the EPS, migrant workers are entitled to the workers' basic rights stipulated by the Labor Standards Act and the Minimum Wage Act (Shin 2009: 107).

4 The estimated number of migrant workers including the undocumented migrants in Korea, as of 2008, was 548,553. Of these, 179,040 were migrant female workers (Korea Immigration Service, Ministry of Justice 2009: 282–371).

5 The Korean government has implemented a number of steps to employ Korean–Chinese or ethnic Koreans with foreign nationalities legally through the Employment Management System and the Visit and Employment system. Korean–Chinese domestic workers are allowed to work in Korean households under these programs (Shin 2009: 99).

6 Most undocumented migrants ship their children home through the help of their documented fellow migrants or Filipino priests in Korea, because undocumented migrants must send their children back home within a month after birth. Otherwise, they have to pay penalties when their children depart from the country (Lee 2006: 167).

7 After the introduction of the EPS, undocumented migrant workers faced considerable difficulty in finding jobs in factories; Korean companies were charged huge penalties if they were caught employing undocumented migrants (Seol 2004: 29).

References

Ahmed, Sara. 2004. *The Cultural Politics of Emotion*. New York: Routledge.

Anderson, Kay and Smith, Susan J. 2001. "Editorial: Emotional Geographies." *Transactions of the Institute of British Geographers* 26(1): 7–10.

Aronson, Jane and Neysmith, Sheila M. 1996. "'You're Not Just in There to Do the Work': Depersonalizing Policies and the Exploitation of Home Care Workers' Labor." *Gender and Society* 10(1): 59–77.

Asato, Wako. 2003. "Kankoku ni okeru gaikokujin rōdōsya no shogū ni kansuru dōkō to shiensoshiki no han-nō" (The Trend of the Conditions of Foreign Workers and the Response of Migrant Support Organizations in Korea). *Keizaigaku Ronsyū* 42 (5): 85–103.

Asis, Maruja M.B., Huang, Shirlena and Yeoh, Brenda S.A. 2004. "When the Light of the Home is Abroad: Unskilled Female Migration and the Filipino Family." *Singapore Journal of Tropical Geography* 25(2): 198–215.

Bosco, Fernando J. 2007. "Emotions that Build Networks: Geographies of Human Rights Movements in Argentina and Beyond." *Tijdschrift voor Economische en Sociale Geografie* 98(5): 545–63.

Chan, Annie H.N. 2005. "Live-in Foreign Domestic Workers and their Impact on Hong Kong's Middle Class Families." *Journal of Family and Economic Issues* 26(4): 509–28.

Cheng, Shu-Ju A. 2004. "When the Personal Meets the Global at Home: Filipina Domestics and their Female Employers in Taiwan." *Frontiers* 25(2): 31–52.

Glenn, Evelyn N. 1986. *Issei, Nisei, War Bride: Three Generations of Japanese American Women in Domestic Service*. Philadelphia, PA: Temple University Press.

Himmelweit, Susan. 1999. "Caring Labor." *Annals of the American Academy of Political and Social Science* 561: 27–38.

Hochschild, Arlie R. 1983. *The Managed Heart: Commercialization of Human Feeling*. Berkeley and Los Angeles: University of California Press.

——2000. "Global Care Chains and Emotional Surplus Value." In Will Hutton and Anthony Giddens (eds), *On the Edge: Living with Global Capitalism*. London: Jonathan Cape, 130–46.

——2003. "Love and Gold." In Barbara Ehrenreich and Arlie Russell Hochschild (eds), *Global Woman: Nannies, Maids, and Sex Workers in the New Economy*. New York: Metropolitan Books, Henry Holt and Company, 15–30.

Hondagneu-Sotelo, Pierrette. 1994. "Regulating the Unregulated? Domestic Workers' Social Networks." *Social Problems* 41(1): 50–64.

Hondagneu-Sotelo, Pierrette and Avila, Ernestine. 1997. "'I'm Here, but I'm There': The Meanings of Latina Transnational Motherhood." *Gender and Society* 11(5): 548–71.

Huang, Liling and Douglass, Mike. 2009. "Foreign Workers and Spaces for Community Life: Taipei's Little Philippines." In Amrita Daniere and Mike Douglass (eds), *The Politics of Civic Space in Asia: Building Urban Communities*. London and New York: Routledge, 51–71.

Ito, Ruri, Ogaya, Chiho, Tenegra, Brenda and Inaba, Nanako. 2008. "Ika ni shite 'kea jōzu na Firipin jin' wa tsukurareruka? Kea gibā to sai seisan rōdō no 'kokusai shohin' ka" (How the 'Good Carer Filipinos' are Created? Caregivers and the 'International Commodification' of Reproductive Labor). In Ruri Ito and Mariko Adachi (eds), *Kokusai idō to "rensa suru jendā": Saiseisan ryōiki no gurōbaruka*

(International Migration and "Genders Interlinked": Globalization of the Reproductive Sphere). Tokyo: Sakuhin-sha, 117–43.

Kim, Woo-Seon. 2007. *Church and Civil Society in Korea after Democratization: The NGOs' Activism for Migrant Workers.* PhD diss., University of California, San Diego.

Kim, Young-Joo. 2009. "Yŏsŏng oegugin nodongja ŭi saenghwal shiltae mi't jiwŏn jŏngjaek bang'an: Ch'ungch'ŏng-namdo sare rŭl chungshim ro" (The Life and Working Conditions of Overseas Migrant Women Workers and the Policy Direction: Focusing on Chung-cheong-nam-do Case). *Han'guk Minjok Yŏn'gu Nonjip* 37: 178–91.

Korea Immigration Service, Ministry of Justice (Pŏpmubu ch'ulipkuk oegugin jŏngjaek bonbu). 2009. *2008 Nyŏndo ch'ulipkuk oegugin jŏngjaek t'onggae yŏnbo* (Annual Report of the Statistics of Immigration Policies for Foreigners in 2008), 282–371, 738–801.

——2013. "Sachŭng palgŭp annae menyuŏl: Ch'eryu jagyŏkbyŏl daesang, ch'ombu sŏryu dung" (A Guide to the Issuance of Visas: The Categories of the Qualifications of Sojourn, the Documents for Application and Others). September 1, 1–300. www.hikorea.go.kr (accessed October 1, 2013).

Lee, Hye-Kyung. 2003. "Gender, Migration and Civil Activism in South Korea." *Asian and Pacific Migration Journal* 12(1–2): 127–53.

——2005. "Changing Trends in Paid Domestic Work in South Korea." In Shirlena Huang, Brenda S.A. Yeoh and Noor A. Rahman (eds), *Asian Women as Transnational Domestic Workers.* Singapore: Marshall Cavendish Academic, 341–63.

Lee, Jungwhan. 2008. "Migrant Workers and HIV Vulnerability in Korea." *International Migration* 46(3): 217–33.

Lee, Minwon. 2006. "Invisibility and Temporary Residence Status of Filipino Workers in South Korea." *Journal for Cultural Research* 10(2): 159–72.

Mai, Nicola and King, Russell. 2009. "Introduction: Love, Sexuality and Migration: Mapping the Issue(s)." *Mobilities* 4(3): 295–307.

McElhinny, Bonnie. 1994. "An Economy of Affect: Objectivity, Masculinity and the Gendering of Police Work." In Andrea Cornwall and Nancy Lindisfarne (eds), *Dislocating Masculinity: Comparative Ethnographies.* London and New York: Routledge, 159–71.

McKay, Deirdre. 2007. "'Sending Dollars Shows Feeling': Emotions and Economies in Filipino Migration." *Mobilities* 2(2): 175–94.

Morokvasic, Mirjana. 2007. "Migration, Gender, Empowerment." In Ilse Lenz, Charlotte Ullrich and Barbara Fersch (eds), *Gender Orders Unbound: Globalisation, Restructuring and Reciprocity.* Opladen and Farmington Hills, MI: Barbara Budrich Publishers, 69–97.

Parreñas, Rhacel S. 2001. *Servants of Globalization: Women, Migration and Domestic Work*. Stanford, CA: Stanford University Press.

——2005. *Children of Global Migration: Transnational Families and Gendered Woes.* Stanford, CA: Stanford University Press.

Pe-Pua, Rogelia. 2003. "Wife, Mother, and Maid: The Triple Role of Filipino Domestic Workers in Spain and Italy." In Nicola Piper and Mina Roces (eds), *Wife or Worker? Asian Women and Migration*. Lanham, MD: Rowman and Littlefield Publishers, 157–80.

Pribilsky, Jason. 2004. "'*Aprendemos a Convivir*': Conjugal Relations, Co-Parenting, and Family Life among Ecuadorian Transnational Migrants in New York City and the Ecuadorian Andes." *Global Networks* 4(3): 313–34.

Romero, Mary. 1992. *Maid in the U.S.A.* New York and London: Routledge.
Seol, Dong-Hoon. 1999. *Oegugin nodongja wa Han'guk sahoe* (Foreign Workers and Korean Society). Seoul: Seoul Taehakkyo Ch'ulp'anbu.
——2004. "Migrant Workers in the Midst of Reforming Foreign Labor Policy in Korea." In Yong Soon Min and Allan DeSouza (eds), *Xen: Migration, Labor and Identity: SSamzie artbook No.27*. Seoul: SSamzie Space, 26–30.
Shin, Julia J. 2009. "The Gendered and Racialised Division in the Korean Labour Market: The Case of Migrant Workers in the Catering Sector." *East Asia* 26: 93–111.
Suzuki, Nobue. 2007. "Carework and Migration: Japanese Perspectives on the Japan-Philippines Economic Partnership Agreement." *Asian and Pacific Migration Journal* 16(3): 357–81.
Tenegra, Brenda R. 2006. "Transcending Dislocations: Narratives from Filipina Domestic Workers in Tokyo." *Annals of Ochanomizu Geographical Society* 46: 29–46.
Tsujimoto, Toshiko. 2003. "Church Organization and its Networks for the Filipino Migrants: Surviving and Empowering in Korea." In Mamoru Tsuda (ed.), *Filipino Diaspora: Demography, Social Networks, Empowerment and Culture*. Quezon City: Philippine Migration Research Network (PMRN) and Philippine Social Science Council, 125–62.
——2013. "Gŭlrobŏlhan ch'awŏn esŏ iruŏjinŭn tolbom nodong ŭi ŭimi pyŏnhwa: P'ilrip'in ijunodongja e chumokhamyŏ" (Global Transformation of the Meanings of Care Labor: Focusing on Filipino Migrant Workers). *Asia Jŏnŏl* 6: 168–89.
Uttal, Lynet and Tuominen, Mary. 1999. "Tenuous Relationships: Exploitation, Emotion, and Racial Ethnic Significance in Paid Child Care Work." *Gender and Society* 13(6): 758–80.
Yeates, Nicola. 2004. "'Global Care Chains': Critical Reflections and Lines of Enquiry." *International Feminist Journal of Politics* 6(3): 369–91.
Yeoh, Brenda S.A. and Huang, Shirlena. 1999. "Singapore Women and Foreign Domestic Workers: Negotiating Domestic Work and Motherhood." In Janet H. Momsen (ed.), *Gender, Migration and Domestic Service*. London and New York: Routledge, 277–300.

Part VI

Affect, modernity and empires

9 Affective attachments to Japanese women's language

Language, gender and emotion in colonialism

Momoko Nakamura

> One morning in June, I had a quarrel with my eight-year-old daughter … When I became very angry, I heard the most unexpected words from her mouth, "Shut your trap!" … To have to hear such dirty language from an innocent girl like her, I wonder what is happening in this society.
>
> (Housewife, 37, *Asahi Shimbun*, July 1, 2006)

Japanese people have a strong affective attachment to Japanese women's language. It brings them such joy to hear polite, soft and indirect women's language uttered from women's mouths. Reflecting the national desire to hear feminine speech, etiquette books for women on how to look beautiful, be loved and gain happiness by learning and manipulating women's language are always on bestseller lists. The emotional attachment to women's language has often been translated into hatred of and refusal to accept any change in women's speech more than that of anybody else. Women with unfeminine speech make people irritated, frustrated and even angry, thus readers' letters to both national and local newspapers all over Japan are filled with daily complaints by people criticizing women's unfeminine speech heard on the street, on the train or at home. Correcting a daughter's speech is a parental responsibility and a means of discipline. If a daughter uses vulgar speech, despite her parents' discipline, as the above reader's letter shows, a mother might even bother to write a letter to a newspaper. The irresistible refusal to change woman's speech is not confined to older speakers. A twenty-two-year-old female student wrote to a newspaper: "Recently, it seems noteworthy that the speech of young women, including that of myself, has gotten worse" (*Asahi Shimbun*, March 11, 1999).

The irritation, frustration and anger evoked by woman's unfeminine utterances can even trigger unexpected action. In November, 2009, a government committee started screening ministries' budget requests. An Upper House female member of the committee, Renho, had several fierce verbal battles with bureaucrats and gained public attention. On the last day of the committee's deliberation, a seventy-year-old male rock musician, Yuuya Uchida, appeared at the screening place. Newspaper reporters were surprised to find him in this unlikely place and asked him why he came. He answered: "The screening itself really shows democracy in action, but watching Renho on TV, I got angry at her rude way of speaking. That's why I came here today" (*Asahi Shimbun*, November 28, 2009). The rock musician came because he was angry at her manner of speaking, not at what she said. The visual and auditory experience of a speaking woman on TV made him come all the way to the screening place, even though he was fully aware that he would not be given an opportunity to show her his anger directly. Importantly, the reporters immediately accepted this musician's anger without him even offering any explanation of his negative emotions, taking it for granted that their readers would do the same. His anger or irritation induced by the coarse-speaking woman were sensed, felt and promptly resonated among the people. This highlights how affectively impactful women's language is in Japanese society. In this chapter I shall demonstrate the importance of affect as an analytical category in examining the relationships between language and gender.

Previous studies of Japanese women's language have criticized it as a linguistic symbol of polite, soft and indirect heterosexual femininity, stating that women's language legitimates and reproduces the gender hierarchy. Researchers point out that the polite, indirect, soft Japanese women's language functions as a norm to justify ways of restricting women's free speech in Japan (Nakamura 2001). Even in a situation where a woman is physically or verbally abused, the norm can prevent Japanese women from stopping the abuse with coarse speech. Nevertheless, the reproduction of the gender hierarchy alone cannot account for the hatred, disgust and aversion induced by hearing women's unfeminine speech. In fact, Japanese people are fully aware that Japanese women's use of women's language is decreasing, especially among younger generations (see Gendai Nihongo Kenkyuukai 1997; Mizumoto 2010). Therefore, why are parents still shocked at their daughters' unfeminine speech? Crucially, from the reader's letter that opens this chapter, we also realize that the mother was not writing the letter so that her daughter's speech could improve, but was informing readers of the newspaper that something was wrong with society: "I wonder what is happening in this society." The mother viewed her daughter's vulgar speech as a sign of some dreadful social change, which warranted public concern.

To investigate emotional attachment to women's speech in Japan, we need to shift the previous focus on gender to a focus on affect and emotion. Indeed, there is something in women's language or, more precisely, in the image and voice of a woman who speaks/does not speak proper women's language, which can be sensed but cannot be entirely captured by a linguistic analysis. In this chapter, I will examine the affect of women's language and the subjectivities of a speaking woman constructed and mobilized by affect.

In examining the affect of women's language, I adopt a historical approach, aiming to show the genealogy of people's affective attachments to women's language in Japan. McElhinny (2010: 311) points out the importance of historicizing studies of language and affect by arguing that "an approach to affect attentive to history and political economy considers when certain kinds of emotional display emerge as novel or problematic and who gets to decide they are such." Similarly, Mitchell (2009: 214), through an analysis of the shifting emotional values attached to Telugu language in South India, demonstrates "how emotional attachments to language, far from being naturally inherent in speakers' relationships to the words that they use, are historically situated." Indeed, affective attachment to Japanese women's language has been developed through a process of preserving the values attached to women's language in one period and layered with new values in the next. The result is the multilayered and sometimes contradictory values attached to women's language today. Mitchell (2009: 213) emphasizes that the unified passion for the language would not have been so strong, were it not for the shifts during the previous century. Returning to the past tells us why women's impolite speech induces hatred and anger as well as fear and anxiety among Japanese people. This study is not about the past but about how the past informs the present state of women's language. What affective values are accumulated in women's language? What are historical and political processes in which women's language has gained certain values? Who had the privilege actively to attach affective values to women's language? What kind of subjectivity of a speaking woman was constructed in the process of such affective value accumulation? Why does a woman who speaks with coarse language invoke negative emotional reactions?

This chapter attempts to answer these questions by delineating the historical process through which Japanese came to have strong emotional attachments to women's language. I analyze metapragmatic discourses about women's speech in two colonization processes. One is Japan's colonization of East Asian countries during World War II and the other is the occupation of Japan by the US Army after the war. The first section shows that women's language, originally denied legitimate status as the national language, was suddenly praised and elevated to an imperial tradition and a symbol of patriarchy during World War II. This change was mediated by the desire of the Japanese government to imagine a superior imperial language over other world languages to legitimate its linguistic colonization of East Asian countries. Linguists, intellectuals and the military government tried eagerly to prove that Japanese language was so refined, civilized and superior that even women and men speak it differently. The second section demonstrates that during the US occupation, when both the emperor and the patriarchal family systems were denied, Japanese linguists stopped associating women's language with an imperial tradition and instead redefined it as a natural reflection of "innate" femininity. De-politicized and naturalized, women's language became one of the few ideologies that used to represent imperial tradition and patriarchy but survived the defeat in the war and the US occupation. During the pre-war and war periods, the emperor and patriarchal system as the major legal, political institutions sustained Japanese tradition, pride and social order. For Japanese intellectuals, the denial and loss of these systems meant the denial and loss of the stability of Japanese society and identity. Thus, they translated the historical trajectory of women's language into their own expectations for and anticipation of women's language to represent, symbolize and sustain Japanese tradition, pride and social order. The Japanese government and intellectuals, in the two opposite power relations, constantly found a felt space of possibility in women's language that could be mobilized and steered to achieve political and economic objectives. In the conclusion, I will argue that these historical processes engendered both an affective attachment to women's language and an ideal subjectivity of a speaking woman who enacts and validates Japanese tradition, pride and social order by reproducing women's language.

The genealogy of women's language

Women's language is presumably constructed through repeated use of particular features by women in individual interactions. This view claims that the category of women's language has naturally evolved because women have always spoken differently from men, reflecting their essential feminine nature. Gal (1995) has argued, however, that the category of women's speech is culturally constructed within social groups; she proposes to see women's language not as just the total of linguistic features whose frequent use distinguishes women from men, but as an ideological-symbolic construct, a discursive construct, which is potentially constitutive of those identities (Cameron 1997: 28). In this sense, Japanese women's language was redefined as a language ideology (Blommaert 1999; Kroskrity 2000; Schieffelin *et al.* 1998); as "the cultural system of ideas about social and linguistic relationships, together with their loading of moral and political interests" (Irvine 1989: 255), and here I want to add that it is affective—full of affection and effective. The ideology of women's language can be examined as the knowledge that serves as a resource for the ongoing construction of gender identity for both women and men, the norms which operate as a powerful hegemonic construct of preferred feminine speech patterns, and the belief that women and men, because of their innate differences, indeed speak differently (Nakamura n.d., forthcoming). This new perspective of regarding women's language as knowledge, norm and belief has inspired historical and discursive studies of the genealogy of Japanese women's language (Endo 1997; Inoue 2006; Nakamura 2007; Washi 2004). By examining what and whose metalinguistic discourses became possible, meaningful and affective in a particular sociopolitical and economic juncture, these studies have attempted to reveal how the belief, knowledge and affective values of women's language have been constructed by metalinguistic discourse.

Inoue (2006) takes up schoolgirl speech at the end of the nineteenth century, which shares some typical features with women's language today, and she demonstrates how metapragmatic discourses of male intellectuals about the speech of schoolgirls enhanced the emergence of schoolgirl speech in building the modern nation-state, language standardization, capitalism and the development of print mass media. In contrast to the positive evaluation of women's language today, studies of the early modern period demonstrate that women's speech was severely condemned and excluded from the national language that was being formed in the same period. Inoue (2006: 67) points out that the speech of female students was criticized as "unpleasant to the ears," because "it disrupts the symbolic alignment between modernity and masculinity." Nakamura (2006) also demonstrates that schoolgirl speech was derogated by being associated with frivolity and sexuality. For that reason, while grammar books and school textbooks increasingly included linguistic features associated with schoolboy speech in the national language, they completely precluded schoolgirl speech features (Nakamura 2008). Thus, how was the derogated schoolgirl speech turned into the women's language so many Japanese love to hear today? Inoue (2006) argues that by being used in print media such as magazine advertisements in the early twentieth century, schoolgirl speech was assigned the symbolic value of the ideal bourgeois lifestyle, becoming the speech of the universal modern Japanese woman. The acquisition of bourgeois value alone, however, cannot account for excessive reluctance and hatred of hearing unfeminine speech from women. To reveal the genealogy of affect accompanying women's language, we should take into account the reverse colonization experiences during and after World War II which disturbed and shook the foundations of the traditional values and stability of Japanese society and identity. This chapter is the first study of the discourses of linguists and governmental officials in the context of colonization in order to examine how and why their discourses were mobilized and steered to assign affective values to women's language.

Affect and language ideologies

Recent anthropological studies of affect have revealed the central role affect plays both in creating political and economic shifts and structuring subjectivities appropriate to such changes (Clough and Halley 2007). They focus on what affect does in the relationship between subjective experience and the social reconfiguration, rather than trying to define what distinguishes affect from other concepts such as emotion, feeling and desire (Ahmed 2004; Richard and Rudnyckyj 2009). This chapter is based on three theoretical arguments of this new perspective. First, although affect studies have been strongly influenced by psychological understanding to consider it as immanent in individuals—the inner state manifested through outward expression—recent studies have focused on how emotions are socially mediated and historically constructed. Ahmed (2004) proposes to analyze how the circulation of emotions between subjects creates the effect of a collective. Such inter-subjective, reflective relations enhance the emergence of imagined communities (Anderson 1983). Similarly, I argue that the circulation of desire, anticipation and expectation for the superiority of Japanese language during the war and the stability of Japanese society and identity during the US occupation made possible, meaningful and acceptable the discourses to redefine women's language as the symbol of tradition, pride and order.

Second, recent studies emphasize both the linguistic and non-linguistic enactments of affect, such as tears and hugging (Richard and Rudnyckyj 2009), voice (Inoue 2006; Weidman 2007), and objects (Navaro-Yashin 2009). Due to the difficulty of obtaining non-linguistic data of the early twentieth century, however, I focus on academic discourse such as publications by intellectuals and grammar books from the beginning of World War I (1914) through the end of the US occupation (1952). The readers will be surprised to find that linguists played a highly political role in producing discourses supporting and sustaining the goals and strategies of the government in each period.

Third, two arguments have been proposed concerning the relationship between affect and subjectivity. Ahmed (2004) regards affect as a phenomenon circulating between bodies and signs. Richard and Rudnyckyj (2009), by contrast, focus on an aspect of affect that forms a medium through which subjects act on others and are acted upon, creating new types of subjects and new relations among those subjects. In this chapter I adopt both perspectives. The first and second sections of the chapter, by analyzing metapragmatic discourses circulating among subjects, delineate how and why particular affective values were assigned to women's language. I then argue that once a particular affect is assigned to women's language, it is mobilized to construct a socially acceptable, ideal subjectivity of a speaking woman. The notion of language ideologies, as shown in the definition cited above, has been concerned with political and moral interests assigned to language. How such interests influence speaking subjects, however, has not been fully investigated. In discussing that affect mediates particular values attached to language and production of new subjects and relationships, I intend to demonstrate how affect theory can shed new light on the study of language ideology.

Women's language as imperial tradition, 1914–45

> Can we see a correct, pure Japanese language spoken in the future Manchuria? This is an important, national task of the Japanese empire. If we realize that the major role to fulfill this task depends on women's speech, however … I feel horrified and cannot help but worry about the future of this country.
>
> (Matsumoto 1941: 28)

Shigeo Matsumoto, a male teacher at an elementary school in the Japanese colony of Manchuria, was offended by the Japanese women's speech he heard in Manchuria in 1941. Matsumoto was disappointed precisely because he was expecting the speech of Japanese women in Manchuria to fulfill "an important, national task" of speaking "pure Japanese language." That is why he paid attention to women's speech and noticed that they were not speaking as he expected. He interpreted this fact as a national problem that would affect the future of Japan. Nevertheless, such nationalistic and emotional expectations of women's speech were unimaginable in the late nineteenth century. The early form of Japanese national language was tailored to male citizens as the primary, authentic speakers. Okano (1964 [1902]: 510) suggests that Japanese language policies set "the language of men in middle class society" as the national language standard. Linguists, in writing grammar books and school textbooks of Japanese national language, completely ignored women's speech so that it remained either the object of feminine norms or the target of criticism (Nakamura 2008). For Shigeo Matsumoto to make such a statement, some changes must have occurred in the way Japanese people conceptualized the speech of Japanese women from the early to the mid-twentieth century. What did Matsumoto mean by "national task" of speaking "pure Japanese" in Manchuria, the colony of Japan, in the mid-twentieth century? Why did Japanese people change their views of women's speech and what political and economic processes enabled such a change during the war period?

The exclusion of women's speech from the national language changed when Japan started invading and colonizing other countries in East Asia. After victory in the Sino–Japanese war in 1895, Japan occupied Taiwan. After winning the Russo–Japanese war in 1905, Japan annexed Korea in 1910. The Kanto earthquake (1923) and the Great Depression (1929) moved the government to react with a colonial policy utilizing armed aggression. Japan occupied and began ruling Manchuria in 1932. In 1937, Japan went to war with China and the invasion of Asian countries continued. The Japanese military government tried to advance colonization by teaching Japanese language to those in the colonized areas to implement the Japanese spirit, meaning loyalty to the Japanese emperor at the time (Kubota 2005; Lee 1996; Osa 1998; Shi 2003; Yasuda 1997). Japanese colonization was carried out based on the assimilation policy of educating people in the colonies to become Japanese citizens loyal to the Japanese emperor. The military government planned to establish an Asian imperial realm under the sovereignty of the emperor. For the people in the colonized areas, however, the emperor was not the subject of religious worship but simply the leader of the colonizer. Lacking both historical and religious reasons to inculcate the Japanese spirit, intellectuals opted for teaching Japanese language as an effective strategy (Kubota 2005; Shi 2003; Yasuda 1998).

Teaching Japanese language was considered an effective tool to implement loyalty to the emperor, since it had already been claimed that Japanese language embodied the Japanese spirit. Japanese national language was ideologically constructed to enhance nation-state building since the late nineteenth century (Lee 1996; Osa 1998; Yasuda 1997), based on the nationalistic ideology of one language, one nation, one state (Woolard 1998: 17). Kazutoshi Ueda (1968: 110), a professor at the Imperial University, stated that "the Japanese language is the spiritual blood of the Japanese people," asserting the close connection between Japanese spirit and national language. Language policy makers during the war directly expanded his conception of national language to overseas, claiming, "Now that Taiwan and Korea have became part of our country, teaching Japanese spoken language is the best way to transform those people into Japanese" (Kokugo Choosa Iinkai 1980: introduction). In Korea, Japanese-language education was forced by the educational laws issued in 1911, 1922 and 1938. In 1940, Koreans were obliged to use Japanese names. In the 1940s, the military government proposed the idea of the Greater East Asia Co-prosperity Sphere and Japanese linguists repeatedly claimed that "the Japanese language is expected to take an active part as the common national language in the Greater East Asia Co-prosperity Sphere" (Ishii 1941: 235). Japanese national language was not a mere language but was expected to become the symbol of "Japanese polity" and "Japanese spirit" (Shi 2003: 208), binding together all the people in the colonies through loyalty to the emperor. What Shigeo Matsumoto, a teacher in the Japanese colony of Manchuria, meant by "an important, national task" of speaking "pure Japanese language," therefore, was the task of Japanese people in the Japanese colonies to speak and teach Japanese national language aiming to transform people in the colonies into Japanese citizens loyal to the emperor.

Nevertheless, in addition to resistance against the compulsory use of Japanese, teaching Japanese in the colonies faced another difficulty—there was no single Japanese language even inside Japan. To establish a national language, Ueda (1964: 506) claimed to choose the speech of "educated Tokyo residents" as the national language standard. However, even among educated Tokyo residents, wide speech variations were used (Tanaka 1983: 156). Just as the Japanese people were speaking their own regional dialects inside Japan, Japanese language teachers in the colonies spoke regional varieties. Lee (1996: 297–99) documents that in the Second National Language Measure Conference, held in 1941, the major theme of the discussion was not how to teach Japanese in the colonies but discontent with the speech of the teachers. The more the language policy makers tried to set one national language as the goal of colonial education, the more they were annoyed that there was not one Japanese language inside Japan. As Komori (2000: 258) points out, "It was because of this discrepancy that the myth of a single national language had to be desired" in the colonies more than inside Japan. Hoshina (1942: 199), a student of Ueda and a member of language committees in the Ministry of Education, insisted that: "Since the language of a superior nation always possesses strong influence, it is obvious that the Japanese language, the language of the leader of the Co-prosperity Sphere, meets the qualifications." To make sense of such a statement, it was urgent to declare those characteristics of Japanese language that proved its superiority and legitimated Japan's invasion.

The desire to imagine a Japanese imperial language superior to all other world languages as a ploy to legitimate Japanese colonization necessitated two changes to the ideology of women's language inside Japan. One was the emergence of discourses praising women's language as part of the imperial tradition. The other was that academic discourse as in grammar books and language textbooks started referring to linguistic gender differences, gendering

Japanese national language. These two changes both reflected the desire to emphasize the superiority, peculiarity and fineness of Japanese language to legitimate teaching Japanese language in the colonies.

Concerning the first change, many intellectuals suddenly praised women's language as a tradition of the imperial realm and constructed women's language as a symbol of Japanese cultural superiority. They started talking about the origin of women's language, citing either *nyooboo kotoba* (court-women's speech) or *keigo* (polite language). Court-women's speech is a set of words and expressions invented by women serving in the imperial palace in the fourteenth century to refer to domestic items such as food, kitchen utensils and clothes. The first paper connecting women's language to court-women's speech, by Kikuzawa (1929: 67), defines women's language in the 1920s by four characteristics of court-women's speech: use of polite language, use of elegant language, an indirect way of speaking, and avoidance of unrefined Chinese words (Washi 2000: 20). Repeatedly cited, the paper made court-women's speech the origin of women's language. Ishiguro (1943: 227) reiterates: "The characteristics of women's language are making a refined and elegant impression, not expressing anything directly, being polite, and avoiding Chinese words that sound awkward as a part of the Japanese language." Kindaichi (1942: 296), on the other hand, associates women's language with polite language: "To consider the origin of polite language … is to consider the origin of women's language."

To answer why women's language was claimed to derive from court-women's speech and polite language, we need to know what they putatively represent. Above all, court-women's speech was understood in terms of its connection with the emperor's family. Kikuzawa (1933: 40) asserts that the elegance of the emperor's family has continued in the form of court-women's speech: "Court-women's speech originated in the gracious Imperial Court, spread to women in the Shoogun families, on to the wives of feudal lords, then to good families in the common population, and it is still used today." Nevertheless, it was not the emperor's family but women working in the court who started using court-women's speech. Court-women's speech was not initially considered elegant speech. Tayasu (1964 [1771]: 693–94), already in the eighteenth century, criticized it for changing beautiful, traditional names. Polite language was also considered to be a characteristic of the Japanese language of which the entire country could be proud. Kindaichi (1942: 307) asserts: "Our national language has nothing else we can be proud of compared to Western languages … This category of polite language usage is what we can be fully proud of." Court-women's speech and polite language, in other words, were invented as a symbol of the emperor system during the war. Accordingly, to produce discourses that redefined these speech styles as the origins of women's language is to achieve the connection between women's language and imperial tradition (Hobsbaum 1983). Re-inventing women's language as imperial tradition made Japanese language superior and unique by tying its provenance to the emperor system.

At the same time, there emerged other discourses that constructed women's language as a symbol of Japanese cultural superiority. Tanizaki (1975: 157), one of the major writers of modern Japanese literature, states: "That languages spoken by men and women are different is an advantage only the Japanese spoken language possesses. This cannot be found in any other national language than Japan." For Ishiguro (1943: 236), women's language is "one of the beauties of the Japanese language that no other national language is allowed to follow." These discourses, by characterizing women's language as a phenomenon found only in Japan, used it to prove the superiority of Japan.

Women's language was so closely identified with the imperial tradition because the temporal incongruity of nationalism is often resolved by metaphorically invoking gender distinction. Nationalism necessarily embraces the contradiction of simultaneously looking to both past and future. The nation-state cannot be imagined simply by possessing a certain space of land. It is necessary to look to the past to invent its shared history and tradition, and to the future to visualize the present as a process yielding the glorious days to come. "[T]he temporal anomaly within nationalism … is typically resolved by figuring the contradiction in the representation of *time* as a natural division of *gender*. Women are represented as the atavistic and authentic body of national tradition … Men, by contrast, represent the progressive agent of national modernity" (McClintock 1995: 358–59). If nationalism necessarily associates tradition, nature and continuity from the past with femininity, and modernity, progress and discontinuity with masculinity, it was a logical consequence that women's language was chosen during the war as the symbol of the imperial tradition, making gender an affective space that can be invested politically or ideologically. The idea of a superior country with a superior language served to justify Japanese domination of its colonies. As part of this process, women's language was used to the fullest to give substance to the discussion of the superiority of the Japanese language.

In addition to the redefinition of women's language as imperial tradition, the second change in academic discourse occurred: inclusion of linguistic features associated with women into the standard grammar, gendering the national language. This was promoted by the desire to prove that Japanese language was so refined, civilized and superior that women and men use it differently. The biggest difference between pre-war and wartime academic discourse is an increased reference to linguistic gender differences. While few references to these were found in the pre-war period (Nakamura 2008), more intellectuals began to claim during the war that Japanese do and should speak differently according to gender. It was the military government that most strongly emphasized the importance of maintaining linguistic gender differences. In 1941, when the Pacific War broke out, the Ministry of Education issued *Reihoo yookoo* (Gist of Manners), which requires "All men to use manly language and all women to use womanly language," making a strict linguistic distinction between female and male citizens (Reihoo Yookoo Kenkyuu Kai 1941: 65–66).

Gendering the national language was further promoted by grammar books. Nakamura (2004) analyzed sixteen grammar books published from 1922 to 1944 and found two changes compared to those published in the pre-war period. First, grammar books published for overseas use emphasize gender differences much more than those published for use in Japan. For instance, *Japanese: Standard Spoken Grammar of the Greater Co-prosperity Sphere* (Fujiwara 1944) was a textbook for people in Manchuria and China. This book genders the greatest number of features, such as personal pronouns and sentence-final forms, among the sixteen textbooks, as if these different usages prove the uniqueness and superiority of Japanese language. Gendering the national language was most clearly embodied in the textbook for the colonies exactly because it was not what was spoken inside Japan but was an ideology created by the desire to imagine a superior imperial language.

Second, linguistic features, such as *teyo*, *dawa* and *noyo*, which had been called schoolgirl speech and severely criticized during the pre-war period, were included in standard grammar books. Nagata (1976 [1935]: 95) presents both *teyo* and *wa* simply as feminized forms without any criticism. Sakuma (1983: 78) even defends women's use of *no* and *te* as substitutes for *ka* in interrogative forms: "they were all created to soften the demanding connotation implied in *ka*." Grammar books suddenly included schoolgirl speech in standard Japanese to emphasize gender differences within national language. In fact, grammar books rigorously criticized some other usages of female students, such as the masculine personal pronouns *kimi* and *boku*. Kikuzawa (1940: 303) states: " … we should not let women use the masculine *kimi* or *boku*." Kieda (1943: 85) even claims that "women should never use [*boku*]. If a young woman uses *boku* or *kimi* … such a woman is not a Japanese woman." These grammar books incorporated schoolgirl usages that reinforced gender distinction, while criticizing those that crossed the border of gender distinction, aiming to construct a gendered national language. In so doing, they thus adopted the language of "educated" female students, which fitted the definition of standard language, rather than the language of non-Tokyo or lower-class women. Grammar books integrated the schoolgirl features into their prescription of Japanese national language to emphasize gender differences.

The ideology of gendered national language was created to reproduce in the language the patriarchal family system crucial to the war effort. Gendering the national language symbolically enhances gendering Japanese citizens (Gal and Irvine 1995). In 1938, the National Mobilization Law was issued and women, who had been outside of the framework of Japanese citizens, were required to contribute to the war (Suzuki 1997). National Mobilization, however, required women to "serve the country behind the guns" as wives and mothers, in contrast to the role of soldiers for men. Even during the last years of the war, the military's top brass vehemently refused the idea of female conscription (Ooe 1988: 442), claiming that "the destruction of the [patriarchal] family system is the destruction of the country" (Wakakuwa 1995, 2000: 45). One reason for refusing the conscription of women, therefore, was to maintain the patriarchal family system, which had been effective at controlling and mobilizing the nation. The Great Japan Imperial Constitution (1889) established the patriarchal family, based on absolute power of the father, turning the private sphere of the family into a minimum unit of the state. By creating continuity from the patriarchal family to the imperial state, the ideology of "state-as-patriarchal family" successfully mobilized the whole nation as the children of the emperor. During the war, when national mobilization was promoted by expanding patriarchal aspects of the family to the state itself, it was crucial that national language, the linguistic symbol of the nation-state, be gendered. Nagao (1943: 131) explains: "The power of women's language, the language of love, comfort, and friendship, during this time [of war], along with the solemn, simple language of soldiers [which expresses] determination and responsibility, strengthens the unity of those who fight and promotes the will to cooperate with each other." Here, women's language is contrasted with soldiers' language, which are conceptualized as together supporting the military regime. Gendering national language, thus symbolically gendering citizens, functioned to maintain the patriarchal system, which was the effective system to control people as a minimum unit of the emperor system. Redefining women's language as part of the imperial tradition and gendering national language were promoted by the desire for a superior Japanese language legitimating Japanese colonization and the desire to mobilize the patriarchal family for war efforts.

Essentializing women's language, 1945–52

> [Prime Minister Yoshida Shigeru states] that as a consequence of the emperor's more explicit detachment from politics, his "position"—presumably meaning his spiritual role—"will become that much more enlarged, and his position will increase in importance and delicacy."
>
> (Dower 1999: 390)

Fifteen days after World War II ended on August 15, 1945, the Supreme Commander of the Allied Powers (SCAP), General Douglas MacArthur, arrived in Japan and launched the seven-year occupation of Japan. While the Allied Powers sought to have the emperor take responsibility for the war, SCAP planned to terminate the occupation as quickly as possible by governing Japan through the emperor system. To get rid of his militaristic image, the emperor declared his transformation from "god" to "human" in January 1946. As a result, the *Showa* Emperor, generally known outside Japan as Hirohito, was not designated a war criminal in the International Military Tribunal for the Far East, and the Japanese Constitution issued in 1946 maintained the emperor as the symbol of the state and the unity of the people. This section shows that just as the emperor endured by giving up his sovereignty, the ideology of women's language survived by abandoning its connection with the imperial tradition and being newly redefined as a natural representation of femininity.

Post-war academic discourses show three changes concerning women's language. First, in discussing the relationship between women's language and court-women's speech, they no longer mentioned the emperor system. The US occupation authorities ordered deletion of school materials linked to militarism, ultra-nationalism and *Shintoism*. Under such conditions, it is likely that researchers voluntarily decided not to refer to the emperor in their discussions about women's language. Second, along with the first change, some linguists began to state that both men and women were now using court-women's speech. Mashimo (1948: 72) states: "few [court-women words] are used only by women today … " It became difficult to associate directly court-women's speech with women's language. Third, they continued to talk about four characteristics of women's language proposed by Kikuzawa (1929) and its relation to polite language. Yoshida (1952: 34) completely repeats four characteristics of Kikuzawa in stating that: "[Women's language is characterized by] first, use of elegant or special feminine words, second, frequent polite speech, third, an indirect way of speaking and fourth, avoidance of Chinese words." Yazaki (1960: 209) also repeats the four characteristics: "Women's language uses words specific to women, avoids vulgar, violent words, prefers elegant, polite expressions, and an indirect way of speaking. Thus, women's language frequently uses polite language." Accordingly, linguists continued to associate polite language with women's language, following the argument proposed by Kindaichi (1942) during the war. Mashimo (1948: 168) states: "Women and polite expressions are inseparable." Kindaichi (1948: 91) himself maintains his argument: "Polite usage is inseparable from women's language." As a result, while women's language was de-politicized by being dissociated from the imperial tradition, it remained a symbol of the tradition of Japanese language and the ideology of gendered Japanese language was maintained.

Meanwhile, the US occupation authorities denied the patriarchal family system, actively promoting gender equality. Of the five reform orders SCAP announced on October 11, 1946, the first was the liberation of Japanese women by granting suffrage to women over twenty years old. The Constitution of Japan stipulated fundamental human rights, including two articles, Article 14 "Equality of the sexes" and Article 24 "Equality of husband and wife." The women's equality and rights guaranteed in these articles "went far beyond what the U.S. Congress, the state legislatures, and many Americans are willing to accept in their own country" (Pharr 1987: 222). The amendment to the Civil Law the following year dissolved the patriarchal family system and allowed equal inheritance for women and men.

The policy of the occupation authority elicited two responses among Japanese intellectuals. One was to welcome the democratic ideas of the policy. They stopped talking about women's language as imperial tradition and started criticizing women's language as an obstacle to gender equality. The other response was ostensibly to accept the policy while trying hard to preserve at least the patriarchy. The latter group took pains to preserve women's language which had symbolically embodied imperial tradition and patriarchy during the pre-war and war periods.

The first group criticized the negative effect of women's language on equal rights of the sexes. As the journalist Bunshiroo Suzuki (1948: 60–61) states, "Although people talk about … equal rights among the sexes, as long as men's speech differs from women's speech so clearly, women themselves cannot help but violate that equality on a daily basis." The critic Furuya (1953) argues that "the past 'soft women's language' is the language of weak, unconfident women who, their power deprived by men, had to live assiduously studying the pleasure of men and trying painfully to show coquetry and flirtation … It is the language of slaves."

To compete with this denial of women's language, several discourses vindicating women's language emerged. The most prevalent feature of such discourses is essentialization, the process that turns a phenomenon related to gender into one based on biological sex distinction. These discourses turned women's language into a naturally determined, biological construct—i.e. merely an outgrowth of femininity, which was conceptualized as women's innate nature. A typical example is found in Mashimo (1948), who introduced the distinction between social equality and biological differences. When the US occupation launched women's liberation, only biological differences could be used to deny social equality, so he tried to protect women's language by redefining it as the natural representation of women's innate femininity: "Although men and women are originally equal …, they have different natures and distinctive roles according to the difference … For example, love, tenderness, modesty, and prudence are characteristics with which women are endowed, and they constitute that which we call femininity. Therefore, humble, respectful speech, which flows naturally from femininity, represents women's language" (Mashimo 1948: 132). The subsequent essentializing discourses followed Mashimo's strategy. By making a distinction between features of women's language that are based on social condition and those based on women's nature or physiological characteristics, they argued that we should abandon the former but should keep the latter. Nagano (1955: 81) claims: "Features of women's language based on differences in social class or education—social conditions—will fade away … However, those features based on women's psychological, physiological conditions—natural conditions … will ultimately remain." Rather than directly asserting the natural, innate foundation of women's language, they first distinguish features of women's language based on social conditions from those based on nature, then proclaim that the latter features will survive. Such a strategy was necessary because simply to compel the use of women's language did not work under the democratization policy of the post-war occupation. To develop a laudable argument under such social change, they had to show their recognition of the problem of women's language. Associated with "natural" features, the ideology of women's language was redefined as a natural phenomenon that continued irrespective of social change. Japanese linguists and intellectuals separated women's language both from the emperor system and social gender inequality and associated it with "natural" gender distinction. Both the separation of women's language from the imperial tradition and the essentialization discourse successfully preserved women's language.

Two factors affected the vigorous attempt of Japanese linguists and intellectuals to preserve the ideology of national language gendered by women's language. First, for the intellectuals who lost confidence with Japan's demise in the war and under the US occupation, the two language ideologies (women's language, a symbol of the imperial tradition, and gendered national language, a symbol of a patriarchal family system) were recognized as among the last means to recover Japanese pride and order. Under the occupation, the emperor, who had been worshiped as a living god, declared his humanity and was redefined as the symbol of the state. The divinity of the emperor, founder of the Japanese family system, was easily refuted by the foreign occupation army. To consolidate social order, therefore, some intellectuals considered it crucial to preserve patriarchal institutions as much as possible.

Second, for many Japanese, the patriarchal family system and the emperor system were inseparably intertwined. It was evident in the controversy in the Japanese government concerning the US draft of the new Japanese Constitution. The controversy reveals that the seemingly unrelated issues of women's liberation and the emperor system were understood nevertheless to be closely linked. Thus, regarding Article 24, guaranteeing the equality of women in family life, the Japanese government offered objections "as strong as in the matter of the emperor system" (Doi and Gordon 1996: 19–20). At a plenary session of the House of Representatives discussing Article 24, Fujiroo Hara states: "It is needless to say that the family system and the emperor system in Japan are very closely related ancient customs … The family system can be referred to as God's road for our nation, the system we have maintained since the beginning of the world. We believe that it is our family system that leads us along the wide road to the foot of the emperor" (Shimizu 1962: 501). It is not surprising, therefore, to discover that those people, even after the patriarchy was denied its legal foundation, made great efforts to keep citizens gendered by preserving other institutions. One of these was the ideology of national language gendered by women's language.

De-politicized by its dissociation from the imperial tradition and naturalized by the association with "natural" femininity, women's language became one of the few ideologies that had formerly represented the imperial tradition and patriarchal family system but survived the defeat in the war and the US occupation. As testified by the above Fujiroo Hara's statement, during the prewar and war periods, the emperor system and patriarchal family system were closely intertwined with each other to sustain Japanese tradition, pride and social order. The Japanese government and intellectuals, in seeking to recover and rebuild the stability of Japanese society and identity after the war, thus translated the historical trajectory of women's language into the expectation and anticipation towards women's language to represent, symbolize and sustain Japanese tradition, pride and social order. Song (2009: 201), in discussing close relationships between colonialism, sexism and racism in Korea, points out that "[sexist] tradition is often invented, reinterpreted, or reinforced by those males whose pride has been damaged after the domination by different races." It was through the historical process in which women's language survived the total loss of Japanese tradition, pride and order in the war that Japanese intellectuals found this language as a site for affective and ideological investment in order to recover Japanese social order and identity at the intersection of women and language.

Conclusion

Japanese people came to sense and feel the possibility and potentiality to sustain Japanese tradition, pride and social order in women's language, through the sociopolitical processes of two opposite colonization experiences during and after World War II. To legitimate linguistic colonization of the East Asian countries during World War II, women's language was suddenly praised as an imperial tradition and a symbol of patriarchy. After the war, under occupation by the US Army which denied both the emperor system and patriarchal system, Japanese intellectuals viewed women's language as a felt space of possibility to recover Japanese social order and identity. Throughout these historical and political processes, linguists played a crucial role in producing metalinguistic discourses about women's speech that could be mobilized for political and economic purposes.

This does not mean that the affect of women's language in Japan has not been changed for the past seventy years after the war. Nor does it mean that every time a woman speaks women's language, she preserves Japanese tradition. Rather it means that to be able to talk about Japanese women's language or to be able to say that Japanese language has women's language enables people to confirm themselves that there is a space in which Japanese social order and identity can be reproduced, preserved and sustained; the belief that Japanese women speak women's language endorses the stability of Japanese society. The result of empirical studies that Japanese women's use of women's language is decreasing makes no effect on the belief exactly because it is the belief irrelevant to empirical facts. Instead, the feelings, belief, anticipation and possibility attached to women's language intensify people's attachments to it. No matter how much Japanese society changes and how insecure we may feel, as long as Japanese people can believe that Japanese women are speaking women's language, Japanese tradition, order and identity are secured.

Such emotional commitment to women's language constructs a historically unprecedented subjectivity of a speaking woman. Richard and Rudnyckyj (2009: 60) argue that affect serves as a medium through which the subjects appropriate to social shifts are formed and produced. Similarly, affective attachments to women's language were mobilized to construct a socially acceptable or ideal subjectivity of a speaking woman. An ideal speaking woman validates and legitimates Japanese social order and identity by reproducing women's language. Many studies on affect focus on how affect is mobilized to enhance emerging social changes such as globalization and new liberalism. In contrast, women's language, translated as a possibility to sustain Japanese tradition and order, became a national notion not allowed to change. Thus, the use of women's language was regarded as the primary task of female citizens. Kindaichi (1942: 309) declares: "To become a complete Japanese woman, she must, more than anything, acquire this traditional Japanese woman's language." Such an emotional statement reflects a latent fear of losing or experiencing any change in women's language; the fear and anxiety, as mentioned, shared by the mother who wrote the letter to a newspaper about her daughter's impolite speech in 2006. Polite, indirect and soft women's language uttered from women's bodies can be mobilized into the possibility to believe that Japanese tradition, pride and social order are safely inherited through which Japanese identities can be established.

Women's unfeminine, impolite speech, on the other hand, makes people irritated, frustrated, angry, fearful and anxious exactly because such speech refuses the possibility to believe in social order and makes their own identities insecure. The image and voice of an impolite, unfeminine speaking woman inevitably make people aware of the fragility and vulnerability of affective possibility attached to women's language. It is thus legitimate to comment, evaluate and criticize a woman's speech solely based on how she speaks rather than what she says. Affect mediates people's attachment and perception about women's language.

Acknowledgements

An earlier version of this article was presented at the joint meetings of the Canadian Anthropological Society and the American Ethnological Society held at the University of British Columbia, Canada, in May 2009. I owe many thanks to Jie Yang, organizer of the panel and editor of the book, for giving me insightful comments and advice. I am also grateful for the Grant-in-Aid for Scientific Research (B) (grant no. 20310155) provided by the Japanese Ministry of Education, Culture, Sports, Science and Technology.

References

Ahmed, Sara. 2004. "Affective Economies." *Social Text* 22(2): 117–39.

Anderson, Benedict. 1983. *Imagined Communities: Reflections on the Origin and Spread of Nationalism*. London and New York: Verso.

Blommaert, Jan. 1999. "The Debate is Open." In Jan Blommaert (ed.), *Language Ideological Debates*. Berlin and New York: Mouton de Gruyter, 1–38.

Cameron, Deborah. 1997. "Theoretical Debates in Feminist Linguistics: Questions of Sex and Gender." In Ruth Wodak (ed.), *Gender and Discourse*. London: Sage, 21–36.

Clough, Patricia T. and Halley, Jean, eds. 2007. *The Affective Turn: Theorizing the Social*. Durham, NC and London: Duke University Press.

Doi, Takako and Gordon, Beate Sirota. 1996. *Kenpoo ni danjo byoodoo kisoo hiwa* (The Secret Story of Including Equality of the Sexes in the Constitution). Tokyo: Iwanami Shoten.

Dower, John W. 1999. *Embracing Defeat: Japan in the Wake of World War II*. New York: W.W. Norton & Company.

Endo, Orie. 1997. *Onna no kotoba no bunka shi* (The Cultural History of Women's Language). Tokyo: Gakuyoo Shobo.

Fujiwara, Yoichi. 1944. *Nihongo: Kyooeiken hyoojun koogo hoo* (Japanese: Standard Spoken Grammar of the Greater Co-prosperity Sphere). Tokyo: Meguro Shoten.

Furuya, Tsunatake. 1953. "Onna kotoba" (Women's Language). *Mainichi Shimbun*, March 4.

Gendai Nihongo Kenkyuukai. 1997. *Josei no kotoba: Shokuba hen* (Women's Speech: At Work Place). Tokyo: Hitsuji Shobo.

Gal, Susan. 1995. "Language, Gender, and Power: An Anthropological Review." In Kira Hall and Mary Bucholtz (eds), *Gender Articulated: Language and the Socially Constructed Self*. New York and London: Routledge, 169–82.

Gal, Susan and Irvine, Judith T. 1995. "The Boundaries of Languages and Disciplines: How Ideologies Construct Difference." *Social Research* 62(4): 967–1001.

Hobsbaum, Eric. 1983. "Introduction: Inventing Traditions." In Eric Hobsbaum and Terence Ranger (eds), *The Invention of Tradition*. Cambridge: Cambridge University Press, 1–14.

Hoshina, Kooichi. 1942. *Daitooa kyooeiken to kokugo seisaku* (The Greater East Asia Co-prosperity Sphere and National Language Policy). Tokyo: Toosei Sha.

Inoue, Miyako. 2006. *Vicarious Language: Gender and Linguistic Modernity in Japan*. Berkeley, Los Angeles and London: University of California Press.

Irvine, Judith T. 1989. "When Talk isn't Cheap: Language and Political Economy." *American Ethnologist* 16(2): 248–67.

Ishiguro, Yoshimi. 1943. *Utsukushii Nihongo: Josei shinsho* (The Beautiful Japanese Language: Women's Book). Tokyo: Koofuukan.

Ishii, Shooji. 1941. "Chuutoogakkoo no kokugo kyooiku" (Language Education in Secondary School). In *Kokugo bunka kooza 3: Kokugo kyooiku hen* (Lectures on Language and Culture 3: National Language Education). Tokyo: Asahi Shimbun Sha, 222–35.

Kieda, Masuichi. 1943. *Kotoba zukai no sahoo* (The Manner of Language Use). Osaka: Osakadoo Shoten.

Kikuzawa, Sueo. 1929. "Fujin no kotoba no tokuchoo ni tsuite" (On Characteristics of Ladies' Language). *Kokugo Kyooiku* 14(3): 66–75.

——1933. "Kokugo isooron" (Variations of National Language). In *Kokugo kagaku kooza 3: Kokugo gaku, ippan to tokushu* (Lectures on National-language Science 3: National Language Study, General Usage and Special Usage). Tokyo: Meiji Shoin, 3–67.

——1940. *Kokugo to kokuminsei: Nihon seishin no senmei* (National Language and Nationality: The Clarification of Japanese Spirit). Tokyo: Shuubunkan.

Kindaichi, Kyoosuke. 1942. *Kokugo kenkyuu* (A Study of the National Language). Tokyo: Yagumo Shorin.

——1948. *Nihongo no shinro* (The Course of the Japanese Language). Kyoto: Kyoto In Shokan.

Kokugo Choosa Iinkai. 1980 [1916/1917]. *Koogohoo, Doo bekki* (Spoken Language Grammar, separate edn). Tokyo: Bensei Sha.

Komori, Yooichi. 2000. *Nihongo no kindai* (The Modern Age of the Japanese Language). Tokyo: Iwanami Shoten.

Kroskrity, Paul V., ed. 2000. *Regimes of Language: Ideologies, Polities, and Identities.* Santa Fe, NM: School of American Research Press.

Kubota, Yuko. 2005. *Shokuminchi Choosen no Nihongo kyooiku: Nihongo niyoru "dooka" kyooiku no seiritsu katei* (Japanese Language Education in Korean Colonies: The Formation Process of Assimilation Education by Japanese Language). Fukuoka: Kyuushuu Daigaku Shuppan Kai.

Lee, Yeounsuk. 1996. *Kokugo toiu shisoo* (The Ideology of National Language). Tokyo: Iwanami Shoten.

Mashimo, Saburoo. 1948. *Fujingo no kenkyuu* (A Study of Lady's Language). Tokyo: Tooa Shuppan Sha.

Matsumoto, Shigeo. 1941. "Manshuu no fujingo" (Ladies' Language in Manchuria). *Manshuu Kokugo* 9: 25–28.

McClintock, Anne. 1995. *Imperial Leather: Race, Gender and Sexuality in the Colonial Contest.* New York and London: Routledge.

McElhinny, Bonnie. 2010. "The Audacity of Affect: Gender, Race and History in Linguistic Accounts of Legitimacy and Belonging." *Annual Review of Anthropology* 39: 309–28.

Mitchell, Lisa. 2009. *Language, Emotion, and Politics in South India: The Making of a Mother Tongue.* Bloomington and Indianapolis: Indiana University Press.

Mizumoto, Terumi. 2010. "Terebi dorama: 'Dorama go' toshiteno onna kotoba" (TV Dramas: Women's Language as "Drama Language"). In Momoko Nakamura (ed.), *Jendaa de manabu gengogaku* (Learning Linguistics from Gender). Kyoto: Sekai Shisoo Sha, 89–106.

Nagano, Masaru. 1955. "Danjo dooken de nai Nihongo" (Japanese Language is Not Equal for Men and Women). In Haruhiko Kindaichi (ed.), *Kooza Nihongo 3: Nihongo no shushusoo* (Lectures on Japanese 3: Aspects of Japanese). Tokyo: Ootsuki Shoten, 67–81.

Nagao, Masanori. 1943. *Josei to kotoba* (Women and Language). Tokyo: Tsukuda Shobo.

Nagata, Yoshitaroo. 1976 [1935]. "Kyuu shiiki no onin gohoo" (Phonemic Usage in the Old Quarters of Tokyo). In Shuuichi Saito (ed.), *Tokyo hoogen shuu* (Dialects in Tokyo). Tokyo: Kokugo Kankoo Kai, 19–143.

Nakamura, Momoko. 2001. *Kotoba to jendaa* (Language and Gender). Tokyo: Keisoo Shobo.

——2004. "Discursive Construction of the Ideology of 'Women's Language': The Impact of War (1914–45)." *Nature-People-Society* 37: 1–39.

——2006. "Creating Indexicality: Schoolgirl Speech in Meiji Japan." In Deborah Cameron and Don Kulick (eds), *The Language and Sexuality Reader.* London and New York: Routledge, 270–84.

——2007. *Onna kotoba wa tsukurareru* (Constructing Women's Language). Tokyo: Hitsuji Shobo.

——2008. "Masculinity and National Language: The Silent Construction of a Dominant Language Ideology." *Gender and Language* 2(1): 25–50.

——n.d. (forthcoming). *Gender and Language Ideologies: The Genealogy of Japanese Women's Language.* Amsterdam and Philadelphia, PA: John Benjamins.

Navaro-Yashin, Yael. 2009. "Affective Spaces, Melancholic Objects: Ruination and the Production of Anthropological Knowledge." *Journal of the Royal Anthropological Institute* 15: 1–18.

Okano, Hisatane. 1964 [1902]. "Hyoojyungo ni tsuite" (On Standard Language). In Sumio Yoshida and Yuuichi Inoguchi (eds), *Meiji ikoo kokugo mondai ronshuu* (Collection of Papers on National Language Issues after Meiji). Tokyo: Kazama Shobo, 509–14.

Ooe, Shinobu, ed. 1988. *Juugo nen sensoo gokuhi shiryooshuu 9: Shina jihen daitooa sensoo kan dooin gaishi* (A Collection of Secret Documents in the Fifteen Years of the War 9: The Short History from the China Incident to the Great East Asia War). Tokyo: Fuji Shuppan.

Osa, Shizue. 1998. *Kindai Nihon to kokugo nashonarizumu* (Modern Japan and the Nationalism of National Language). Tokyo: Yoshikawa Koobunkan.

Pharr, Susan J. 1987. "The Politics of Women's Rights." In Robert E. Ward and Yoshikazu Sakamoto (eds), *Democratizing Japan: The Allied Occupation*. Honolulu: University of Hawaii Press, 221–52.

Reihoo Yookoo Kenkyuu Kai. 1941. *Reihoo yookoo kaisetsu* (A General Commentary on the Gist of Manners). Tokyo: Kookoku Seinen Kyooiku Kyookai.

Richard, Analiese and Rudnyckyj, Doramir. 2009. "Economies of Affect." *Journal of the Royal Anthropological Institute* 15: 57–77.

Sakuma, Kanae. 1983 [1940]. *Gendai Nihon gohoo no kenkyuu: Kaiteiban* (A Study of Modern Japanese Usage, revised edn). Tokyo: Kuroshio Shuppan.

Schieffelin, Bambi B., Woolard, Kathryn A. and Kroskrity, Paul V., eds. 1998. *Language Ideologies: Practice and Theory*. New York and Oxford: Oxford University Press.

Shi, Gang. 2003. *Shokuminchi shihai to Nihongo: Taiwan, Manshuukoku, tairiku senryoochi ni okeru gengo seisaku* (Ruling Colonies and Japanese Language: Language Policies in Taiwan, Manchuria, and Chinese Occupied Territory). Tokyo: Sangen Sha.

Shimizu, Shin. 1962. *Chikujoo Nihonkoku kenpoo shingiroku 2* (Report on the Article-by-article Discussion of the Japanese Constitution 2). Tokyo: Yuuhikaku.

Song, Youn ok. 2009. *Datsu teikoku no feminizumu o motomete: Choosen josei to shokuminchi shugi* (Searching for the De-imperialistic Feminism: Korean Women and Colonialism). Tokyo: Yuushi Sha.

Suzuki, Bunshiroo. 1948. *Bunshiroo zuihitsu* (Bunshiroo Essays). Tokyo: Chuuoo Kooron Sha.

Suzuki, Yuko. 1997. *Shinpan feminizumu to sensoo: Fujin undooka no sensoo kyooryoku* (Feminism and War Revised: War Cooperation of Woman's Liberation Activists). Tokyo: Maruju Sha.

Tanaka, Akio. 1983. *Tokyo go: Sono seiritsu to tenkai* (Tokyo Language: Its Formation and Transformation). Tokyo: Meiji Shoin.

Tanizaki, Junichiroo. 1975 [1934]. *Bunshoo tokuhon* (A Writing Reader). Tokyo: Chuuoo Kooron Sha.

Tayasu, Munetake. 1964 [1771]. "Kusa musubi" (The Grass Tie). In Yuriko Kunita (eds), *Nyooboo kotoba no kenkyuu* (A Study of Court-women's Speech). Tokyo: Kazama Shobo, 693–719.

Ueda, Kazutoshi. 1964 [1895]. "Hyoojungo ni tsukite" (On Standard Language). In Sumio Yoshida and Yuuichi Inoguchi (eds), *Meiji ikoo kokugo mondai ronshuu* (Collection of Papers on National Language Issues after Meiji). Tokyo: Kazama Shobo, 502–8.

——1968 [1894]. "Kokugo to kokka to" (National Language and State). In *Meiji bungaku zenshu 44: Ochiai Naofumi, Ueda Kazutoshi, Haga Yaichi, and Fujioka Sakutaro Shuu* (The Complete Collection of Meiji Literature 44: Naofumi Ochiai, Kazutoshi Ueda, Yaichi Haga, and Sakutaroo Fujioka). Tokyo: Chikuma Shobo, 108–13.

Wakakuwa, Midori. 1995, 2000. *Sensoo ga tsukuru josei zoo: Dainiji sekai taisenka no Nihon josei dooin no shikakuteki puropaganda* (Portrait of Women Created by the War: Visual Propaganda for Promoting Women's Corporation Under the World War II). Tokyo: Chikuma Shobo.

Washi, Rumi. 2000. "Nyooboo kotoba no imi sayoo: Tennoo sei, kaisoo sei, sekushuariti" (The Semiotic Process of Court-women's Speech: Imperial System, Social Hierarchy, and Sexuality). *Joseigaku Nenpoo* 11: 18–35.

——2004. "'Japanese Female Speech' and Language Policy in the World War II Era." In Shigeko Okamoto and Janet S. Shibamoto Smith (eds), *Japanese Language, Gender, and Ideology: Cultural Models and Real People*. Oxford: Oxford University Press, 76–91.

Weidman, Amanda. 2007. "Stage Goddesses and Studio Divas in South India: On Agency and the Politics of Voice." In Bonnie McElhinny (ed.), *Words, Worlds, and Material Girls: Language, Gender, Globalization*. Berlin and New York: Mouton de Gruyter, 131–55.

Woolard, Kathryn A. 1998. "Language Ideology as a Field of Inquiry." In Bambi B. Schieffelin, Kathryn A. Woolard and Paul V. Kroskrity (ed.), *Language Ideologies: Practice and Theory*. New York and Oxford: Oxford University Press, 3–47.

Yasuda, Toshiaki. 1997. *Teikoku Nihon no gengo hensei* (The Language Organization of the Japanese Empire). Kanagawa: Seori Shobo.

——1998. *Shokuminchi no naka no kokugogaku* (National Language Studies in the Colonies). Tokyo: Sangensha.

Yazaki, Genkuroo. 1960. *Korekara no Nihongo* (Modern Japanese Language). Tokyo: Mikawa Shobo.

Yoshida, Sumio. 1952. *Kinseigo to kinsei bungaku* (Language and Literature of Modern Times). Tokyo: Tooyoo Kan Shuppan Sha.

10 The politics of *haan*

Affect and the domestication of anger in South Korea

Sung Kil Min

In a newspaper column, Kim Eun-pyo (2013) delineates the role of *haan* (roughly suppressed anger) in overcoming poverty and discrimination through two events experienced by the late Korean President Park Chung-hee and Samsung Chairman Lee Keun-hee. When Park Chung-hee visited West Germany to get a loan in 1963, he went to see Korean coal miners and nurses working in Ruhr. As he listened to the Korean national anthem sung with tears by five hundred mud-covered miners, he was unable to read his prepared speech. He said spontaneously, "Blood-tears flow from my heart. Let us hand over a well-off country to our descendants." He himself began to cry. The whole event became a sea of tears. Such crying was triggered by smoldering *haan*, anger and pity because of the poverty of their country caused by colonization and the Korean War. The second event was experienced by Lee Keun-hee, chairman of Samsung. In 1993, he was shocked to see Samsung products displayed in the remote back corner of a home appliance store in Los Angeles. His resulting anger and shame led him to devote himself to making Samsung the best; such *haan* of anger and shame became a driving force for Samsung to develop quickly and ceaselessly for twenty years.

Similarly, in recent years when South Korea was facing the neoliberal crisis caused by the International Monetary Fund (IMF), at a lecture for college students former President Kim Dae-jung said, "I had laid the cornerstone of democratization with *haan* and tears. As long as we do not escape from but keep the affect of *haan*, we can overcome the IMF event [crisis in foreign exchange] and national division."[1] These instances offer a glimpse of how *haan* has been utilized to motivate entrepreneurs, government leaders and ordinary people in South Korea to strive forward to achieve various social, economic and political goals.

This chapter examines the affective dimension of the rapid, condensed growth of Korea in the modern period, and bases its conclusions on a mixture of affect theory, psychodynamic theories of human behavior, and personal clinical experiences. *Haan* as a keyword comprises all aspects of the affective dimension in relation to rapid social change. Particularly I analyze *haan* and its historical transformation in order to examine the affective dimension of modernity and nation-building in contemporary South Korea. The chapter considers *haan* not only as a personal or psychological attribute but also as a political affect which can be channeled as a social and political force that intensifies people's attachments to social, economic and political processes. Using examples of *haan* derived primarily from media and historical events, I argue that the use of affect as an analytical framework can highlight the way people's potentiality and creativity are mobilized and actualized in social and political movements against poverty, discrimination and exploitation.

Indeed, suppressed *haan* can be channeled through *haan-puri*—dissolving or resolving *haan*—which produces a force or energy for actualizing social, economic, or political potentialities. This process of *haan-puri*, while resonating with what Peter Lyman (2004) calls the domestication of anger—redirecting the energy of anger in the form of force, authority, moral indignation, care and technique and mobilizing it in defense of the social and political order (ibid.: 133–34), has much deeper impacts and more functions—personal, social, political and economic—in South Korea, because *haan* is a more encompassing concept and affect (see below).

Social scientists have described elsewhere the chronological processes of development in relation to international and domestic social, political and economic conditions (Ahn 2001; Kim 2007; Kim 2009), but have rarely extended these explanations to incorporate either psychological or affective dimensions. As an attempt to expand beyond these studies, I analyze one of the key affects in South Korea—*haan*—and the way this affect has been channeled and mobilized for various social, economic and political objectives. In this way, *haan* can be understood specifically as a keyword for affect or, rather, as a *structure of feeling* that is manifest in imperial and global economic systems, the production and productivity of affective labor, and the propagation of specific emotional states, such as hatred, anxiety, excitation, or forgiveness (McElhinny 2010: 310). *Haan* will be considered below not only as a personal or psychological attribute, but a *political* affect that can be channeled as a force that deepens people's attachment to certain social, economic and political processes.

This analysis aims to understand how *haan*, as a *political* affect, is embedded in larger historical and material forces that privileged particular types of *haan* and *haan-puri* over others, with the intention of supporting certain kinds of nation-building projects. More specifically, the focus of this analysis is two types of new *haan* formed during and after the three military regimes since President Park and their differences from the traditional *haan* formed during the Japanese colonization, national division and the civil war as well as their different ways of *haan-puri*—dissolving *haan*.

Under the dictatorship of Park Chung-hee (1961–79), ordinary people, especially those advocating democracy and human rights, were politically suppressed or even arrested. This type of new *haan*, related to military suppression, was channeled—through practices of *haan-puri*—in efforts of democratization in South Korea. Such *haan-puri* differs from the *haan-puri* of the traditional *haan* of poverty and social suppression, which was mainly through getting rich and national liberation. Meanwhile, throughout the various periods of industrialization another type of new *haan* was spawned by rapid modernization and widening economic gaps. As a result of these feelings of inequity, market relations began to emerge, particularly under the "economy first" policy (proposed by military dictators such as Presidents Park Chung-hee and Chun Doo-hwan) through which rapid economic development engendered an increasingly aggressive, individualistic culture. With the growing influence of corporate plutocracies, some groups in South Korea—i.e. manual laborers and the new working poor—have begun to feel a new *haan* of relative poverty and of being unfairly exploited.[2] This *haan* was called the new *haan* of the people, a term generally referring to lower classes, who were more likely influenced by leftist or socialist regimes in North Korea. This type of new *haan* commonly finds its forms of resolution through acts of vengeance, social violence, or suicide. I suggest that this new type of *haan* poses certain challenges for Koreans as they develop new kinds of social cohesion in an increasingly globalizing world.

In the following, I will first discuss the uniqueness of the phenomenon of *haan*, and the general process of *haan-puri*. Then I will contextualize the significance of *haan* as both a keyword and a political affect and the practice of *haan-puri* in the political and economic transformation in contemporary South Korea.

What is *haan*?

Haan can be defined as a mixed mood of loss and anger, a feeling of unfairness, hatred and revenge or a victim's complex (Min *et al.* 1997).[3] Kim Young-ae defines *haan* as follows:

> *Haan* is the Korean people's collective emotion which is embedded in community as well as the individual, and inherited through generations. This repressed, emotional sediment is accumulated through the repetitive process of experiencing multi-layered suffering due to existential and environmental conditions which inhibit the community or persons from realizing their full potential, and deprive them of the means to eliminate or correct the causes. *Haan* is also a dynamic energy which can be directed, either constructively or destructively, to others or to oneself.
>
> (Kim 1991: 10–11)

Haan is a key concept for understanding the culture, history, and individual and collective mentalities of Korea, where traditionally the suppression of anger has been regarded as a social virtue. Feelings associated with *haan* are accumulated and layered in people's hearts by acts of conscious or unconscious suppression, marking out a space of potentiality for both individual and collective action, thought and feeling.

Specifically, *haan* involves a number of slightly different definitions: it may be defined as pathos; a mass-formation in the chest, along with some feelings of hatred and revenge; a chronic mixed mood of loss and anger; or the feeling of experiencing unfairness, regret and sorrow (Min *et al.* 1997). Regardless of what affective state it is used to define, the basic underlying components of *haan* are anger and a feeling of unfairness, both of which appear as reactions to distress, depression, or personal or collective trauma.[4]

These feelings may be caused by external events (i.e. at the international, national, organizational and familial levels) or by the specific interactions between such occurrences and one's life or destiny. As mentioned, the suppression of these feelings of anger or inequality has traditionally been recognized as a social virtue in Korea and, in fact, when contextualized by social and cultural conditions, these suppressed affects may be accumulated and layered deep in the mind for long periods of time (Min *et al.* 1997).

The affective state of this suppression, its main etiological factor being the feelings of anger and a perception of unfairness, is called *haan*. For instance, such suppression can be witnessed in the popular Korean film *Seopyeonje*, in which the feelings of sorrow of a daughter caused by her relationship with her straightforward step-father's strong wish for her to become a true *pan-sori* singer are generally seen as exemplars of *haan*:[5] the events of the film express the presence of suppressed anger and the feeling of unfairness, for the daughter in the film is forced to experience not only the event(s) that led to her being blinded by her father, but also slowly to come to terms with this destiny, however painful that realization may be. The father, too, is confronted by *haan*, in that he must feel sorrow and guilt not only as a result of realizing the consequences of his violent, irrational actions for his daughter, but also enduring those sensations as they arise in the act of confessing his wrongs.

Political and economic channeling of *haan*: *haan-puri*

As Park Jae-hong (2008: 46) observes, the philosophy that Koreans have shown in furious economic development is the philosophy of *hae-won* (resolving a grudge), and *haan-puri* (resolving *haan*). It is like a *ssigim-gut* (shaman ritual for cleansing and wish fulfillment) through which people free themselves from grudges caused by suppression, illness, poverty and war and resolve the *haan* of suppressed anger, tears and unhappiness.

During the last fifty years, Korea has developed from a traditional poverty-stricken agrarian society to an open, capitalistic industrial society. This rapid change is often referred to in Korea as "condensed growth," or "compact modernization." Such rapid development has led to questions about how Koreans could have developed their country so quickly while at the same time, people have also wondered why they remain so unsatisfied with their country and their lives (Min *et al.* 2002). Indeed, there is an affective dimension of Korean modernity. As former President Kim Dae-Jung wrote, reflecting on the history and future of the Korean nation, when he was put in the army jail in 1980 for planning and directing revolution:

> As we Koreans are excellent people, our country will become democratic and economically developed in the near future. But in history, there has been a vicious cycle of so many unfair sacrifices, *haan*, hatred and retaliation in relation to party strife during Yi dynasty, Japanese colonial rule, 6.25 War [see below for explanation], and military dictatorship. If we cannot overcome these, we will not be able to develop a true, advanced and humanistic society. The ways to stop this cycle of *haan* is forgiveness and reconciliation beyond the dimension of law.[6]

In the following, I trace the psychological and collective development of *haan* and its relationship with social and political movements in Korea—that is, the historically situated expressions of *haan* and its transformation. I argue that Korea's rapid development from a closed, poor agrarian society to an open, capitalist industrial state is attributable to the channeling (*puri*) of this collective *haan* to the extent that the Korean government has utilized *haan* as a political affect, which intensifies attachment to the goals of nation-building.

By considering the historical trajectory of collective *haan* in Korea—from its colonization by Imperial Japan, to its division into separate nations and the Korean civil war—I will trace the traditional *haan* of poverty and social suppression, and its transformation—how, once ignited, its latent, fire-like force (in Korea fire, *hwa*, is synonymous with anger, *hwa*) stimulated a culture of creativity and determination in Korea. In so doing, I will examine the transformation of political and economic communities through actualizations of collective potential, particularly through the *haan-puri* process. The functions and event-ness of *haan* in South Korea may help us understand the role of sentiment as a political affect (i.e. historical trauma and the sense of crisis or national shame). It may offer suggestions for mobilizing people in other areas of East Asia, such as Taiwan, Hong Kong and China, which have also experienced rapid economic development within a short period of time.

Haan as affect and a keyword

Korean poets (Koh 1980), critics (Moon 1985), social scientists (Han and Kim 1980), anthropologists (Kim 1997), theologians (Suh 1984), and even economists (Lee 2009a) refer to Korea as a nation of *haan*, Korean national history as a history *of haan*, and Korean culture as a culture of *haan*. In fact, the association between *haan* and Korean society and culture is so strong that it can be considered a keyword for understanding the history of Korea and Korean culture, a key site at which feelings, emotions and social experiences have been constructed, negotiated and contested for collective action and change (see McElhinny 2010). Lee Won-bok, in an article titled "Esthetics of *Haan*," writes:

> We Koreans are a nation of *haan*. Distinctively Koreans have many *haan* in their chest [heart]. Though young Koreans of these days seem to be different, they will have to have at least a mass of *haan* knotted in their chest as they step into age of 40s: *haan* of not having received higher education, *haan* of poverty harboring desire to retaliate [against the] world by earning much money, *haan* of not [being] properly treated in spite that they do not feel at all being inferior to others … , etc.
>
> (Lee 2009a)

Such *haan* does not disappear with age, but may change one's coping behavior, and may continuously provoke a tenacious intention to retaliate. In many cases, *haan* may provide dynamic power for industriousness and growth, but it is not infrequent to see people with *haan* suffering unhappy feelings caused by dissatisfaction about their social reality and wishes to solve *haan* somehow. Such *haan-puri* is seen often in politics. Among presidents of Korea, many of them revealed their own *haan* and tenacious intentions in their policies and administration during their time in power (see below *Haan* of Leaders).

As a unique traditional collective sentiment for Koreans, collective *haan* appears to be an example of a collective affect that is signified through particular forms of collective sentimentality (i.e. collective feeling *and* action). Moreover, its emergence as a keyword for affect arises in the context of its promise for addressing the ways in which imperialist, colonialist and neoliberal interactions have historically occurred in Korean social and personal life; for coming to terms with the uses of Korean affective engagement as a means for industrialization and democratization, as these apply both to institutional power and political and social mobilization; and for appreciating the impact and resonance of specific forms of affective speech in Korean social life (see McElhinny 2010: 310).

By recognizing the value of *haan* in terms of its capacity to produce potentiality and creativity in social, economic and political movements, one may begin to see how it establishes a political vector through which the need for present action may be portended. In so doing, the discussion provides opportunities for exceeding the structural worlds of formal political institutions, which have tended to rely greatly on binary distinctions and ideological or hegemonic positions. The propositions for using affect as a keyword for social change, then, increasingly offer meaningful engagements with a more thorough account of the emotional conditions that arise in the personal and inter-personal events of everyday life (see McElhinny 2010: 310).

The complexity of the concept of *haan* can be clearly understood, therefore, as it includes all these affective conditions as part of its potential arrangement, so the possibilities for political, social and economic mobilization become clearer: the accumulation and layering of suppressed anger and inequality permit the realization of *regimes of anticipation*, in addition to the regimes of truth that are typical of traditional historical and structural analyses (McElhinny 2010: 249). The complexity of *haan* is also seen in the specific arrangements of affects, individuals and collectives, and in the specific ways that affects, as keywords for motivating action, are present, presented and used by and within particular political communities and groups.

Hwa-byung, for example, meaning "anger disease" or "fire disease," is categorized as a culture-related syndrome that is associated with specific types of etiological events (Min *et al.* 1986; Min 1989) and characteristic temperamental predisposition (Lee *et al.* 2012). As Kang Jun-man states, "While Westerners feel angry ten times a day, Koreans feel so fifty times a day. The death rate of Korean males in their forties is known to be the highest in the world. Korea is a country which has the most serious stress-type social structure in the world. Accordingly, who would fear World Cup frenzy, if it could resolve stress and prevent death due to *hwa-byung*."[7]

Hwa-byung is a pathological example of *haan* (Min 1991), different from depression (Min *et al.* 2009). *Haan* is regarded as not simply a symptom but an etiological event *of hwa-byung*. Its symptoms are similar to those associated with *haan* (Min *et al.* 1997), though signs of the latter are somewhat milder and more endurable. While anger in *haan* appears to be more suppressed, as well as more passively and healthily expressed, sublimated, or managed, anger in *hwa-byung* is only partially suppressed, somatized, or openly expressed. *Hwa-byung* appears to resemble a dormant volcano, within which suppressed hot flame, leaking steam and smoke, and boiling lava are ready to erupt. *Haan*, on the other hand, is comparable to an extinct volcano, with a surrounding positive appearance, vibrant with life and beauty.

While *hwa-byung* is best associated with personal suffering, *haan* is a collective experience and, paradoxically, has positive emotional dimensions that may motivate people to endure and find creative solutions for the accumulated and layered sensations of anger, difficulty, etc. In this way, *haan* emerges as a possible function of political mobilization—specifically in the instances of its resolution (i.e. *haan-puri*)—insofar as it has been used by the Korean government as a means of economic and political transformation, such as in the developments and implementations of free market industrialization and democratic institutions. The mobility and productive impact of *haan* and *haan-puri*, then, appear to establish an important distinction between the personal and inter-personal, or collective, and suppose its significance not simply to be an important psychoanalytic concept, but more importantly—for the purpose of this chapter—a sociopolitical one.

The significance of *haan*, and affect more generally, in terms of its sociopolitical value also supposes an important function in anthropological analyses of political life, for it suggests the need for understanding non-linguistic, non-structural definitions of political institutions and social movements. That is, it proposes the necessity of recognizing the force or flow of energy that exists within political communities and between political subjects. In the following, I will highlight the ways *haan* and *haan-puri* have changed historically and how these particular affective experiences can be situated as central to the social, economic and political transformations in contemporary Korea.

Collective *haan* and political affect

At the personal level, *haan* is generally considered to be a complex feeling associated with the intertwining of life experiences. It is often caused by difficulties, involving frustration, victimization, trauma, feelings of regret, or twists of fate.[8] All of these various states may overlap each other and co-exist in one's life. The focus of this chapter, however, is to examine *haan* as a collective, political affect, as a result of which it becomes possible to speak of *haan* and *haan-puri* as politically impactful forms of potentiality and creativity that are mobilized in terms of shared energies or intensities.

The suppressed and accumulated feelings of anger or unfairness that typify the collective experience of *haan* are embedded in and motivate the developments of Korean national history (Koh 1980; Han and Kim 1980; Moon 1985; Kim 1997). The various forms of social unfairness, injustice, or suppression that are present in Korean history can induce *haan* in a certain class or group of people. For instance, there are those in the lower classes who have been suppressed by bureaucrats or the upper class, women suppressed by men who exploit the gendered political strength in the patriarchal social system (Chung 1991), and a social class that includes servants, butchers, tanners, shamans and roaming entertainers (like hero and heroin in *Seopyeonje*) who have been known to live with painful *haan* because of their exploitation and difficult lives. In all of these instances, what is witnessed is the transformation from personal to collective *haan*, one which is inherited by the next generation in the forms of expressed and experienced Korean history and cultural life. The popularity of the film *Seopyeonje* serves as an example of this transmission: it represents a cultural image of the aesthetic of *haan*, producing a sense of sorrow and unconscious anger that can be shared collectively, and the potential of resolution that can be felt through the experience of the heroine's struggle, misery and pain.

In the contemporary Korean social, political and economic life, international injustices and violence throughout the nation's history may also provide an etiological basis for inducing a collective *haan* (Koh 1980; Han and Kim 1980; Moon 1985; Kim 1997). In particular, by looking at historical events that may have led to the development of South Korea's collective *haan* one ought to look back to the period of the old three kingdoms (57 BC–676 CE) and the territorial loss of Koguryo, the largest kingdom in the south of Manchuria and north of the South Korean peninsula, and to the eras of invasion and exploitation by aggressive neighbors, such as the Chinese dynasties (Song, Tang and Qing), the Mongolian Empire (1231–70 CE) and Japan (1592–98 CE). From the beginning of the twentieth century until the end of World War II in 1945, an enfeebled Korea had been the battlefield of foreign countries (the Sino–Japanese War in 1884–85, the Russo–Japanese War in 1904–05, and World War II in 1941–45, and finally was colonized by Japan). Throughout this period of colonial subjection, many Koreans were killed or suffered traumatic experiences, including the robbery of national treasures, labor exploitation, the conscription of civilians for military service, and the use or enslavement of

Koreans as laborers, including as sex workers (Min *et al.* 2011). Koreans who managed to escape to, perhaps, Russian Manchuria were displaced, yet again, into the wilderness of modern-day Uzbekistan in 1937 by Stalin, the leader of the former Soviet Union. Many of them died from socio-environmental factors, such as frigid temperatures and starvation in the wilderness.

Following this period, and with Japan's surrender to Allied Forces in 1945, Korea found itself divided into two states, according to the post-war agreement made between the United States and the Soviet Union: South Korea was occupied by the United States, and North Korea by the Soviet Union. In 1950, five years after this division, North Korean troops marched South, bringing conflict and anguish yet again to the population of South Korea.

All these tragic experiences during the Korean War were traumatic for Koreans and resulted in the well-known expression, the "*haan* of 6.25" (the term signifies the date of the war's commencement, June 25, and associates the period and the events of the war with hatred, the "*haan* of family separation," and of the trauma of leaving home) (see MacKie, Chapter 11, this volume). This commemoration demonstrates the targeted use of affect as a means for intensifying a particular collectivization and mobilization of national experiences. In so doing, the memory of the period creates a potentiality in which certain collective memories and political rhetoric may be used in supporting nation-building projects.

Thus, while prior to these post-war conflicts, the Confucian emphasis on social order, compliant modesty and social harmony, and the teaching of self-cultivation through education (Ham 2000), social hierarchies and obedience to superiors and elders were highly valued in Korea, the breakdown of these practices and forms of life can be said to have resulted in the upsetting of social bonds.

However, the persistence of such cultural norms and requirements suppressed the anger and feelings of unfairness, thereby establishing the experience of *haan* as a culturally normalized sensation (Chung 2007). Koreans are said therefore to have developed the unique culture of a "we" relationship, or a family-oriented we collectivism (Chung 2006). In Korea, sons are supposed to have to study hard to attain a higher social position, become rich (to resolve the *haan* of poverty), and make their parents and whole family happy as they can be sure their family will continue. This social pressure on education has impacted girls with the women's liberation movement and has led to "education fever" and serious competition among younger generations. However, the daughter-in-law is liable to have *hwa-byung* because of suppressed anger related to the traditional women's *haan*. Women frequently attribute their *hwa-byung* to betrayed *jeong* (loving affect of attachment) by their unfaithful husbands (Min 1989). If one is separated from his or her community, he or she will feel disappointed, lonely, angry, or *haan*. These experiences are directly related to the national histories of conflict and separation.

However, recovery of *jeong* and the *han* philosophy (theory about one-ness), and shaman ritual (exorcising evil spirits), as well as Western Christianity, have played a part in the *haan-puri* process. For example, shamanism in Korea is known to be a secular, pragmatic and materialistic thought system, through which people wish for a blessed life. However, despite such hopeful efforts, everyday life is considered to be unfair and full of *haan*; people's desires are often frustrated by irresistible forces, including illness or misfortunes possibly made by evil spirits, natural disaster or social unfairness. It is in these instances of everyday life that new forms of political understanding may be demonstrated; sites where considerations of social, economic, political and cultural life can offer opportunities for understanding the variety of ways that critical discussions and transformations may be made the basis for mobilization and used as tools in political maneuvering (McElhinny 2010: 321).

If there is, in fact, a thought system that underlies these Korean cultural phenomena, I believe that these cultural systems are examples of the prominence of the *han* philosophy in Korean political life, for *han* represents Koreans' ideal or desire to become one (the wholeness as described by Kim (1991)), to reconcile, or to harmonize with other people, nature and God (or gods) (Kim 1995).

Taken as an example of these irresistible forces and of the demand for such reconciliation and harmony, the violent treatment of his daughter by a stepfather in the film *Seopyeonje* offers a culturally significant representation of the dynamic that exists between Korean forms of collectivity and individuality, as these comprise both those energies and forces that are beyond any particular form of rationale or control as well as the need to maintain social relationships and connections in order to feel whole or oneness; it is a representation of *haan* inasmuch as it suggests the need for oneness and conviviality despite, and even as a result of, whatever torment and trauma may be experienced.

Western religious systems, moreover, brought new systems of knowledge and, more specifically, have helped Koreans by highlighting the importance of work, altruism, industriousness, economics, thrift and human rights, and of *haan-puri* as well (Hwang 1995). For instance, with the influence of Christianity from the West, its presence and impact in Korea have produced specific collective, community-oriented practices through which *haan-puri* may come about: during Japanese colonization and Korean War, many Koreans, especially mothers, used to pray with tears at dawn in the church to God for solving their *haan* in relation to national affairs (independence and security), familial affairs (husbands' health or sons' success) or personal affairs (suffering from illness, poverty or husbands' violence). And during democratization, pastors may become "priest[s] of *haan*" for victims of social unfairness (Suh 1984). Forgiveness has been proposed as a positive method of *haan-puri* (Oh 1995).

To the extent that Korean culture has been affected by a recomposition of traditional and Western ideological and knowledge systems, Chung (2007) argues that today's Korean society can be figured as a complex of both premodern Korean and superficial Western modernist systems. These cultural influences, I suggest here, are related to the affect of *haan*.

Haan of leaders

Many Korean presidents themselves harbored *haan*, resonances that were reflected in the policies and administration styles that characterized their rule.

For instance, President Rhee Syng-man, the first president of the Republic of Korea (1948–60), had harbored *haan* for a long time during his independence movement since 1900. He could resolve his *haan* (*haan-puri*) by becoming the first president of the newly independent country. President Rhee took a course for orienting policy directives to solve people's *haan* toward a free, democratic and capitalist society by calling for changes in land ownership, educational systems, the recognition of women's rights, trying to develop a strong military, and spreading the values and beliefs of Christianity (Lew 2012). Other Korean presidents following President Rhee often promised that *they* could resolve the issues of Korea's collective *haan* because they themselves came from the poor class and understood the hardships of life, as shown in the example of President Park Chung-hee that opened this chapter. Park Chung-hee, a military dictator, contributed a great deal to economic development, advocating a "can do" attitude, igniting the fire of *haan* which had been latent or dormant for 5,000 years. His political propaganda, which focused on perseverance and hard work, is now found to be timely and generally successful.

State leaders who supported democratization are exemplified in President Kim Young-sam (1993–98) and President Kim Dae-jung (1998–2003), who emerged from earlier anti-military government movements. After long and difficult struggles against various injustices, they worked to transfer power from military dictators to democratic officials, without resorting to violence or the injustices of authoritarian takeover. However, President Kim Young-sam (1993–98) was blamed by his political opponents for having a *haan*-ful wish to be president, and in fact put into place a process of *haan-puri* in the name of justice and reform by imprisoning two previous military general presidents (Chun Doo-hwan and Noh Tae-woo) as part of the country's democratization. President Kim Dae-jung (1998–2003), moreover, said in one of his addresses that he had built democracy on the foundations of "*haan* and tears". The next president, Roh Moo-hyun (2003–08), on the other hand, tried another more leftist approach, which has been criticized as being the wrong political approach for instituting *haan-puri* due to his neglect of the market system. President Roh committed suicide when confronted by various legal problems, and he reportedly died with *haan* caused by the frustrations of his failed political ambition. President Lee Myung-bak (2008–13) appealed to people's *haan* as well by saying that he came from a poor family and had worked hard to be a successful CEO of the Hyundai *Jaebol* group, and he is the most suitable man to overcome economic difficulty (again "economy first") as a follower of President Park. Current President Park Geun-hye is the daughter of former President Park Chung-hee. She is supposed to have her own *haan*, as, when she was an adolescent, her father was assassinated by one of his staff, and before that her mother was also assassinated by a communist from North Korea. Many Koreans, especially the older generations voted for her, expecting her strong leadership in the economy (resolving the new *haan* of poverty among seniors who remember that they had worked hard together with president Park Chung-hee) and securing national security like her father (Suk 2012).

Generally politicians including presidents have been blamed for aggravating the factional strife in Korean society, which is derived from localism-related *haan*, an extension of family-related *haan*. Therefore becoming president is seen as not only a successful *haan-puri* for those elected to office, but also for the electorate. Even leaders in economic development, including the founders of *jaebeol*, used to say in fact that they have succeeded in business as a result of their personal experiences of challenges and struggles in life, thus linking personal *haan* with the notion of collective *haan*.

Haan-puri: the domestication of anger

Personal haan-puri

With *haan* as a central part of Korean culture, people have developed systematic strategies for coping with or overcoming *haan* through *haan-puri*, or the dissolution of *haan*. Such *haan-puri* can be achieved through, for instance, traditional cultural resources, such as shamanism or *shin-baram* (wind of high spirit). Shamanism, as a traditional thought system, explains and deals with nature, fate and human suffering. In so doing, it has provided various means for healing and *haan-puri*. A typical shaman ritual practiced by *mudang* (a shaman ritual practitioner) for the healing of *haan* or *hwa-byung* is called *sal-puri*, which involves entertaining with music, dance and foods the spirits of the dead, asking them to solve their *haan* and leave for the other world, and exorcising evil spirits with the help of good spirits who hold a stronger power.[9] What is witnessed during these rituals of *haan-puri*, as community festive events, is the use of confidence, excitement and other positive sensations and emotional states that occur alongside creative and productive practices. Thus, the participants, including *mudang*, clients and observing neighbors expectedly experience positive emotional states such as relief, reconciliation, harmony, enthusiasm, indulgence, or joy at the completion of the ritual of *haan-puri* (see Park and Lee 2009).

Haan therefore appears to provide the basis for gaining and using energy in one's life. For example, *haan-puri* can indeed include experiences of wish-fulfillment, restoration of self-esteem, or the achievement of success. For example, the *haan* of an illiterate mother who has suffered from poverty and the violence perpetrated by an abusive husband may find *haan-puri* years later in the success of a son: her sacrifice and endurance through the hardships of the life she has led find purpose or fulfillment in the endeavors and successes of her son.

Or, again, as in the depiction of the daughter singing *pan-sori* in *Seo-pyeonje*, what is described is a father's attempt to produce the complex latency of *haan* in his daughter, as he believes that the more extreme the *haan* that is harbored in her heart, the more perfect her *pan-sori* might be; thus, he sees his poor treatment of her, and the accumulation of *haan*, as creating an energy through which she can achieve success. Her experience of *haan-puri*, on the other hand, is drawn directly from the trauma she experienced, necessitating both the suppression of her anger and the acceptance of her fate.

When someone dissolves *haan* successfully in a productive, creative, artistic, heroic, or humorous manner, he or she is often praised for having "*mut*," that is, smartness, elegance, or "cool." Or one's *haan* can also be resolved by impulsively releasing or expressing anger or violence (*hwa-puri*). However, while *haan* may be resolved in such a manner, *hwa-puri* is not desirable, because it may induce *hwa* or *haan* in another person who is present at the *hwa-puri*. People are thus discouraged from losing control of their anger until the proper time comes for resolving anger or *haan*. Again, in the film *Seopyeonje*, the heroine fails to understand why her step-father would cause her such pain and misery, but works hard to suppress that anger until she is capable of resolving it at the appropriate time, by accepting her father's violent treatment as part of her destiny; to resolve her *haan*, therefore, she forgives her father and reaffirms her love for him. The film demonstrates the process of *haan-puri* by showing the daughter sing *pan-sori* for the guests whom, because of her father's violence, she cannot see; however, it is ostensibly because of that same violence that she is capable of singing the *pan-sori* perfectly, for the layered, accumulated *haan* is what gives her the potentiality of a creative, diligent spirit.

Enthusiasm and productivity in collective *haan-puri*

What has been described above is how the long-term suppression of *haan* may lead to the accumulated latent emotion of *haan*, or fire-like anger, and how this accumulation and latency may constitute a dynamic and forceful energy. Bae Soon-hoon, former CEO of Daewoo Electronics, said in an interview that because *haan* and *shin-myung* (enthusiasm or high spirit induced during shaman rituals) dwell together in the genes of Koreans, one more miracle is possible if Koreans can solve *haan* and revitalize *shin-myung*.[10]

In terms of the impact that *haan* and *haan-puri* have on Korean society as a whole, however, its presence is used specifically to instigate a particular form of Korean culture and inter-personal politics: to work hard, to engage in industrialization, or to "fight" for democratization. The rapid social, political and economic development associated with this dynamic and forceful energy of *haan* has generally been coupled with Koreans' strong will, industriousness and creativity, and with leaders' decision-making abilities. As mentioned, there has been an energy to affect Korean people and Korean leaders positively through various processes of *haan-puri*.

In fact, *haan-puri*, through escaping the crippling effects of a history of war, poverty and social suppression, is considered to be key in supporting the "furious" developments of modern Korean history (Park and Lee 2009). The latent fire-like power of *haan*, or suppressed anger, can therefore be ignited and awakened through collective practices of *haan-puri*; it motivates people to work hard, and to be creative and efficient in the specific uses of their resilience.

Haan can thus become an exploding energy for social movements and industrial development. Policies on industrialization and exports were driven powerfully by the military dictator Park Chung-hee (1961–79), who assumed power by *coup d'état* during the disturbance in 1961 that followed the 4.19 student revolution (April 19, 1960), which ended Rhee Syng-man's government. Park and the Korean people shared a sense that "we Koreans should not repeat the same history of *haan* anymore," as a popular slogan. As Lee (2009a) argued, Koreans believe that people deserve to enjoy a happy life after having endured so much hardship. Social scientists like Park and Lee (2009) agree that "The miracle of Han river" was the result of *haan-puri*.

New *haan* and *haan-puri*

The economy's first motto became the dominant message during 1961–88 under the rule of military dictators (Presidents Park Chung-hee and Chun Doo-hwan). As a result of this shift in economic thinking a few companies rapidly grew because of their access to government support, becoming large corporate groups, or *jaebeol*. This plutocratic system is considered to have led the charge in the industrialization and economic development of Korea. In terms of the way that *haan* was used as a political, social and economic tool in the collectivization of a national vision, military dictators' policies succeeded in transforming previous iterations of *haan*, which were, as discussed above, linked with poverty and war, into the energy and potentiality for success in economic development and in direct competition with North Korea.

The shift to a competitive market-based economic system has triggered a transformation of collective *haan* in South Korea, as well as a change in *haan-puri* which had become primarily focused on resolving *haan* through the means of economic development since Park Chung-hee's *coup d'état* in 1961. In so doing, Koreans have also begun to recognize the importance of freedom and human rights, which has coincided with a problematization of the traditional political institutions and policies of South Korea. As mentioned, the two types of *haan* are interrelated.

As Lee (2009a) has argued, the most prominent *haan-puri* to take place in the political realm was initiated in 1960, during the 4.19 student revolution against the then president and dictator, Rhee Syng-man (1948–60). In 1961, General Park raised a *coup d'état*. While dictator Park's economic policies throughout 1961–79 caused rapid industrial expansion, they simultaneously limited access to freedoms and human rights, a move that was justified by appeals to national security rationales.

Eventually, however, as industrialization spurred along gains in the distribution of wealth, education and economic opportunity, a new *haan* derived from industrialization and democratization emerged, particularly among a politically conscious student population, human right activists and laborers.[11]

The process of industrialization has widened the income gap between the rich and the poor, and intensified class stratification in Korea. Now, relative poverty has become one of the most significant social issues in the country, and often results in violent social conflict and *haan*. The feelings of relative poverty and unfairness are perceived as being as painful as absolute poverty, stimulating the emergence of new *haan*. Kahng Gyoo-hyoung, a professor from Myongji University, presented at a seminar of Korea Economic Research Institute on February 13, 2013:

> Though Korea has developed so rapidly, it became such a country as being divided by winners and losers. As gap between social classes has broadened, feelings of relative deprivation have prevailed, and anger and hatred have accumulated and layered in people's minds … Korea got out of "hungry society" with amazing rapidity, and too easily got into "angry society."

Labor movements and their supporters, including student leaders, labor union leaders, other social activists for the urban poor, and anti-government political activists, have experienced numerous examples of political suppression, claiming that they have become the victims of military governments and economic exploitation by a government-supported plutocracy. At the same time, poor farmers have migrated to the cities seeking employment, to the extent that more than 80 percent of Koreans live in cities (Ha 2012). The rapid urban growth during the 1960s–80s was also coupled with many of the repercussions that accompany increases in urban populations and declines of rural communities: for instance, an emerging urban poor, who suffer from feelings of deprivation, persecution and inequality.

What is witnessed is a new type of *haan* which has developed since the 1970s in the repercussions of economic development, urbanization and democratization. This kind of new *haan* has become prevalent throughout various spheres of Korean society, especially among the unemployed, urban paupers, low-achieving students, the chronically ill, victims of gentrification and impoverished seniors. These people have insisted that they are victims of social injustice. Their slogans, as part of a larger socialist movement, pronounce, "Let us live with dignity as human beings!" or "Let our living be worthy of the name of human." Leftists, who had been silenced or suppressed since the Korean War, have also recently begun to voice their discontent and join forces with other social activists, even going so far as to adopt some North Korean ideologies. For example, they claim to have become victims of the exploitation of a wolfish pro-Japanese followed by pro-American military dictatorship, and now of a plutocratic business community.

Beyond industrialization, there has emerged a process of democratization, which spreads, for example, through women's liberation, unionization and citizens' environmental movements, and political action on behalf of the urban poor. Even socialist or leftist movements have begun to emerge, taking root during Japanese "imperial" rule, the Korean War and the establishment of national division; such movements had, in fact, been strongly suppressed during the Cold War period, by military regimes in the name of national security. Thus, as the uses of *haan* and *haan-puri* emerge as significant political, economic and social instruments, what also arises are the new champions of political struggle and challenge; new forms of emotional display become possible as "novel or problematic" (McElhinny 2010: 311), so a new *haan* reflects a changing dynamic within Korean political and cultural society.

The traditional *haan* of poverty, which was layered once more by *haan* of economic exploitation during Japanese rule (1910–45) and *haan* of economic destruction during the Korean War (1950–53), had been resolved (*haan-puri*) by working hard with industrialization starting from the 1960s. The traditional *haan* of social suppression, which was accumulated once more by the *haan* of Japanese rule was resolved by liberation from Japan, but the "new" *haan* due to dictators' political suppression (1961–88) had to be resolved by fighting against dictatorship with democratization.

With economic development, people's sensitivity for deepened economic parity, harsh competition and other social fairness increased, and another *haan* developed due to relative poverty and human rights violation not only in the labor market but in other social areas including social minority (women, farmers, the ill, the disabled, urban paupers and immigrants). This new *haan* and the ways of resolving it (*haan-puri*) are now subjects for hot discussion among leaders, intellectuals, critics, human right activists and researchers on how to develop a social welfare system and promote enthusiasm (*shimyung* or high spirit) and social integration.

The negative impact of *haan* and *haan-puri*

The energy of *haan*, like the power of fire, can be positive or negative. The educational fever in South Korea is an example of a *haan-puri* process that may benefit or do harm to children. *Jeong*, Confucianism and family-oriented "we" collectivism, as examples of the positive effects of *haan*, have motivated Koreans to work together enthusiastically, as discussed above; however, *haan* may also cause social corruption: too much enthusiasm may induce self-righteousness and even authoritarian rule. Probably these changes are reasons that many Koreans do not yet regard their own country to be an advanced nation (Kim 2007), and they do not rate their quality of life as high as is witnessed in advanced Western countries, despite increased income (Min *et al.* 2002).

During Korea's condensed growth, the government has supported a few select business groups to enhance their profit and efficiency. The system of subsidies and political favoritism—of the *jaebeol*—has been criticized for its use of special privileges and its support of a culture of bribery and corruption.

Sudden richness of Korean society is now blamed for having intensified materialism, Mammonism, negligence of life and a shallowness emergent in capitalist culture.

Few people now follow the traditional Confucian culture of temperate living; young Koreans tend to prefer brand-name goods to show off their success and wealth.

Contemporary Koreans are said to have acquired characteristics of being quick-tempered—the so-called "*pali-pali*" (hurry-hurry) syndrome—during these last decades of rapid economic development. The syndrome is associated with the prioritization of outcomes rather than processes, resulting in incomplete achievements. Examples of this include the collapse of an apartment building and a central bridge in the 1980s, as these projects focused much on the final product being completed than assuring the processes of their construction as consistent and effective. Such a syndrome can, moreover, be manifest in politics. Every new regime hurries to highlight the benefits of their particular agenda, undertaking "reformation" programs that involve large-scale replacements of personnel and policy.

Rapid economic growth was accompanied by widespread urbanization, beginning in the early 1960s, a move that has produced a large number of aggressive urban paupers and widespread social unrest.

Such impulsivity is exemplified by impulsive purchases, typically afforded with credit and other borrowed capital, which is regarded as the spirit of setting fire or *jirum-shin* (possessed by the spirit of impulsive shopping). Feelings of pent-up anger can be expressed impulsively through acts of hatred and violence. In fact, the rapid development of Korea has witnessed an increase in social uprisings, violence, crime, depression and suicide (Ha 2012). Moreover, as the new economic *haan* has intensified, resistance has grown in size and impact. A recent example of this was the popular anti-government and anti-American candlelight vigils as demonstrations against the importation of American beef. As these events gain in popularity, however, the fighting spirit of Koreans has become a very real threat, as violent engagements are increasingly being used during anti-government or labor protests.

It is no longer rare to see Koreans expressing anger openly (*hwa-puri*) in daily life. Kristof (1997) describes Koreans as passionate but cantankerous, and people, particularly politicians, tend to attribute one's failure of achievement to others' ill intentions or acts of malice against them. Tolerance, in this sense, seems to have developed into aggression, resulting in increased violence or suicide; the culture of *jeong* and familial "we" collectivism is increasingly expressed through negative acts, such as xenophobia and discrimination against immigrant laborers (see Tsujimoto, Chapter 8, this volume).

Struggles between social organizations have taken on the tone of non-conciliation and self-centeredness, for to accomplish the stated goals of rapid economic development with limited natural resources, competition appears as the only unavoidable condition. People must compete at all times, from kindergarten to employment. Desires to be "the first and the best" have extended beyond monetary wealth, to matters of social prestige and even physical appearance. Parents are now willing to get into debt for their children so that they might receive extra-curricular studies, an overseas education and even cosmetic surgery.

Losers, on the other hand, are expected inevitably to suffer from the frustration, anger and feelings of unfairness—*haan*—that result from lacking in achievement and having no access to resources. Harsh competition and uncertainty have made many people turn again to shamanism, as a final attempt to secure good fortune and blessings.[12] What are seen in these instances of negativity are the results of structures of feeling in which forms of neoliberal capitalism lead to feelings of alienation and distress. In this way, the anticipatory feelings of hope and fear are increasingly made into the main political vectors through which social, economic and political expression can take place; these sensations of futurity, then, produce urgencies in the present and permit the enactments of specific forms of action (i.e. forms of violence, suicide, etc.) (McElhinny 2010).

Conclusion

Korea has recently transitioned from a poverty-stricken and traditional agrarian society to an open industrial and free market-based democracy. *Haan*, chronically suppressed anger and feelings of unfairness, has acted as a significant political affect in this transition, mobilizing the population for rapid economic development. *Haan-puri*, moreover, has acted as a channel for managing and directing transformative practices of economic and political action. Once ignited, *haan*'s latent fire-like power has awakened a resilient Korean society, stimulating new forms of creativity and productivity. Traditional cultures of shamanism, family-oriented we-collectivism, Confucianism, affect, *jeong* and the *han* philosophy (philosophy of one-ness, a spirit of standing together) have also supported processes of *haan-puri*, in combination with imports from Western culture (i.e. Christianity, education and science).

While political and social freedoms were suppressed under the "economy first" policies of previous authoritative administrations, the *haan* of the politically suppressed has led to struggles over democratization; additionally, with rapid industrialization and the appearance of *jaebeol*, some Koreans, including laborers, began to feel the new *haan* of relative poverty and economic exploitation. From the emergence of these new energies come demands to improve the general quality of life for all South Koreans, and the advocation of democratization.

Such rapid economic and democratizing development in South Korea has a negative impact (new *haan*, suppressed anger and feeling of unfairness) on individuals and society; for example, an increased likelihood of expressed anger and aggressiveness in the whole society and economic development has induced destructive Mammonism. Thus with democratization and rapid economic transformation, South Korean society has found itself bound by a certain type of affective confusion because the various demands of and conflicts between social organizations have created contradiction or conflict. Such unintended complications have led to a lag in terms of Korea's ability to develop responsible and effective social policies and directives, resulting in a new developmental challenge: to determine how best to cope with new *haan*, to rebuild social cohesion around new sets of social relationships, and to develop a more truly advanced, "cultured" society in the midst of the pressures of a globalizing world.

Notes

1 *Hanguk Ilbo*, July 1, 1998.

2 Relative poverty refers to the widening gaps that exist between the rich and the poor in free market economies, and the extent to which the new poor increasingly

comprises former members of the middle class and those who find themselves confronted by un-/under-employment and economic vulnerability.

3 The bodily signs of *haan* include chest stuffiness or oppression, epigastric mass, palpitation, crying and a lot of talking. Typically patients express *haan* through long narratives with tears and sighing about how they have suffered from unfairness, how they have tried to control anger, endure hardship, or forgive people.

4 The expression of anger, translated from the Korean as "*hwa*," means both "anger" and "fire." To feel very angry is a fire-like state. Koreans seem to "like it hot" not only in temperature, but also in color, taste, temperament, emotion and behavior, for living with *haan* is described as living with a "mass of fire" deep in one's chest or heart (Kim 1997).

5 *Pan-sori has* been considered a typical Korean traditional vocal art. Such art products as traditional ceramic wares have been widely praised as representing the aesthetics or beauty of the "sorrow" of Korea.

6 *Pressian*, August 15, 2012.

7 *Hankyoreh*, 21 May 2006; vol. 611: 15

8 These negative life experiences that cause *personal haan* may include: 1 frustration, caused by poverty, academic failure, difficulties in romance, sexual or reproductive complications, and experiences of other hardships (*won-haan*); 2 being a victim of physical and social violence, discrimination, corruption, injustice, or betrayal (*won-haan*); 3 enduring difficulties in failing romantic relationships (typically *jeong-haan*), separations from spouses and family, or the early death of parents; 4 feelings of regret (*hoe-haan*), including regret for not having the chance to show one's filial piety before a parent's death; and 5 experiencing an unfair fate, such as a chronic disease, handicap, or loss of property due to natural disaster (Min *et al.* 1987; Min 1991).

9 Popular powerful spirits of good nature are heroic generals who died tragically with *haan* and *uk-wool* (unfairness) (Lee 2009b).

10 *Kwangju Ilbo*, March 24, 2009.

11 Laborers felt angry and thought themselves the victims of the *jaebeol*, which led to demonstrations and protests throughout Korea: anti-government demonstrations and strikes continued throughout the 1960s; with the completion of the Seoul–Busan expressway in 1970, which was touted as a monument to Korean development, a young labor leader, Jeon Tae-il, immolated himself to protest political suppression; the Gwangju democracy campaign against the country's military regime was exploded in 1980, killing hundreds of people; in 1987, after a massive civic protest, a democratically elected civil president took power from the military regime; and finally, from 1993, democratically elected presidents representing Korea's civil society (Kim Young-sam, Kim Dae-jung, Roh Moo-hyun, Lee Myung-bak and Park Geun-hye) have focused on strengthening democratic institutions and relations, particularly as these relate to economic strength. In fact, the last president, Lee Myung-bak, dubbed the "CEO president," made headway in advancing the Korean economy.

12 Secret customers of shaman rituals and fortune telling include parents of students facing entrance examinations for college, candidates running for parliament, businessmen planning a start-up, or women who are confronting marital problems.

References

Ahn, Byung Jik. ed. 2001. *The History of Economic Growth of Korea*. Seoul: Seoul National University Press.

Chung, Christopher. 2006. "Conceptualization of jeong and Dynamics of hwa-byung." *Psychiatry Invest* 3: 46–54.

Chung, Hyun Kyung. 1991. *Struggle to be the Sun Again*. Maryknoll, NY: Orbis Books.

Chung, Soo-bok. 2007. *Cultural Grammar of Koreans*. Seoul: Tree of Thought Pub Co.

Ha, Kyu-sub. 2012. *Suicide Prevention in South Korea. Trend and Current Status*. Presented at the Mental Health and Mental Health Care in Korea. Seoul National University, July 9–19.

Ham, Jae Bong. 2000. *Confucianism, Capitalism and Democracy*. Seoul: Tradition and Modern Times.

Han, Wan Sang and Kim, Sung Ki. 1980. *An Essay on haan in Popular Sociological Concept*. Seoul: Hangil-sa,

Hwang, Young Hoon. 1995. *A Study of hwa-byung in Korean Society: Narcissistic and Masochistic Self-disorder and Christian Conversion*. A dissertation for degree of doctor of philosophy. Princeton Theological Seminary.

Kim, Eun-pyo. 2013. "Anger of Park Chung-hee, Anger of Lee Keun-hee." *Maeil Kyungje*, April 25.

Kim, Joon Yeon. 2009. "Political Suppression and Non-cultural haan-puri." *Chosen Ilbo*, May 27.

Kim, Kyung Dong. 2007. "Social Change in Korea: A Bird's-eye View." *Korea Herald*, October 23.

Kim, Sang Il. 1995. *Han Philosophy*. Seoul: Onnuri.

Kim, Yeol Kyu. 1997. "Won-haan and hwa-zung (hwa-byung)." In *The Academy of Korean Studies (Editors). Proceeding of "Hwa-byung of Koreans—The Cultural Diagnosis and Treatment"*. March 20, Seoul, Korea, 5–17.

Kim, Young-ae. 1991. *Haan: From Brokenness to Wholeness*. PhD dissertation. Clairmont School of Theology, 10–11.

Koh, Eun. 1980. *For the Purpose to Overcome haan. Stories of haan*. Seoul: Bori.

Kristof, Nicholas D. 1997. "The Great Divide." *The New York Times*, April 27.

Lee, Jieun, Min, Sung Kil, Kim, Keung-hyang, Kim, Borah, Cho, Sung Joon, Lee, Sang-hyuk, Choi, Tae Kyou and Suh, Shin-young. 2012. "Differences in Temperament and Character Dimensions of Personality between Patients with *Hwa-byung*, An Anger Syndrome, and Patients with Major Depressive Disorder." *Journal of Affect Disorder* 138: 110–16.

Lee, Kyung-hee. 2009b. "Historical Persons who became Gods in Shamanism." *Joongang Ilbo*, November 26.

Lee, Won-bok. 2009a. "Aesthetics of *Haan*." *Munhwa-ilbo*, January 31.

Lew, Young Ik. 2012. "Achievement of President Rhee Syng Man." *Aeguk News*, July 2.

Lyman, Peter. 2004. "The Domestication of Anger: The Use and Abuse of Anger in Politics." *European Journal of Social Theory* 7(2): 133–47.

McElhinny, Bonnie. 2010. "The Audacity of Affect: Gender, Race, and History in Linguistic Account of Legitimacy and Belonging." *Annual Review of Anthropology* 39: 309–28.

Min, Sung Kil. 1989. "A Study on the Concept of *hwabyung*." *Journal of the Korean Neuropsychiatry Association* 28: 604–15.

——1991. "Hwa-byung and the Psychology of Haan." *Journal of Korean Medical Association* 34: 1189–98.

Min, Sung Kil, Lee, Chang Ho, Kim, Joo Young and Shim, Eun Ji. 2011. "Posttraumatic Stress Disorder in Former Comfort Women." *Israel Journal of Psychiatry and Related Science* 43: 161–69.

Min, Sung Kil, Lee, Chang Il, Kim, Kwang Il, Jung, Young Chul, Suh, Shin Young and Kim, Dong Ki. 2002. "Development of the Korean Versions of WHO Quality of Life Scale and WHOQOL-BREF." *Quality of Life Research* 11: 593–600.
Min, Sung Kil, Lee, Jong Sub and Hahn, Jeong Ok. 1997. "A Psychiatric Study on haan." *Journal of Korean Neuropsychiatry Association* 36: 603–11.
Min, Sung Kil, Lee, Man Hong, Kang, Hong Cho and Lee, Ho Young. 1987. "A Clinical Study on hwabyung." *Journal of Korean Medical Association* 30: 187–97.
Min, Sung Kil, Lee, Man Hong, Shin, Jong Ho, Park, Mook Hee, Kim, Man Kwon and Lee, Ho Young. 1986. "A Diagnostic Study on *hwabyung*." *Journal of the Korean Medical Association* 29: 653–61.
Min, Sung Kil and Namkoong, Ki. 1990. "An Epidemiological Study of hwabyung." *Journal of Korean Neuropsychiatry Association* 29: 867–74.
Min, Sung Kil and Suh, Shin-young. 2010. "Anger Syndrome, hwa-byung and its Comorbidity." *Journal of Affect Disorder* 124: 211–14.
Min, Sung Kil, Suh, Shin-young and Song, Ki-joon. 2009. "Symptoms to Use for the Diagnostic Criteria of Hwabyung." *Psychiatry Invest* 6: 7–12.
Moon, Soon Tae. 1985. *What is haan?* Seoul: Isak.
Oh, Young Hee. 1995. "The Use of Forgiveness in the Healing of 'haan': A Psychological Approach." *Korean Journal of Counseling and Psychotherapy* 7: 90–94.
Park, Jae-hong. 2008. *Quality Management Based on the Analects of Confucius*. Seoul: Ewha Womans University Press.
Park, Woo-hee and Lee Eo-ryeong. 2009. *Spirit of New Capitalism in Korea*. Seoul: Bakyoung-sa.
Suh, Nam Dong. 1984. *A Theological Study of haan*. Seoul: Hangil-sa.
Suk, Nam-joon. 2012. "Tasks of Park Geun-Hye." *Chosun Ilbo*, December 20.

11 Familial communism and cartoons

An affective political economy of North Korea

Craig MacKie

In December 2011 Kim Jong-il, the "Dear Leader" of the Democratic People's Republic of Korea (North Korea) passed away after a reign of seventeen years. As with his father before him, this event precipitated a staged public mourning, a performance often greeted with puzzlement or ironic humor by Western observers, who also frequently questioned the authenticity of the emotions expressed. This response—confusion, bewilderment, incredulity and suspicion—is typical of observations by Westerners regarding events in North Korea, in many cases with very good reason. However, what was particularly interesting in this case was the repeated insistence on the difficulty of this deliberate fakery (see Lamar 2012): the manifestation or performance of "genuine" sorrow for a man who, it is assumed, perhaps correctly, is secretly despised. It is suggested by certain powers that were these people not so repressed, their true hatred would have taken form in performances of freedom, rather than the cynical mourning of a craven and beaten people. In line with intervention in Iraq, Afghanistan, Libya, Tunisia, etc., or in the coverage of such events as the recent death of Hugo Chávez, the stated assumption of the intervening military power or liberal hegemony is that the oppressed Others unconsciously or, more likely, *covertly* crave liberalization; that even in cases where a group shows evidence of loyalty to an alternative system they are either unaware that they crave liberation or are unable to express that they crave it. This nice piece of enlightenment hopefulness, introduced systematically by thinkers such as Hegel (1984), takes human freedom to be the secret truth of our being, and awaits the spirit's revelation that will inevitably result in liberation, in this case in outpourings of hatred. However, I want to challenge this idea, not the idea that an emotional performance was occurring in these displays of mourning, but the idea that a "true" response could have occurred in the first place, for is there such a thing as "true" mourning? We can at best hope for "appropriate" mourning, I think and in the case of the national mourning of the Kim family it is certainly more productive to examine such aspects as national identity and the promises and uncertainties of the future than it is to hold to some sort of simplistic notion of cultic or "false" delusion.

Emotion is not simply a truism come about *sui generis* and locked inside of us to be discovered. It is learned, and as a learned experience it is amenable to manipulation by those who would have us feel one way or another. In short, it can be wielded as a political technology to mobilize action and unify groups. In particular, feelings of national inclusion and exclusion, not to mention a whole host of emotions thereby linked, are experiences that must be taught to the citizen-subjects. In fact, as with a familial (kinship based) or a religious community, the national community may be a *predominantly* affective construct, a point Benedict Anderson (2006) emphasizes. Indeed, as he suggests:

> Part of the difficulty is that one tends unconsciously to hypostasize the existence of Nationalism-with-a-big-N and then to classify *it* as an ideology … It would, I think, make things easier if one treated it as if it belonged with "kinship" and "religion" rather than with "liberalism" or "fascism."
>
> (Anderson 2006: 14)

Thus, for theorists such as Anderson, the national community extends organically from the same motive forces that bound the community of kinship, the bonds of the religious congregation, and the intimate familiarities of the dialect group, with the rise of national vernaculars, systematized and circulated by means of print media and later by film, video and the internet (Anderson 2006). Rather than the Nation being something altogether historically novel, the inclusion/exclusion mechanism of group sociality itself was instead maximised and refounded at a different scale of operation. If this is the case, it may just be that the *emotionality of the nation* can be understood through an analytic mobilization of the theories and history surrounding the affectivity of family ties. In concert with this perspective, by adopting an affect-based approach to nationalism in this chapter, I will examine North Korea's use of children's cartoons in establishing certain basic emotional coordinates in the daily comportment of North Korean citizens.

However, before I push on too far, it is important for me to clarify what I mean by affect and to define exactly how I understand affect to be used as a political technology. First let me say that I do not think that affect and the affection of people toward particular objects (by which I mean literal "things" as well as people and concepts such as "nation," "brother," "other" and "neighbor") can be wielded in an entirely instrumental fashion. It is *steered* or *navigated*; it is *shaped*, and its forces are mobilized, as with any other material force (de Courville Nicol 2011). It has this in common with electrical energy; it is found and mobilized from things (fuel, for example) and in the relation between things, and is never created *sui generis*. In North Korea the affective forces available and ready to hand included a profound sense of loss and a sense of outrage derived from the traumatic experiences of war and imperialism faced during the late nineteenth and early twentieth centuries. These experiences undermined the foundation of the dominant ethnic and dynastic identity from which North Korea had previously been composed. Thus the continuity of affective forms and expectations that had already been established during the

Korean feudal period had to be re-engineered to suit the contemporary conditions, while at the same time taking into account the new emotional landscape and emerging affects that attended to the changing character of group identity in the modern period. Affect is thus a kind of comportment or behavior linked to a thing, person or idea, and premised on an emotional impulse. For though we do not learn our emotions, we do learn how to deal with them; we learn to behave. We learn when and where we can appropriately express certain passions, and learn how we should feel toward certain things, people, ideas, groups and objects. We may feel differently about these things than we've learned we should feel, but all the same we know how we *should* feel, how we are *expected* to feel by the group(s) to which we are beholden (Hochschild 1979).

For though North Korea certainly fashions itself in the tradition of Soviet totalitarianism, a system of disciplinary shaping that proved untenable in the long run, its systems of control are also intimately bound to the obligations of familial loyalty and legacy, giving it a (re)generative quality that borders on the literal. Or in other words, by use of the kinship network, and through its symbolic association with party, military and labor discipline (see Lankov 2013), the Northern Korean state achieves the same capillary distribution of disciplinary effects as those in force in the more uniquely European system of discipline identified by Foucault (1995). By mobilizing the affective force of love, loyalty and protectiveness and through memorialization and manipulation of the sympathetic wounds of families in mourning, it is thus arguable that the North Korean government achieved disciplinary penetration rivaling that of Western capitalist societies. So while the widespread use of police surveillance, modern technologies of audio and visual recording, show trials, auto-critiques, the radical and deliberate manipulation of records and statistics, and so on were all essential in the development of a uniquely totalitarian style of discipline on which North Korean leaders draw heavily (Armstrong 1995), the North Korean practice of ruining the social lives of family members through diminished Songbun,[1] and later, following a 1972 dictate by Kim Il-sung, incarcerating relatives up to three generations distant in concentration camps after a verdict of disloyalty has an affective utility that would appear to outstrip the synonymous mixture of fear and guilt that acts to order a more conventional police state. The family's integration as an object of everyday discipline and social shaping appears constantly in the practices of the North Korean state. In the realm of jurisprudence as well as in such arenas as the military and international diplomacy, the totalitarian ideal of complete saturation of social space does not only express itself in socialist language but, at every step, includes the family as well. In this sense, family becomes a part of the social infrastructure.

To illustrate this I will focus on one of the premier sites of affective ordering and training today, stories for children, a uniquely delimited and conservative space of cultural production even in countries whose artistic heritage engenders the European modernist tendency toward ceaseless innovation. It is thus one particularly useful in revealing dominant social norms. Specifically, I will analyze the affective pedagogy and the settings in both American and North

Korean children's cartoons representing the military, in order to examine the relationship posited between the national community, the family and the role of the soldier therein.

The separation of families and the figure of the orphan

James A. Foley (2003: 1) refers to the separation of families as "one of the most urgent and pressing humanitarian issues" facing Korea. Not only a case of the isolated North being cut off from the South, expatriate Korean communities in Japan, Manchuria, the United States, Eastern Russia and, indeed, across the world also lack the ability to contact their relatives. With diasporic pressure exerted during the Japanese occupation of 1910 and again during the Korean War in 1945, the scope of the problem is understandably wide, and with estimates of 520,000 wartime refugees fleeing the North, the scale of the problem is also of no small magnitude (Foley 2003). Over half a century of separation has borne families who often have no idea what has become of their relatives, a fact that underlines Foley's account of the "common … seemingly superfluous [greeting] 'Ah, so you survived then?' on the rare occasions when [the families] are reunited" (ibid.: 2). However, the symbolic or what might be better referred to as the "national semiotic" impact of this displacement goes far beyond the mutual isolation of families. The problem of family separation, through attachment to the national imaginary and by its inclusion into a narrative of postcolonial heroism and familial reunification, became constitutive of the affective legitimacy of the new republic amongst its citizenry. This legacy was in turn actively mobilized in the discursive practices of the state and its agents, repeated over and over in constellations ranging from the juridical to the literary, whereby a status politics of racial-cum-political purity was developed through a modernist formulation of inherited kinship politics.

In the literature of North Korea, this is most clearly mythologized by various stories of orphans written about in the socialist realist novels of the country, with the implication being that the Republic of Korea (South Korea) was accordingly "adopted" by the wrong (bourgeois, decadent, American) family during the Korean War. This genre, which was imported from the Soviet Union in the 1940s but became thoroughly "Korean" by the late twentieth century (Gabroussenko 2010), also began to develop the theme of a parent-leader and child-populace, though at the beginning it was Stalin and Soviet ideology that played the role of leader-father and master text. As Brian Myers suggests, "The genre was evidently meant to flatter the Soviets with the implication of filial subservience, and at the same time to plead for motherly protection of a race too pure to survive on its own" (Myers 2010: 25) as in, "the depictions of the colonial era, novelists and painters focused on the forced labor of little girls and boys, thus reinforcing the impression of a child race abused by an adult one" (ibid.: 24). Though Myers's formulation of the "child race" is deeply problematic as a result of the instrumental way he uses it in his text, the work does correctly register the incessant recitation of filial and familial themes and the fixation on the dead father that characterizes propaganda in North Korea. This figuration is also repeated in Korean American literature, as is noted by Tracy Wood, who argues:

> When a diasporic perspective is applied to Korean American literature, what rises to the surface is the figure of the orphan, a figure that is facing forward and yet always looking back. The figure of the orphan, of course, is not restricted to Korean American literature, but the frequency with which it appears and the layers of meaning bound in its deployment distinguish the Korean orphan from his literary counterparts. Besides the nearly 200,000 actual orphans that have been exported since the Korean War, the image of the orphan resounds throughout Korea, a country which often refers to itself as "a dissected body, a fractured mind or a separated couple of family" … And while Korean American writers also use the figure of the orphan to signal their own isolation and distance from American hegemony, it is impossible to ignore these *Korean* feelings of loss and abandonment which are bound up in the figure of the orphan.
>
> (Wood 2008: 131)

This duality in the formulation of Korean "nationness," the separation of "Korea" into a "North" Korea and a "South" Korea, can never be forgotten in any discussion of the Korean national consciousness.

While it is important to emphasize the family as it is imagined from the perspective of the North Korean nation and in terms of this country's unique discursive claims to represent the national family, the complicated snare of overlapping identity claims must always be kept in mind. Indeed, it is as a result of the scission of Korea into two halves, each with its own radically different social structure, that the history of this peninsula has been called by some Korean scholars "the best living laboratory for comparativists" (Yang 1999: v), and if one is compelled to look, the primordial history of international Bolshevism and the gaudy adventure of capitalism does seem in many ways manifested into these state forms. So the relationship between North and South Korea, while providing a parodic version of capitalism and communism for Western journalists and academics, also powerfully and clearly incarnates the interwoven passions and techniques of state and economic formation as they impact identity in general.

Family: the happy object of the nation

In North Korea we have, then, the logic of identity and nation-state working against the logic of what Sara Ahmed would call the "happy object" or affectively rooted promise. As South Korea and North Korea are pitted against one another in a conflict of national identity, this very conflict simultaneously frustrates the "promise" of the national community itself, the state of happiness, flourishing or belonging which acts as the metaphysical and emotionally mediated guarantee of the compact between citizen and state. As Ahmed argues, the happy object is both intentional and anticipatory, being something we deliberately turn ourselves towards in hopes of future pleasure. In fact, for Ahmed, as for North Korea, this state of anticipation may, in fact, be more important than the object itself. Ahmed writes:

> The object is not simply the cause of the feeling, even if we attribute the object as its cause. The object is understood retrospectively as the cause of the feeling. Having understood it in this way, I can just apprehend the nail and I will experience a pain affect, given the association between the object and the affect has been given. The object becomes a feeling-cause. Once an object is a feeling-cause, it can cause feeling, so that when we feel the feeling we are expected to feel, we are affirmed. The retrospective causality of affect … quickly converts into what we could call an *anticipatory causality. We might even anticipate an affect without being retrospective insofar as objects might acquire the value of proximities that are not derived from our own experience.*
>
> (Ahmed 2010: 28, my emphasis)

The shared notion of a pre-established community is thus one of these "retrospective causalities," where the very predilection toward sociality seen in every human culture is manifested as a generalized favorable disposition toward the dominant group identity. In the case of Korea, this relatively distinct identity also has the unusual trait of being over six hundred years old (Foley 2003). The heritage of ethnic identity that authenticated Korean kinship and early statehood following the Chosun period, thus became the obligatory tradition by which both nations had to legitimate themselves. As the very loss of that identity in 1910 to Imperial Japan retroactively constructed "Korea" as the lost happy object, the stage was set for its emergence as a national entity. The affective legitimacy and nostalgic power of the ancestral field of relations imbricated itself within the emerging structure of a wholly modern nationhood.

Thus, more than even North Korea, Kim Il-sung, or even the peninsula of Korea, the reunified Korean ethnic family is the anticipated happy object of North Korea's affective training. While what we might call this *prime* happy object lends positive affect to objects around it (i.e. Kim Il-sung, socialism, the military) and always references social history, what Ahmed (2004) calls the "sticky" and "backward" linking nature of affective circulation, the promissory nature of happiness over-determines the social bond by acting as a point of shared aspiration. Again, in the language of Ahmed, "To be affected in a good way by objects that are already evaluated as good is a way of belonging to an affective community. We align ourselves with others by investing in the same objects as the cause of happiness" (Ahmed 2010: 38). Indeed, one might suggest that a perpetually frustrated promise holds a special kind of longevity. As the subject invests more time into commitment to the promise, the possibility of non-receipt gains an edge of desperation. As with millennial cults that fail in their predictions of rapture, it is easier to forestall and re-imagine the millennial judgment, or, in this case, the reunification, rather than give up on the promise altogether (Stone 2000); as Ahmed explains:

> a happy object [can] accumulate positive value even in situations of unhappiness: we can live with disappointment by imagining the promise of happiness will be given to those who follow us … Happiness can involve a gesture of deferral, as a deferral that is imagined simultaneously as a sacrifice and gift: for some, the happiness that is given up becomes what they give.
>
> (Ahmed 2010: 33)

Ahmed's signal example of such a deferral is the act of a parent sacrificing happiness for a child, an act which implicitly promises, first, an ultimately greater happiness in the child's life paid for with the happiness renounced by the parent and, second, the "happiness" of the sacrifice itself, the self-assured knowledge that the final happiness of the child is reason enough to be content in present unhappiness. While the happy family "is both a myth of happiness, of where and how happiness take place," it is also "a powerful legislative device, a way of distributing time, energy and resources" (Ahmed 2010: 45). In other words, the family can also be a legitimating force in the maintenance of an economy; a legitimating force that, further, is structured on a sense of anticipation and sacrifice to the group rather than on the more immediate pleasure of the late capitalist economy. Through this anticipatory mechanism whereby happiness is "found," or at least located in the future of the family, and where the family simultaneously acts as an impetus to defer one's happiness to posterity, the family can thus become a powerful force of libidinal disinvestment premised on a pleasure to come in the future, a disinvestment that was used strategically by the North Korean leadership.

This affective manipulation of these families in mourning to the ends of political legitimation, economic production and nation-building was unprecedentedly effective, the contradictory temporal orientation of the group's future commitment to the happiness of legacy lending a strange durability to the North Korean state after the collapse of the Soviet Union. Having founded the state on the dual principles of both of constituting and recapturing the nation, while likewise having developed the essence of the nation as an extended, yet homogenous family unit, Kim Il-sung was able to set up the state as a surrogate for those lost to war, colonialism and, later, ideological contamination. At the same time, directing the efforts of the citizens toward the object of a re-founded, national happy family, understood as both that day-to-day life in North Korea and that of the eventual unification to come, the North Korean leadership was able to continually direct the aspirations of its citizens toward the prosperity future generations while maintaining daily rank-order discipline. This was achieved through the mechanism of familial loyalty, a mechanism whose motive trajectory moves seamlessly from the past in the form of emotional obligations to the dead. With a special sense of totality that connects the family as biological unit to the family as national community, it is, therefore, particularly true in North Korea that, "the family is also an inheritance … [and t]o inherit the family is to inherit the demand to reproduce its form" (Ahmed 2010: 45).

In the context of the nation-state this helps to explain Anderson's (2006) paradox of the "novel antiquity" underpinning every republic, whereby the empirically modern origins of nations, national boundaries and nationalism exists despite an almost universal claim by nationalists to origins in antiquity. This effort to authenticate national group identity by means of an ancient origin story can be seen in the DPRK, and interestingly contrasts against the chronological orientation of Ahmed's "happy object". While for North Korea the happy object of the national discourse is unambiguously the reclamation of an (ostensibly) authentic and unfragmented Korean nation, what is perhaps a bit more peculiar is how this prime happy object of Korean nationalism is also analogical to an idealized version of the Korean ethnic family unit in abstract and to the Kim patrilineage (that of Kim Il-sung, Kim Jong-il and Kim Jong-un) in particular. This is a metaphor that has been pushed so far in the country that today the state is conceptualized in a one-to-one relation directly linking not only the nation and the family, but also the individual body of the leader, where "the life of every citizen [is] conceptually part of the leader's personified sovereign body and the citizen's economic life part of the superorganic household economy headed by the leader—hence, the slogan 'We are the general's family' (*janggunnim sikso*), which is widely displayed in the domestic space of North Korean households" (Kwon and Chung 2012: 155). The Kim patrilineage has thus come to represent a transcendental nexus of Koreanness, institutionalized in the corpus of the state philosophy *Juche*,[2] wherein the Korean nation is explicitly linked to the leader's body in a suprabiological formulation and whereby the citizenry is to understand itself as simultaneously the leader's children, the general's family, and the bearer of Korean ethnic purity in the form of their blood. This last notion, that of genetic purity, becomes quickly complicated by the need to dismiss South Korean national authenticity as an illusory form while maintaining a doctrine of racial destiny that includes their "subjugated" capitalist brothers to the South and the global Korean diaspora in general. For North Korea, then, the "nightmare of history" is not found in the same rootless, anomic breakdown of traditional bonds that we experience in the West; rather, North Korea's unique nightmare is to be ensnared within an unending generational obligation to a suprabiological family.

However, the idea of genetic purity, of lineage and the importance of kin and heritage, cannot be extracted from a social system whose legitimacy rests on an appeal to the family. As with all feudal dynasties, the clenched knot that binds the order of society, the dominant coterie of families that establish and arrange the systems of resource distribution, must explain to the dominated classes and to themselves why it is that their pre-eminence is justified. Moreover, in the nation the penultimate figure of the system, the leader, who stands second only to that modern player, the people, must be able to emblemize, unite and serve as the ideal prototype of the citizenry. Seen in the political dynasties of such figures as the Clintons, the Bushes, the Trudeaus and the Gandhis, we continue affectively to invest in the charismatic figure of the ruler. This *charismatic affect*, loosely compatible with Weber's (1947) formulation of charismatic authority, is not an office to be filled but a role to be embodied, and in this capacity runs into contradictions in a society whose transfer of power is based on the holding of offices.

Charismatic affect at the level of the leader is the analogue of our investment in the family and the immediate, corporeal relations of our day-to-day lives; it enables us to personify the incomprehensible unity of a disintegrated group identity (North and South Korea) into the body of an existing person. It gives the national citizen, not a face, but an exemplar (see Kwon and Chung 2012). Thus, while the Kim dynasty stands as an example of an unusually successful application of charismatic affect, its very existence as a dynasty without the assurances of the divine mandates of yore, has produced contradictions which may prove to be insurmountable. A process that is reflected in the problem of "emotional fakery" in the mourning of Kim Jong-il, and encoded throughout the culture apparatus of the DPRK, not in the least of which is the cartoon industry.

Affect norms and cultural production for children

To understand the animation of North Korea it is imperative to grasp the centrality of the Kim patrilineage and the family in general, but one must also keep in mind the role of the military and its unique relationship to the family. The first fact to remember about the relationship between the individual citizen of North Korea and the apparatus of the military in North Korea is that, in all likelihood, oneself or someone in the immediate family has recently, or is currently, doing service. With a population of 25.5 million and a standing reserve of 8.2 million men and women (for a total 9.3 million when one factors in active personnel), along with a period of three- to five-year mandatory service between the ages of seventeen and twenty-two, there is roughly a one in three chance of a young person having an immediate family member in the military at any given time, and one is almost guaranteed of having a relative one relation distant in active service. This connection to the military, in and of itself, serves as enough of a contrast to make the affective foundation of the citizen or military relationship profoundly different than that between, say, a citizen of the United States and their armed forces (there being a roughly one in one hundred and forty-three chance of having an immediate relative in active service).[3] This increased likelihood of growing up amongst family who are soldiers necessarily implies that a different emotional relationship will develop between that person and the military. When one's immediate relatives are soldiers—indeed, when one is obliged to become a soldier oneself for at least five years—the related affectivities surrounding the figure of the soldier will in all likelihood be much stronger. Certainly the root symbols of childhood comfort and security will be differentially distributed.

The People's Army of North Korea is, thus, an institution that is included in the system of North Korean affective economy as primarily linked to the object of the home, while simultaneously being inscribed with the symbols of security and protection as guarantors of its affective legitimacy and as with practically everything "good" about North Korea, this symbolic and affective figure, that of the soldier who defends the home, has, from the beginning, been tied to the body of Kim Il-sung as revolutionary leader. It is for this reason that any leader of the country must hold, simultaneously, the titles of leader of the Korean Workers Party and General of the military. On the simple and brutal level of political pragmatics, it is prudent for any dictator to ingratiate themselves with the military elite, a motivation clearly at work in the "military first policy" (*Songun chongch'i ui ponjiljok t'uksong*—Essential Attributes of Military First Politics), formally enacted by Kim Jong-il in 2002, which accorded soldiers priority in the distribution of food and other necessary commodities following in the wake of multiple famines (Koh 2005). The politics of crisis aside, however, the efforts of the North Korean leadership to deliberately tie the military to the affective force of an idealized home and the related notions of security, safety and tranquility is nowhere clearer than in propaganda produced for and performed by children.

Terry Woronov (2007), in her study of the construction of national subjects in China, writes about this propaganda in the related context of Chinese national communism, where she explores the gap between the expectations state officials had of children and the reality of the children's affects during a heat wave at the fiftieth anniversary celebrations of the founding of the Young Pioneers. The resulting scene of 10,000 irritable children gathered in Tiananmen Square standing up and sitting down, yawning, talking and crying during the speeches of communist leaders was omitted from state coverage of the national celebrations, which precipitated Woronov's interest. She argues, "both that the organization is *not* an anachronistic holdover from the socialist era, and that a close study of children's daily activities as Pioneers provides privileged insight into the nature of contemporary Chinese nationalism … [while also holding that] … a performative approach to nationalism … augments our understanding of the ways that children are produced as national subjects" (ibid.: 650). Woronov's Butlerian understanding of political performance mirrors my approach in understanding North Korea, for, like leadership transition, "children's nationalism requires repeated performances, reiterations of an ideal that can never be entirely achieved" (Butler, cited in Woronov 2007: 651). Simultaneously, however, "the norms for performances of nationalism are constantly changing in the context of … rapid social and economic changes, rendering them impossible to achieve fully" (Woronov

2007: 651). The mass games of North Korea and the indigenous paramilitary children's organization, called the Pioneer corps after the Soviet fashion, are the obvious correlates in the case of North Korean children's political performances (Martin 2004). With 30,000 children elected and drilled every year to perform in the airing games it has recently won the Guinness record for the largest event of its kind (Watts 2005; Reuters 2007).

In addition to the expectation that children repeatedly perform acts of nationalism in their production as civic subjects, the issue of children's affective training is equally crucial. The content of the national identity must be made palatable to the more delicate, or at least more embryonic emotional sensitivities of children, a challenge similarly faced in the transmission of any emotional norm to the young, be it centered around danger and fear, hope and realism, morality and immorality or national identity: the proper affect of the group and the improper affect of the Other group. What's more, the proper orientation toward what *is* to be considered dangerous, immoral, Other, etc., must be made pedagogically transmissible, while at the same time that the proper affects are accorded to appropriate symbols, ideas and concepts. Zipes comments on this phenomenon:

> Literature for children is not children's literature by and for children in their behalf. It never was and it never will be. Literature for children is script coded by adults for the information and internalization of children which must meet the approbation of adults … It is the adult author's symbolically social act intended to influence and perhaps control the future destiny of culture. At heart are notions of civility and civilization. Adults who write literature for children want to cultivate raw sensibilities, to civilize unruly passions, and to reveal unsocial forces hostile to civilization.
>
> (Zipes 1981: 19)

This imperative to correctly organize the distribution of positive and negative affects while providing children with edifying educational and moral lessons has obvious extensions into other media produced for children, such as cartoons or the decorations of a kindergarten class. One only has to think of the different representational logic seen in pictures of, say, kittens versus snakes, especially when these animals are included as illustrations for very young children and as long as the audience of children is putatively threatened by snake bites. The anxieties adults have about the safety of children and their orientation toward safe or unsafe realities, toward improper emotional orientation and toward proper affective socialization, the establishment of which will later be known as "healthy fear" or "realistic expectations," will be coded into any children's media produced, even a single illustration or the framing of a photograph, and certainly will be included in the *civilizee* productions of Western children's literature and the animated shorts of North Korean children's propaganda.

In a similar vein, for de Courville Nicol (2011: 3), "Fear emotions, as felt incapacities, should not be thought of outside of their relationship to desire emotions, or felt capacities, toward which they tend." Instead, they are always related in a dynamic of the designation of an object of fear or insecurity, a threat (from cigarette smoke to terrorism) and the designation of an object of desire, which implements security. For me, it helped to conceptualize de Courville Nicol's description of the economy of desire and security as the "securing" of the object of desire. In the above example of the adult's fear for the child's security, the establishment of the child's appropriate fear designations actually satisfies the desire for security in the adult's relationship with their child.

De Courville Nicol's model also usefully conceptualizes the experience of "moral outrage" as a fear-based compulsion to escape the Other's illegitimate ability to inflict harm on the self and, by extension, on the community and familial ties with which one identifies—a point that has multiple implications in the case of North Korea. Fear, along with desire, are here astutely described as being involved in a linked state of felt anticipation, mediated through the embodied pain of fear and the embodied pleasure of desire, where, "Simply put, fear is the painful anticipation of pain that produces the urge to overcome danger, while desire is the pleasurable anticipation of pleasure that produces the urge to implement security" (Nicol 2011: 16). With pain being the originary point that motivates individuals to "avoid through fear-driven anticipation" (ibid.: 17), experience lends "subjects knowledge of the means of averting pain … and of seeking pleasure … [which] may be inborn or embodied more recently, but, like their knowledge of the forces that cause painful and pleasurable consequences—like their knowledge of objects of fear and desire—it is in any event a result of prior interactions with their environment" (ibid.: 22). To translate this into the North Korea context: while being educated as to the appropriate objects of fear, imperialist soldiers and vicious foreigners, the very daily proximity of family members who are soldiers reaffirms the child's sense of security and the identification of the military with the family as related object of security and desire. Moreover, the learnt means of avoiding pain and producing security that have been socially engendered by the revolutionaries who have been running the country since 1945 include a militaristic policy of belligerent anti-imperialist sovereignty, alliance with counter-hegemonic countries (now strained in the case of China), isolationism and reliance on the bonds of family, all of which have been promulgated and internalized as related affective structures and distributed through a powerful propaganda apparatus.

The cultural expression of these systemic vectors can be seen in the animation, in particular the still-frame cartoons, of North Korea. One of the only examples of a North Korean industry that is able to hire foreign experts, the inner workings of this unusually important state apparatus was described and dramatized in an autobiographical piece of graphic non-fiction by Montréaler Guy Delisle entitled *Pyongyang* (2007). When one considers the emphasis placed on the production of propaganda by Kim Jong-il, particularly televised propaganda,[4] it is no surprise that cartoons are part of the state's propaganda machine. Given the fact that North Korea is listed seventy-six out of two hundred and fifteen in terms of numbers of televisions per capita, and that many televisions are located in public sites intended for regular group viewing (Kim 2010),[5] the importance of still-frame, animated cartoons, a creative form that is amenable to production by large numbers of laborers with few tools or electronic devices, perhaps becomes clearer.

By North Korean standards, its animation industry is enormous. With cinema the country's only official export and the only area of the economy that can hire foreign experts, one of its high waters was revealed when it became known that the ultra-popular South Korean cartoon character Poporo the Penguin was in fact produced by a South and North Korean joint venture (Park 2011). The North Korean animation industry faltered at the beginning, only finding its place in 1957 when the Party established the "April 26 Children's Film Studio," out of which later grew the Scientific Educational Film Studio of Korea (SEK) in 1997. SEK became internationally important, shooting stop-motion sequences for companies in Spain, Italy and France. Even Disney is reported to have delegated production to this studio (Schonherr 2012).

Though the proportion of infrastructure devoted to the mediation of nationalism through television is unprecedented in North Korea, its emphasis, notwithstanding Kim Jong-il's personal interest, is completely understandable. As with print media and radio before it, these constantly innovating technologies of communication have long been identified as a crucial vector in nation-building (Anderson 2006). In the same way that Hegel imagined the national community coming to consciousness by the daily prayer of newspaper reading (Pinkard 2000), the centrality of the electrically transmitted moving image cannot be underestimated as it applies to the far-flung national communities of today. By way of illustration then, I will now focus on the content of affective pedagogy within two North Korean cartoons representing the military (*The Frog Guard* and *Squirrel and Hedgehog*), with an emphasis on how the complicated issue of inter-state violence (who, when, where, why and how much) and the related legitimacy tale of the military is constructed for the young. Included in this analysis will be a minimal comparison to the US cartoon of the same *taxa*, *G.I. Joe* (Sunbow Productions 1985), which in many ways fills the same role for US national identity. By highlighting the instrumental use of affective forces such as shame in the production of a national subject, we can thus better understand how other affective mediations influence, shape and interpellate us as people who "have" a nationality. As in the act of pointing out where we live on a globe, by watching such cartoons as children we are engaged at the most elemental level in the act of making ourselves national.

In the analysis of *Squirrel and Hedgehog* I will focus on the establishment of a shame- and-outrage-based national origin story, with the first episode establishing some of the most basic coordinates that will persist throughout the series. I will then point out some of the narrative adaptations that have been made to the cartoon series as the geopolitical position of North Korea shifts during the late twentieth century, while at the same time discussing the representation of violence in the cartoon as it changes over time as well. Finally, turning to *The Frog Guard*, I will show how the narrative settings of these North Korean cartoons are consistent between themselves while standing in marked contrast to the settings elected for *G.I. Joe*. To sum, while Joe's combat terrorism is in abject and foreign landscapes (the arctic, unrecognizable swamps, deserts and islands), the anthropomorphic squirrels, frogs and hedgehogs of North Korea always protect the home and family.

Frog[s squirrels, ducks and hedgehogs] *Guard* vs. *G.I. Joe*

Squirrel and Hedgehog, a cartoon for young children, was first released in the 1970s, a period that saw an emphasis by Party leadership on distinguishing themselves from the USSR and promulgating an indigenous model of self-sufficiency, the aforementioned *Juche* philosophy. The series centers on a village called "Flower Hill," where a community of anthropomorphic animals lives a simple, rustic existence. From the very first episode the village of Flower Hill finds itself under assault by a collection of weasels, wolves, rats and carrion birds, wielding high-tech weaponry and using unscrupulous tactics. This in turn leads to the village's defense by hedgehogs (the army proper), ducks (the navy and air force), and a lone, drunken bear (the Soviet Union), who is nonetheless very strong and well-intentioned. These characterizations are very broadly drawn and, given the audience, have been made deliberately simple to interpret. The depictions in these cartoons also change significantly from the first episode onward as the beleaguered North Korea of this era faced the thaw of the Cold War and the ultimate demise of the Soviet Union. However, *Squirrel and Hedgehog*, which has reached its thirty-second episode and continues to be produced today, also maintains certain basic narrative elements throughout its development: the village's predominance, a perpetual state of invasion and a mandate to educate the young. With an uncanny similarity to the didactic "Knowing is Half the Battle" segments that frequently conclude episodes of *G.I. Joe*, *Squirrel and Hedgehog* furnishes the audience with a lesson at the end of the first episode that will set the tone for the rest of the series. Having erroneously relied on the Soviet-bear character to defend the village, the protagonist citizen-squirrel prostrates himself before the hedgehog commander, and then pleads:

SQUIRREL: Can you forgive me hedgehog commander?
HEDGEHOG COMMANDER: Have courage! Let's unite our strength and pay them back a thousand-fold!

[Depiction of the weasel soldiers crawling onto land, badly hurt.]

WEASEL COMMANDER: Hedgehogs … [this isn't over.]
HEDGEHOG COMMANDER: You only relied on bear for protection, without preparing yourself for battles.
SQUIRREL: I've learned now. Just watch how I change myself.

[Depiction of the squirrel and hedgehog driving together in a tank; hedgehog addresses the audience.]

HEDGEHOG: And so the squirrels, who regretted their mistake, will from now on be the defenders of Flower Hill.
SQUIRREL: I'll make sure I never make the same mistake again! In fact, when I think about that day, I get a little embarrassed …

(n.a. 2009: 8:49–9:57)

The affective pedagogy here is unambiguous, using shame to underline the point that the squirrel's failure to defend the community was a mistake never to be repeated again. Equally worthy of note, however, is the statement by squirrel, "just watch how I change myself", which also unambiguously indicates the presence of the emotional work expected of the child viewer. This point is also reiterated at the start and finish of each episode by means of the theme music, the lyrics of which run:

> Brave and smart comrades of Flower Hill
> Let's keep our hill in unity.
> Though fierce enemies attack …
> By our strength and wisdom we shall defeat [them]!
> Let's make our hill a fortress!
>
> (n.a. 2009: 8:10–8:40)

Thus Flower Hill, and by extension the home, the community and the nation, is in a single stroke transformed in the imagination into a fortress by means of an idealized re-telling of the Korean War story.

However, as North Korea found itself increasingly isolated and reliant on international espionage to achieve military and national aims, the themes of *Squirrel and Hedgehog* are adapted from the repetition of the myth of Korean nationhood to an emphasis on spying, double agents and subterfuge, with the now radicalized citizen-squirrel protagonist volunteering for surveillance and intelligence work in a kind of guerrilla capacity. While providing ample material for storylines, the high-espionage period of *Squirrel and Hedgehog* also allowed the authors to explain the complex realities of such things as legitimated treachery, lying for political or military purposes, and vigilance against saboteurs and double agents to their child audience, carefully balancing the essential moral goodness of the protagonist against the urgency of wartime and his responsibility to protect Flower Hill. Again, much like *G.I. Joe*, the cartoon is constructed in such a way as to orient the child viewer correctly vis-à-vis the soldier and the nation, both encouraging the audience to identify with the national military, and by extension the national family, through a recollection of their fantastic adventures that explain the where, when and conditions under which violence and wartime treachery are legitimate. However, whereas *G.I. Joe* distantiates the home-front from the scene of conflict, the normal North Korean child's cartoon locates the action at the heart of the community, and calls the citizen to take on a military role in everyday life.

By the time the series reaches its twenty-seventh episode, "The Snare," these themes are depicted in a recycled form, with the now veteran squirrel-soldier-citizen returning to his home village. It is worth noting that the scene in which Squirrel flies over his local village (1:30–2:22) weeping while soft patriotic strains of music are heard, is a stylistic standard in the *Squirrel and Hedgehog* series, with the protagonist frequently overcome with emotion at the beauty of his homeland (indeed, it leads to his capture in episode two), and serves as a concrete example of the North Korean nation as the aforementioned "happy object." In these sequences the countryside is always layered with the movements of the community in harmony, a thing to be treasured as full of emotional wonder and meaning, while simultaneously being something to defend unto death. As Squirrel re-unites with his civilian younger brother the constituent affect norms of the series are repeated, with the younger brother constantly commenting on how he would have liked to have become a soldier if his brother had not killed the enemy already, which left him no option but to become a doctor's assistant. However, as luck would have it, and much as with the Squirrel of episode one, the kid brother is unaware of the nearness of harm that waits for both himself and his family, not to mention Flower Hill. Squirrel's younger brother is then radicalized in turn, as was Squirrel before him, from a sense of shame when his actions enable an enemy spy to access crucial military information that brings harm to his people. In the final scene of the episode Squirrel is almost killed and in what may be a final utterance of filial loyalty, says to his comrade:

SQUIRREL: As long as [my younger brother] is safe, I'm okay.

[Squirrel passes out. Squirrel's comrade strikes Squirrel's younger brother.]

SQUIRREL'S COMRADE: What did you do!? Do you even know what you just did!?

[Scene fades to a shot of warships and then cuts to Squirrel, explaining himself to his commanding officer.]

SQUIRREL: Sorry about the situation [my younger brother] caused.

COMMANDER: Our enemy is planning to steal Flower Hill by taking advantage of unsuspecting kids. However, that's a big mistake … because their "snare plan" to snare Flower Hill will put them into their own snare.

(n.a. 2011: 9:40–10:14)

The themes of enemy aggression, vigilance, the community under continued threat and a lesson learned are thus re-articulated here to enable Squirrel to "pass on" the civilian-soldier role to the next generation: an attempt by the party to maintain the efficacy of their previous mobilization of affectivity and war memory amidst radically changing global conditions, the stagnation of the command economy and the peaking power of the capitalist West.

Yet in so many ways North Korea's animation is consistent with the semiotic and narrative structures dominant in Western cartoons. The terrorist is replaced with the imperialist aggressor, and the soldier is an object of love and affection but otherwise, the themes of vigilance, safety and, ultimately, the necessity of the military is the foundational narrative of all of these various stories. The need for adults to explain to children the strange idea of "legitimate" violence, the who, how, where, when and why of adults fighting with other adults, is imperative and would seem inevitable, as a result of the child's ontic insecurities and the impulse (rooted in the parent's fears), to produce an affective and practical awareness in the child of the means by which to ensure their security. In the West, though I suspect just as frequently in North Korea, this pedagogy of security is often located in the need to differentiate, usually "bad men" from "good people," along with the concordant designation of the "police" or other "adult you trust" (teacher, crossing guard, friend's parents, etc.) as objects of security, while my expectation is equally that the "bad men" in North Korea include Americans, Japanese and capitalists amongst their number. In the 1980s, the recuperation of late Cold War American militarism took the form of the globe-trotting *G.I. Joe*, while signally, and in contrast, North Korean children's cartoons almost always distantiate violence from the inside of the home, positioning the military in the interstice between the inside or outside of the home rather than the American convention which locates the soldier in the interstitial space between nation-states.

In this capacity, *The Frog Guard* and *Squirrel and Hedgehog* are excellent examples of this scheme of fear and security in an articulation based on North Korean history, with the locale of the village or home as a site of violence.[6] These pieces, which in most ways are structured identically to American children's cartoons, both contain one significantly unfamiliar element: a deliberate attempt to produce an affective link between the military, home and security. As can be seen at 3:07 of the clip, the arrangement of the nearby settlement, the guard tower and the crops are integrated in such a way as to make the relationship undeniable. As opposed to the symbolic logic of *G.I. Joe*, the soldier is not only a "guard" of the American (or North Korean) way of life but is also a member of the community, inscribed within the village. Also centrally significant in the piece is the fact that when violence occurs it is distantiated yet more present than in *G.I. Joe*, with the frog guard firing arrows from his gun rather than bullets. This essential but minimal difference seems to be operating according to the same principles that led to the North American decision to allow hand-to-hand combat instead of the penetration of bodies. It is as if the real violence cannot ever be symbolized, but must always have a "symbolic cap" that covers it up, even when there would be no significant difference if violence were expressed more realistically. In any case, the theme of the soldier's affective inscription into the community is much more powerfully evident in *Squirrel and Hedgehog*,[7] but *The Frog Guard* presents the semiotic constellation in its basic constituent parts: the soldier, the community, and its defense; the military is the principle by which the community is constituted. So while the family is not directly represented, the way it is in *Squirrel and Hedgehog*, the implication is that the community is sustained under an affectively rooted sense of loyalty, a loyalty that takes place in the context of a life-and-death struggle. The historical circumstances that make the familial orientation of this affective constellation cognizable are the colonial history of the Korean peninsula.

A simple viewing of both clips will convince the reader of what is a rather uncontroversial claim: a group's history with violence will determine the kinds of stories it tells its children about violence, especially where, when and who takes part in it. In the differential affective economies of the United States and North Korea, the soldier either resides in or outside of the community, with the North Korean child being made to understand that it is the military that has enabled the survival of the local group, a stark contrast to the American practice of representing the military in a variety of symbolically distantiated locales when producing media for their young.

Conclusion

Without the assistance of an affective political economic approach in understanding power in North Korea, I am not certain that the dynamics and importance of kinship within the disciplinary mechanisms of the national community would have become clear for me. It took the combination of a material and historicist method, along with a willingness to embrace the role of the *irr*ational and emotive in social order for these processes of community identity and disciplinary shaping to rise to the surface, for though the Soviet-style discipline of the country persists, its longevity cannot be attributed to these draconian measures when almost all of the similar systems to appear in history have collapsed. Instead, through the medium of wholly modern communication systems, eventually presented in such forms as the child's cartoon, a call of loyalty to the family was advanced, parsed in the language of socialism and premised on the separation of families and the erosion of traditional identities during the nineteenth and twentieth centuries; a call that was heeded. Thus, the riddle of North Korea's longevity would appear to be found in that most parochial of institutions, that made up by our mothers, fathers, siblings and grandparents, dressed in the uniforms of their lives: those figures that reach from the past and point to the future, directing us to those things that brought them pleasure, and warning us of those things that brought them pain.

Notes

1 According to Andrei Lankov (2013), the Songbun system is the formal class hierarchy, or caste system, of North Korea. It is a fully endorsed public system; detailed records are kept by cadre as to the value of each person's Songbun throughout the country. It is premised on a complicated system of appellations that are transmitted by means of the family unit, with one's Songbun rating directly influencing one's marriage prospects and the possibility of finding gainful employment.
2 *Juche* philosophy emphasizes self-reliance, autonomy, military defense and an almost direct relationship between the body of the leader and the "body" of the people. For more on this topic see Kim 1993.
3 These figures are taken from James Hackett (2010) for North Korea and from the United States Department of Defense (2013) for the United States, with very rough figures gleaned by dividing the country's total population by the number of reserve and/or active military personnel in service.
4 North Korea is unique as a famine-wracked "Third World" country with roughly 1.2 million televisions—a huge number when compared to other Third World countries such as Ethiopia, at 682,000 televisions; Cambodia at 94,000; and Sierra Leone at 53,000.
5 Wikipedia, en.wikipedia.org/wiki/List_of_countries_by_number_of_personal_televi sions.
6 www.youtube.com/watch?v=3CE8q5K66_0.
7 www.youtube.com/watch?v=YiHJ7t2vscU.

References

n.a. 2007. *North Korea Animation 4*. www.youtube.com/watch?v=3CE8q5K66_0&feature=youtube_gdata_player (accessed on September 29, 2013).

n.a. 2009. *A Squirrel and Hedgehog*. Ep. 01, Part 2. www.youtube.com/watch?v=Jf-Zjx4Bdk&feature=youtube_gdata_player (accessed on September 29, 2013).

——2011. *A Squirrel and Hedgehog*. Ep. 27, Part 2. www.youtube.com/watch?v=kHeBpyXal3w&feature=youtube_gdata_player (accessed on September 29, 2013).

Ahmed, S. 2004. "Affective Economies." *Social Text*: 117–39.

——2010. *The Promise of Happiness*. Durham, NC: Duke University Press.

Anderson, Benedict. 2006. *Imagined Communities: Reflections on the Origin and Spread of Nationalism*. London: Verso.

Armstrong, Charles K. 1995. "Surveillance and Punishment in Postliberation North Korea." *Positions: Asia Critique* 3(3): 695–722.

Delisle, Guy. 2007. *Pyongyang: A Journey in North Korea*. First edn. Montreal: Drawn and Quarterly.

Foley, James. 2003. *Korea's Divided Families: Fifty Years of Separation*. London: Psychology Press.

Foucault, Michel. 1995. *Discipline & Punish: The Birth of the Prison*. Second edn. London: Vintage.

Gabroussenko, Tatiana. 2010. *Soldiers on the Cultural Front: Developments in the Early History of North Korean Literature and Literary Policy*. Kapolei: University of Hawaii Press.

Hackett, James. 2010. *The Military Balance*. London: Routledge.

Hegel, Georg Wilhelm Friedrich. 1984 [1975]. *Lectures on the Philosophy of World History Introduction*, trans. Hugh Barr Nisbet. Cambridge: Cambridge University Press.

Hochschild, Arlie Russell. 1979. "Emotion Work, Feeling Rules, and Social Structure." *American Journal of Sociology* 85(3): 551–75.

Kim, Seok-hyang. 1993. *The Juche Ideology of North Korea: Socio-political Roots of Change*. Athens, GA: University of Georgia Press.

Kim, Suk-young. 2010. *Illusive Utopia: Theater, Film, and Everyday Performance in North Korea*. Ann Arbor: University of Michigan Press.

Koh, Byung Chul. 2005. "'Military First Politics' and Building a 'Powerful and Prosperous Nation' in North Korea." Nautilus Institute for Security and Sustainability. nautilus.org/napsnet/napsnet-policy-forum/military-first-politics-and-building-a-powerful-and-prosperous-nation-in-north-korea/#axzz2OlxCiBg8 (accessed March 27, 2013).

Kwon, Heonik and Chung, Byung-ho. 2012. *North Korea: Beyond Charismatic Politics*. Lanham, MD: Rowman & Littlefield Publishers.

Lamar, Cyriaque. 2012. "Footage of Synchronized Mass Mourning for Kim Jong-il is Unsettling." November 19. io9.com/5869249/footage-of-synchronized-mass-mourning-for-kim-jong+il-is-unsettling (accessed on September 29, 2013).

Lankov, Andrei. 2013. *The Real North Korea: Life and Politics in the Failed Stalinist Utopia*. Oxford: Oxford University Press.

Martin, Bradley K. 2004. *Under the Loving Care of the Fatherly Leader: North Korea and the Kim Dynasty*. New York: St Martin's Press.

Myers, B.R. 2010. *The Cleanest Race: How North Koreans See Themselves and Why it Matters*. Reprint. New York: Melville House.

Nicol, Valérie de Courville. 2011. *Social Economies of Fear and Desire: Emotional Regulation, Emotion Management, and Embodied Autonomy*. First edn. New York: Palgrave Macmillan.

Park, Ju-min. 2011. "Iconic South Korean Penguin Character Actually Half-North Korean." uk.reuters.com/article/2011/05/16/oukoe-uk-korea-penguin-idUKTRE74F17V20110516 (accessed on September 29, 2013).

Pinkard, Terry. 2000. *Hegel: A Biography*. Cambridge: Cambridge University Press.

Reuters. 2007. "North Korea Halts Mass Games Due to Flood." uk.reuters.com/article/2007/08/27/uk-korea-north-arirang-idUKSEO29172020070827 (accessed on December 28, 2010).

Robbins, Thomas. 1997. *Millennium, Messiahs, and Mayhem: Contemporary Apocalyptic Movements*. London: Routledge.

Schonherr, Johannes. 2012. *North Korean Cinema: A History*. Jefferson, NC: McFarland.

Stone, Jon R., ed. 2000. *Expecting Armageddon: Essential Readings in Failed Prophecy*. London: Routledge.

Sunbow Productions. 1985. *G.I. Joe: A Real American Hero*. Claster Television Hasbro.

United States Department of Defense. 2013. Armed Forces Strength Figures for January 31, 2013. siadapp.dmdc.osd.mil/personnel/MILITARY/ms0.pdf (accessed on October 29, 2013).

Watts, Jonathan. 2005. "Welcome to the Strangest Show on Earth." *The Guardian*. www.guardian.co.uk/world/2005/oct/01/northkorea (accessed on December 28, 2010).

Weber, Max. 1947. *The Theory of Social and Economic Organization*, trans. Talcott Parsons. New York: The Free Press.

Wood, Tracy. 2008. "The Ghostly Presence of the Korean Orphan." *Bajo Palabra. Revista de Filosofía* 3: 127–33.

Woronov, Terry W. 2007. "Performing the Nation: China's Children as Little Red Pioneers." *Anthropological Quarterly* 80(3): 647–72.

Yang, Sung Chul. 1999. *The North and South Korean Political Systems—A Comparative Analysis.* Revised edn. Seoul: Hollym.

Zipes, Jack. 1981. "Second Thoughts on Socialization through Literature for Children." *The Lion and the Unicorn* 5: 19–32.

Index